The Crescent Remembered

Islam and Nationalism on the Iberian Peninsula

Patricia Hertel

Translated from the German by Ellen Yutzy Glebe

sussex
ACADEMIC
PRESS
Brighton • Chicago • Toronto

First published in German under the title *Der erinnerte Halbmond. Islam und Nationalismus auf der Iberischen Halbinsel im 19. und 20. Jahrhundert* © 2012 by Oldenbourg Wissenschaftsverlag GmbH, München.

Published in English translation 2015 and 2016 (paperback) in Great Britain by
SUSSEX ACADEMIC PRESS
PO Box 139
Eastbourne BN24 9BP

SUSSEX ACADEMIC PRESS
Independent Publishers Group
814 N. Franklin Street, Chicago, IL 60610

and in Canada by
SUSSEX ACADEMIC PRESS (CANADA)

British Library Cataloguing in Publication Data
A CIP catalogue record for this book is available from the British Library.

Library of Congress Cataloging-in-Publication Data
Hertel, Patricia.
[Erinnerte Halbmond. English]
The crescent remembered : Islam and nationalism on the Iberian peninsula /
    Patricia Hertel.
pages   cm. — (Sussex studies in Spanish history)
Includes bibliographical references and index.
ISBN 978-1-84519-654-7 (hardback)
ISBN 978-1-84519-793-3 (paperback)
    1. Islam—Public opinion. 2. Muslims—Iberian Peninsula. 3. Islamic
countries—Relations—Iberian Peninsula. 4. Iberian Peninsula—
Relations—Islamic countries. I. Title.
BP65.I25.H4713 2015
946'.00088297—dc23

2015007259

MIX
Paper from
responsible sources
FSC® C013056

Typeset & designed by Sussex Academic Press, Brighton & Eastbourne.
Printed by TJ International, Padstow, Cornwall.
Printed on acid-free paper.

Contents

Preface by Series Editor
Nigel Townson

Since the fall of the Franco regime in the 1970s, historical work on Basque, Catalan and even Galician nationalism has thrived in reaction to the stiflingly centralist vision of the nation-state propagated under the 37-year dictatorship. Scarcely surprisingly, Spanish nationalism has been stigmatized and eschewed as a subject of research on account of its (unfair) association with the intolerant and exclusive outlook of the Franco regime. Only in the last two decades has the study of Spanish nationalism come into its own, not least as a result of the publication of José Álvarez-Junco's pioneering *Mater dolorosa*. Patricia Hertel's study adds to our understanding of nation-building in the modern era, but in a highly distinctive fashion. Her framing of the process reaches beyond Spain to embrace the entire Iberian Peninsula. Moreover, she tackles a much-neglected facet of nationalism: religion. Accordingly, *The Crescent Remembered* endeavours to break new ground by examining how the historical 'memory' of Islam, and its reconfiguration within the popular imagination, contributed to the cultural construction of national identities in Iberia.

The author adopts an explicitly comparative approach in seeking to delineate the similarities and the convergences of nation-building in both Spain and Portugal. Astonishingly, the two nations are rarely compared at all, despite their patent geographical, linguistic, religious and other proximities. They are, as the Spanish saying goes, "Two countries back to back". Still, as Hertel highlights, the comparative approach can yield rich rewards. It plays a fundamental function insofar as it identities what is specific about a particular process, event or collectivity, while, conversely, it enables us to calibrate the extent to which we are talking about a common or even transnational phenomenon. Another advantage is that it can raise questions that challenge the pieties of long-established orthodoxies.

The Muslims may have been expelled from the Iberian Peninsula long before the modern era, but they lived vividly on in the collective 'memory' and popular imagination. Hertel compares and contrasts the role of Islam in the nation-building of Spain and Portugal alike by drawing on an enormous array of sources: paintings, photographs, newspapers, festivals, colonial documentation, school textbooks, propaganda, and so on. Her multi-faceted and interdisciplinary reconstruction reveals not merely the importance of Islam, but also that there did not exist a straightforward dichotomy between a Catholic 'Us' and an Islamic 'Other'. On the contrary, the author stresses the changeable and nuanced nature of the relationship between the two. Thus historic Islam may have been denounced in the nineteenth century as the adversary *par excellence*, but under the twentieth-century dictatorships of Salazar and Franco it was, curiously, reevaluated in much more positive terms.

The Crescent Remembered therefore presents a deeply-layered analysis that interweaves the nation-building process in Spain and Portugal over two whole centuries. Further, in view of the current debate within Europe and beyond over the nature of Islam, this scholarly study constitutes a timely historiographical corrective to Manichean representations of the religion.

Preface and Acknowledgements

Perched on the top of a hill in the northern part of the historical district of Toledo is a little square structure with miniature arches reminiscent of those of the Great Mosque of Cordoba. Its name has changed over the centuries, a reflection of history: in 999 or 1000 its construction as a mosque—just steps away from the city gate, Bab al-Mardum (Gate of the Majordomo), for which it is sometimes named—was financed by a private donor, and it served as a place of worship for the wealthy Muslim families in the neighborhood until the Christian conquest of Toledo in 1085. A hundred years later, it was given to the Order of the Knights of Saint John, and in 1186, it was consecrated as the Chapel of Santa Cruz. In the course of this appropriation, the Muslim prayer niche, the mihrab, was destroyed, and an apse was added to the eastern side of the building. Today the structure is called "Cristo de la Luz" (Christ of Light), a reference to a legend in which a miraculous candle in an ancient Visigoth chapel is said to have remained lit during the centuries of Muslim presence.

The photo on the cover of this book shows the meeting of the Islamic arches and the Christian apse. The wall paintings—pseudo-Arabic characters next to a Maltese cross—are reminders of the two religions which have celebrated their holy services in the building. This detail of the mosque-church visually depicts the topic of this book, the memory of the Muslim past in the nineteenth and twentieth centuries on the Iberian Peninsula. The building embodies the topic's historical roots: the Middle Ages and the complex relationship between Muslims and Christians in this period—a history which was constantly present and hotly debated in Spain and Portugal centuries later.

At the same time, the remnants of those paintings can be seen as an allegory of memory. Some aspects are highlighted in bright colors, retouched, or even further embellished, while others remain pale and hard to see, even falling into oblivion. New, shifting images of the past emerge, which often have little or nothing to do with historical reality, but which reveal a great deal about the concerns of the present. This study essentially asks which aspects of the Islamic past were painted in bright or dark colors, what was remembered, what forgotten, and why. It analyzes the various ways in which the crescent lived on in collective memories and imagination in Spain and Portugal.

This book is a translation of my Ph.D. thesis, which was published in

German in 2012. That project led to many contacts and encounters for which I am deeply indebted: my advisors, Siegfried Weichlein (Fribourg) and Martin Baumeister (Munich/Rome) accompanied me on the intellectual journey that such a study requires, inspired me with their analytical and historical expertise, and offered valuable advice each step of the way. Maria Isabel João (Lisbon), Sérgio Campos Matos (Lisbon), Jesús Millán (Valencia), Xosé Manoel Núñez Seixas (Santiago de Compostela), and José Manuel Sobral (Lisbon) encouraged me by being constantly interested in my project and willing to share their extensive knowledge. Alberto A. Abreu (Viana do Castelo), Carmen Cardelle de Hartmann (Zurich), Mariano Delgado (Fribourg), Susana Gómez Martínez (Mértola), Geoffrey Jensen (Lexington), Eva Maria von Kemnitz (Lisbon), Ramón López Facal (Santiago de Compostela), Bernabé López Garcia (Madrid), Toni Morant i Ariño (Münster), David Parra Monserrat (Valencia), Paulo Raposo (Lisbon), Reinhard Schulze (Bern), Christiane Stallaert (Leuven), Nina Clara Tiesler (Lisbon), AbdoolKarim Vakil (London), and Rafael Valls (Valencia) offered valuable input from their respective disciplines and fields of expertise. Discussions with my colleagues and with the participants of the workshops and conferences I attended while conducting my research were invaluable in shaping the project.

I am grateful to Anthony Grahame from Sussex Academic Press and Nigel Townson, editor of Sussex Studies in Spanish History Series, for including this book in the series. The translation was made possible by generous grants from the Research Fund of the University of Fribourg (Switzerland), the Christine Bonjour-Stiftung in Basel, and the Professorship for Modern European History, Professor Martin Lengwiler, Department of History, University of Basel, for which I would like to express my gratitude. A very special thank you goes to Ellen Yutzy Glebe, not only for her competent and thorough translation, but also for the contributions she made as a fellow historian.

List of Illustrations

FRONT COVER: Interior of the former Mosque Bab al-Mardum/Cristo de la Luz, Toledo. © Patricia Hertel. BACK COVER: Celebratory banner of the moros y cristianos festival from Alcoy, 1907. © Asociación de San Jorge de Alcoy (Museu Alcoià de la Festa). Reproduced courtesy of the Museu Alcoià de la Festa and the municipality of Alcoy.

The plate section (after page 100) includes substantive explanatory captions and source details.

Introduction

"Is not the Ishmaelite close at hand,
With whom you have waged countless wars?
If a fresh crusade is your purpose,
Does he not bow to the faith of Arabia?
If it is land and riches you desire,
Does he not own a thousand cities?
Or if it's fresh battle honours you covet,
Is he not still a formidable target?"[1]

Luíz Vaz de Camões, *The Lusíads* (1572)

"History of Don Quixote de la Mancha,
written by Cide Hamete Benengeli, an Arab historian."[2]

Miguel de Cervantes Saavedra, *The Ingenious Hidalgo Don Quixote de la Mancha* (1605/1615)

EUROPE AND ISLAM: ENCOUNTERS, MEMORY, IMAGINATION

Are "Islam" and "Europe" irreconcilable opposites? Are they two sides of the same coin? Or is this apparent contrast extraneous in the context of postmodern challenges to dualistic worldviews? From a historical perspective it is at least clear: for centuries "Europe" and "Islam" were used as potent but often ambiguous categories to describe and interpret the past and the present.

Europe's historical encounter with Islam, both the contact itself and the interpretation which ensued, was formative.[3] Since the Middle Ages, concepts of a Christian "Europe" and a non-European "Islam" have been seen to be at odds. However, this antagonism was not a given prior to the historical contact between Christians and Muslims. It is rather the result of a history of encounters characterized by conflict and cooperation, cultural assimilation and rejection. In the Middle Ages, the Iberian Peninsula became a space for such encounters in which concepts of "Ourselves" and the "Other" formed under the influence of Islam. This process continued even after there was no longer a significant Muslim presence on Iberian soil. The heterogeneous and evolving notions of Islam on the Iberian Peninsula during the nineteenth and twentieth centuries and their influence on national perceptions of "Us" and "Them" are the central topics of this monograph.

At the European level, the historical contact between Christians and Muslims was widely marked by the struggle for power and territory. European rulers banded together against their respective Muslim opponents in bloody conflicts like the Crusades, the Ottoman Wars, and the battles for territory on the Iberian Peninsula and in the Balkan region. As an ideological unity developed among Christians in the West, Europeans developed analogical views about Islam as well:[4] Moors on the Iberian Peninsula, Saracens in the Holy Land, and Turks in the Balkan region were all perceived by Europeans as different facets of the same foe, Islam. The notions and images[5] of Europe and Islam developed within an expansive geographical and chronological context during repeated military conflicts from the battle which halted Muslim expansion near Tours and Poitiers in 732 to the Fall of Constantinople in 1453, the naval Battle of Lepanto in 1571, and the Battle of Vienna in 1683. Countless texts, pictures, and stories commemorated (and mythologized) these victories and defeats, these heroes and their exploits. Though Islam hardly presented a real territorial threat to Europe in the nineteenth century, it retained a prominent and important role in the repertoire of European myths. This was shown iconographically, for example, in the exhibition *Mythen der Nationen* (Myths of the Nations) in the German Historical Museum in Berlin, in which nine of the seventeen countries presented some form of an encounter with the Islamic world.[6] Conflicts with their respective Islamic opponents were perceived not only as political struggles but mythologized as battles of fate in which the salvation of Europe was at stake.[7] "Islam" represented a single united enemy which personified Europe's adversary par excellence: political and territorial opposition was linked to religious, cultural, and ethnic antagonism. These lines of opposition overlapped and reinforced each other.

However, Christians and Muslims did not only meet on the battlefield. Europeans also encountered the Islamic world in the reception of scientific discoveries, in diplomatic relations, and in the portrayals of Islam and the Orient in music, literature, and art, some of which originated in actual experience and others which were more the product of their own romantic imaginations.[8] A variety of cultural phenomena stylized the Muslim world, positioning it as an exotic antipode to contemporary European society, which was perceived to be sober, prudish, and lacking in fantasy. Examples of this genre include: Antoine Galland's translation of the fairy tales of *One Thousand and One Nights* into French between 1704 and 1717; the "Turkish Style" at the hundred year anniversary of the Battle of Vienna, characterized forever by Wolfgang Amadeus Mozart's opera *Die Entführung aus dem Serail* which debuted in 1782;[9] the enthusiasm for everything Egyptian following

Napoleon Bonaparte's campaign from 1798 to 1801[10]; the paintings of Eugène Delacroix; and the books of the British adventurer Richard Burton, who succeeded in participating in the pilgrimage to Mecca, which was forbidden for non-Muslims.[11] These cultural developments combined with political events like the demise of the Ottoman Empire and the colonization of Islamic areas to feed the idea that Islam was both politically and culturally controllable.

Over the centuries, cultural impressions of the Orient and the Occident developed out of this mixture of stereotypes, antagonisms, myths, and caricatured descriptions. These conceptions became influential in the historiography despite their logical shortcomings; for example, ancient Greece was associated with the Occident while the Byzantine Empire was considered Oriental.[12] From a European perspective, countries in the Far East, like Japan or China, could also be considered part of the Orient. Due to the geographical proximity and historical recollection, however, Islam and Muslims dominated the concept of "the Orient." Modern studies have examined the relationship between Orient and Occident and deconstructed these antagonistic stereotypes in depth.[13]

The regions in which there was a centuries-long Muslim presence were especially important for the contact of Europe with the Islamic Other, namely the Balkans, the Iberian Peninsula, southern Italy, and Sicily. Within these complex processes of antagonism, coexistence, and cooperation, there were struggles for political and cultural dominance, alliances both with and against fellow believers, and feuds and romances. Over time, these all crystallized in the collective memory as historical narratives and myths. These zones of contact were defined not by fixed borders, but rather by flexible "frontiers,"[14] a concept which emerged from the study of the American West, but which has been adapted to refer to other zones of contact within which behavior ranges from acceptance to confrontation.[15] The zone of contact on the Balkan Peninsula has received the most scholarly attention due to the significance of medieval Constantinople and the Byzantine Empire, the long reign of the Ottomans, the Balkan Wars in the twentieth century, and the continuing Muslim presence in the region. The contact in Sicily was quite limited since the period of Muslim rule lasted only from 832 to 1072. Elements in the architecture of structures like the cathedrals in Palermo, Cefalù, and Messina testify to the Arab influence, as do aspects of the theatrical rituals for local festivities.[16] Following the foundation of the Kingdom of Italy in 1861, the regions of Sicily and southern Italy, which had been previously influenced by Islam, became incorporated into a larger picture of a backwards, more African than European *mezzogiorno*. It was seen by the North Italians to be an ongoing problem for scholarship, politics, and the economy. At the same time, however, they idealized the South as a picturesque contrast to the industrialized North.[17]

The Iberian Peninsula was a zone of contact between Muslims and Christians for nearly eight hundred years. In 711 Tariq ibn Ziyad, a Berber who had converted to Islam, led an army across the narrow straits between Africa and Europe while serving Musa ib Nusayr, the Arabian governor of North Africa. The straits came to bear his name in memory of this turning point: Gibraltar, or in Arabic, Dschabal at-Tariq, "Mountain of Tariq." Because the Visigoths were too weak to provide any significant resistance, Tariq's troops were able to take over most of the peninsula within a short time: at its most expansive, the Islamic Al-Andalus (Land of the Vandals) included the entire Iberian Peninsula, except for parts of the northern coastal region, as well as an area around Narbonne, in the south of modern-day France. The ensuing centuries were characterized by battles between Muslim and Christian kingdoms, but also among followers of the same religion, as territorial lines shifted back and forth.[18] The Islamic rule on the peninsula ended with the fall of the Nasrid dynasty in Granada in 1492; the rulers of Aragon and Castile and Portugal subsequently forced Jews and Muslims to either accept baptism or emigrate. Ferdinand of Aragon and Isabella of Castile aimed for religious conformity within the areas unified by their marriage and strove to become exemplary Christian monarchs. Manuel I of Portugal expelled Jews and Muslims from his territory because this was a condition of his marriage to Ferdinand and Isabella's daughter.[19] The Iberian monarchs institutionalized the Inquisition and, after 1609, banished the offspring of baptized Muslims.[20] From the early modern perspective, which equated religion with ethnicity, this ended the Islamic presence on the peninsula. However, this did not end the contact of the Iberian Peninsula with Islam, for it persisted in the collective memory, which, with the passing of time, however, was no longer based on any real experience or contact.[21] The period of Muslim influence became a reservoir of impressions, fantasies, and stereotypes which helped to shape self-image(s) and identity(s) within the society of the peninsula. The Islamic past thus remained an important part of Iberian "cultural memory."[22]

This past was personified and thereby especially memorable in the figure of the Spanish *moro* and the Portuguese *mouro*.[23] These terms, derived from the Latin *maurus* (dark), became common in both scholarly discourse and general slang. Originally the term referred to natives of the former Roman province Mauritania in northern Africa,[24] but after the Arabs Islamized the North African Berber tribes, *moro* became a synonym for all Muslims and was used by medieval chroniclers in Europe to describe the invasions of the Almoravids and Almohads from the eleventh to thirteenth centuries.[25] The term was applied to Turks, Arabs, and Syrians—in short, to all followers of Muhammad—while in Spain the contact and memories solidified around the stereotype of the North African *moro*.[26] *Moro* became a collective term for *árabes* (Arabs) and *bérberes* (Berbers); many authors presumably did not even know that the Muslims who crossed the strait with Tariq in 711 were descended from the Berber tribes that had been Islamized by the Arabs. The terms *sarraceno* (Saracen) and *agareno*, used frequently in medieval Europe, are rooted in medieval Christian understanding, which traced the ethnic roots of the Arabs back either to Abraham's wife Sarah or to Hagar, Sarah's servant, who bore Abraham's first son, Ishmael. Both expressions are used less frequently in Spanish texts, and only for the medieval context.[27] The term *morisco*, the diminutive form of *moro*, was used to refer to those Muslims who were forcefully baptized after the demise of the Kingdom of Granada and lived under Christian rule.[28] The popularity of the term *moro* is evidenced in archaic expressions in which *moro* is used as a synonym for "not Christian": for example, an unbaptized child is *un niño moro. Vino moro* is an expression referring to undiluted (i.e. "unbaptized") wine. *Moro* carried various negative connotations: of danger, for example, in *haber moros en la costa*[29]—an image based on the frequent attacks by North African pirates in the early modern era; of chaos, as in *estar como moros sin señor*;[30] or of combat, as in *haber moros y cristianos.*[31] Due to its derogatory use in past times, the term is no longer considered politically correct. However, it conveys modern anti-Islamic prejudices: a jealous husband who keeps close watch over his wife is called a *moro*; *bajarse al moro*[32] is slang for the sale of hashish in North Africa.[33]

The Portuguese term *mouro* is only a partial semantic equivalent to the Spanish *moro*. Historically, it has similarly referred to North Africans and followers of Islam.[34] Although Portuguese also uses expressions like *andar mouro na costa*[35] for "there's trouble ahead" or *trabalhar como um mouro*[36] for "to work hard," the term *mouro* has been used less frequently in Portuguese historical narrative than its Spanish equivalent *moro*.[37]

In addition to the historical connotations, in Portuguese there is a mythological association: in traditional folkore, the *mouro* is a fabled creature who guards over a bewitched treasure. His female counterpart, the *moura encantada*,[38] a Portuguese siren, beguiles mortal men with song and her blond tresses. In the same way, the term *tempo dos mouros*[39] is used in rural areas of Portugal as well as in culturally adjacent Galicia to refer not to the actual period of Muslim presence but rather to a long past, pre-Christian epoch.[40] The Portuguese *mouriscos* are also not to be equated with the Spanish: the term did not refer to the comparatively small group of Muslims who were forcefully baptized under Christian rule following the expulsion of 1497, but rather to converted Muslims who were brought to Portugal as slaves from the colonies in North Africa and to a few *moriscos* who had emigrated from Castile.[41]

Images of *moros/mouros* and *moriscos/mouriscos* pervade the historical and literary works of the peninsula. They are especially prominent in the works of early modern writers, witnesses to the debates over the living conditions of the *moriscos* within the Christian kingdoms of Iberia.[42] Two outstanding examples are *The Lusiads* by Luís Vaz de Camões (1524/25–1580) and *Don Quixote* by Miguel de Cervantes Saavedra (1547–1616). Although they are vastly different—an epic about Portuguese global exploration versus a parody of medieval romance novels—both works relate in their own way a search for purpose and identity. The respective protagonists encounter representatives of Islam: as Vasgo da Gama's caravel casts off, the Old Man from Restelo, who embodies pessimism towards the discoveries and condemns them as "futile lust," warns the sailors about being excessively ambitious, especially considering the Islamic presence and dominance in North Africa and elsewhere.[43] Most of *Don Quixote* is supposedly translated from a manuscript by an "Arabian Chronicler" named Cide Hamete Benengeli, which is merely a pseudonym for Cervantes himself. Under this guise, Cervantes, despite the censorship of his era, was able to present both fiction and parody, all the while referring to the "falseness" of the supposed Arabs. One of the most thought-provoking scenes is the protagonist's meeting with the exiled *morisco* Ricote, who understands the political reasons for the king's eviction decree but cannot hide the personal regret and unhappiness he feels about the decision:

> So in the end we were justly punished with exile, a mild enough penalty in some people's opinion, but for us the most terrible punishment that could have been inflicted upon us. Wherever we are we weep for Spain—after all, we were born here, it's our native country. Nowhere have we found the welcome we long for in our misfortune, and it's in Barbary and everywhere else in Africa, where we'd thought we'd be accepted, welcomed and feasted, that we're most insulted and ill-treated.[44]

Ninenteeth-century nationalists replaced Camões's and Cervantes's question marks with exclamation points and declared the works to be literary embodiments of the nation and their virtues. Don Quixote presents an ideal of a Christian-Castilian knight, about which even the twentieth-century historian Claudio Sánchez-Albornoz wrote: "Who would dare to ascribe Islamic roots to the ingenious nobleman Don Quixote de la Mancha?"[45] The Portuguese sailors were accordingly seen as missionaries spreading civilization and culture.[46] Many interpretations overlooked the ambivalence of the works.[47]

Cervantes and Camões became protagonists of political myths[48] that acquired new significance in nineteenth-century Europe. They offered meaningful narratives which were used for political communication and to interpret the present. These political myths were a reaction to the need for the young model of the nation to claim legitimacy by incorporating a "conceived order"[49] and presenting itself as an autonomous subject.[50] The imaginary boundaries of the myths fused with the demands for political borders from both a territorial as well as a cultural perspective. For example, the myths around Schiller and Dante served as a cultural basis of the movements for national unity within those authors' respective homelands, for such states seemed to have been already achieved in the poets' works.[51]

The territorial border between Spain and Portugal—excepting the city of Olivença/Olivenza, which both countries still claim today—has been stable since the Middle Ages,[52] but the imaginary contours of the Iberian nations nevertheless had to be first shaped and fashioned. Wars like those against Napoleon or in the colonies,[53] the celebrations to honor national heroes,[54] and other corresponding historical narratives[55] catalyzed nationalist thinking. The struggle with Islam played a key role, and became central to Castilian and Portuguese nationalism's conception of both the past and the present even though there had been no notable legal Muslim presence since the expulsion of the *moriscos* in 1609.[56] The physical absence of a rival group does not prevent its continued development and use as an antagonist. The medieval Jewish presence played a similar role: Anti-Semitism was widespread in nineteenth-century Spain, though practically no Jews lived there.[57] Islam was seen as particularly dangerous because, unlike Jews, Muslims had exercised territorial power and posed a very real political threat in the Middle Ages. The crescent remembered was crucial in the development of national identity on the Iberian Peninsula. When nineteenth-century historians evoked Islam as a religious enemy, when romantically inspired scientists were enthused about the Muslim cultural heritage, and when colonial politicians used the past in their attempts to legitimize contemporary colonial rule, they were all actually dealing only superficially with Islam. The variable and often contradictory memories of the Islamic past were reflections of the search for a national identity.

ISLAM AND NATIONALISM ON THE IBERIAN PENINSULA: RESEARCH QUESTIONS

This study uses the example of the Iberian Peninsula—a zone of contact with an Islamic presence spanning centuries—to examine the meaning and function of Islam in the process of cultural nation-building in the nineteenth and twentieth centuries. How was the medieval Muslim presence remembered? Which pictures, descriptions, and judgments were associated with the *moro*, and why? These memories were shaped by the medieval heritage and early modern historiography, which presented Islam as an enemy in the context of the Crusades and the conflicts with the Ottoman Empire. Furthermore, in the nineteenth century the political myth of a supposed *reconquista* (reconquest) of Muslim areas emerged. The campaign against Islam was accordingly presented as a coordinated action of all Christian rulers, in which religious and political goals were inextricably joined.[58] This created the perception that Islam was the Other par excellence. It was impossible to deny the Muslim past. At the same time, this created a constant need to explain how this history could be reconciled with the image of a Catholic nation.

The study inquires about mechanisms of inclusion and exclusion of Islam and the Muslim heritage. These were not invented in the nineteenth century; they already existed in the early modern era, although at that point the mechanisms of exclusion were consistently dominant.[59] From the nineteenth century on, however, they acquired a new dimension in the context of nation formation. Why could the Islamic past be integrated, at least selectively, into the image of a Catholic nation? How did preconceived notions of Islam evolve, and under what conditions was it possible to abolish the conceptual boundaries of Islam?

These questions lead to an examination and comparison of the concept of Islam within the Spanish and Portuguese national identities. Both states share a similar history. Both nations viewed the medieval struggle against Islam as a heroic act. As colonial powers, both had contact over centuries with Muslim peoples. Did the processes of inclusion and exclusion of Islam work the same way in the formation of both nations, or were there differences in the quality and significance of the memories of these encounters? Did they occur chronologically parallel or offset? How can the differences be explained?

Such comparisons necessitate the partially artificial construction of comparable units, which has recently led to criticism of the comparative method.[60] Any study of multiple factors, however, demands the construction of a starting point and procedure.[61] The designations "Spain" and "Portugal" are used here as necessary simplifications and are not to be understood as absolute, closed entities. They are the result of cultural nation formation, not its prerequisite. Within this development, the memories of a Muslim presence in the territories of the future nation-states are the *tertium comparationis* used to compare the later constructions of "Islam" and associated understandings of the nation, their change over time, and the factors contributing to the outcomes.[62] To this aim, the respective political, social, and cultural developments are described, and similarities and differences outlined. From the beginning it should be made clear that some of these processes in Spain and Portugal occurred along differing chronologies: for example, the establishment of advanced academic study of Arab culture and language or the affinity with the Muslim populations in colonial areas. This is a commonly recognized problem with the comparative method: the selection of objects for comparison must find a balance between similarities, which make the comparison possible, and differences, which shed new light on the things compared.[63] In respect to the cultural context, the comparison of Spanish and Portuguese understandings of Islam is less asymmetrical than that of geographically distant civilizations. There are nevertheless significant qualitative and quantitative differences which make the comparison somewhat asymmetrical.[64] These asymmetries and delays can be used to better understand hidden, foundational commonalities and disparities. For example, differences in the development of institutions for academic study of Arab culture and literature as well as varying levels of cultural assimilation in the colonies point to differences in literacy, scholarly inquiry, and colonization.

Spain and Portugal share many historical commonalities: with the exception of Basque, their languages are similar; both claim a Roman and Visigoth (not Muslim!) heritage; their constitutional monarchies were challenged in the nineteenth centuries by liberal movements and anti-clericalism; both rose and fell as colonial powers; both monarchies were abolished in the early twentieth century and followed first by short-lived republics (from 1910 to 1926 in Portugal and from 1931 to 1936 in Spain) and then by longer periods of dictatorship (until 1974 in Portugal and 1975 in Spain). Furthermore, the geography of the two nations would seem to lend itself to a sense of common identity. Closer examination, however, reveals that these political parallels and the geographic proximity of the two countries belie the heterogeneity that was a serious obstacle to any kind of unification.

In the nineteenth century, the consolidation of nation-states in Italy and Germany and the marginalization of the Iberian Peninsula revitalized plans to create an Iberian Union to counteract the perceived deficits of Spain and Portugal in the European sphere.[65] Especially in Portugal, the Iberian question and the possibility of a unitary, federal, republican, or monarchical union with Spain was the subject of intense debate among intellectuals. Although the audience for this debate was socially limited, it encouraged a dialogue among intellectuals over Portugal.[66] The historian Joaquim Pedro de Oliveira Martins (1845–1894), despite his skepticism about a political federation, created a sort of "cultural Iberism"[67] by presenting Iberia as two states (and their respective colonies) bound culturally by a common destiny.[68] Except for such isolated intellectual contacts, however, public exchange and travel between Portugal and Spain was minimal except in the border regions: the relationship of the two was characterized more by ignorance than encounter.[69] In the end, the strong identification of the Portuguese with their nation and the Spaniards' affinity for their respective regions precluded the collective understanding that could have unified the region as a historical actor.[70]

Within the respective nationalist movements, the picture is even more complicated: the debate over the Spanish national concept continues within both historical and political circles there.[71] The historical peculiarities—for example, the heritage of the independent medieval kingdoms, the industrial imbalance between the regions, and the failure of comprehensive nationalization—encouraged the emergence of peripheral nationalist movements in the last third of the nineteenth century.[72] The centralist, Castilian nationalism invoked Islam as a common, external enemy, which served to define and unify a heterogeneous land. In contrast, Basque and Catalan nationalists used the supposed absence of a Muslim presence to distance themselves from Castilian centralism. This study therefore concentrates on Castilian nationalism and considers the peripheral nationalisms in the examples of the Basque Country's historiography and in the festivals of Moors and Christians in the Valencian Community.

On the other hand, in Portugal few questioned the existence of a single nation. In the nineteenth and twentieth centuries, intellectuals did emphasize the contrast between north and south, which was strengthened by the climatic differences between the Atlantic and Mediterranean zones. There was—and in some respects still is—a popular understanding of the "Christian North" as the origin of Portugal in opposition to an "Islamic South," a *mourolândia*; this dichotomy surfaces primarily in the competition between Porto and Lisbon.[73] However, this Portuguese regionalism has had little political significance.[74] The territorial demarcation which occurred during the Middle Ages was decisive in the formation of a later Portuguese identity.[75] Medieval events formed the basis for a political entity within which national identities subsequently slowly crystallized.[76]

This study must set some limits. Conceptions of Islam beyond the context of the national and colonial realm of Spain and Portugal—for example Spanish or Portuguese perceptions of the Ottoman Empire or the Arabian Peninsula—are not addressed for this reason. Similarly, this study does not address Islamic sources about the Muslim presence in Iberia. The impression could admittedly arise thereby that "the in-group discusses the outsiders, who have been condemned to silence," and that the analysis deconstructs Eurocentric perspectives, only to rebuild them in the end.[77] This approach, however, highlights the formation of national identities and the role of antagonistic stereotypes therein. The perception of Islam changed over time depending on the surrounding social, political, and cultural context. Studying this change can help historians to understand mechanisms of nation-building over an extended period. In this process, the evolution of the representations of Islam is a constant indicator of the changing national definition of "Ourselves" and the "Others."

METHODS AND SOURCES

Intellectual and cultural historians have described nation-building as a process of religious, historical, ethnic, and linguistic integration. Since the nearly simultaneous publication of the now canonic works by Benedict Anderson, Ernest Gellner, and Eric Hobsbawm in 1983, the study of nation as an "imagined community" (Anderson) via historical master narratives, political myths, jubilees and celebrations, exhibitions, monuments, music, and visual art and architecture—has become quite substantial.[78] Numerous investigations have analyzed mechanisms by which the nation became established as the central political model in the nineteenth century[79]: partly by an "invention of tradition" (Hobsbawm), of a supposed national past in historiography, myths, and architectural memorials, partly by oblivion or oppression.[80] The intentions of activists from the scholarly elite and supporters of nationalism, however, are not to be equated with the relevant experience and perception of the wider population, to which historians often have only limited access. However, it is at least possible to outline historical narratives which aimed at a wider audience, for example in school books or at public festivals. It is difficult to draw conclusions about the impact of such narratives on the population, but they indicate a potentially wider social reach than treatises that circulated only among the elite.

On the basis of these observations, this study seeks to illuminate the tensions between competing elite conceptions of the nation and the related struggles over their interpretation. Further, it attempts to determine which of these conceptions were aimed to reach a wider audience. A selection of examples shows how ideas of Islam were reflected in certain social contexts and everyday practices,[81] not only in the nineteenth century, the formative phase of European nationalism, but also in the twentieth century, an era often neglected by research on nationalism.[82]

Chapter one analyzes the depiction of Islam as a medieval opponent in the historiography of the nineteenth and twentieth centuries. The time span stretches from the liberal historiographies of the mid-nineteenth century, in which the nation was portrayed as a historical protagonist, through the establishment of the dictatorships in the 1930s, which changed the conditions for historiography in ways that made liberal interpretations especially difficult if not impossible. The approach centers on the historical actors, examining selected historians' works to determine how and why the Muslim presence was integrated or excluded from a national narrative. The chapter focuses on authors who had no or only rudimentary understanding of Arabic, who were thus neither specialists for the Muslim past nor experts in Arab language or culture.

Chapter two continues by focusing on Islam as an object of scholarship as reflected, on the one hand, in the institutionalization of Arab scholarship and the associated concepts of history and Islam and, on the other hand, in the examples of conservators, archaeologists, and historians who dealt with Muslim architecture. The distinction between the two was hazy in the early phases of professionalization. Chronologically the chapter deals with the period of formation of academic Arab studies, which coincides with the debate about national monuments. In Spain this occurred from the second half of the nineteenth century until the Civil War in 1936, in Portugal from the establishment of the republic in 1910 until the end of the Estado Novo in 1974. The approach is discursive, concentrating on the discussions of the pioneers of both institutional and non-academic Arab studies by analyzing national concepts which sought to incorporate the Muslim past into the image of a Christian nation.[83]

Chapter three turns to Islam as a "colonial Other": it begins with an overview of the developments during the nineteenth century and then proceeds to address the Iberian dictatorships in depth up to the point at which they lost the important Muslim colonies with the independence of Morocco from Spain in 1956 and the demise of the Portuguese colonial empire following the revolution of 25 April 1974. The analysis centers on the discourse about Islam in the colonies between governments, colonial politicians, members of the military, and ecclesiastical authorities. Given the traditional image of Islam as an adversary, which had dominated political and official discourse for centuries, the question arises as to why, at a certain point, both dictatorships positively reevaluated Islam. Even though many pejorative stereotypes about Islam survived these political caesuras, domestic events like the Spanish Civil War together with global processes like the wave of decolonization after 1945 led to an adjustment in the view of Islam. These strategies of differentiation and approximation are substantiated in this chapter.

While chapters one and two are dedicated to images of Islam that circulated among the intellectual and political elite, chapter three looks at the link between internal communications (e.g. colonial documents) and publications intended for a wider audience (e.g. propaganda). Chapter four goes on to address the depictions of Islam that were intended to have an extensive social reach. It is not about proving which social classes adopted which images of Islam, for this is nearly impossible with the available sources: instead the focus is on the intended reach of the historical images rather than their impact. Publicly performed stagings of national myths during historical jubilees are examined in addition to the portrayal of the (Muslim) past in school textbooks, though the latter only became relevant in the twentieth century, which accounts for that period's dominance in this section.

Chapter five completes the study by addressing Islam at a local level. The approach is performative: the analysis of annual ritual stagings of battles with Islam as part of urban and village festivals shows how representatives of the Islamic Other were imagined and incorporated into the local identities and also how changes in such festivals over time reflected the political and social developments. The conclusions of the earlier chapters about the images of Islam are here tested once again.

This study is based on a wealth of sources: historiographical texts; school books; academic scholarship on the Arab language, culture, and architecture; documents about colonial politics; textual and pictorial propaganda produced during the Spanish Civil War; commemorative publications; newspaper articles; iconographic portrayals (historical paintings, photographs); and descriptions of national and local festivals. Given the length of the study's timeframe and the abundance of material available, only printed material was considered; the aim was to adequately address the extensive geographic region in question and the richness of the relevant printed source material. A further limiting of the source selection was necessary: textual and pictorial sources were considered which were available for the entire period examined here, but more recent audiovisual materials—for example, Morocco films of the Franco period—which have been examined in other studies, were not.[84]

Similarly, it was beyond the reasonable capacity of the study to analyze the plethora of literary treatments of the figure of the *moro*, the Muslim past, and the Islamic presence in the colonies. There are already numerous studies that deal with these topics, among them relevant overviews of the genre of the *comedías moriscas*, which included influential sixteenth-century authors like Lope de Vega.[85] The recurring literary theme of the *moro de Granada*, which fascinated authors far beyond Spain, provides another significant example of literary idealization of Moorish figures.[86] These were often presented in contrast to a militant or religious hostility towards the Moors, which was exacerbated by actual conflicts. In the nineteenth and twentieth centuries, authors produced abundant texts featuring Jews and Moors.[87] Romantic authors conceptualized the bygone Muslim Middle Ages with dread and fascination and used it as an element of drama.[88] The colonization of Morocco was also a widespread theme in the literature. The distinction between fiction and autobiography was blurred in the *Diario de un testigo de la guerra de África* (*Diary of a Witness to the War in Africa*)[89] by Pedro António de Alarcón (1833–1891), who came to terms in this work with his experiences as a soldier and correspondent. Other studies have pointed out the heterogeneous nature of these texts, their authors, and their central tenets supporting and opposing colonization.[90] Many twentieth century authors addressed the relationship between Spain and North Africa and literature's attempt to come to terms with the past, including Francisco Ayala (1906–2009), author of the short story "La cabeza del cordero" (The Lamb's Head), in which the protagonist encounters his supposed relatives in Morocco.[91] The most prominent representative of Moorish culture at the end of the twentieth century was Juan Goytisolo (*1931), a novelist[92] and essayist[93] who, influenced by Américo Castro, addressed the Muslim past in his complex, multifaceted, and controversial works. Goytisolo reworked and revised a variety of historical myths, for example, the year 711 in his novel *La reivindicación del Conde don Julián* (*Count Julian*)[94]. Though literary depictions of Islam were not directly used for this study, they are an important source of inspiration and are accordingly quoted at the head of each chapter.

RESEARCH OVERVIEW

This study includes several aspects of cultural history and diverse geographic areas and thereby combines several fields of research. At the European level, it contributes to the study of the relationship between religion and nation. Furthermore, it attempts to explain the parallel and divergent developments at the level of the Iberian Peninsula and to describe Islam's role there. At the national level, there are continuities and interruptions in the historical narrative within Spain and Portugal as well as inclusive and exclusive processes. These are grounded in the main areas of conflict during the period examined: between liberalism and conservatism in the nineteenth century, and between dictatorship and democracy in the twentieth century.

Religion and nation

Within the cultural historical research on nationalism, many studies have investigated religion and national identity and thereby supplemented the classical studies of Gellner, Anderson, and Hobsbawm, who ascribed no especial importance to religion.[95] While the original secularization theory posited that national identity supersedes religion, later studies showed that religion changes and can in turn serve nationalism.[96] According to this interpretation, identification with the nation is a continuation of, rather than alternative to, religious identity. Research on religion and nation thus necessarily includes the interlacing of religious and secular understanding of modern society,[97] mechanisms of sacralization of the nation,[98] and the catalytic effect of armed conflict within these processes.[99] As part of territorial rivalries, nationalism could take on especially virulent religious dimensions.[100] Research on religion and nation in the multiconfessional societies of central Europe has concentrated on competing confessional concepts of the respective nations, while inter-religious references have at most dealt with the question of Jewish participation in the process of nation-building.[101]

The question of antagonism between religions, rather than confessions, and thus the role of Islam in fostering or hindering nation-building has thus far been addressed primarily for the Balkan states. Research on religious conflict with Islam during the early modern era has concentrated on the study of perceptions of the Ottoman Empire, and for the nineteenth and twentieth centuries on studies of the memory of Ottoman rule.[102] Studies of multiple countries in the Balkan region have shown how these nations rejected everything related to Islam after they gained independence from the Ottoman Empire. Not only did they consider it to have been forced upon them, but was also seen to be antiquated and to hinder their reaching out to Western Europe.[103]

There is no comparable body of research for the Iberian Peninsula on the connection between the legacy of Islamic rule and nation-building. The tensions between religion and nation in these confessionally homogenous societies formed primarily between Catholic and anticlerical groups. After the turn of the nineteenth century, Spanish society was characterized by antagonism between conservative and progressive parties, between ecclesiastical authorities and their opponents, between those who saw Spain as a (Catholic) Christian bastion and those who fought for a secularist or even anticlerical state. Starting with the Liberal Triennium from 1820 to 1823, the model of Two Spains emerged to describe this rift; it sparked political discussion during various crises in Spanish history and became a literary motif.[104] The latter was especially successful in this poem by Antonio Machado (1875–1939): "Little Spaniard, just now coming into the world, may God keep you. One of those two Spains will freeze your heart."[105] The crucial question of what role religion should play in the Spanish nation was a constant theme in intellectual circles of the nineteenth and twentieth centuries.[106] Similar discussions in Portugal about the relationship between Catholicism, republicanism, and secularism culminated in the establishment of a secular republic in 1911.[107] This division of state and church was later preserved in the Estado Novo. The Islamic legacy remained ambiguous during this process of religious nation formation: it was used for anti-Catholic, anti-national, and also anti-atheist purposes.

Iberian history

Historians have been slow to show interest in the question of Iberia as a whole, partly due to a lack of mutual interest between the Iberian states. This explains why the first comprehensive overview of Iberian history from Roman times to the twentieth century was produced in the USA rather than on the peninsula itself.[108] More recent political factors like democratization and Spain and Portugal's joint entrance into the European Community in 1986, combined with the fact that scholarship

has become more focused on comparative studies of two or more countries, have increasingly prompted historians to address the Iberian
Peninsula as a whole. The use of the term "Iberian," does not, however,
indicate balanced coverage of both Iberian nations: Spain often domi-
nates, as evidenced both in the names of various chaired professorships
and research institutions for Iberian Studies[109] and in the contents of
essay collections ostensibly about the Iberian Peninsula.[110] Due to the
complexity of Spanish nationalism, which remains a cause of political
discussions, Catalonia and the Basque region have received dispropor-
tionate attention compared to the politically autonomous state of
Portugal.

Beginning in the mid-1990s, a number of comparative studies of
nationalism were published which examined similarities in the political
structures of Spain and Portugal, especially in the twentieth century,[111]
political and cultural processes of nation formation,[112] national and
Iberian identity,[113] and the relationship between the two countries. While
these collections mostly grouped essays which focused on only one of the
countries under collective headings and attempted to unify them with an
introduction or commentary on the Iberian relationship, more recent
volumes of essays offer a more holistic discussion: they approach questions less from a national perspective than from a structural one, looking
at liberalism, authoritarianism, or the transition to democracy.[114] Further
studies have examined the neighboring countries' perceptions of each
other[115] and their respective roles in international relations.[116] Recent
cultural historical analysis has revealed similarities and differences in the
historical identities along with overlapping and intertwined aspects of the
national narrative in the nineteenth and twentieth centuries.[117] The
public festivals sponsored by the Iberian dictators have also been
compared.[118] These studies illustrate how profitable it can be to utilize
Portugal, which too often has been historically marginalized, as a counterpart for analytical comparison to Spain, because the national
history(s) are thereby seen in a new light. The potential for such studies
has in no way been exhausted.

Images of Islam in Spain and Portugal

Despite the growing body of research on the Iberian Peninsula as a whole,
the perception of Islam has been addressed only within the paradigm of
the national states. The considerable differences between the two countries in this respect, however, make it a logical subject for comparative
study.

In Spain the relationship between the nation and Islam has been a
topic of interest and object of scholarly attention since the nineteenth
century. Depending on their political, religious, and academic back-

ground, historians have viewed the Muslim past as either integral or contrary to the Spanish nation. This discussion climaxed, not as one might assume, between the opposing parties in the Civil War, but rather between similarly educated former colleagues: Claudio Sánchez-Albornoz (1893–1984) and Américo Castro (1885–1972) were republicans who fled Franco's Spain to live and publish in exile.[119] Their work on the medieval foundations of the Spanish nation and identity sparked heated discussions.[120] Castro, a philologist and cultural historian, argued in his books *España en su Historia: Cristianos, Moros y Judíos* (1948) and *La realidad histórica de España* (1954, *The Structure of Spanish History*) that the coexistence of Christianity, Islam, and Judaism was fundamental to the Spanish nation:

> Christian Spain was not something that preexisted in a fixed reality of her own, upon which fell the occasional influence of Islam, as a "mode" or a result of the life of "those times." Christian Spain "became"— emerged into being—as she incorporated and grafted into her living process what she was compelled to by her interaction with the Moslem world. . . . I wish to submit that that which is most original and universal in the Hispanic genius has its origin in a living disposition forged in the nine centuries of Christian-Jewish-Moorish interaction.[121]

Sánchez-Albnornoz, a medievalist and legal historian, countered this thesis with a series of articles and his two-volume account of Spanish history, *España: un enigma historico* (1956, *Spain, a Historical Enigma*).[122] He admitted to an Islamic influence in a cultural linguistic sense, but maintained that the "Spain's vital structure" had never been "Arabized."[123] Furthermore, he blamed Islam for the historical feudalization, fragmentation, and economic marginalization of Spain, which had been consumed by the fight against Islam in Europe's name:

> In summary, one should see here the tragedy that Islam caused in Spain, the legacy that Muhammad left behind: . . . an inexistent and multifaceted Spain, highly feudal, divided amongst differing kingdoms, . . . with diverging ideals and a disjoined economy.[124]

These opposing views shared a common focus on Castile, which they equated with Spain, and hardly considered other regions.[125] Beyond the content of their scholarship, the intensity of the language exchanged in this debate testifies to the sensitivity of the question of the "Spanish essence," especially in the claims made by Sánchez-Albornoz.[126]

Following the democratic transition, historians and scholars of Islam produced studies of Spanish perceptions of Islam along the entire spectrum of cultural scholarship. The development of the conception of Islam[127] – so central for Spain – was examined for all periods using individual genres of sources including iconographic portrayals,[128] historiography, school books,[129] and Spanish scholarship on Arab culture and language.[130] In addition, the role of Islam in the Moroccan wars[131] and in the central event of the twentieth century, the Spanish Civil War,[132] earned special attention. Within scholarship on nationalism and nation-building, further studies examined the foundation of a department of Arab Studies at the University of Madrid;[133] Islamic archaeology;[134] national myths like the Battle of Covadonga;[135] and the mobilization in the Spanish Civil War.[136] Scholars of social anthropology and communication studies have complemented and enriched the historical analysis by contributing interpretations of stereotype formation;[137] studies on the early modern notions of ethnic and religious purity (*casticismo*) and their transfer into modern concepts;[138] and descriptions of Islam's role in popular festivals.[139] Research on the paradigm of the "three cultures" (Jewish, Christian, and Muslim) analyzes its significance for Spanish identity in the twentieth century.[140]

While the Spanish portrayal of the *moro* has been the subject of much research, study of the perception of Islam and its role in the nation formation of Portugal has only just begun. The effects of the Islamic presence in Spain became the subject of heated debate, but its fundamental significance was widely accepted. Scholars remain divided, however, on the question of Islam's relevance in Portuguese history. The literary scholar Eduardo Lourenço (*1923), one of the most influential contemporary Portuguese intellectuals, posits the struggle with Islam as the catalyst for a militant pilgrimage myth and the medieval conception of a chosen people.[141] He praises the trend of more recent research in which "our Arab side, which had been deeply suppressed, is coming to the surface and will force us . . . to reconsider our canonical national myth, which was born, consciously or unconsciously, out of this suppression and of active forgetting." [142] In contrast, the historian João Medina (*1939) did not even include Islam in his recent study of the "images which define the identity of Portugal." Instead, he emphasizes the expulsion of the Jews: the simultaneous expulsion of the Muslims, who unlike the Jews had once ruled the territory, remains in the background.[143] Similarly, in 1996 the Portuguese government commemorated the 500th anniversary of the expulsion of the Jews while never mentioning the Muslims' similar fate.[144]

There are historical reasons for this deficiency. Following nineteenth-century historians' efforts to deal with Islam in medieval Portugal, the historiography of the Estado Novo consciously ignored the minorities and was primarily devoted to fashioning heroic Christian monarchs and explorers. This changed in the 1990s with the exposure of the selective vision of historical research to date. An especially important new field of research investigates the conception of Islam within the realm of Portuguese colonialism and its influence on the formulation of a national narrative.[145] Other recent studies have taken the first steps towards understanding the role of Islam within Portugal itself by investigating Arabic scholars and Arabic studies.[146] In addition, historians, religious scholars, and political scientists have examined the first (modern) Muslim community in Portugal (Comunidade Islâmica de Lisboa) and the Muslim presence there.[147]

The discrepancy in the state of research on Spain and Portugal cannot be explained solely by external factors like the difference in size or the shorter Muslim presence within what is the modern state of Portugal. This is not only the starting point for the present study, but also an object of inquiry: it is not only the *explanans* but an *explanandum*, as well. It is impossible to entirely correct the imbalance, which is endemic in the current scholarship. The study does, however, select examples from the plethora of Spanish studies and grant the heretofore mostly marginalized Portuguese examples comparable attention.

1

Islam as a Historical Enemy: The Middle Ages as Portrayed in the Historiography

"His eyes were Portuguese,
an abiding reflection of inner thoughts,
turbulent tempests of the heart, and an utter inner peace.
The name of his homeland was written in the boy's face:
he was a son of Hispania:
The colors, the gestures, the look—all indicated,
that the spirit of a Goth resided within,
and, at the same time, that
the blood of an Arab coursed through his veins."[1]

Alexandre Herculano, *O Monge de Cistér ou a Epocha de João I* (1848)

ISLAM IN THE SEARCH FOR A "SER DE ESPAÑA"

In the nineteenth and twentieth centuries, Spanish historians produced historiographical concepts that reflected the political and social divisions in their country. The various groups—conservatives[2] and liberals, clerics and secularists, monarchists and republicans—struggled between and even amongst themselves to define a state which was gradually losing its grip on the former South American colonies and felt robbed of its former glory. The Carlist Wars, the short-lived First Republic, the restoration of the Bourbon monarchy, and the frequent changes of government around the turn of the twentieth century clearly demonstrated these fissures between the "two Spains." There were in fact far more than two. Spanish intellectuals responded to these turbulent times by asking themselves what constituted "Spain." In their search for a *ser de España*, a quintessential Spanish nature, they sought a model for the future in Spain's past. They inevitably viewed history, however, through the lens of their present.

These concepts of the nation were as varied as the political and religious views of their authors, but they all sought to create a sense of unity lacking in their contemporary society. The Islamic domination of the Middle Ages was an obstacle in the formulation of a continuous Spanish narrative. The early modern monarchs—from Ferdinand and Isabella to Philip III—had attempted to effect territorial and political unity by shoring up the religious identity of Spain by forcing baptism and expelling religious minorities. The historiography of this period was inclined to portray Islam negatively, written as it was under the influence of the Reformation and Counter Reformation, conflicts with the Ottoman Empire, and the attacks of the Barbary Pirates along the Spanish coast. The Jesuit Juan de Mariana (1536–1624), whose *Historia de rebus Hispaniae* was published in multiple languages and editions and remained a standard work through the nineteenth century, characterized the Saracens as "rabble" and Islam as "evil superstition." [3] Despite scattered support, Islam served as a sort of negative backdrop against which Spanish society defined itself into the nineteenth century.[4] The dualistic understanding which nineteenth-century historians had inherited led them to perceive the Islamic past as somehow "un-Spanish."

Nevertheless, historians recognized the significance of the Middle Ages and therefore felt obliged to somehow smooth over these fractures and integrate them into a coherent national concept.[5] They had to both explain how Islam had been able to defeat the Christian Visigoths in the first place and then integrate the influence which Muslims had had on the peninsula over the course of the nearly nine hundred years between Tariq's invasion in 711 and the expulsion of the *moriscos* in 1609. Ignoring or denying their importance was not an option: there were undeniable traces of the Islamic past in the laws, culture, language, and architecture of Spain. In addition, there was an ethnic dimension: whereas sixteenth-century statutes concerning *limpieza de sangre*, purity of blood, had equated religion and ethnicity and favored "northern" blood as purer and nobler,[6] the nineteenth century, influenced by theories of race, paid more attention to ethnic lineage. The question of physical relationships between Muslims and Christians and the corresponding influence on the gene pool within Spain was present but seldom directly addressed. Nevertheless, it lent the search for a *ser de España* a concrete biological aspect.[7]

In the search for these answers, the so-called *reconquista* became a central concept. This term, used by historians since the eighteenth century, took on new meaning in the mid-nineteenth century. The term *restauración*, prominent in the early modern period, had primarily described the restoration of the Visigoth kingdom and the Christian faith. The term *reconquista*, on the other hand, suggested that the territorial conquest had had a significant martial component, not only a necessary defense against an enemy of the faith but also a territorial stranger.[8] The latter had the advantage of portraying the struggle with Islam as a national achievement which set Spain apart from the rest of Europe.[9] At times both terms were used simultaneously.[10] However, in the nineteenth century, *reconquista* gradually came to dominate.[11] This is evidenced in the fact that *reconquista* was used not only to describe the struggles between Muslim and Christian rulers or the concrete conquest of a town or fortress, but rather increasingly to refer to the centuries of Islamic rule themselves.[12] *Reconquista* thus became the most successful Spanish national myth: the fight against Islamic domination, in which religious and political goals seemed to be inextricably linked, was depicted as the deciding characteristic of an entire epoch.[13] The mythical *reconquista* allowed nineteenth-century historiography to brush aside the religious and political heterogeneity of the Middle Ages—even though these were manifest in the alliances and battles with and against fellow believers. They replaced it with a simplified master narrative in which countless individual narratives took on mythical proportions: for example, the Battles of Covadonga, Clavijo, and Las Navas de Tolosa; the legend of Saint James the Moor Slayer (Santiago Matamoros); or the "Cid," Rodrigo Díaz de Vivar.

The *reconquista* thus provided a historical framework from which the attitudes of the individual authors towards Islam could be discerned. There were key moments which had to be included in any national narrative: Tariq's invasion in 711; the Battle of Covadonga in 722, which heralded the beginning of the supposed *reconquista*;[14] Granada's fall as the last outpost of Islamic power in 1492; and the expulsion of the *moriscos*, the baptized descendants of the Muslim population, in 1609.[15] Historians incorporated these events differently depending on the political significance they ascribed to religion. There were as many explanations as there were authors. Given this wealth of scholarship, the following selection can present only a few examples of the most influential and prominent authors within important political factions: the liberal (Modesto Lafuente) and the conservative-neocatholic (Marcelino Menéndez y Pelayo, Manuel Merry y Colón), in addition to the liberal (Rafael Altamira) and conservative (Ramón Menéndez Pidal) representatives of the *regeneracionismo* after 1898. The historical position of Cláudio Sánchez-Albornoz, who would later vehemently oppose Castro, also emerged in this period. Based on this body of scholarship, basic positions on the incorporation of medieval Muslim history can be outlined which competed with and influenced one another. As varied as the accounts listed are, they nevertheless share a Castilian, centralist conception of the Spanish nation. They are supplemented here by Basque conceptions of history as an example of the portrayal of Islam in peripheral national concepts.

Between aversion and fascination: Modesto Lafuente y Zamalloa

The historian, theologian, and journalist Modesto Lafuente (1806–1866) made the nation the protagonist in his thirty-volume work, *Historia general de España*. He is thus considered the founder of the liberal historiography of the Spanish nation, and, because of its large number of editions, the *Historia general* was regarded as a sort of "Bible of the Spanish Middle Class" during the era of Isabella II.[16] Lafuente, who was educated in a Catholic institution but never tooks clerical vows, was not anticlerical like many liberals. He viewed the Spanish nation as clearly Catholic, but favored the separation of church and state.[17] This search for a balance between religion and politics, between national pride and tolerance, is also evident in his position regarding Islam. He clearly saw the year 711 as "one of the worst catastrophes ever to befall Spain, one of the most horrifying revolutions, perhaps the worst of all."[18] From Lafuente's point of view, the nation was an organic subject with roots stretching back to the pre-Roman Iberians, and this crisis had been its test of character: "The nation has disappeared; she will rise again."[19] The religious semantics reflect Lafuente's interpretation of the event as somehow sacred.

Thus Lafuente viewed the struggle with Islam as a national defense against a foreign entity. He dealt with the "conquerors of Spain" in depth and described Muhammad's biography, the teachings of the Quran, and the deeds of the Muslim rulers over the peninsula.[20] His attitude oscillated between disgust for their atrocities and admiration of their religious tolerance, especially during the caliphate. He hid this ambivalence in his many questions: "How can our rulers' mix of wildness and gentleness, of generosity and cruelty be explained? The Arab, impetuous and fiery like his warhorse, violent in his passions and emotional outbursts, is generous, gallant, and thankful, but fierce in his hate, blind in his wrath, and relentless in his revenge."[21] Lafuente's description resonates with many of the characteristics which the Orientalists of the nineteenth century conveyed in their stories, images, and poetry. This combination of high culture and bellicosity, of patience and violence towards those of other faiths, was a stereotype of Islam common in European Romanticism. Lafuente's questions were not meant to be answered; indeed, definitive answers would only have detracted from Islam's fascination.

His ambivalence towards Islam carried over into similar attitudes towards the Catholic monarchs. On the one hand, he admired what they had achieved in terms of national unity, but, on the other hand, he was outraged by their religious intolerance. He enthusiastically celebrated Isabella I of Castile as "the" Spanish heroine and attempted to draw parallels to the successor who bore her name, Isabella II,[22] even though this required that he legitimize forced baptisms, expulsions, and the establishment of the Inquistion. "A worthy prince and the most gracious princess who ever sat on Castile's throne left their heirs with the most malignant, darkest, most oppressive institution for human rights and thought, the most contradictory to Christianity's mind and spirit."[23] His verdict on the expulsion of the *moriscos* was similarly skeptical. Although it had contributed to a religious unity of sorts, "we do not believe that it is a great accomplishment ... to achieve unity by extinguishing those who are of another faith. The accomplishment would have been to convert the unbelieving and angry by way of doctrine, conviction, wisdom, gentleness, and the superiority of our civilization."[24] Lafuente's views clearly opposed those of conservative Catholic authors like Menéndez y Pelayo, who explicitly approved the expulsion.[25] Such diverse positions on controversial points within the past reveal the ideological heterogeneity of Spanish historiography.

Lafuente viewed Islam as a destroyer of national unity but nevertheless ascribed it a prominent role in his narrative. He praised Christian deeds but was outraged by the fate of the non-Christians. The search for contemporary balance was reflected in his search for historical balance. His careful negotiation between fascination and aversion provided many liberals with model attitudes towards the Islamic past.

Exclusion: Marcelino Menéndez Pelayo

The historian Marcelino Menéndez y Pelayo (1856–1912) from Santander, one of nineteenth-century Spain's most influential scholars, essentially equated Spanishness with Catholicism; in his eyes, therefore, the Islamic past was anti-Spanish. This interpretation made him an important figurehead for the Catholic parties which agreed with him on this point. The young scholar was admired by the *integristas*, supporters of an antiliberal, traditional Catholicism, the most radical of whom had abandoned the ranks of the monarchist Carlists in 1888 to form their own party.[26] Menéndez y Pelayo himself (together with the founder of the Catholic Union party, Alejandro Pidal y Mon), however, switched for practical reasons to the liberal conservative party of Antonio Cánovas del Castillo.[27] Despite his (professed) political disinterest, Menéndez y Pelayo served two terms in the Senate for this party, which indicated a revision of his earlier skepticism towards the Restoration and a favorable reconsideration of the parliamentary monarchy. The *integristas* resented this transition because, in their opinion, the constitution of the Restoration did not go far enough[28]: although it established Catholicism as the state religion, articles eleven and thirteen ensured the freedom to practice other religions privately as well as the freedoms of thought and assembly. From the *integristas'* point of view this could not be reconciled with Spain's Catholic essence.[29]

Menéndez y Pelayo may have succeeded for a long time at walking a tightrope between the various Catholic groups, but in his writing his position was clear. He popularized Christianity as a vise which held the nation together. Accordingly, his *Historia de los heterodoxes españoles* (*A History of the Spanish Heterodox*)[30] recounts a history in which, over the course of centuries, various heretical movements had been successfully repressed, including, for example, the Arians, Albigenses, and Protestants. Though members of these groups may have been Spanish by birth, their rejection of Roman Catholicism, which Menéndez y Pelayo saw as an intrinsic part of Spain, made them outsiders in his eyes.[31] This attitude was influenced by Menéndez y Pelayos' contemporary experiences. Given the social, economic, and regional conflicts which plagued the state during the Restoration, he viewed religion as the key to Spanish greatness and unity: "Without a shared god, a shared altar, a shared sacrifice, without calling themselves children of a shared father, and being renewed via a shared sacrament . . . , which people could be strong and grand? . . . Christianity grants Spain this unity."[32]

The sheer volume of Menéndez y Pelayo's scholarship makes it difficult to summarize his attitude towards the Muslim presence. He praised Muslim and especially Jewish thinkers like Maimonides and expressed appreciation for the cultural blossoming of Al-Andalus, which certainly would have dismayed the more conservative of his followers.[33] This does not mean, however, that his conception of a *ser de España* left room for other religions or even for other non-Catholic Christian denominations. He considered the Muslims of the year 711 "foreign invaders, different in race, language, and culture [than us]," whom he at least credited with being tolerant towards those who practiced the Christian religion.[34] He criticized the methods used to drive out the *moriscos*, but he felt that the expulsion itself had been a historical necessity:

> A hundred times worse than the professing Muslims, whose religion is an obstacle to every civilization, there were dissembling Christians, dissenters and apostates, furthermore disloyal subjects and godless Spaniards, enemies of their own land, born supporters of every foreign invasion, a race unable to be assimilated, as the tragic experiences over one and half centuries teach [us]. Does this mean to excuse those who broke the treaty of surrender from Granada or those who participated in the rebellion in Valencia . . . ,[35] who baptized the *moriscos* in a sacrilegious way? Not at all. But . . . after every hope of a peaceful conversion was exhausted, the expulsion was unavoidable, and I reiterate that Philip II's mistake was to not do so at the right moment.[36]

At the same time, Menéndez y Pelayo was not blind to the fact that the expulsion represented a loss of labor power and knowledge which had disadvantaged Spain in many ways. In his view, however, this material loss could be more easily compensated for than the potential effects of a prolonged conflict.[37] As a scholar Menéndez y Pelayo valued the cultural accomplishments of Jews and Moors in the Middle Ages, but for the Spanish nation these were insignificant. He viewed the expulsion of the *moriscos*, perceived to be foreign, in a social Darwinist light as confirmation that the "inferior race always loses out in the end to the stronger and more robust principle of nationality."[38] The historical accounts influenced by Menéndez y Pelay saw Catholicism as integral to the nation, equated religious and political unity, and thus excluded Islam a priori from a *ser de España*.

Marginalization: Manuel Merry y Colón

If one focuses on the political history with its rulers and territories instead of the cultural and intellectual history as Menéndez y Pelayo did, it is impossible to ignore the Islamic kingdoms. Nevertheless historians, including the Sevillian Manuel Merry y Colón (1835–1894), developed strategies to marginalize the political and cultural importance of this period. A member of the Unión Católica, he, too, was interested in defending a Catholic Spain, though it was not his goal to support the theses of the Carlists. He defended his view of an intrinsically Catholic Spain, not only in his six-volume account of Spanish history, but also in a shorter, more succinct narrative accessible to a wider audience, which he wrote together with his son, Antonio Merry y Villalba. This *Compendio de la Historia de España* (Compendium of Spanish History) was widely used in Catholic schools and seminaries during the Restoration period.[39]

Most Catholic authors agreed with Merry y Colón that the conversion of the Visigoth king Reccared from Arianism to Catholicism in 589 was the naissance of Christian Spain. The subsequent disruption introduced by Islamic rule was, in Merry y Colón's opinion, divine punishment for the intrigues, decadence, and moral decay under the Visigoths: "Providence's highest purpose was to punish any people whose lives were limited to debauchery and baseness with disintegration and ruin."[40] In the eyes of conservative Catholic authors, this was the only fitting explanation for the end of Christian rule in the Middle Ages. They strained to salvage some meaning from events which they viewed as a definitive catastrophe.

The description of the *reconquista* takes up about forty percent of the *Compendio*,[41] within which the description of "Arabian Spain" covers just two pages. Compared to the extensive descriptions of Christian heroics during the Middle Ages, Merry y Colón's brevity here is a clear expression of disdain. This quantitative disregard is intensified in his dismal depictions: "The Moors sowed dismay throughout the peninsula, for the terror which they spread was so great that it was comparable . . . to the damage done in Troy, Babylon, and Jerusalem with their inhumane behavior."[42] Merry y Colón echoed here the judgments of the *Crónica Mozárabe* of 754, an eyewitness account of the first decades of Muslim rule by an anonymous cleric who was presumably from Murcia or Toledo.[43] The account gave the impression that the social order was breaking down and compared the situation with biblical tragedies.[44] Merry y Colón only summarily referred to the Muslims' cultural achievements, especially during the caliphate, and he denied their "originality." He blamed "despotism in the political organization, [and] the moral decay to which this religion leads, which encourages every liberty and sensuousness [i.e., carnality]," for the demise of the caliphate.[45] Parallel to this brief account, he described Christian heroics at length. In his account, the Battle of Covadonga between the Visigoth leader Pelayo and the Muslim troops became an emotional lesson for seminarians about the indivisibility of the throne and altar in Spain:

> The first king of Asturias leads his few troops to the battlefield. In one hand he holds the holy cross, in the other his sword. They gather in the grotto of Covadonga, before the icon of the Virgin Mary, to say a fervent prayer, and so they attack the hostile Moors near Monte Auseba, defeat and humble them. It was heaven's will to help those valiant Christians, and so it happened that the mountain began to disintegrate, cascading down upon the Muslims, and burying the majority of them. Pelayo advances with his small regiment, captures Gijón, defeats Munuza [a Muslim general in northern Spain] near Orates, and the territories of Asturias are freed from the Muslim yoke.[46]

The vivid description and the use of the present tense not only serve to make the account dramatic and haunting, but they also place the historical battle against Islam in a practically contemporary context. This vision of a glorious *reconquista* serving to unify Spain clearly illustrates how the memory of Christian heroism was intended to garner support for Catholicism in the nineteenth century. The Islamic opposition appeared throughout such accounts as intimidating and brutal, but in the end it remained somehow dim and ill-defined. Islam provided the dim background against which Christian deeds could be portrayed as rays of light.

From religion to civilization: Rafael Altamira y Crevea

Whereas the historians addressed thus far adapted the religious dichotomy to mean that the medieval Islamic past was "un-Spanish," one of the most influential liberal historians, Rafael Altamira (1866–1951), offered another perspective: he treated Islam first and foremost as a civilization and only secondarily as a religion. An important proponent of the Spanish *regeneracionismo* after 1898, Altamira was convinced that the *regeneración* of the Spanish nation could be achieved only through education and awareness of historical and social accomplishments. Neither the church nor the nation took on the role of protagonist in this account; instead, Altamira focused primarily on the social and cultural contributions of those ethnic groups who had settled the peninsula, including the Muslims in the Middle Ages. In his most significant work, *Historia de Espana y de la civilización española (A History of Spanish Civilization)*,[47] Altamira outlines Islamic law, finer points of Arabic languages, the Islamic instructional system, philosophy, and literature alongside their Christian counterparts. The Islamic influence, such an uncomfortable topic for conservative historians, was dealt with here on multiple levels:

> The opposing political interests and the ongoing struggle between the Christian centers of the peninsula and the invaders should not lead to false conclusions about the everyday relationship between the two. Off the battlefield, the two peoples often dealt with each other with compassion and familiarity. . . . This mingling must have been significant in all social classes, necessitated by the shortage of women among the ranks of the militant interlopers. . . . On this point individual agreements prevailed over religious feelings, which, on the other hand, were not always a barrier which separated the two parties with insurmountable hate. This is seen in the fact that there is hardly any war in which Muslims fought on one side and Christians on the other, but rather much more often that there were mixed troops of both origins on each side.[48]

Just as Altamira dealt openly with the topic of interreligious marriage, he similarly deconstructs the often mythologized *reconquista*. He differentiated between a "unifying effect" of the *reconquista*, which united the Christians themselves, and a "disassociating effect," which led to particularism within the Christian kingdoms.[49] In Altamira's opinion, these parallel developments explained the diverse mentalities in Spain and the contemporary tension between the central (Castilian) state and the movements for autonomy on the peripheries. He highlighted the connection between medieval Christians and Muslims and described the latter in depth, but in the end he, too, thought of them as not "Spanish." In a later work, he portrayed the spread and conservation of the Jewish and Islamic cultural heritage as an accomplishment, but also credited Spain with having been "Europe's salvation from the Muslim and Turkish danger."[50] With this conclusion he accommodates the conservative narratives of *reconquista* and *convivencia* in his work.

His work was widely read and acclaimed by many, including Menéndez y Pelayo, who explicitly praised the *Historia de Espana y de la civilización española*.[51] This can be explained by the fact that Altamira shared the opinions of conservative authors, even if his conclusions were motivated by other goals. His example shows that the Spanish historical narrative varied less in its content than in the way the historians presented and weighed their arguments.

Cultural influence with reservations: Ramón Menéndez Pidal, Cláudio Sánchez-Albornoz

The debate over the *ser de España* intensified after 1898 and led to an increased interest in the past far beyond the circles of academic historians. Influential intellectuals drew attention to the *ser de España* and the question of whether their nation was experiencing *europeización* or *africanización*. These included Ángel Ganivet (1865–1898) as a trailblazer of the Generación del 98 (Generation of 1898) in addition to authors as varied as Miguel de Unamuno (1864–1936), Ramiro de Maeztu (1875–1936), and José Ortega y Gasset (1883–1955).[52] Religion played an undeniable role in these questions. Altamira represented the secular view of the Middle Ages. However, the changes in thought appeared within a new generation of traditionally oriented historians and their judgment of this epoch. Ramón Menéndez Pidal (1869–1968), a prominent representative of the Generación del 98 and the first leader of the Centro de Estudios Históricos, established in 1910, had been a student of Menéndez y Pelayo's. Unlike his teacher, however, Pidal did not marginalize the Islamic Middle Ages but viewed this epoch as an important turning point for the national history.

His literary scholarship attempted to define the essence of Spain, and even more so, its Castilian being, especially his studies on the heroic epic *Cantar del mio Cid* (*Poem of the Cid*). Based on Arabist scholarship, he developed the topos of Spain as a link between Christianity and Islam. He emphasized that "the great cultural successes of the Middle Ages were due to the Muslims, especially from the eighth to the twelfth century, during which the language of progress is Arabic, not Latin."[53] As an example of the cultural exchange between Christians and Muslims, he offered an example taken from his personal area of research, the historical Cid: "In Valencia the Cid became interested in Arabic authors; he would have been a barbarian if he had not been infused with the literature of the conquered."[54] Although Menéndez Pidal's comments went further than many other conservative nineteenth-century authors who denied there having been any such exchange at all, in his account the Cid remained an innately Spanish, Christian hero who understood himself to be "stronger in his Westernness."[55] This was in congruence with Menéndez Pidal's underlying assumption that Spain's historical essence predated the Middle Ages and that the Muslim era had merely influenced this preexisting essence.[56]

Cláudio Sánchez-Albornoz (1893–1984), who studied under Menéndez Pidal, extended this line of argumentation. In 1929, he published an essay in the *Revista de Occidente* on "España y el islam."[57] In later publications, including his *España – un enigma historico*, Sánchez-Albornoz subsequently expanded the initial essay's central theses in response to Americo Castro's *España en su historia.*[58] Sánchez-Albornoz also viewed the Middle Ages as crucial in the national history, but his theses were much more pointed than those of Menéndez Pidal. The sole accomplishment with which he credited Islam was the influence of the "Arabic Spanish culture," which had "produced the most abundant fruits, cultivated the Hispanic spirit, and paved the way for an early reception of the Renaissance on our soil and for the exquisite blossoming of the Golden Age."[59] On the other hand, Sánchez-Albornoz also pointed to a "fatal influence of Saracen rule in Spain on the economic life and the political organization."[60] This criticism was especially biting because Sánchez-Albornoz made medieval Islam a scapegoat, blaming it for Spain's contemporary underdeveloped state:

> Without Islam, a unified Spain, despite feudalism, would have had a sense of solidarity and weight which were lacking in the sixteenth century. . . . Without Islam the wealth of Spain would have grown as quickly as that of its neighboring countries in the West, and Spain would have been a match for them. . . . And without Islam . . . , with a less powerful monarchy, with a leading class concerned most of all with the well-being of the nation, and with a population with normal religious and militant sensibilities, the nation would not have allowed itself to be carried away by the military adventures of the Habsburgs beyond the limits of necessary interests and would have known to defend itself against the despotism of a foreign dynasty which ruined Spain's economy with its foreign policies and left the central problem of Hispanic unity unsolved and extinguished the Spanish spirit for centuries with its domestic policies.[61]

The attack on the Habsburg dynasty as the origin of feudalism, absolutism, and internal disarray did not originate with Sánchez-Albornoz. Nineteenth-century liberals had repeatedly made this suggestion.[62] Sánchez-Albornoz's theses naturally challenged nationalist Catholic interpretations.[63] Seen as a whole, the republican Sánchez-Albornoz had a certain affinity with liberal conceptions, but he combined these with the hostile attitude towards Islam common in conservative Catholic circles.

The examples of Menéndez Pidal and Sánchez-Albornoz clearly illustrate a transition between the scholarship of the nineteenth century and that of the 1920s: the later authors, though decidedly Catholic, addressed the Islamic Middle Ages in depth and assigned them an important if not uncontroversial role in the historical narrative of the nation. The insights of Arabic studies were being incorporated into the broader scholarship.[64] The later debate between Sánchez-Albornoz and Castro had its roots in this environment of the 1920s. The two historians had much in common—similar educational paths at the secular Institución Libre de la Enseñanza, a shared republican, anti-Franco political stance, and the experience of being in exile—but this did not prevent a most vehement historiographical debate over the Islamic Middle Ages from breaking out between them. Perhaps it was precisely the experience of watching Spain's fate unfold from afar that served to catalyze the debate. Although the debate itself began first in 1948, the contested claims predated the Civil War, Francoism, and their exile.

Islam in the "*nacionalismos periféricos*": The example of the Basque Country

The movements for autonomy which emerged in Catalonia, the Basque Country, and Galicia in the last third of the nineteenth century developed their own conceptions of history which challenged those of the central Castilian state. This had an effect on the portrayal of the *moros*. In particular, Sabino Arana Goiri (1865–1903), the founder of the Partido Nacional Vasco (PNV), which advocated a radical Basque nationalism, attempted to attack the Castilian representations of history with its own weapons: although Castilians celebrated the defensive struggle against the Moors as their most important accomplishment, Arana claimed that there had been practically no Muslim presence in the Basque region.[65] Early versions of this topos can be found already in the early modern era. The privilege of the collective nobility (*hidalguía universal*) was granted, for example, according to which Basques were not required to prove their "purity of blood" when entering the monarch's service.[66] Arana, an important advocate of an ethnic basis for the Basque nation, developed an anti-Castilian thesis, claiming that the Basque Country was not only ethnically purer, but also more devoutly Catholic than Spain at large.[67] Instead of using the traditional name of the Basque Country, Euskal Herria, which was a reference to those who speak *euskera*, Arana introduced the neologism *Euzkadi*, which refers to all who are of the Basque race.[68] The idea of racial purity as the basis of the Basque nation was so central to Arana's work that he even viewed the name of a person as an indication to whether they were *euskeriano* or *maketo*.[69] Marriages with non-Basques were to be avoided in order to preserve the racial purity, but also to protest the religious spirit.[70]

Arana judged the Basques to be the oldest race on the peninsula, and he characterized the province of Vizcaya, which he used to illustrate his theories about the Basque Country in general, as the region "which not even the bellicose sons of Muhammad were able to capture and subjugate."[71] During the Melilla War in 1893, when Spanish newspapers evoked the stereotype of the perfidious, bloodthirsty moros, Arana used the animosity between the Spaniards and the moros to characterize the relationship between Spain and the Basque region: "The maketos. They are our Moors. With one difference: the Moors hate the Spaniards because some of them are oppressed by them, and the maketos are those who enslave us . . . and will not stop until they have extinguished our race." The popular expression hay moros en la costa—literally "Moors on the coast," or more figuratively, "trouble is brewing"—did not apply to the Basque region, for the maketos had long since settled there.[72] Arana expressed his hate for "our national parasites"[73] by using the most prominent Spanish antagonistic stereotype against the Castilian central state.

The PNV moderated their founder's obsession with ethnicity in order to widen their potential political base. The question of ethnicity became one of several factors with broader appeal, for example, love of the Basque homeland, fluency in the language, or simply one's birthplace.[74] Nevertheless, the supposed absence of Islam within the region remained an important topos in Basque historiography leading up to the Civil War. Estanislao de Labayru (1845–1904) provided a factually detailed account of the Basque defense against the invading Muslim troops.[75] Bernardo Estornés Lasa (1907–1999), who contested the kinship of the Iberians and the Basques, described the battles of the Basques against Islam as a fight for the existence of a people.[76] The politician from Bilbao and opponent of Basque nationalism, Gregorio de Balparda (1874–1936), on the other hand, in his centralist version of history, emphasized that the Basque Country had not been in the least exceptional during the Muslim takeover of the peninsula. He thereby countered the separatist Basque historical accounts.[77]

The anti-Islamic attitudes of Basque nationalism were actually veiled anti-Castilian sentiments. This historic Muslim presence was suppressed and marginalized rather than addressed. Though this could be achieved for the past, it was not as much an option for the contemporary period. The group Aberri (Fatherland), for example, sided with the Moroccan independence fighter Abd el-Krim during the Rif War in the 1920s.[78] In the magazine bearing their name, they attempted to counter the depiction of the wild, barbaric moros, which prevailed in the majority of the Castilian press, by substituting the image of Abd el-Krim as a courageous, patriotic freedom fighter.[79] Even though Arana's racial attitudes were still present, this case shows that it was primarily about independence and autonomy. Aberri, which suggested forming a four-party alliance including the Basque Country, Catalonia, Galicia, and the Rif Republic to support Morocco, was more radical than the Catalan nationalists.[80] Within Catalonia, the position of nationalist groups towards the wars in Morocco changed from the patriotic fervor of the middle classes during the war from 1859 to 1860—and a corresponding anti-Moroccan atmosphere[81]—to declarations of solidarity with the Moroccans in the 1920s and an insistence that the war was a purely Spanish affair of no concern to Catalonia.[82] When "Muslims" fought against Spain, they could also garner support from the nationalists on Spain's periphery.

ISLAM IN THE SEARCH FOR PORTUGUESE ORIGINS

The question of Portugal's Islamic past emerged as part of that country's search for its political, cultural, and ethnic origins. Nineteenth century-historians felt called to explain how the small County of Portucalia on the edge of the peninsula was able to ascend to the status of independent kingdom and, excepting the Iberian Union (1580–1640), maintain this for seven centuries. Portuguese historians agreed that this course was inextricably linked to Portugal's military success, against both Christians and Muslims alike.

The Islamic adversary thus became a prominent figure in Portugal's foundational myths. Historians had to deal with Islam's role and influence in the rise of the Portuguese nation. Religious interpretations viewed the Christian nature as essential and portrayed the struggle against Islam as a divine mandate which made Portugal's independence sacred. Secular authors discounted religious factors and influences, emphasizing the political, voluntaristic elements of Portuguese nation-building: in such accounts, Islam was only one of several political opponents. A third approach emphasized Portugal's ethnic roots and rejected both the religious and the purely political interpretations.

These varied authors did not agree on the key moments of medieval history, offering varied interpretations of conflicts with Islamic opponents like the Battle of Ourique (1139) or the Siege of Lisbon (1147). The encounter with León or Castile—for example, the Battle of Aljubarrota in 1385—was considered more relevant. A line could be drawn from the historical opponent to neighboring Spain, which the Portuguese intellectual elite of the nineteenth century viewed skeptically. The year 711 was considered less important from this perspective: since Portugal was equated with the rise of an independent nation, events prior to the twelfth century were relegated to a sort of pre-history.

The myth of the *reconquista* broke down not only on religious, but also on political grounds, because the southern expansion of the new kingdom actually represented more of a *conquista*, i.e., a campaign to enlarge the territory. Thus these historians were not so much interested in specific events like battles but rather in the processes that had stabilized Portugal's autonomy or otherwise fostered development.[83] This is evidenced, for example, in the fact that the definitive fall of the last Muslim town, Silves in the Algarve (1249), garnered no particularly strong attention and was not incorporated into the national mythology. In their descriptions of Portugal's origins, the historians were more inclined to question the manner and extent to which Muslims had been a significant contact and to investigate Islam's cultural and linguistic influence.

The examples here are intended to illustrate significant historiographical lines of argumentation: the political-secular (Alexandre Herculano, Joaquim de Oliveira Martins), the ethnic (Teófilo Braga), and the Catholic (de Sousa Amado, Fortunato de Almeida).

Demystification: Alexandre Herculano de Carvalho e Araujo

The scholarship of Alexandre Herculano (1810–1877), the most influential nineteenth-century Portuguese historian,[84] represents a turning point in the depiction of the Islamic past: he assigned Islam an important role and purged the older accounts of the mythological elements with which they had described the contact between Muslims and Christians, myths which had persisted into the nineteenth century.

Influenced by Romantic notions, Herculano considered race, language, and territory constitutive for a modern nation,[85] but these did not actually apply in the Portuguese case. He disputed any ethnic, territorial, or linguistic continuity between the Celtic Lusitanians and the Portuguese nation.[86] This was a break with one of the most successful Portuguese foundational myths, dating back to the fifteenth century.[87] According to Herculano, Portugal's statehood had originated with a political act 1096–1097, when Henry of Burgundy received the fiefdom over the County of Portucalia from King Alfons VI of León. Herculano viewed the revolt of Henry's son Afonso Henriques against León and the conquest of territory which had been ruled by the Muslims as crucial paving stones on the path to Portuguese independence:[88]

> The new monarchy was composed of two parts, one with roots in León and another with Saracen roots: it had its origins in the former, and it shared, if we want, the structure and form of the society. As victor, it imposed its own characteristics on the latter, although, as must happen, it was thereby fundamentally changed itself. These facts

belong to the history of the civilization of our country; they represent the source of this civilization.[89]

Herculano emphasized the Islamic aspect of the new state, which is hardly surprising given his attitude towards religion. In fact, he was an important representative of the anticlericalism common among Portuguese intellectuals and an open critic of ultramontanism and the nineteenth century's controversial dogmas of the Immaculate Conception and Papal Infallibility.[90] At the same time, he highlighted the social role of the Catholic Church and advocated Christian instruction in schools.[91] He viewed historical scholarship as a secular endeavor and distanced himself from the clerical historical interpretations.

This distance is evidenced in the way he relativized mythical conceptions like the so-called Miracle of Ourique. The *Crónica de 1419* (Chronicle of 1419) had adopted and intensified the mythical, religious aura around Afonso Henriques's battle against the Moors in older chronicles: on the eve of the battle, which supposedly took place on the feast day of Saint James, the patron saint of the Crusades, Christ appeared to the Portuguese leader and foretold the victory.[92] This was essentially a Portuguese version of the legend around Emperor Constantine and the Battle of the Milvian Bridge, and it became a vital element of the foundational myths which presented the rise of Portugal as part of Providence's plan. Into the nineteenth century Ourique was considered the foundational event of the nation; religious authors used this myth as evidence of a divine blessing for the political advance. Others distanced themselves from the religious interpretation but nevertheless viewed the battle as foundational for the Portuguese monarchy, because, according to legend, Afonso Henriques had been proclaimed the first king of Portugal subsequent to this victory.[93] Herculano, on the other hand, portrayed Ourique as nothing more than a "*fossado*," a run-of-the-mill invasion and raid in enemy territory, and denied that it had any political significance.[94] His claim sparked one of the most bitter nineteenth-century debates within Portuguese scholarship, a passionate exchange which lasted for over a decade.[95]

By denying the mythical character of events like the Battle of Ourique, Herculano also challenged the traditional depiction of the Middle Ages in which two religious parties were absolutely opposed to each other, but he did not supplant it with a romantic conception of *convivência*. Instead, he highlighted examples to illustrate that differences of religion had not presented insurmountable obstacles: the mercenary service of the Castilian Cid, who had fought on both sides of the religious divide, and the alliances of Afonso Henriques with Muslim rulers. This was a decided break with the portrayal of medieval and early modern chroniclers:

Fascinated by the spectacle of religious zealousness, the historians had forgotten that in addition to this there are also other human passions . . . , they had forgotten that power struggles, revenge, pride, fear, cowardice and every other of the numerous human passions which oppose or subjugate religious zeal infringe upon the social unity that was created by this religious ideal. And they created, in opposition to that, relationships and bonds which reflected shared interests and political commonalities.[96]

In addition to academic scholarship, Herculano composed historical novels, which, thanks to Sir Walter Scott, became a popular literary genre in the nineteenth century. While *O Monge de Cister* (The Cistercian Monk) deals only tangentially with the life of the Muslims under the rule of King John I, *Eurico o Presbytero* (Eurico the Presbyter) describes the tragic love of a Visigoth priest for a sister of the Visigoth leader and hero of Covadonga, Pelayo. The Arabs are portrayed as fearsome, bloodthirsty invaders. In one dramatic scene, the young nuns of a monastery allow their abbess to stab them on the altar and die as martyrs in order to spare them from being ravaged by the enemy. The abbess herself is then slain by the scimitar in the Arabs' raid. In his romance novels, Herculano indulged the overly simplified perspectives which he attempted to deconstruct in his historical scholarship: melodramatic scenes like this served to create tension and can be seen as a concession to the audience's expectations.

In addition to spanning the bridge between fiction and scholarship, Herculano's work connects politics and culture. The Islamic heritage was, in his eyes, rather insignificant. He credited the Mozarabs more with preserving the Hispanic-Roman culture than with instilling Arab culture on the peninsula.[97] Herculano's theory of Portugal's political nation formation corresponds to his perception of Islam as one of several political opponents. His discounting of the providential myths shaped subsequent scholarship.[98] His national narrative presented Islam without resorting to a religious dichotomy and thereby paved the way for a fundamentally more nuanced interpretation of Portuguese history.

Instruction: Joaquin Pedro de Oliveira Martins

The historian and politician Joaquim de Oliveira Martins (1845–1894) emphasized Islam's civilizing influence in his account. Like Herculano, Oliveira Martins rejected the ethnic origins of the nation and emphasized its political nature. In his opinion, Portugal was not a nationality rooted in ethnicity but rather a nation grounded out of deliberate solidarity which persisted as a moral force.[99] This moral force originated, however, in Oliveira Martins's eyes, in an act which had hardly been moral: The Portuguese nation's foundation was due to the "valiant, [yet] mediocre, ambitious, brutal, and insidious character of Afonso Henriques,"[100] and its continuing existence to the acquiescence of the subsequent generations.

This interpretation—by a republican historian who had sympathized with the socialists in his youth—was far removed from the providential, monarchial interpretations of his predecessors. At the same time he rejected any sense of geographical determinism of the nation and viewed the territorial borders as pure convention.[101] Oliveira Martins, unlike Herculano, judged the Portuguese character to be anemic and weak. For this reason his *História da civilização ibérica* (*A History of Iberian Civilization*)[102] and numerous other pieces of scholarship inquired after the originality of a civilization, the causes of social and political decadence, or a national spirit that included the entire peninsula. The Arab invasion was the "greatest historical good fortune of the peninsula."[103] Oliveira Martins reversed the argument of Catholic authors who pointed to the longer history of Christianity as evidence of its superiority compared to the younger Islam:

> The old Arab, who had achieved the ease and smile of a mature age, took the ill-mannered Asturian, in whose breast [youthful] passions still raged, into his lap, fondled him, soothed him, and led him, thus inebriated into his mosques, true forests of stone, let him sip the Oriental nectar and hear enchanting legends; he blinded him with gold, colors, and the jewels of the temple, the palaces, the gardens, the robes; he bewitched him with fantasies of harems and finally told him, smiling, as he stroked his hands through his long white beard, "Believe in your Christ, we don't resent it."[104]

In this unusual metaphor, Islam surpassed Christianity in maturity and wisdom, appearing not as a martial soldier but rather as a benevolent grandfather, somehow magical, who instructed the inhabitants of the peninsula in sensuousness. Oliveira Martins thus showed that he considered the civilizing accomplishments more significant than the date of origin of each religion. Among these accomplishments was religious tolerance. The conversions were the result of conquests, but not forced by the victors; Islam had first become intolerant as it spread into Africa and Spain.[105] Religious fanaticism was found among Muslims and Christians alike.[106]

Oliveira Martins's assessment of Islam as a civilizing force had much in common with Rafael Altamira's.[107] However, unlike Altamira, he did not view the Muslim influence as inherently foreign. Instead, he emphasized the "*génio irmão*," the shared spirit between Christianity and Islam. Given the age in which Oliveira Martins lived, this should not be viewed as an ecumenical confession but rather as an indication that he did not view religion as a critical factor in defining the nation. This stemmed from his fundamentally reserved attitude towards church and religion. Such attitudes often resulted, as the example of Herculano has already shown, in a reassessment of the Islamic past.

Romanticization: Joaquin Teófilo Fernandes Braga

The writer and politician Teófilo Braga (1843–1924) credited the Muslim influence with having had a significant role in the formation of Portuguese culture. Inspired by Romantic literature, he collected popular narratives, customs, and legends and sought to divine their ethnic basis. There were two aspects to Braga's interest: As a scholar researching what was considered national literature, he developed theories about the cultural influence of the Mozarabs;[108] as a member of the Partido Republicano Português, he used these theories to shore up his political stance. Braga became the first transitional president after the monarchy was overthrown and later served a short second term after he was reelected in 1915. His scholarship served to demonstrate his republican ideals.

From Braga's historical viewpoint, the Visigoths embodied backwardness and feudalism while the Arabs appeared to be a motor of progress, especially in regards to the legal system. The Arab invasion was thus not seen as a catastrophe, but rather as a blessing for the peninsula:

> In the absence of the Arabs, the Visigoth princes would have driven Hispania into feudalism and the principle of the local assembly, the source of all freedom, would have degenerated into a an assembly of gangs of thieves and murderers . . . ; without the Arab rule, the working class would know no civil respect and . . . be destined forever to slavery.[109]

Braga connected the ahistorical term "civil" with his political demands for the nineteenth century. His portrayal of the assimilation of the Mozarabs also depicts the Arabs as pioneers of modern liberties. This assimilation was not the result of pressure by the victors, but stemmed rather from the combination of the "sympathy" of the Mozarab population towards their new rulers, who practiced "political and religious tolerance."[110] The Islamic rule and the contact with the Islamic culture had inspired the Mozarabs to cultural greatness, which Braga saw as constitutive for the nation:

> The Mozarab race is the essence of the Portuguese nation, [and] it would have been destined to make the literature unique and rich, had

it not been destroyed and razed by Catholic suppression and the triumph of the absolutist monarchy.[111]

The criticism of Roman Catholicism, however, did not lead Braga to praise Islam. On the contrary, he asserted that the Mozarabs had practiced "a pure form of Christianity, not corrupted by the authoritarian and worldly appetites of Roman Catholicism."[112] It was not easy to reconcile his Mozarabic theory with that of the political origins of Portugal. His solution was to minimize the political role of Afonso Henriques. Braga claimed that Afonso Henriques and his successors had acceded to the pressure of the Mozarabs, who sought to ensure the success of their political institutions through independence.[113] In effect, in order to underline his theory of ethnicity, Braga presented the Mozarabs as subjects and the first kings of Portugal as objects in the formation of the Portuguese nation.

Braga's theory was often incoherent, especially because he repeatedly revised it in the course of engaging the topic. His contemporaries were also critical. Oliveira Martins accused Braga of having been forced to invent a romantic concept of Portuguese origins, because he had found none in the actual history.[114] As a prominent example of ethnic-based concepts of the Portuguese nation, it shows the weaknesses unavoidable in the Portuguese context. There was no clear ethnic, cultural, or geographical explanation for Portugal's political boundaries, especially given that northern Portugal had more in common culturally and geographically with Galicia than with the Algarve. Braga's theory also shows how the influence of the Islamic past could be used against the monarchy and Roman Catholicism—against the very elements which the traditionalists viewed as genuinely Portuguese. In the search for a new political and social focus, which Braga represented, the image of Islam—the epitome of the Other—could be used to catalyze renewal and change.

Reluctance and acceptance: Catholic authors

As the examples of Herculano, Braga, and Oliveira Martins suggest, positive assessments of the Islamic past often coincided with republicanism, secularism, and the rejection of clerical authority. Among Portuguese intellectuals, these attitudes were quite common. Nevertheless many remained loyal to the Catholic Church and emphasized Portugal's religious character while cultivating and propagating a dislike of the Islamic past.

An example of such a text is the ten-volume *Historia da Igreja católica em Portugal* (History of the Catholic Church in Portugal) by Father José de Sousa Amado (1812–1878), which proclaimed Christianity to be the core "Portuguese" trait. According to de Sousa, Portugal thus predated its own political independence. Portugal's Christian roots were so strong that "neither three to five centuries of Moorish tyranny, nor the new Saracens' despotic deceit of the modern doctrine were able to fundamentally shake its [the Catholic folk's] faith."[115] He attacked the position of anticlerical authors like Herculano, whom he called a "destroyer of Portuguese history."[116] The peninsula had profited from the Arab invasion, because the "raging current" of Islam had obliterated the immorality of the Visigoth princes and priests, while those "least guilty" had remained true to the Catholic faith.[117] De Sousa's portrayal and arguments coincided on many points with those of conservative Catholic authors: in the topoi of Visigoth decadence and its abatement under Islamic rule, in the emphasis of the Christian character of the peninsula, and in the depiction of secularists as "modern Saracens." The language used also reflects this similarity: whereas de Sousa used the identifier "*mouros*" (analog to "*moro*," which is omnipresent in Spanish accounts), Herculano and Oliveira Martins seldom used this terminology.

While de Sousa's accounts embodied the spirit of the cultural battles taking place within the monarchy, the comprehensive historical descriptions of Fortunato de Almeida (1869–1933) originated in the secular First Republic, in which the Catholic Church was searching for a new role. De Almeida's *História da Igreja em Portugal* (History of the Church in Portugal) and the *História de Portugal* (History of Portugal), both of which remain important reference works due to a wealth of factual detail, have an apologetic tendency in regards to the church and religious orders.[118] De Almeida, like other authors sympathetic to the church, emphasized the "invincible [mutual] antipathy of the religions, [which was] the most important origin of conflicts and violent acts after the first years of the conquest,"[119] and thus accentuated the religious character of the medieval struggles. On the other hand, he did not revert to the mythologizing viewpoint of the nineteenth century and mentioned the Battle of Ourique only briefly without any religious or providential interpretation in the vein of Herculano. Once again, the terminology used to refer to the medieval Muslims is revealing: as a synonym for the neutral "*muçulmanos*," he uses the more judgmental "*infiéis*" when describing the medieval battles. Perhaps he wanted to denote the perspective of medieval Christians, in whose view the Muslims were exactly as infidel as the Christians were from the Muslims' viewpoint. This linguistic mingling of contemporary and historical terminology lent his account a pejorative undertone.

Religious portrayals of Portugal's history emphasized the nation's Catholic character and assumed a continuity of religious difference. However, there are indications that the religious historians did adopt the reassessments of their secular colleagues, at least in some cases. The local priest and historian of Valongo, near Porto, Joaquim Reis, for example, stressed that the Arabs had "not always" been "vandals" and that they had "only used the scimitar with which they had come armed to Hispania on the battlefield."[120] His account made clear that religion alone was insufficient to classify anyone as friend or foe. Using similar language to that which the religious authors had used to portray Muslims, Reis described atrocities which had been committed by the neighboring Christian kingdoms:

> It is sad but true: the Arabs, who practiced a religion diametrically opposed to ours, initially plundered many churches and monasteries, destroying and burning them, but they also spared many others, including the unrestricted practice of the Christian cult [there], in exchange for specified tribute. The Catholics from León, Castile, and Galicia, on the other hand, robbed us in their invasions, burned the monasteries, killed the monks, raped the nuns, demolished the churches, and left the communities distressed and terrified through which they came. They left scared, tear-stained faces, blood, corpses, and ruins in their wake.[121]

Apparently this claim seemed so bold to the author that he hid it in a footnote, perhaps out of respect for the many bishops to whom he dedicated his tome. Thus it can be seen only as an isolated opinion with little ambition of gaining a wide audience. Nevertheless it shows that in religious historical accounts, differences of religion could be bridged if the political situation called for this. It is an indicator that the Catholic historical conception was not sacrosanct, even in the politically turbulent period directly preceding the regicide in 1908 and the environment in which the clerical hierarchy demanded a united Catholic front against the secular currents. It also suggests that the Christian neighbors on the peninsula were seen as more of a threat than the Muslim Other from Africa.

COMPARATIVE CONCLUSIONS

The images of Islam used by Spanish and Portuguese authors in the nineteenth and twentieth centuries emerged from similar political, social, and cultural situations. Foreign policy crises like the loss of colonial territories and economic inferiority compared with their European neighbors damaged the powerful empires' self-perceptions. The political and intellectual elites sought to orient themselves anew amidst the tension between conservative and liberal, clerical and anticlerical, republican and monarchal ideas. In this process, historians made it their task to provide guidance for the future by examining the past.

In spite of the fact that each country was largely oblivious to the history of the other,[122] there were many similarities in their parallel histories. In the mid-nineteenth century, the concept of the nation increasingly took over the role of protagonist from the monarchy. Within this process, Modesto Lafuente and Alexandre Herculano were pioneers of a new civic historiography for their respective homelands. As in the case for practically all European nations, the Middle Ages were viewed as a critical phase of nation formation in Spain and Portugal. The struggle against Islamic opponents, who superficially and nearly exclusively embodied the Other, was portrayed as a national heroic act. Depending on the authors' understanding of the contemporary Spanish or Portuguese nation, this heroism could entail a victory over a religious, political, or dynastic enemy or the ability to embody tolerance, assimilation, or the riches of civilization. The heterogeneous concepts of Islam illuminate the contradictory national concepts which competed within Spain and Portugal.

In the Spanish case, the authors of very different accounts included the same historical events but varied greatly in their evaluation of these. The image of a *reconquista* became prolific in the nineteenth century. It could take the form of a religious process—as in the scholarship of Merry y Colon—or of a patriotic one—as in that of Altamira, but all sides considered it to be a formative aspect of the epoch. At the same time, the essentialist character of the question of a *ser de España*, inherited from the early modern expectation of a congruence of religion and politics, complicated the efforts to integrate seemingly foreign influences like Islam.[123] In addition, due to the colonial wars in Morocco, the *moro* was continually present as an opponent, which made the topoi of exclusion seem plausible.[124]

Portugal's religious historians emphasized the Christian character of the nation, as well. The suggestion that Portugal had risen from the battle against Islam, however, had its limits, because there were just as many crucial battles against the Christian kingdoms on the peninsula. Intellectuals who were ideologically further from the church did not view the providential but rather the political aspect as formative. Nevertheless, there were important differences in their accounts of history: the struggle with Islam naturally played a role in all of them, but the attitude of the author significantly influenced whether and how each depicted events like the Battle of Ourique. Islam as an opponent appeared historicized and no longer presented a threat, unlike the great rival Spain on the peninsula itself. Although some Portuguese intellectuals did pose the question of an Iberian Union,[125] the majority of them resented Spain.[126] The fact that Castile-León appeared the more threatening of the medieval foes was due not only to the secular viewpoint of the nineteenth century, which ascribed less importance to the religious conflicts. In fact, defending their independence against a powerful neighbor was a continual concern throughout Portuguese history. The Portuguese victories were accordingly mythologized and glorified through the centuries: the monumental monastery Santa Maria da Vitória (Saint Mary of the Victory), for example, the final resting place of the Portuguese kings of the fourteenth and fifteenth centuries, was erected to memorialize the victory in Aljubarrota over Castile-León in 1385. The Battle of São Mamede, in which Afonso Henriques defeated his mother Teresa of León and the Galician count Fernando Peres de Trava in 1128, was celebrated as the "First Portuguese Afternoon."[127] There are no comparable celebrations within Portugal related to Islam.[128]

In the periodization of these historical concepts, positive judgments of the Islamic eras may not be seen as a progressive process. The portrayal did not become increasingly positive over time: in Spain there was a noticeable conservative reaction starting in the 1880s, as conservative authors began responding to the success of liberalism by marginalizing or suppressing the Islamic past. They were thereby seemingly oblivious to the sympathetic portrayal of the Moors in the work of their predecessor Lafuente a decade earlier.[129] The formative phase of the national historiography was rather characterized by a coexistence and competition of understandings and assessments. The debates after 1898 represent a break in the national conception of Islam, after which the Islamic past and its historical significance were no longer a frequent topic of discussion. The relevant assessments and interpretations, however, continued to spark intellectual discourse—as the debates of Castro and Sánchez-Albornoz show. In Portugal the political break of the republic had little impact on the contents of the historical image of Islam, because the Islamic Middle Ages was not the epoch about which historical discussions were taking place—unlike the Age of Exploration or of Absolutism.[130]

The dictatorships later hearkened back to the strategies of the late nineteenth and early twentieth centuries of degrading and annexing Islam. The rhetoric of religious accounts from the Crusades was especially important in the regimes influenced by Catholicism. At the same time, tactical considerations led to the use of positive images, too. Both Franco's regime and the Estado Novo used older conceptions, although they also modified them to their own ends.

2

Islam as an Object of Research: Integration of the Islamic Cultural Heritage

"Every significant person born
within the boundaries of modern Portugal
is a fellow countryman who ennobles us."[1]

António Maria de Oliveira Parreira, *Os Luso-Arabes* (1898)

SPAIN'S WELL-KNOWN HERITAGE: THE IDEA OF A "SPANISH ISLAM"

Al-Andalus as national reference: Spanish Arabists interpret the past

In his study of the construction of the Orient in the nineteenth and twentieth centuries, Edward Said characterized Orientalism as "a Western style for dominating, restructuring, and having authority over the Orient."[2] His study of those who participated in this discourse included not only colonial politicians and romantically-inclined writers, but also scholars whose research was associated with Oriental languages and cultures. According to Said's argumentation, such research perpetuated the practical and ideological dominance of the West. Said's controversial theses[3] made new connections between scholarship, colonialism, and nationalism in the nineteenth century and led to a great deal of further research and debate.

Spanish Arabists had not previously considered themselves to be Orientalists.[4] However, Said's argument sparked research comparing the peculiarities of the situation in Spain to Said's French and English cases. On the one hand the academic Arabists who were active starting in the mid-nineteenth century in Spain were a "small, isolated guild,"[5] who fought for national and international recognition of their scholarship. They understood themselves to be researching the "national essence," which is why, prior to the twentieth century, they focused primarily on the history of Al-Andalus. On the other hand, this Spanish Orientalism looked less to Arabia or Asia and more to neighboring North Africa. Although Spanish scholars did play a role in developing this "domestic Orient"[6]—for example by participating in military envoys—their role within the colonial endeavor of their home country was noticeably smaller than that of their counterparts in France or Italy.[7] Meanwhile the *africanistas*—colonial politicians, intellectuals, soldiers, and businessmen—were trying to colonize Morocco both militarily and economically.[8] Both groups, those with a historical focus and those with a contemporary colonial interest, contributed to the African focus of Spanish Orientalism,[9] which made it more limited than in the leading European countries.

Arab studies in Spain was primarily a historical discipline of which philology was in turn a part.[10] Scholars throughout Europe—Stanley Lane-Poole (Great Britain), Reinhard Dozy (Netherlands), or Carl Brockelmann (Germany)—produced influential scholarship in the field of Arabic philology and created early standard works, but there was no comparable Spanish scholarship. Instead the pioneers of academic Arab studies in Spain posed the question: How can the undeniable historical presence of Muslims in Spain be reconciled with the conception of a Catholic Spain? In answering this question, historians had heretofore generally neglected the language, culture, and history of Al-Andalus, due either to a simple lack of expertise or more explicitly to their political standpoints; the Arabists, however, began searching Arabic sources for answers. The question of integration was doubly important for them: if the Islamic heritage could be conclusively integrated into the national history, then the integration of Arab studies within Spanish academia would also be ensured.[11] Which possibilities for the interpretation of the nation's past did the Arabists provide, and how?

In the nineteenth century, there was already a centuries-long tradition of research on Arabic language and culture in Spain: Philip II (1527–1598) had acquired an impressive number of Arabic manuscripts; his collection of Arabic works remains one of the most important in the world today.[12] After a period of disinterest in the seventeenth century, Arab studies experienced a revival in the 1700s due to the increased proximity of the Ottoman Empire and the attempt to expand Spanish influence in northern Morocco. This renewed interest led to the establishment of centers for Arabic language at the Reales Estudios de San Isidro, the university in Valencia, and the library of the Escorial.[13] At the same time, the field of Arab studies was evolving from a primarily clerical endeavor into a secular scholarly discipline along the lines of the Enlightenment.[14] In the late eighteenth and early nineteenth centuries, both members of the clergy and educated lay people took up the Arabic language: they translated texts, worked as librarians to expand and index collections of Arab knowledge, and compiled historical studies.[15] Especially noteworthy among these is the *Historia de la dominación árabe* (*History of the Dominion of the Arabs in Spain*)[16] by José Antonio Conde (1766–1820), the first comprehensive historical account of the Islamic Middle Ages in Hispania. According to Conde, the previous historical accounts had been of little use "for the era of our [*sic*] Arabs."[17] On the very first page, he pointed out the discrepancies in the assessment of the Cid in Christian and Islamic sources: "in one as humane and valiant, . . . in the other [as] perfidious and cruel."[18] In an attempt to close the gap in the research and to round out the picture painted by Spanish historians, Conde minutely described the history of the territories under Islamic rule between 711 and 1492. With his admiration for Arab culture, Conde viewed the Middle Ages as a sort of golden age, and his account served to nourish later romantic fantasies which sympathetically portrayed the Moors.

In the early nineteenth century, therefore, there was already a certain tradition of addressing such topics, and important scholarship had already been produced.[19] However, the field was first institutionalized at the larger universities as part of a comprehensive restructuring of the Spanish academic system: in 1836 the university of Alcalá de Henares was relocated to Madrid. It was called Universidad Central and had important privileges: it was, for example, the sole university allowed to award doctoral degrees.[20] A year later the Arabist Pascual de Gayangos y Arcre (1808–1807) suggested that a professorship for Arab studies be established. When this happened in 1843, Gayangos was the first to be appointed to it. Three years later, the University of Granada introduced a professorship for Arab studies, followed by the University of Saragossa in 1887.[21] These universities became the leading institutions for Arab studies in the nineteenth century. Beyond the walls of these institutions there was a wider field of scholarship in which local historians, archaeologists, art restorers, and high school teachers dealt with Arab language and culture.[22]

Scholars in this new discipline of Arab studies aimed to close the gaps in the traditional historiography, gaps which had been caused not only by a lack of popular appeal but also by shortcomings in the language abilities and knowledge of academic historians. This scholarship seemed ideally poised to investigate the "own" and the "foreign" in the Spanish context, and especially, starting in 1850, the idea of the nation as a political concept. The Arabists thus understood themselves to be contributing to Spanish national history. The royal decree which established the professorship on 5 October 1843, argued that valuable Arab treatises and cultural remnants were "resting, forgotten, without being put to use for the general history of Spain."[23] The Arabists took up this argument in their quest to be recognized as legitimate scholars. Orientalist studies were accordingly presented as the *nosce te ipsum* of the nation,[24] and, unlike in other European lands, were thus to be regarded as an "intrinsic and beloved necessity" rather than "mere scientific curiosity."[25] Indeed, the classical arsenal for nationalist historiography was readily available to scholars working on Al-Andalus, including language, culture, ethnicity, and, at least partly, religion. The Arabists especially emphasized the Arab influence on Castile and thus negated the centralist concept of the nation. Towards the end of the nineteenth century there was similar research on Catalonia, Galicia, and Aragon.[26] Although scholars of Arab studies dedicated themselves to Arab language and culture, they did not necessarily endorse these. Their scholarship created models of inclusion and exclusion of the Arab heritage, and they varied in their assessment of its relevance for the national past.

One of the most important pioneers in the field, the Andalusian Francisco Javier Simonet y Baca (1829–1897), provides a fitting example. When, in 1862, at the age of 33, Simonet was appointed to the chair of Arab studies at the university in Granada, his mentor and teacher, the Arabist and author Serafín Estébanez Calderón, wrote to him: "We Malagans . . . have an interest in Arab things. If you are able to establish this subject in that university on a sound basis and with the purpose of [elucidating] what is Castilian and of good Spanish race, you will be deserving of much gratitude."[27] Simonet seems to have taken these comments to heart: his extensive research and countless publications for both academic and popular audiences highlighted the Islamic heritage of Spain.[28] At the same time he clearly showed that cultural integration into the national collective as he understood it was always limited. As part of the ceremony to confer his doctoral degree at the Universidad Central, Simonet gave a presentation on Arabic literature in which he claimed that "the Arab influence was never able to permeate into the depths of our literature, but remained superficial and formal."[29] His definition of religious boundaries was even narrower. On the Arabic title page of his *Descripción del reino de Granada* (A Description of the Kingdom of Granada) from 1860, he referred to himself—in Arabic—as "the servant of the Messiah . . . from Málaga."[30] The tendency to discount or demonize everything related to Islam became more pronounced in the course of Simonet's career.[31] It is also evident in his *Historia de los mozárabes* (History of the Mozarabs): the Christians who had lived under Islamic rule—whom Simonet called "Spaniards"—had "consistently preserved the national spirit and the culture of the ancient Roman-Visigothic and Christian Spain over many centuries."[32] The Mozarabs were presented in this account as a bulwark against the Arab-Islamic intruders, which completed the narrative of a continuous Christian Spain despite the break of 711. While many conservative Catholic historians had minimized the Islamic influence as a result of ignorance, Simonet did so with the authority of a reputed scholar. At times this even took on absurd proportions, as illustrated in this anecdote told by his student, Antonio Almagro Cárderas: when the First Spanish Republic was proclaimed in February 1873, and the university students in Granada revolted against their instruction, Simonet and several students willing to attend classes ascended the Alhambra. There Simonet led them through the exercise of translating Arabic inscriptions and rebuked thereby the liberals as "new Saracens."[33]

Simonet's numerous references to religion made him an exception among the Arabists, however, for they mostly avoided such questions in their scholarship.[34] This was perhaps due to the fact that the topic was considered too delicate to be addressed within an academic discipline which was already fighting for recognition. In a society in which religion and politics were as intricately connected as they were in Spain during the Restoration, language, literature, and music offered easier opportunities to integrate the national heritage. The Arabists took advantage of their foreign colleagues' interest in the history of Al-Andalus, for this was their overriding contribution to the liberal account of the nation: scholarship on Islamic Spain suggested a culturally rich nation in a period in which other European peoples were still (supposedly) mired in the ignorance of the "Dark Ages." Even before the political and ideological crisis in 1898, Spain's intellectuals were painfully aware of their inferiority compared to their European neighbors. In such interpretations, the medieval influence of Islam could be presented as evidence of Spain's cultural superiority, for example as emphasized by Francisco Fernández y González (1833–1917):

> Because the Spaniards are united via their Semitic and African elements with the earliest lineage of the human race, we can boast before our neighbors who brag of their more significant cultural accomplishments: peoples of the North, you are children and know nothing more than today and yesterday. Our history is ancient, our literature immense, linguistically diverse . . . , our culture is full of shining lights which once shone brighter than yours today.[35]

If Arabists had persisted in negating the influence of the Islamic past, they would have diminished the long-term potential of their field.[36] The geographical determinism which emerged from the climatic theories that had been so influential in the eighteenth century offered an alternative.[37] Arabists of various political and ideological persuasions made the case in their scholarship for a distinctively "Spanish Islam," which could not be compared with that in Africa or Asia. Islam in Spain had been shaped by the Muslims' contact with the native Iberian population, and the invaders had simply appropriated much of the native Iberian culture.

This unique amalgamation had resulted in the renowned and widely recognized architectural, literary, and musical contributions of Al-Andalus. Depending on the individual perspective of the respective scholars, this assimilation was presented as unilateral—meaning the Muslims were Hispanicized, as Simonet claimed,[38] —or bilateral, in which case religious boundaries were the least permeable. Such accounts allowed all the political parties to integrate the undeniable historical Muslim presence on the peninsula into a coherent narrative and to recognize the Arabists' service to the nation. The topos of a "Spanish Islam"—in varied incarnations—became entrenched in the Arabists' historical narrative in the twentieth century.

An outer sign of this transition towards a conception of a "Western" Islam was a change in terminology: instead of the terms common in the nineteenth century like *"España musulmana"* (Muslim Spain) or *"arte hispanomusulmán"* (Hispano-Muslim art), twentieth-century scholarship preferred to discuss "Al-Andalus"—which was also the name of a journal founded in 1933.[39] At the same time, under the influence of the Valencian Julián Ribera y Tarragó (1858–1934), Arab scholars in Spain succeeded in broadening their thematic focus to include not just medieval Spain but also the Middle East, which in turn led to a wider recognition. Ribera, unlike many of his predecessors, focused on the cultural history of Al-Andalus rather than politics or language.[40] As professor for Hispano-Arabic literature at the Universidad Central, Ribera conceived of a historical narrative in which territory and not religion determined membership in the national collective. His argumentation clearly illustrates the rhetorical images and historical analogies which Ribera and his successors used:

I repeat (and will tirelessly repeat, for justice demands it), that the Muslims of the peninsula were Spaniards: of Spanish race, of Spanish language, of Spanish character, preferences, tendencies, and spirit. I think that every impartial and unprejudiced person must recognize that Abd-ar-Rahman III was just as much as a Spaniard as Trajan, with the distinction that Abd-ar-Rahman was King of Spain in Spain while Trajan was Emperor of Rome in Rome; that Averroës was as Spanish as Seneca, except that Averroës was born in Córdoba, [where he] studied, lived, and wrote, while Seneca, although born in Córdoba, worked in Italy, and that the popular poet Abencuzmán was just as Spanish as Martial, except that the former spoke and wrote colloquial Spanish and the latter classical Latin. Thus these Muslims have just as much—or even more—right to be called Spaniards in our history and literature as those Ibero-Roman figures who have long since been included [as such] and to whom we lovingly refer as fellow countrymen and friends although they were heathen. And [thus accordingly] we must also recognize the accomplishments of these Spanish Muslims as our own, national, Spanish achievements.[41]

In this way it was possible to claim ancient and medieval figures for the Spanish nation regardless of their religion. A sort of *jus soli* (citizenship based on birthplace) projected the territorial concept of modern Spain back into antiquity and the Middle Ages, providing an alternative to categorization based on religious affiliation without completely replacing it, as the term "heathen" suggests.

Despite these new possibilities for interpretation which the Arabists created for a Spanish nation, they met with some resistance, especially in the first phase of their activity in the mid-nineteenth century. Many historians reacted to the conclusions of their colleagues with displeasure or disbelief. In 1879 Vicente de la Fuente, Rector of the Universidad Central, accused the modern school—"squadron of new invaders of our classic history"—of siding "with the Moor, or, as he is called today, the Arab. For he who is scorned in his homeland [Morocco] and Algeria as a deadbeat, lazybones, liar, thief, and scoundrel is hailed today in Spain as a gallant, genteel, truthful type, a troubadour, mystic, poet, artist, farmer, and even theologian—granted of a theology *sui generis*."[42] In a later positivist phase, the Arabists sought to earn recognition by producing detailed translations and literary editions and by publishing articles in recognized historical journals with a general focus.[43] In 1910 scholars affiliated with the liberal Institución Libre de la Enseñanza founded the Centro de Estudios Históricos to reform instruction and scholarship; it included several research groups working on Arab topics under Ribera's direction.[44] Six years later, following personal and ideological disagreements, Ribera and his students left, reinforcing the very isolation of Arab studies which had nearly been surmounted.[45] This, combined with the fact that the conception of a Christian Spain still dominated the historiography leading up to the Civil War, limited openness to the idea of a "Spanish Islam."[46]

The colonial expansion in Africa led only to a partial reassessment of the necessity for Arab studies. The wars of 1859–1860 and 1893–1894[47] certainly increased public awareness of and interest in the field. Some Arabists participated in the Junta de Enseñanza en Marruecos (Junta of Education in Morocco), which aimed to improve the public education of the native population. One controversial point in this context was the question of whether to teach classical or contemporary colloquial Arabic.[48] The departure of Ribera and his colleagues from the Centro de Estudios Históricos provided an obvious breaking point beyond which historians of Al-Andalus and the *africanistas* interested in the military and economic situation of Africa no longer moved in the same circles.[49] This division was certainly not absolute; in order to legitimize colonization, the *africanistas* were happy to adopt the Arabists' claim that Spanish and Islamic cultures could be compatible. The example of the magazine *Africa*[50] shows how they popularized their findings about the proximity of Christians and Muslims in Al-Andalus and presented the past as a potent model for negotiating the present.

Within the institutions founded after the Spanish Civil War to emphasize the historical link between Spain and the Arab world—an attempt to provide a scholarly foundation for Franco's claim to Morocco—Arabists mostly dealt with topics concerning Al-Andalus, not Morocco.[51] Miguel Asín Palacios (1871–1944) was an exception: one of the most important Arabists of the early twentieth century and a devoted follower of Franco, he delivered an academic legitimatization for the participation of Muslim soldiers among the ranks of the Christian *caudillo* in a prominent essay on medieval Spain, "Por qué lucharon a nuestro lado los musulmanes marroquíes?" (Why did the Moroccan Muslims fight on our side?). Asín Palacio threw his entire weight as a priest and scholar behind his argument: Islam was, he claimed, a "true and real, albeit illegitimate son"[52] of Judaism and Christianity. Shared practices like fasting and almsgiving were undeniable, as was the Muslim veneration of the patriarchs of the Old and the saints of the New Testament. His essay did not address the actual motivation of the Moroccans: material needs resulting from hunger and poverty as well as a psychological need for adventure.[53]

In addition to these theological arguments, Asín Palacios added anecdotes from the front as further evidence of an "enthusiastic and active participation in our cause"[54]: in response to the suggestion that an icon of the Virgin Mary should be removed from a military hospital in deference to the religious feelings of injured Moroccans, the patients had requested that the image remain, saying "The Virgin good for all."[55] Asín Palacios responded directly to the stereotypes exploited in Republican propaganda, according to which the Moroccans were sexually perverse and insatiable[56]: the Moroccans were so chaste and honorable that they had shredded the pictures of scantily clad women in the Spanish magazines which were distributed for their amusement in the hospitals.[57] Last but not least, he introduced evidence from the Arabists' original domain, language: the common Spanish expression, *ojalá* ("hopefully" or "Lord willing"), a derivation of the Arab *inschallah*, suggests a shared piety and corresponding modes of expression.[58]

The era from the mid-nineteenth century to the early phase of Franco's regime shows how the contribution of Arab studies to the construction of a Christian nation could change: for Simonet, religion had represented a sacrosanct boundary between Christians and Muslims. Asín Palacios, a student of the Arabist Ribera and the Catholic historian Menéndez y Pelayo, was the ideological and biographical personification of the reconciliation of Catholicism and the Islamic heritage in which the historiography of the nineteenth century had invested so much energy. This connection of Catholicism and Islam was certainly not symmetrical, but rather asymmetrical and paternalistic. Nevertheless it offered a legitimatization which proved especially useful in Franco's regime.

Islamic architecture as national monument: The example of the Alhambra

Within the field of nineteenth-century Arab studies, the integration of the Islamic past was not only a question of dealing with an abstract cultural heritage but also the very concrete matter of how to deal with the architectural heritage. The research on historical structures and national ideologies was linked.[59] The Alhambra, the Great Mosque of Córdoba, and the Giralda in Seville, on which the former minaret could be clearly recognized, provided witness in stone to the influence of the erstwhile medieval rulers. Given the importance and sheer dominance of these edifices, the question of how to integrate these buildings into the Spanish cultural heritage was particularly visible and urgent. Was the Alhambra less "Spanish" than the Cathedral of Santiago or the palaces of the Habsburgs and the Bourbons? How could these renowned Islamic structures be integrated as cultural treasures of a nation whose intellectual elite sought to downplay the historical Muslim influence?

The arguments in favor of or against certain monuments and architectural styles were also motivated by financial considerations. The more convincingly the significance of a particular structure could be established, the greater the chances of its receiving subventions from the limited public funds available in nineteenth-century Spain for the renovation and preservation of historical monuments. Two primary deficiencies hindered the preservation of the architectural heritage into the early twentieth century: there was a shortage of both funds and educated art historians.[60] Legislation concerning the architectural heritage aimed foremost to regulate structural changes to monuments and protect them from intentional or inadvertent damage.[61] However, in the nineteenth century the first political measures were taken to manage and classify the cultural treasures: in 1844 the Comisión de Monumentos (Commission for Monuments) was founded on the French model, with subsidiary chapters responsible for the protection of historical buildings and the establishment of museums at the local level.[62] The goal was to create a body responsible for a central catalog of historical structures and archaeological excavations.[63] The centralization also included requirements for the restoration of historical buildings. The law of 14 September 1850 was a first attempt to control the renovations of historically significant public buildings. It stipulated that renovations were to preserve the original character of the structures such that the old and new sections be indistinguishable from one another.[64]

The political and intellectual elite in Spain—just as in other European nations—were aware that the architectural legacy had a tremendous potential to enhance national prestige both within and beyond the national boundaries. This legislation—as insufficient as it might appear from a modern standpoint—included measures to make the cultural heritage accessible to those who were interested in it. On 8 October 1850, the Ministerio de Comercio, Instrucción y Obras publicas (Ministry of Commerce, Education, and Public Works) issued a decree providing funding for the series *Monumentos arquitectónicos de España*, a collection of elaborate publications which were to include numerous illustrations and lithographs of Spain's most important architectural treasures. The historical monuments were meant to testify to "Spain, as it once was," while the series aimed to present "Spain, as it is," i.e., as a land of splendid, monumental architecture spanning centuries.[65] In order to convey this message to interested foreigners, the volumes included a parallel French translation. The ambitious project had to first overcome some practical obstacles: the members of the commission had to acquire the instruments and machines for production elsewhere because within Spain neither suitable printing presses, folio-sized paper, nor engravers and lithographers were available.[66]

One of the first works the series covered was the Alhambra. The opening lines of the text highlighted the "ongoing popularity" of this structure and its association with a "race which is different from ours in religion and customs," while insisting that the latter was not to be seen as an impediment.[67] The editors of the *Monumentos arquitectónicos* actually classified the works according to their religious origins: heathen, Christian, and Muslim. Due to the religious dichotomy, these experts did not view the Middle Ages as a single epoch.[68]

Some of these buildings covered in the *Monumentos arquitectónicos* were officially classified as national monuments in the latter half of the nineteenth century (once again following the French model). This classification, created by decree on 19 February 1836, placed buildings with historical and artistic significance under the protection of the state. It was intended to prevent unchecked changes or even looting of these sites by archaeologists, especially those from abroad.[69] However, because the decree was accompanied neither by legal changes nor by financial means to this effect, it did not necessarily improve the situation. In addition, the nominations for this status were only sporadic and limited. The governmental agency responsible conferred this status on seventy-five buildings in Spain—mostly religious structures—between 1844 and 1903. During this same time period, its French counterpart recognized 3,684 buildings within France.[70]

By 1900, three important structures of Islamic origin had been recognized as national monuments: the Alhambra in 1870, the Great Mosque in Córdoba in 1882, and the Mosque Cristo de la Luz (Christ of Light) in Toledo in 1900.[71] The ministry reacted thereby to the nominations of architects, conservators, and scholars interested in the arts, who were mostly members of the Institution Real Academia de Bellas Artes de San Fernando (Royal Academy of Fine Arts of San Fernando), which was responsible for the application process. José Amador de los Ríos y Serrano (1818–1878), for example, a professor of literature at the Universidad Central and co-editor of the *Monumentos arquitectonicos*, described the former mosques in Toledo, Cristo de la Luz and de las Tornerías, as "two of the oldest and most completely preserved Muhammadan structures" in Spain.[72] His son, Rodrigo Amador de los Ríos y Fernández de Villalta (1849–1917), succeeded in having the Mosque Cristo de la Luz classified as a national monument in order to prevent incompetent restoration and to renew the building's "original simplicity."[73] A small group of dedicated Arabists recognized the significance of Islamic architecture and worked against the religious boundaries which had traditionally prevented the national importance of these structures from being acknowledged. Amador de los Ríos placed himself metaphorically in the Enlightenment tradition:

> This systematic aversion ... prevented ... anyone from having the idea to examine Arab artistry which had created so many delights on our soil; this systematic aversion wrested the glory away from us of being able to show Europe a complete picture of the artistry of this [Arab] people, [a people] among which the torch of human knowledge shone with all its brightness, while the whole world still reposed in deepest ignorance.[74]

In order to compensate for this negligence, professional Arabists and self-educated historians now processed the artifacts of the Islamic era; they researched, described, and cataloged Arab coins, inscriptions, and also entire architectural structures.[75] The Alhambra in Granada played a central role in these efforts. It not only invited projection of foreign Oriental ideals, but was the veritable incarnation of a fantasy from *A Thousand and One Nights* on European soil and the embodiment of an ambivalent history. The debates surrounding these structures crystallized to an exceptional degree around the Alhambra because of its fame both within and beyond the national borders.

Unlike the Mosque of Córdoba, the Alhambra did not represent the highpoint of Islamic power during the caliphate but rather a sort of architectural swansong: following the Christian conquest of the important centers of Córdoba (1236), Valencia (1238), Seville (1248) und Silves

(1249), the small Emirate of Granada, nestled between the Sierra Nevada and the Mediterranean coast, survived as the last area of Islamic rule on Iberian soil for nearly 200 years. As the only royal residence of the Nasrid dynasty (1237–1492), the Alhambra was built and constantly changed and expanded, blossoming as a symbol of their ascension and, in the end, of their demise.[76] On 2 January 1492 the last Nasrid emir, Muhammad XII (in Spanish popularly called "Boabdil"), capitulated to Ferdinand and Isabella, on whom Pope Alexander VI then bestowed the honorary moniker of "Catholic Monarchs." The Alhambra thus became one of the most magnificent trophies in history. The royal couple displayed an interest in preserving the structure from the very beginning, whether out of pride as a concrete symbol of their victory or out of secret admiration for the artistry of those defeated.[77] Their political decisions gave the Alhambra new meaning, as it became a symbol of the Catholic monarchy and their victory over those of other faiths: the Alhambra Decree published in 1492 forced Sephardic Jews to either accept baptism or emigrate. From 1499 on, Cardinal Jiménez de Cisneros, Isabella's confessor, took a series of severe actions against the Muslims of the city: he burned heaps of Islamic manuscripts and hundreds of Muslims were forcibly baptized. These were only the first of many measures and decrees intended to enforce religious unity, a process which came to a head in the expulsion of the *moriscos* in 1609.

Although rulers had expressed appreciation for the Alhambra— including Charles V, who built a Renaissance palace within the Nasrid fortifications,[78] the monument's distance from Madrid doomed it to obscurity in the seventeenth and eighteenth centuries. During the late eighteenth century and the era of the Napoleonic Wars, the Alhambra was especially neglected and, lacking any official protection, suffered destruction and looting.[79] It was primarily foreign travelers, under the influence of Romanticism in the nineteenth century, who discovered in the Alhambra an outlet for their craving for the exotic. Flamenco, bull-fighting, and its Oriental flair on European soil all contributed to Andalusia's picturesque allure.[80] Here was the possibility of an Orientalist escape within the more comfortable confines of Europe.[81] The American author Washington Irving spent several months in the Alhambra and compiled a collection of stories (*Tales from the Alhambra*, 1829) which made the building famous far beyond Spain. Like other travelers, he lamented its decay. Only in the mid-nineteenth century did the Alhambra profit from this growing architectural and archaeological interest (Plate 14).[82] It became an icon of Orientalism abroad and inspired the Crystal Palace in London (1851), the Wilhelma of King Wilhelm of Württemberg (1842–1846), and countless Orientalist salons in the houses of the wealthy bourgeoisie and nobility alike.[83]

The history of the conservation and restoration of the Alhambra connects several families: Rafael Contreras y Muñoz (1824–1890), the son of the civic architect José Contreras, practically grew up in the Alhambra and served for over forty years as the official "*restaurador adornista*" ("decorative conservator").[84] As such he was more concerned with ornamentation in accordance with nineteenth century fashion than with the preservation of the structure itself. Isabella II commissioned him to create an "Arab salon" in the palace of Aranjuez along the lines of the Alhambra's Sala de las Dos Hermanas (Hall of the Two Sisters). Contreras subsequently received similar commissions from other Spanish nobles and from throughout Europe.[85] His son and successor, Mariano Contreras Granja, shifted the focus from a historicizing restoration to preservation of the structure.[86] In addition, the painter and archaeologist Manuel Gómez-Moreno González (1834–1918), along with Francisco Javier Simonet, successfully applied on behalf of the Comisión de Monumentos Historicos y Artísticos (Commission for Historical and Artistic Monuments) in Granada to have the Alhambra classified as a national monument and wrote numerous monographs and travel guides about the structure. His son, Manuel Gómez-Moreno Martínez (1870–1970), wrote a doctoral dissertation on Mozarabic architecture and became the first professor of Arab archaeology at the University of Madrid in 1913. The journalist, historian, and author Luis Seco de Lucena Escalada (1857–1941) held the position of a "*vulgarizador de la Alhambra*" and was responsible for introducing measures to popularize the history of the Alhambra. The texts he produced provided a foundation for travel guides up until the 1980s and were translated into many languages. His son, Luis Seco de Lucena Paredes (1901–1974), became a professor of Arab language and literature in Granada in 1942.[87] This small, closely knit group was in the vanguard of having the Alhambra recognized as a Spanish national monument.

Despite this common goal, however, their assessments of the Moorish origins of the structure were quite varied. The Alhambra was the central example used in a fundamental debate among Spanish archaeologists of the nineteenth century about whether the Visigoth-Catholic or Islamic heritage had been more significant to Spain.[88] The degree to which this debate became heated is evident in Rafael Contreras's pointed judgment of 1878:

> The Visigoth epoch . . . did not produce anything on our soil which we can equate with a national artistry. For that one has to look to the eighth century, when the Christian society disappears and our soldiers flee from the glint of the scimitar, for the theocratically ruled homeland is not able to set any civic values in opposition to the invaders. . . . Are we still unable to recognize with gratitude what the ancient Spanish civilization owes these guests who sowed their blood and their Oriental

endeavors on our soil? The Spaniard, in his essence, this race which is somehow distinct from the European family and especially from the Nordic peoples, today embodies in decay that culture, and neither brutal religious persecution, nor the unity imposed by the iron [fist of the] monarchy, nor the emigrations could destroy the soul which burns for Muslim art, literature, and poetry.[89]

Contreras's ahistorical use—at least from a modern perspective—of terms like "civic" make clear that this discussion of architecture was actually a veiled critique of religious privileges. At the same time his description of the Muslims as "guests" and his praise for the Oriental world reveal the influence of foreign Romanticism. Contreras's argument was countered by Gómez-Moreno and his son. In their *Guia de Granada* (Travel Guide to Granada), published in 1892, they combined architectural commentary with appraisals of Muslim character in essentialist interpretations:

[Arab architecture] lacks stability, knows no brilliance, and is poor in regards to technical skills, but in the decorative aspect it exceeded all other styles of the Middle Ages, though it did not achieve the unique freedom of the Gothic. In sum: it is a highly faithful representation of the people it served, it portrays their refined and sensuous culture, their profuse poetry, and their instability.[90]

Whereas Gómez-Moreno saw in the year 711 the "terrible catastrophe of the Arab invasion,"[91] Contreras alternated between fascination with and aversion to this "fanatic and noble people"[92] and admitted that Spain owed them "eight hundred years of steady progress."[93] Despite their differing attitudes towards the Muslims, both scholars viewed the Alhambra as an achievement of the "Spanish Muslims" and therefore as an artistically original part of the Spanish national treasure.[94]

As the Alhambra became better known and Spain felt increasing pressure to respond to its marginalization within Europe by referring to its former grandeur, the history of this monument became one of the most important national myths: Muhammad XII's relinquishing of the city key to the royal couple was a popular subject of historical painting, most prominently in the monumental work "La rendición de Granada" (The Capitulation of Granada), which Francisco Pradilla y Ortiz completed in 1882 for the Spanish Senate. It was widely reproduced on a variety of everyday utensils and accessories like fans (Plate 3).[95]

The historiography commemorated this event as the end of the so-called *reconquista*. The potential for conservative interpretations led to increased prominence of the Alhambra at the ideological level; meanwhile, at the practical level, the development of a culture of educational tourism within Spain—embodied, for example, in the Sociedad Española de Excursiones, which was founded in 1892—led to more visitors. Although the growing public interest was continually confronted with a chronic shortage of funding for the complicated preservation of the large complex,[96] the Alhambra was an entrenched part of the Spanish architectural heritage by the turn of the century.

The ambivalence concerning the Islamic origins of the building had been overcome for two reasons: first, Arabists had developed the concept of a "Spanish Islam" and, second, the Alhambra was recognized as a symbol of the triumph of the Catholic kings, as here in the appraisal of Seco de Lucena Escalada:

> One of the greatest and undeniable accomplishments of which Spain can boast is that we possess and maintain the Alhambra; for by possessing it we show that we had the patriotism, courage, and strength to reconquer the national territory that had been wrested away from us by the Muslim invaders, and by preserving it we show the sacrifice and effort entailed . . . to fulfill our duties as guardians of a monument so extraordinary that it interests the entire civilized world and affects the spirit of all humanity.[97]

The Alhambra was a target for projection from all sides: conservatives viewed it as a symbol of Christianity's triumph over Islam, while liberals considered it a witness to bygone cultural heights. In any case, it distinguished Spain from its European neighbors and therefore embodied Spain's national grandeur and originality. The question remains to what extent this consciousness of the Alhambra's national significance transcended the wishful thinking of its supporters, who continually sought funding for the expensive conservation of the structure. The movements for autonomy which emerged in the Basque region and Catalonia around the turn of the nineteenth century strove to distance themselves from Spanish centralism and thus contested any connection to the historical Muslim presence.[98] In this respect the literary and architectural Islamic heritage served as a divisive rather than inclusive factor. Meanwhile, the founder of the historical *andalucismo*, Blas Infante (1885–1936), fostered pride in Andalusia's archaeological heritage, which linked Spain to the civilizations of the Orient.[99] The field of Arab studies included such varied approaches to the Islamic past that practically all the political and intellectual parties within Spanish society could avail themselves of those which best served their cause. The Alhambra ascended thereby from a stumbling block for conservative nationalists in their conception of Catholic Spain to a veritable pillar of Spain's Christian character, and provided liberals with welcome evidence of Spain's erstwhile cultural greatness.

PORTUGAL'S FORGOTTEN HERITAGE: THE LATE DISCOVERY OF ISLAMIC ROOTS

Portugal's origins: Portuguese Arabists interpret the past

The question of Islam's historical role was also relevant in the formation of a Portuguese nation. Nineteenth-century historians considered the struggle with the Moors to be constitutive. The past contact with the Islamic world was an obvious topic for extensive scholarship: Portugal seized Ceuta in 1415, and, in the following decades, fortifications were erected along the coast from Tangier to Santa Cruz do Cabo de Gué (modern-day Agadir), which predated those of their neighboring Spanish rivals. Despite a colonial empire which stretched over four continents and diverse international contacts, Portugal suffered a distinct lack of academic scholarship in the field of Arab language and culture. Only after the loss of the last North African—and thus the last Arab-influenced—territories, Azamor and Mazagão (modern-day El Jadida) in 1769 did monasteries and ecclesiastical institutions take up a systemic study of Arabic.[100] In contrast to other European states like Poland, Spain, or the Habsburg Empire, the pioneers of Arab studies in Portugal in the late eighteenth century were nearly exclusively clerics rather than lay scholars.[101]

A key figure in the development of a systemic, though not, in a modern sense institutionalized, approach to Arab studies was the Franciscan friar Manuel do Cenáculo Vilas Boas (1724–1814), bishop of Beja and later archbishop of Évora. As an advisor to the Marquess of Pombal, who was inspired by the Enlightenment to reform the system of education, Cenáculo advocated for the instruction of Oriental languages—Hebrew, Syrian, and Arabic—in order to better interpret and translate the Old Testament.[102] Under his guidance the Convento de Nossa Senhora de Jesus in Lisbon became the first center of Arab studies in Portugal. In 1772 Friar António Baptista Abrantes (1737–1812) became the first professor of Arabic language there.[103] A twist of fate advanced the institutionalization of Arab studies in Portugal in 1749 (or, depending on the report, 1750), when Yhuanna min Dimashq, a learned Christian from Damascus, was stranded in Lisbon after a storm interrupted passage of the French ship on which he was a passenger.[104] Cenáculo took the young man, who began calling himself João de Sousa, under his wing: de Sousa joined the Franciscan order, became a priest, and participated in multiple diplomatic mission trips to North Africa. In addition, de Sousa—himself a "self-made scholar"[105]—promoted the study of his native Arabic and went on to succeed Abrantes as professor in 1794.[106]

De Sousa's influence and contacts paved the way for nineteenth-century scholars of Arab studies in Portugal, though their realm remained quite limited. De Sousa's students mostly published in Portuguese, which restricted the audience for their research, especially since they were not backed during this phase by any university.[107] At the same time, Portugal as a whole became less focused on North Africa in the nineteenth century, meaning that Arab language and culture lost political importance.[108] After the professorship once held by de Sousa was dismantled in 1869, there was no institutional scholarship in the field of Arab studies within Portugal. Furthermore, few Portuguese intellectuals addressed the topic. Most of those who did had biographical ties to the Arab world: José Daniel Colaço (1831–1907), for example, was born in Tangier to a family of diplomats who had served in Morocco for generations. Aside from his political function, Colaço worked as a painter and historical author, producing a variety of works which dealt with Arab culture and language.[109] Other Arabists like José Pereira Caldas (1818–1903) and João Leite Neto (1838–1883), both of whom were high school teachers in Braga, published research on Arab music and numismatics, in addition to a conversational language guide.[110] In the late nineteenth century, however, these projects remained isolated without any institutional support. The lack of interest in the Arab world during this time, despite the many historical ties to Portuguese society, can be traced back to the structural and financial weaknesses of the Portuguese educational system. Attempts to create an institution for Arabic studies during this period were thus limited to clerics and their students.

This situation changed only when the First Republic restructured the system of higher education. In order to improve the system of public education and establish counterparts to the University of Coimbra, the provisory republican government founded universities in Lisbon and Porto in 1911; in both cases, the new institutions incorporated existing academies of higher education.[111] This laid the foundation for academically institutionalized Arab studies in Portugal: the literary scholar and historian David Lopes (1867–1942) became the first professor of Arab studies in Lisbon. Lopes's interest in the Arab-Islamic world had been sparked by reading the work of Alexandre Herculano, the first nineteenth-century historian to address the role of Islam in the formation of the Portuguese nation.[112] Herculano's work had been based on secondary literature, but Lopes, aiming to work with the primary sources, had gone to Paris to study Arabic because his native country offered no possibility to do so.[113] Lopes, and later his students, were interested primarily in two dimensions of the contact between Portugal and the Islamic world: first, the contact of the Portuguese with Muslims during the Age of Exploration, primarily in Morocco and India, and, second, the Muslim presence on the Iberian Peninsula.[114] The latter dimension is most relevant for the integration of the Islamic heritage into the national narrative because this era was seen as foundational in the formation of the Portuguese nation.

Lopes used his training and institutional position to correct, expand, and update Herculano's already canonical work,[115] and he published a new annotated edition of Herculano's seven-volume *História de Portugal*. His work succeeded in popularizing the Islamic history of Portugal beyond academic circles. His booklet *Portugal contra os mouros* (Portugal against the Moors) was sold for the moderate price of five centavos in the series *Os livros do Povo* (The Books of the People). His use of the term *mouros* in the title, a term which he avoided in his academic works, shows that Lopes aimed to attract a readership familiar with the legends, myths, and popular literature surrounding this stereotype and then deconstruct these. It is one of the few Portuguese texts produced in the nineteenth and twentieth centuries in which a historian with a command of Arabic reflects on the term *mouro*:[116]

> We call them "Moors," because they came from the region called Mauritania, part of which is today called Morocco. This term is not very precise, it refers not only to the Moors, but also to other peoples who fought under the same flag: Arabs, Syrians, Persians. However, it has been maintained over centuries, and thus we also use it. Others call these invaders "Arabs," but the Arabs were only one part, the most noble and leading in this group. Especially beyond our peninsula they are called "Muslims," and this term is the most precise, for it refers to "one who follows the teachings of the Quran," which is the holy book of these people. . . . Among us, as well, "Moor" had a religious connotation from the very beginning. That is why the Portuguese, after they had sailed around the Cape of Good Hope and met adherents of this same religion . . . in Africa and Asia, called these Moors, as they still call them in the Portuguese territories in India and Mozambique.[117]

Lopes's anchoring of the Islamic past in the historical scholarship had a lasting influence. He penned the chapter "O domínio árabe" (The Arab Rule) for the *História de Portugal*, which became known as the *História "de Barcelos,"* after the city in which it was published. This work, which appeared between 1928 and 1935,[118] was the longest historical narrative of Portugal to date; it embodied the spirit of nationalist, patriotic historiography under the military dictatorship and the early Estado Novo. Nevertheless, the *História "de Barcelos"* should not be dismissed because of its ideological background. The publisher, Damião Peres (1889–1976), was a professor of history in Porto and later in Coimbra, and he recruited historians with varied historical and political views for the individual chapters. Joaquim de Carvalho, for example, who had democratic sympathies, worked on the chapter covering the political history of the nineteenth century, an epoch which the Estado Novo scorned because of the liberal and republican ideas in circulation. On the other hand, there was no historian among the authors as friendly to the regime as João Ameal.[119] The *História "de Barcelos"* should thus be judged less a Salazarist historiography than a historical narrative written in the time of Salazar's rule.[120] At the same time, the chronological divisions and the weight given to the individual epochs reveal much about the significance accorded them and the state of the research which existed at that point: the one hundred fifty years of transoceanic exploration from 1411–1557 cover more than 1,200 pages, for example, while the first volume of the series describes the more than twelve centuries from pre-Roman times up until the Battle of São Mamede in 1128 in just five hundred pages.[121] Within this introductory volume, Lopes's chapter on the five hundred years of Muslim presence in Portugal is a mere forty pages. The events and cultures which predate Portuguese independence are treated as a sort of national pre-history, which garner little attention compared to the later centuries.

As limited as Lopes's influence was, he remains the first modern Portuguese historian familiar with the primary sources from the epoch of the Muslim presence, and he worked to integrate this period into the national narrative. His position is similarly ambivalent to those of his Spanish colleagues: he described the Muslims as "intruders" but, like many liberals, judged the expulsion of the *moriscos* a mistake.[122] Nevertheless he emphasized the legacy of the defeated Muslims, "a part of [whose] soul had been left behind in the places which had been soaked with the blood of their parents," and pointed out remnants of their language in place names, administrative structures, and other words borrowed from the Arabic.[123] Like Herculano, Lopes stressed that their coexistence had not been plagued by religious conflicts and that the struggle between Christians and Muslims had been more political and economic than religious.[124] He positioned himself thus in the tradition of secular Portuguese historiography, which emphasized the political character of the Middle Ages. In Lopes's richly illustrated chapter, for example, which covered architecture, coins, and inscriptions, knowledge of the Islamic influence was presented in this context as historical background and not a danger to a unified nation.

Although Arab studies now existed at the university level, the field remained limited both in personnel and influence, in part because the study of Arabic remained an optional rather than fixed part of a degree program.[125] Lopes's students—among others, Abreu Figanier, José Domingo Garcia Domingues, and José Pedro Machado[126]—went on to publish a variety of philological and historical studies. They were especially productive in their research of the Arab past of individual towns like Lisbon, Évora, or the formerly Portuguese areas of Morocco.[127]

Garcia Domingues explored the theory that the Luso-Arabs had, together with the Mozarabs, preserved the ancient Lusitanian traditions and were therefore the precursors of a Portuguese state. Domingues referred to the nineteenth-century discussion along these lines.[128] However, these scholars' work did not create any fundamentally new national narrative.

Beyond the small group of academic Arabists, there were authors in the Estado Novo who dealt with Islam because they were interested in the Muslim presence in the colonies. Among these was Eduardo Dias, the author of the three-volume work *Árabes e Muçulmanos* (Arabs and Muslims), who, as Garcia Dominques observed, could not be considered an Arabist in the true sense because he did not speak Arabic. Dias did, however, incite a degree of public interest with his comprehensive work.[129] In addition, the scholars who focused on colonial Islam were interested in other questions because they were much more concerned with integrating the Muslim present into the Portuguese national narrative rather than the Islamic past.[130]

The structural deficiency of Arab studies which predated the Estado Novo was exacerbated by the marginalization of Islam in the dictatorship's formulation of the past: Islam was a foe which, once conquered, could be forgotten in favor of grander deeds. This reading dominated the regular festivals commemorating the Conquest of Lisbon.[131] Particularly in the early phase of the Estado Novo in the 1940s, historical accounts which in any way challenged the regime's monolithic vision of the nation were not tolerated. There was no interest in scholarship which could possibly endanger the historical concept of a Christian nation.[132] While research on the Islamic past was not expressly forbidden, it was not supported.

Perhaps this explains why in the last phase of the Estado Novo and the first years under the new democracy, historians who had no formal background in Arab studies became increasingly interested in the Arab past and made valuable contributions to the field. António Borges Coelho (*1928) sent a political message with his scholarship. The first volume of his four-volume edition of primary sources appeared in 1972, two years before the revolution of 25 April. Borges Coelho included Christian and Islamic sources and poems from the Gharb Al-Andalus, the western region of Al-Andalus, a name which lives on in the region Algarve. In the introduction he deplored the fact that the Islamic past of the territory which had become Portugal was being forgotten—due to a lack of interest and knowledge—and its influence was being reduced to something purely superficial:

> Over centuries—during the *reconquista* and then the competition overseas—the fatal crusade mentality did not spare many remnants of the Arab civilization of western Andalusia, especially not the written

ones. And silence invaded the old house. . . . It is this silent civilization which we now want to retrieve from oblivion and whose independent and authentic voices we want to make audible. How much of their blood still flows in our veins? How much of their eroticism became part of our mentality, we . . . who have inherited to a considerable extent their craftsmanship and the procedures with which we still tend our fields and orchards?[133]

Now a Portuguese historian was clearly formulating questions which had occupied his Spanish colleagues for over a century. Borges Coelho was imprisoned in the infamous Peniche Fortress from 1957–1962 for communist activities and became interested during this time in the Islamic Middle Ages within the later Portuguese territory.[134] His edition of source material was published by the magazine *Seara Nova* (New Seed), well known as an organ of democratically minded intellectuals. This sent a variety of signals: given Borges Coelho's biography, the metaphor of breaking the silence and making voices audible which have not been heard can be read in an academic sense as resistance to the Estabdo Novo's historical perspective, and in a political sense as resistance to the system of repression, surveillance, and censorship. After the revolution in 1974, the field of Arab studies was increasingly supported by neighboring disciplines like medieval studies, archaeology, and anthropology in an effort to complete the narrative of the Islamic past and preserve its cultural and architectural legacy. This, too, can be seen as a sign of political and social upheaval.

The discovery of Islamic architecture: The example of Mértola

The disinterest in the Islamic past which prevailed for so long in Portugal is also evident in the treatment of the medieval architecture of this era. This requires some explanation: admittedly, there were no buildings within Portugal as impressive as the Alhambra. Here, too, however, the Islamic past was widely evident in the numerous Moorish fortresses and mosques which had been converted into churches. In Portugal, as in Spain, the Oriental Neo-Mudéjar became fashionable, for example in the Palace of Pena in Sintra (1838–1855), and the Campo Pequeno Bullring (1892).[135] Why was this Islamic architectural heritage neglected until quite recently, both in the sense of preservation and of academic research concerning it?

The parameters for restoration and conservation of the historical structures were fundamentally problematic even compared with the dismal situation in Spain. Nineteenth-century intellectuals were indeed conscious of the need to protect and preserve ancient structures and of their potential significance for the national identity. In 1839 Alexandre

Herculano called upon the government to prioritize protecting "Portuguese" monuments rather than those of Phoenician, Greek, Roman, Visigoth, or Arab origins.[136] However, in the nineteenth century there was an insufficient administrative basis for this. In 1800 a commission led by the architect Joaquim Possidónio da Silva compiled a list of structures deserving protection for the Ministry of Public Works. Two years later Possidónio da Silva was appointed president of the Commission of National Monuments. However, only after a series of additional commissions had been convened and a new list drawn up in 1910, did the ministry declare a variety of historical structures to be national monuments.[137] The buildings were classified by epoch (e.g., prehistorical, Lusitanian, Luso-Roman, medieval, Renaissance, and modern), by type of monument (e.g., churches, fortresses, etc.), and by district.[138] The list included important Islamic works like the São Jorge Castle in Lisbon, the Castle of Silves, or the mosque in Mértola, which had been converted into a church, but it included no references to their history or background.

Beyond the state institutions, several private foundations aimed to preserve the architectural heritage by supporting research and highlighting the need for their preservation. Especially in the latter half of the nineteenth century, there were numerous excavations and reports on Portuguese antiquities.[139] The most influential archaeologist of this age, Sebastião Estácio da Veiga (1828–1891), came from Tavira in the Algarve and was interested in the Islamic legacy. For the Museu Arqueológico do Algarve (Archaeological Museum of the Algarve), he collected pieces taken from excavations for a display on the "Arabian Epochs" in 1880. When the archaeological museum was closed just one year later, the collection was transferred to the Museu Etnografico Português (Portuguese Ethnological Museum), where it was in turn expanded by that museum's founder and Portugal's first influential ethnographer, José Leite de Vasconcelos (1851–1941).[140] One focus of Estacio da Veiga's research was the small town of Mértola in the Alentejo, which was an important trade center in ancient and medieval times, due to the river Guadiana which connects it to the Mediterranean. This past was still very much present in the scattered ruins left behind by the town's early Roman, Christian, and Muslim residents. In a study published in 1880, Estacio da Veiga stressed that the fervor of the Portuguese following their defeat of Islam had nevertheless been respectful of the Islamic culture:

> To strengthen the aversion to the followers of Muhammad and praise the true religion in the national spirit, the [Portuguese] clergy could not portray as barbarians the Arabs who had ruled the Iberian Peninsula, for this would have been an intentional lie and would have dirtied the historical truth. It was sufficient to fight their false doctrine

without hiding the heights of civilization which this people had reached; and the Christian conquerors did not have to destroy the monuments typical of this epoch to reinforce their blessed conquest or convey more power to the banner of the cross, like they did, for example in Mértola, when they used tombstones from the Arab cemetery in the construction of their tower.[141]

Such expressions, however, which explicitly linked the Islamic past to the Portuguese nation, were rare. Unlike in other European nations, archaeology and historical architecture played an insignificant role in the formation of a national identity, neither during the monarchy nor during the ensuing republic. Such a relationship emerged only after the foundation of the Direcção-Geral dos Edifícios e Monumentos Nacionais (General Direction of Buildings and National Monuments) in 1929, the stated goal of which was to cultivate the "highest reverence for religion, nation, and art."[142] Fortresses were the preferred structures used to symbolize the nation which had been gained through the struggle with Islam.[143] This was evident in the celebrations in 1947 of the anniversary of the Conquest of Lisbon, in which the São Jorge Castle served as the stage at the center of the festivities,[144] and in a monumental volume with the programmatic title *A gloriosa história dos mais belos castelos de Portugal* (The Glorious History of Portugal's Most Beautiful Fortresses).[145] The book mentioned whether a fortress was of Islamic origin, but it did not reflect any further on the question of to what extent such a structure deserved to be called "national" or not. The Estado Novo's historical perspective was focused on heroism and sought to establish continuity between the glorious past of the fortresses and their symbolic meaning for the present. There was considerably less interest, however, in Islamic components of the structures. The efforts of the academic Arabists, on the one hand, and of local historians motivated by regional patriotism, on the other, to highlight the Islamic heritage of cities like Silves, the last Moorish stronghold in Portuguese territory,[146] remained isolated: unlike Andalusia, southern Portugal, including the regions with the longest historical Muslim presence, Algarve and Alentejo, had developed no significant tourist industry before the 1970s. The lack of infrastructure hindered a wider public interest.

The Estado Novo did take some measures to preserve buildings of Islamic origin. These appear to have been a rather haphazard assortment of individual initiatives which hardly reflect a structural interest of the state in Islamic architecture. The Direcção-Geral dos Edifícios e Monumentos Nacionais extensively restored the church in Mértola in the late 1940s; it aimed thereby not only to preserve the historical church, but also to restore it to its "original condition as much as possible."[147] Partitions from the sixteenth and seventeenth centuries were removed, while doors from the Almohad era were once again exposed, as was the mihrab, the Muslim prayer niche (Plates 2 and 5).[148] A new architectural arrangement was created: the high altar, which had stood for four hundred years on the northeast site of the church across from the main entrance, was relocated in front of the mihrab. This was a return to the spot it had once occupied after the mosque was initially converted into a church. The projects of the Direcção-Geral dos Edifícios e Monumentos Nacionais thus took some steps to make Islamic components of this building visible once again. There were excavations of Islamic sites under the Estado Novo, for example, in Cerro da Vila (Faro) starting in 1971.[149] However, such archaeological and architectural activities dealing with the Islamic era remained sporadic and isolated during the Estado Novo. The Islamic Middle Ages remained in the shadows compared with other epochs (for example, the Roman).

Only after the revolution in April of 1974 was there a greater emphasis on Portugal's Islamic heritage. The fledgling democracy reacted to the one-dimensional national identity propagated under the Estado Novo by seeking to recognize the cultural and religious diversity of the architectural landscape. The archaeologist and historian Cláudio Torres (*1939) returned from political exile and initiated a comprehensive excavation and museum project in Mértola. He intended to counter a history driven "by a colorless, political factuality, by a parade of heroes and warriors, which, on the one hand, hid the grayness of the present, and, on the other hand, justified the endless colonial wars in Africa."[150] Mértola was certainly not the only town in Portugal with an Islamic archaeological heritage, nor was the legacy here necessarily richer than in other locations. However, the preconditions for an excavation were advantageous in several ways: first of the all, the relevant sites had been hardly built over, which simplified the archaeological excavation. Secondly, the project was of interest to the local municipal administration, which had an important say in the approval of such projects following the political break.[151] In 1978 Torres and his colleagues could begin working on the site. Their exhibits, publications,[152] and lectures incited so much interest—both from the public and the media—that Mértola became an icon for the Islamic Middle Ages in Portugal one hundred years after Estácio da Veiga's efforts. The entire region of the Algarve was affected: as the tourist industry was developed there, the Islamic past was also rediscovered and celebrated.[153] Furthermore, the rediscovery of Portugal's Islamic heritage was the topic of a variety of books starting in the 1980s which made this historical and literary legacy available to a non-specialist audience.[154]

The "Mértola effect" was criticized because this media coverage tended to convey and entrench a myth of a Mediterranean multiculturalism.[155] Additional criticism pointed to the danger of equating "Arabs" and "Muslims," which could result in misperceptions of contemporary Portuguese Muslims.[156] This happened in the exhibition *Pelas Ruas e Lugares de Loures* (Through the Streets and Places in Loures), which took place in the museum of this small town in the vicinity of Lisbon in 1996. The catalog included texts in the respective languages to accommodate the diverse immigrant groups of the town. The Muslim community was "represented," certainly with the best intentions, with Arab texts. In fact, the Muslim residents of Loures are Indians from Mozambique and Africans from Guinea: they speak Portuguese, varied Creole languages, and Gujarati, but not modern Arabic.[157] The still incipient research on Portugal's Islamic past will require a more nuanced handling of the Muslim present, as well.

COMPARATIVE CONCLUSIONS

Compared to the rest of Europe, Orientalism in Spain and Portugal had unique features. Academic research on the Arab world was directly relevant to the understanding of contemporary Iberian society. Spanish scholars' work on the Arab language and culture helped to define the essence of their own nation. In Portugal, however, the example of David Lopes shows that foreign findings could be applied to the local situation to illuminate a chapter of history which had been neglected and considered to predate the nation. Scholars in the emerging field of Arab studies had to deal with the sheer magnitude of potential locations and objects left behind over the several centuries of Muslim presence but also with the weaknesses of their discipline in regards to formal structures and personnel. The manifest crisis among intellectuals and Arabists' peripheral position in the academic landscape alone cannot explain the fact that the discipline was forced to fight for recognition and even eliminated at times. There was a disregard for the Islamic past in both lands which ranged across a spectrum from aversion through disinterest to ignorance.

The field was institutionalized at universities in both countries along similar lines, albeit not chronologically parallel. In the eighteenth century, it was primarily monasteries—those traditional centers of learning—which sought to foster study of the Arab language, because clerics were intrigued by the reports of envoys and travelers, especially from North Africa. Simultaneously, an educated laity developed Arab research as a object of academic study. Arab studies was established in both countries when their systems of higher education were restructured. This happened seventy years earlier in Spain than in Portugal, due to general structural factors. The topos of a "Spanish Islam" had already been developed in the national discourse of the nineteenth and early twentieth centuries, prior to its being co-opted by Francoism as a legitimizing chapter of historical and contemporary Spain. During the period of dictatorship in Portugal, however, the Islamic past and accordingly the Arabists themselves were relegated to obscurity. The political break in 1974 thus also became a cultural break in regards to the relationship of Portugal to its Islamic past. Within the timeframe investigated here, Portugal's transition to democracy is the most obvious example of coinciding political and cultural dimensions.

Beyond this process of institutionalization, the small and, as shown in the Spanish case, heterogeneous group of scholars, archaeologists, and conservators interested in Arab research made important contributions to the collective knowledge of Al-Andalus. Questions of exclusion and inclusion crystallized around the architecture. In Spain the architectural witnesses to the Muslim presence were undeniable and obvious to foreign travelers and the local population alike. Claims to power were manifest in these structures. The origins of the structures had to be made "Spanish" to legitimize their continued existence, conservation, and promotion. This was meant to shore up the nation and its history in return. The topos of a "Spanish Islam" offered a coherent explanation which could be reconciled with the general orientation of Catholicism, with the postulate of a unique nation, and with the academic efforts to define the Islamic legacy. It integrated the cultural accomplishments of Islam which were easier to accept without touching on the religious boundaries, at least for the time being. However, these boundaries could be weakened when necessary, as shown by the example of Francoism.

This obvious heritage in Spain contrasts with the forgotten heritage of Portugal. The *mouros* were no more than a weak echo of a distant past in which they had been rulers who constructed fortresses and mosques. Neither the monarchy, the republic, nor the dictatorship had reason to promote the concept of a Portuguese Islam. The former two governments did not see the Muslim as dangerous to the system, the latter read history in such a way that Portuguese heroes eclipsed all minority facets of the past. A small group of Arabists notwithstanding, academic research on Arab language and culture was deemed unimportant. Furthermore, the social class which could have profited from such study was especially limited, given the high illiteracy rate. In addition, Salazar was of the opinion that there were more important things than teaching the masses to read and write.[158] The study of exotic languages and cultures was naturally even further removed from his goals.

Despite the isolation of Arab studies on the peninsula, perceptions of Arab history and the general history of the nation were not hermetically separated. Seen as a whole, Arabists—both academic and lay scholars— were able to shape and supplement the master historical narrative over time. This is especially true of Spain: there were already pertinent historical and philological works available which offered insights into the

Islamic Middle Ages before conservatives reacted to liberalism's advances in the 1880s and 1890s. The fact that conservative master narratives ignored or marginalized these was thus not the result of a lack of research but rather of resistance to integrating this information into the narrative of a Catholic Spain. At the same time it was the field of Arab studies which developed the concept of a distinctly "Spanish Islam" and helped the classical historiography out of this dilemma. Study of the Arab past thus created an interpretive problem but also offered a solution. Under Franco, especially, many historical accounts took advantage of this.

3

Islam as a "Colonial Other": The Iberian Dictatorships

"I am God. Do you not recognize that in my new jellaba, my white robe?"
"God is a Spaniard."
"I have defected to the Moors—
God is always on the side of those who can do more."[1]

Ramón J. Sender, *Imán* (1930)

SPAIN: STRUGGLE TO EXPAND POWER (1898–1956)

Reluctance: Images of Islam in the Moroccan wars (1859–1921)

To compensate for the gradual loss of colonies elsewhere in the nineteenth century, Spain became increasingly interested in North Africa. In the Spanish imagination, this was the homeland of the *moros*, whom historians had traditionally portrayed as bloodthirsty medieval warriors and insidious early modern enemies of the state. In the conflict in Morocco, the traditional antagonist, the *moro*, and the centuries-old system of religious and cultural exclusion, were appropriated and adapted for the rhetoric of Spanish colonialism.

Leopoldo O'Donnell's campaign from 1859 to 1860 against Morocco under Muhammad IV marked the beginning of Spain's political push to expand into northern Morocco. Spanish historians triumphantly labeled this campaign the "Guerra de África" (African War). The Treaty of Wad-Ras ended the war and granted Spain additional territory around Ceuta and Melilla as well as the enclave Ifni. The Moroccan government, the makhzan, was bankrupted and unable to substantially oppose the Europeans by the end of the conflict.[2] For the next hundred years, Spain's efforts at militaristic expansion were centered in Morocco, where they competed with neighboring France. In 1912, the Treaty of Fes established Morocco as a protectorate with Spanish and French zones, but this was only a formal recognition of the fact that over the preceding decades

Europeans had seized control of territory despite the opposition of Moroccan nationalists.

O'Donnell's campaign sparked a wave of patriotism which swept far beyond Madrid. During this period, the populations of Catalonia and the Basque region still identified strongly with the central Castilian state.[3] Newspapers competed to portray Spain's mission in Morocco as "civilizing"[4]: this provided moral cover for their expansion, just as in other European nations.[5] The memories of the era of grand conquests in South America contributed to a historically inflated sense of patriotism. In the public debate, Spain's history served as a witness to the contemporary venture, as, for example, in the newspaper *La Correspondencia*:

> If Isabella I will always be remembered for having driven the Moors out of her kingdom, then Isabella II should be remembered for seeking them out and conquering them in their dens in Africa; the injured national pride, the embarrassed civilization, the scorned religion—it all leads us to cross the strait with our weapons, which might still be those of Gonzalo de Córdoba, Cortés, and Pizarro.[6]

By mentioning Isabella I, the explorers Francisco Pizarro and Hernán Cortés, and the general Gonzalo de Córdoba, this single paragraph spans a broad spectrum of Spanish heroes. According to this argumentation, contemporary colonization was a natural result and duty of past. Even those who were not prone to exaggerated patriotism were swept up in this enthusiasm. Emilio Castelar (1832–1899), a professor of Spanish history at the Universidad Central in Madrid and later president of the First Republic, also called for the conquest of Morocco:

> God, who placed us in western Europe, . . . who separated us from Africa by the strait, who gave us so many characteristics similar to the African race, who scattered so many treasures of that rich, inexhaustible nature on our soil, God himself is pointing out the way to Africa with his immortal finger. If we approach this race, which is slumbering in a natural state, we can promote their human dignity, inform them of their rights, and prepare them to work with faith for the advance of the universal civilization, which requires the efforts of all mankind. Our sword must cut the swath to civilize Africa.[7]

Castelar combines metaphors of divine legitimization with civilizing values—by which he means a liberalism based on Christianity—and the necessity to propagate these with military force. At the same time, he emphasizes the similarities of Spain and North Africa: nineteenth-century Moroccans were equated with medieval Muslims, whose significance for the Spanish nation was becoming a central topic in the emerging field of Arab studies during this period.[8] This provided a supposedly historical link of Spain to the regions colonized, a link which made Spain's rhetorical position unique within Europe and set it apart from its rivals, including France, which could make no such historical claim. This historical justification of colonization was so often repeated in the subsequent decades that it became a cliché. It was an attempt to use cultural arguments to compensate for the political weakness of Spanish colonization.

Spain's involvement in Morocco led both liberals and conservatives to become interested in the idea of a Spanish nation. The scholarship of Modesto Lafuente, a liberal and devout Catholic, for example, had attempted to provide a theoretical Catholic foundation for the Spanish nation, while enthusiasm for the war in Morocco brought together liberal and Catholic concepts of the nation.[9] The rhetorical strategies varied more in the values they stressed than in the images they used, for example, in the divergent historiographical appraisals of the so-called *reconquista*: while the Catholic narrative described a religious struggle in the medieval tradition, the liberal narrative highlighted values like "progress" and "civilization."[10]

This is especially apparent in the case of the Melilla War between October 1893 and April 1894. This short but bloody conflict between the Rif tribes and Spanish troops under General Juan García y Margallo was sparked by the construction of a Spanish fortress in the vicinity of the Muslim holy site Sidi Guariach and resulted in a diplomatic agreement which required substantial reparations from the makhzan to Spain.[11] The early days of the war, during which the Moroccans were berated as traitors, and the reaction of the press to these events serve as a sort of lens through which the nationalistic reaction and the antagonistic depictions of the *moros* can be more closely examined. Marcelino Menéndez y Pelayo applauded the Melilla War in 1893 and praised the Spaniard's "true enthusiasm," which had come "at the right moment to arouse the energy of a national spirit."[12] Indeed many intellectuals hailed the war as a convenient distraction from other persistent problems. In the popular magazine *Blanco y negro,* one author noted ironically: "In the absence of the attack in Melilla, one would have to invent it either there or somewhere else. We needed a scapegoat. Now we have the Moors. That is enough to diffuse our bad tempers."[13]

This brief war sparked a patriotic wave that dredged up the old stereotypes. The traditional newspaper *El Correo Español* equated the *moros* of the year 1893 with their medieval counterparts: "For the Moors— lawlesss barbarians—the war continues, international law is meaningless, and they attack Spain as often as they can, robbing and assailing the Spaniards, and thereby keeping alive centuries-old feelings of racial hatred."[14] Liberal newspapers also ascribed to historical prejudices and emphasized the Moors' "differentness":

> Generally speaking the character of the Rif people is gruff, proud, shrewd, and suspicious. Most of all, they are filled with distrust, partly because they have historically suffered certain burdens under the Arabs, partly because in their limited trade relations in the past, they have been swindled. They are sober and ignorant, but diligently work their fields, and they are truly savage and brutal when they go to war, even more so, when it is this battle against the *Christian dogs* [emphasis in original].[15]

Conservative and liberal portrayals of the *moros* were practically inter-changeable, and the press was only one medium for the distribution of such stereotypes. They were also disseminated in books by soldiers and accounts of the war like those by Adolfo Llanos y Alcaraz, an officer in the Spanish Moroccan War of 1859–1860 and a correspondent in Melilla for the Real Academia de la Historia in 1893. His accounts included a somewhat more nuanced depiction of the *moros*, because they were motivated by a civilizing impulse rendered futile if the oppo-nent had been completely degenerate and base. Llanos y Alcaraz did claim that the Moors "leave much to be wished for in terms of morals," but he blamed this deficiency on their lifestyle and customs.[16] These belied an essentially good nature, which could be shaped by the Spaniards' positive influence:

> Despite his fanaticism, his hate of Christians, and the barbarian customs which have earned him a bad reputation, the resident of the Rif is no person incapable of improvement. Much to the contrary: in his emotions and his character there is a sound inner nature, a moral nature, a bud which can be used to develop the good. He is no lost crea-ture and no idiot, [and even] amidst his savagery he possesses virtues which other peoples have forgotten. He is neither lewd nor vulgar, and when he wants, he can be loyal, honest, and generous. The raw mate-rial is good, one only has to plant it in civilized soil.[17]

Such accounts sought to give the military enterprise a civilizing, human-itarian note. This resulted in a partial belittlement and banalization of their opponent. Alongside the image of the brutal, terrifying *moro*, there was sympathy for the much less threatening *morito*. This diminution had the advantage of bolstering the Spaniards' confidence that they would win and that the *moros* could be governed. Between 1893 and 1936, there-fore, caricatures that depicted the *moritos* across a spectrum from the ridiculous to the personable were quite common.[18] These pictures and jokes combined with the broken Spanish of the *moritos* to infantilize them, playing into the patriarchal discourse about their becoming civilized. Just as parents may indulge children certain pranks as long as they do not challenge the parents' authority, the *moritos* could poke fun at the Spaniards in jovial anecdotes. Even the grammar became infantile in such accounts:

> "What does the morito say? Don't you like it, seeing so many troops?"
> "So many! So many! You always goes together like lambs. *Morito* go alone and be enough."[19]

Such portrayals of the *morito*, however, remained an exception in the political discourse. The old stereotypes fed into notions which could equally serve those who favored and opposed the war: the former called for vengeance against the "bloodthirsty and wild Riffians" in defense of Spain's honor, while the latter sought to convince the troops that, considering the savageness of the natives, the assignment in Morocco was a suicide mission.[20] The recurrent rebellion of the Riffians and the military setbacks of the Spaniards fed the notion of the bloodthirsty opponent and the hopelessness of the battle. The "Tragic Week" in Barcelona in 1909 brought the conflict from Morocco to the mainland, when demonstrations by anarchists and socialists protesting conscription en masse were violently suppressed. Starting in 1912, in order to spare the Spanish troops, Moroccans were increasingly recruited to fight for the Spanish side in the so-called Fuerzas Regulares Indígenas (indigenous armed forces). These "*moros amigos*" (Moorish friends) reinforced the image of the ruthless *moro* because the Spanish officers at least passively encouraged them to be brutal towards their fellow countrymen. Raids and pillaging in the insurgent villages served as compensation for the minimal or delayed service pay, and rape and armed robbery often went unpunished.[21] In addition, the officers stationed in Africa emphasized the savagery of the Moroccan opponents in their petitions for weapons and funding.[22]

The brutality associated with the stereotypical *moros* was also an element of the image of the *moras*, although such descriptions were less frequent. A war reporter's description of a young Moroccan woman reveals a unique mix of desire and rejection which frequently appears projected onto women of the opposing side:

> Beneath her jellaba . . . it was easy to guess the perfection of her bodily form, with the shape and the firmness of pagan virgins. I observed her uncovered, olive-skinned face; her eyes, with their infinite gaze, with the depth and darkness of an abyss, and her plump, sensual, carmine lips . . . [But in her eyes] was a cynical and horrifying stare in which

could be seen for an instant all the ferocity of these wild women,
hunters of men . . . [23]

Orientalist fantasies produced such real and imaginary images of
"heathen virgins" in which women were both alluringly exotic (the
"Other") while also acquiescent and seductive. The painter Marià
Fortuny (1838–1874), a participant in the campaign of 1859–1860 and
the most influential painter of Moroccan motifs during this period, was
not only known for his monumental depiction of the battle of Tetuán on
canvas. His sensuous portrayal of an "Odalisque" in 1861 embodied
more than a perfect exotic beauty. The naked figure can be seen as an allegory of Morocco, conquered by Spain, although the twist of her body
leaves open to interpretation the question of whether she is facing the
observer (i.e. the Spanish colonizer) or the Moroccan musician at the
foot of her bed (Plate 15).[24] Fortuny's depictions of battles like the one in
Tetuán, his portraits of Moroccans, and his street scenes made him the
Spanish counterpart to France's Eugène Delacroix and Jean-Auguste-
Dominique Ingres.

The conquest of Morocco and its women went beyond the iconographical level and became corporal: marketing directed at travelers
became increasingly sexual in the 1920s. The German publisher
Hochherz offered to deliver "photographs of beautiful, exotic girls'
bodies, browned by the sun" in discrete envelopes to Spanish
customers.[25] Photographs of scantily clad Moroccan women and corresponding fantasies circulated among the Spanish soldiers stationed in the
colonies, while their sexual encounters with the natives remained limited
mostly to prostitutes. An episode in Francisco Franco's war diary sheds
light on the portrayal of the genders[26]: in 1922, a Moroccan offered a
young girl from his village to the soldiers in an attempt to prevent the
village from being raided.[27] That such things happened is less remarkable
than the fact that these topics were addressed in a book aimed at a general
bourgeois audience. Moroccan men were also sexualized. Caricatures
such as those on postcards often sent from soldiers to their families and
friends depicted *moros* with oversized genitalia who were unabashedly
lewd towards European women. These illustrations represented the
supposed insatiability and therefore bestiality of the *moros*.[28]

While aversions to the *moros* were fomented in many negative examples dominating the official discourse across the political spectrum, the
personal experiences of the soldiers reveal the potential for positive
encounters, as well. A Spanish veteran declared that he had never seen a
Moroccan who could not have been mistaken for a Spanish farmer.[29]
Indeed, many of the Spaniards who were responsible for coordinating
relations with the Moroccans seem to have been conscious of the fact that
the negative image Spaniards typically had was the result of a history

dominated by war, oppression, and poverty.[30] However, with the exception of nationalist groups in the Basque region,[31] there was hardly any organized movement within Spain to express solidarity with the Moroccans. The communist party did attempt to form "an alliance in the struggle with the colonized" in the 1920s, but their efforts were doomed to failure, given the insignificance of the party in this period and the lack of sympathy among the general public for the cause.[32] Whereas the need to "civilize" the natives was a central topic of discourse in the beginning of the colonial period, in the 1920s this was increasingly supplanted by patriarchal outrage that the *moros* were so resistant to these "efforts." This was especially true during the rebellion between 1921 and 1926, which was led by the Riffian Muhammad Abd el-Krim (1882–1963). In their attempt to control the charismatic insurgent and his followers, the Spanish forces deployed imported mustard gas against the native population.[33] Many defenseless Riffians were killed and their agricultural livelihood devastated; Abd el-Krim surrendered to the French troops and was banished. This most bitter enemy of Spain in Morocco had been educated in Spain, spoke several languages, and worked as a teacher and translator: he was the exact opposite of the constantly evoked stereotype of the uneducated and barbaric *moro*.

Approaches: "*Africanistas*" before the Civil War (1909–1936)

Parallel to the discourses of aversion and antagonism outlined above, proponents of colonization were also discussing cultural assimilation and appreciation for the *moros*. Spain as a nation was plagued with internal tensions, and the involvement in Africa, especially in Morocco, was seen as an avenue of necessary national regeneration. The group of so-called *africanistas* who supported this colonial expansion was socially and ideologically heterogeneous. It included conservative Catholic intellectuals, who justified the African project by inflating a phrase from Queen Isabella I's testament—"that they should not cease their conquest of Africa and the battle for faith against the infidels"[34]—and derived from it a divine mandate for colonial expansion.[35] This understanding, however, was eclipsed by the increasing interest of the liberal middle class in a supposed "*penetración pacífica*" (peaceful permeation).[36] The interests of entrepreneurs, lawyers, politicians, and doctors—who were admittedly motivated by hopes of economic benefits—were evidenced in the foundation of associations like the Real Sociedad Geográfica, the Liga Africanista Española, or the Centros Comerciales Hispano-Marroquíes. A highpoint of the *africanismo* came on 30 March 1884 in Madrid with the Mitin del Teatro Alhambra, in which intellectuals like Joaquín Costa, an important representative of the Spanish *regeneracionismo* at the end of the nineteenth century, campaigned for involvement in Africa. As a cultural element of this "permeation," several Hispano-Arabic schools were founded in Morocco in the early twentieth century, in which a Spanish teacher from Melilla, Francisco Sempere, assumed an especially important role. He wrote to the military regime, advocating that schools be established at which Muslim children could receive instruction including the study of the Quran. The children of Spanish expatriates, on the other hand, should be introduced to the Arabic language and Moroccan culture to prepare them for local administrative and commercial functions as adults.[37] In 1908 thirty children completed their first year at Sempere's Escuela de la enseñanza para los niños indígenas (School for the Instruction of Indigeous Children). Such schools helped the colonial government persuade Moroccan parents that Spain was promoting the development of their country while respecting the Moroccan culture and Islamic religion.

The militarist *africanistas*, on the other hand, were those officers who had made their military careers in the African territories. Under Alfons XIII, the military had become a central element of holding power in Spain, and the officers serving in Africa played a crucial role therein. Service in the colonies could boost a later career in the capital, and this led to friction between those members of the armed forces who had held posts in Africa and those who had not.[38] These conflicts within the army, mounting criticism of the lower classes due to the death toll in the colonies, and growing doubts about the colonial enterprise following the Disaster of Annual in 1921 caused the officers based in Africa to close ranks. The most important players in the coup of 17 July 1936 came from among the relatives of officers stationed there in the first three decades of the twentieth century: José Sanjurjo (1872–1936), Emilio Mola (1887–1937), Gonzalo Queipo de Llano (1875–1951) and Francisco Franco (1892–1975). Some newspapers and magazines became platforms for their ideas; these were intended to foster feelings of solidarity among Spaniards and a positive self-image for their involvement in Africa. The magazine *Africa: Revista de tropas coloniales* (Africa: Magazine of the Colonial Troops) completely dominated this genre, which saw many titles come and go.[39] The magazine was founded under the title *Revista de tropas coloniales* in Ceuta by Franco and other soldiers in 1924, and Franco became the publisher in 1925. In the 1920s it focused mostly on the leading classes of the colonial troops. The Civil War interrupted publication, but it resumed in 1942 with the changed subtitle *Africa: Revista española de colonización* (Africa: Spanish Magazine for Colonization). The new publication was based in Madrid and, after 1945, under the direction of the newly founded Instituto de Estudios Africanos (Institute for African Studies). The fate of this magazine and its contents reflect the more general historical development in this age: the constant paternalistic discourse about rapprochement, colonization, and the "*penetración pacifica*," which dominated the publication before the Civil War, was limited to those officers stationed in Africa and, occasionally interested civilians. After the Civil War, members of this group were at the helm of the Spanish government. The discourse of rapprochement, which had previously been limited to the military or intellectual circles, became a topic of public discourse.

The magazine emphasized the importance of Spain's African territories. Franco repeatedly used it as an organ to accuse the Spanish government of being weak and allowing the insurgency of the natives to escalate.[40] During this period, the magazine also pointed to the assimilation taking place in the colony: the articles dealt with the integration of Moroccans into the Spanish army.[41] These were accompanied by picturesque photographs of the *moros*: the portrait of a Moroccan blacksmith at his work embodied the stereotypical primeval man in his fascinating primitiveness, the close-up of a young woman's face, the epitome of an exotic beauty (Plate 1). In addition to such portraits, the magazine published impressions of daily life in Morocco like, for example, dignitaries meeting over a cup of tea. Another article featured the "typically Moorish" house in Tetuán, which the government of the protectorate established to demonstrate the Moroccan lifestyle for visitors from the peninsula. The author of the article in *Africa* pointed out an important missing element: "there are no feet decorated with henna dancing on the expensive rugs, no dancers with alabaster arms, graceful figures, and dark eyes. No singer beguiles the men with her love songs and poems of war in which the memory of Andalusia lives on. This the state will never achieve."[42] In such passages, the stereotypical Orientalist gender roles were especially apparent.

Beyond such stereotypes, the references to Al-Andalus served primarily as evidence of the historical similarities of Spain and North Africa. Many authors appropriated Arabist scholarship to legitimize the colonization on historical grounds, claiming to "present their theories in a way understandable for the masses."[43] Religion hardly served as a benchmark for ethnic divisions anymore: a four-part article which dealt with the "Muslim influences on Spanish culture" placed the mass conversions of the Visigoth population after 711 in the foreground, claiming that the similarities of the two religions were so significant that "their dogmatic differences were no insurmountable barrier for individuals with [only] a rudimentary religious education."[44] The concept of a religious division was supplanted by that of a common race:

> [On the difference] between the great majority of the Hispano-Roman, Islamicized Visigoths and the descendants of Spain on the maternal side, one can say that within only a few years the entire Muslim population—at least the vast majority—was of Spanish descent, and, as a

result, we must view the Hispano-Muslim folk *as just as Spanish as the rest of the peninsula, even though they are of a different religion.* Muslims, yes, but they belong to our own race.[45] [Emphasis in the original.]

The magazine suggested more than racial, economic, or cultural assimilation: according to a priest, the theological divisions of the religions could be bridged, the "centuries-long battle" notwithstanding. He explicitly praised the Islamic religion in addition to the culture:

> Islam is . . . a spiritual energy, an enormous religious force, and we believe that it is our duty to use this spirituality and bring it in contact with Christian spirituality: there is nothing to fear from its effects [if] directed well, one can expect an alliance on the fields of faith and without a doubt more unity and association than to date.[46]

Muslims occasionally spoke for themselves in the magazine, for example in an article by a Muslim scholar which examines the Quran's attitudes towards women. This appreciation of Islam as a religion would later prove to bolster the officers' argument during the Civil War for the legitimization of the Moroccan troops. It did not, however, place Islam on par with Christianity, for, at least in clerical circles, there was still a clear aim of saving Moroccan souls via the Christian mission. The *africanistas* agreed with the French bishop Henri Viell's call to "let us love and win over the souls, for they love the truth and we possess them."[47]

The narrative of assimilation, which served the extension of power in Morocco and was essentially a form of advertisement for the colonial enterprise, circulated among the officers stationed in Morocco and other proponents of the colonial policies. They drew upon the Arabists' scholarship, adapting and extending it to serve their own purposes. After the Civil War and the subsequent rise of Franco, these narratives and justifications became known far beyond the milieu of the militarist *africanistas*.

Propaganda: Islamic fear as a weapon in the Civil War (1936–1939)

The protagonists in the Civil War did not invent new images of Islam or the *moros*. They did, however, change the conditions for the dispersal and reception of such images. Within a conflict with a particularly high potential for violence beyond the military front,[48] the image of the *moro*—constructed over centuries in the Spanish imagination—was confronted with the reality of the Moroccan soldiers. The rebellion began in Morocco and involved primarily African troops. Failing their support, and that of Hitler and Mussolini, who provided airplanes for the transfer of troops to the mainland,[49] the rebellion would almost certainly have failed. According to a tally based on multiple sources, a total of 78,504

Moroccans participated in the conflict; an eighth of these fell in battle and nearly all of the survivors sustained injuries.[50]

For the first time since 1492, there was a significant Muslim presence within Spain. Although they were unaware of it, the Moroccans of 1936 brought an ideological baggage with them full of ancient clichés and preconceptions. As a result, old antagonistic images were projected onto contemporary Moroccans as though there had been a seamless continuation of Tariq's army from 711. In addition, the leaders of the coup struggled to justify the participation of Muslims in this supposedly Christian endeavor. The rebels viewed the *moros* above all as kind of physical weapon: six months into the conflict, approximately fifty thousand Moroccans were fighting on their side, fully one-seventh of the male population of Spanish Morocco.[51] They had been recruited with promises of wages and food, promises made even more attractive by the destitution of their homeland.[52] However, the *moros* were also a psychological weapon: during the colonial wars they had gained a reputation as primitive, brutal barbarians, who did not hesitate to decapitate, maim, or mutilate their prisoners. Furthermore their sexual appetite was allegedly insatiable. Their involvement in the conflict thus had a psychological aspect. General Queipo de Llano, infamous for his verbal attacks, had a daily radio broadcast on Radio Sevilla, in which he agitated against the Republican forces. Just a week into the conflict, on 23 July 1936, he boasted that "our valiant *legionnaires*[53] and *regulares*[54] have shown the red cowards what it means to be a man—and the women, too, who have finally met true men, not those castrated militias. Kicking and screaming will not save them."[55] These open threats implied that the rebels passively or even actively condoned and fostered such acts.[56] A Soviet observer reported that the insurgent generals had distanced themselves from the Moroccans with cynical remarks: "Those are the matters of the Moors. A wild people. We can do nothing against it. African nature."[57] Even considering the fact that Koltsov was not impartial and sought to portray the rebels negatively, his statements were hardly invented. The hypocrisy was apparent: clearly the brutality of the Moroccan soldiers—as well as that of the Spanish—was tolerated and silently condoned by at least some of those at the forefront of the rebellion. Other witnesses reported, however, that some Moroccans had been executed on the spot for rape.[58] The extent to which such crimes were tolerated depended primarily on the direct superiors in the hierarchy.

In the long term, the rebels were ill-advised to let this "national cause" be sullied by the brutality of their soldiers. Their Republican opponents, however, had no qualms about using the *moros* as a psychological weapon. They began to publicize the atrocities to rally support for the republic, employing both textual and visual propaganda. Many Republican, socialist, and communist caricatures drew on three stereotypical depictions: Franco as a midget—often with a swastika to emphasize his proximity to German National Socialism; obese, complacent clerics; and stupidly grinning Moroccans with and without a turban. To emphasize their "Otherness," the latter were often shown with pitch black skin and exaggerated puffy lips, which hardly corresponded with the appearance of the light-skinned North African Berbers at all. In the first year of the war, Catalan magazines like *L'Esquella de la Torratxa* used caricatures to attack the newfound friendship of these two former enemies. Such caricatures relied on the iconographical union of Christian and Moorish stereotypes, which were ideologically stylized as two sides of the same coin. This is evident, for example, in the picture of a bishop and a Moroccan, both with bloody lips and weapons, walking over an army of corpses (Plate 4). The caption makes a play on words involving the celebrations known as festivals of Moors and Christians: "Moors and Christians. Their savageness has finally been unified." Another scene made a similar point by showing a Muslim "Allah" with turban and crescent and a Christian "God" with the triangle representing the trinity shaking hands upon a cloud in heaven and pronouncing: "Of course we have made peace. We both want to enslave all peoples."[59] Bishops were repeatedly depicted blessing the *moros*, and *moros* were often shown together with the symbol of the cross. The old expectations of the inferior civilization and the savagery of the *moros* resonated in this contemporary context. A drawing, for example, which depicted two grotesquely exaggerated black figures with teeth bared in front of the town of Burgos, the center of Franco's government during the war, featured this dialogue: "'Are you coming, too, to defend Western civilization?'—'No! I have come to defend the Catholic Church.'"[60] These pictures incorporated anticlerical, antifascist, and anti-militarist discourses, which were already circulating in the leftist scene prior to the Civil War, and linked them to preexisting negative stereotypes.

Independent of the caricatures circulated in newspapers, magazines, and pamphlets, the Republican troops attempted to move the Moroccan soldiers to capitulate. Republican generals had flyers distributed which aimed to convince Moroccans to change sides. Parallel to their efforts, leftist networks recruited like-minded Muslim foreigners like, for example, the Algerian Rabah Oussidhoum, who lived in Paris. When he was asked what motivated his involvement, he answered: "Because all the newspapers speak of the Moors who are fighting for the rebels. I have come to show that not all Arabs are fascists."[61] The Palestinian communist Nayati Sidki was sent to Spain by the Comintern to appeal to the Moroccans among the rebels' ranks to defect. His efforts were largely fruitless, as evidenced in the following anecdote: on 25 September 1936, from the trenches on the front lines in Córdoba, he called upon the

Moroccans to change sides, but his fiery speech, delivered in Arabic, was drowned out by the rounds of gunfire.[62] There were only about one thousand Muslim volunteers among the Republican troops, many fewer than on the rebels' side.[63]

While members of the leftist camp intensified the anti-Muslim propaganda, the leaders of the coup were forced to reinterpret this discourse. This was no small task. How could they explain that the supposed archenemy of previous centuries was suddenly their ally, fighting with the rebels against Spaniards? The rebels adapted African interpretations of the Civil War in a way meant to appeal to the masses. They drew on monotheist commonalities of Christianity and Islam. Victor Ruíz Albéniz, who had served in the colonial wars and was familiar with Morocco, excelled particularly at supporting Franco's cause in this way. Under the name the Moroccans had given him, "El Tebib Arrumi" (the Christian doctor), he produced numerous texts and radio broadcasts in which he used his years of experience in Morocco to back his argument:

> To claim that Islam is related to the hordes who deny and anathematize God's existence, that [Muslims] serve the interests of Jewish gold or anarchist politics which reject hierarchies and attack the family, is to completely misunderstand the Arabic-Berber soul. For the Moors, a Christian is a person who lives a misplaced faith, but the Jew or the Atheist is an unclean being who denies divinity, [who commits] an incomprehensible blasphemy for the soul of a Muslim, that is, of a believer. Furthermore, the Moor can never side with the cowards who fight without honor. In their essence and their potential they are courageous and gallant, and the [atheist] hordes disgust them. That is why they are on our side.[64]

Religious differences which had seemed insurmountable in the nineteenth century now became the basis of the insurgents' discourse. As the passage quoted shows, however, the discourse remained limited: because of Franco's anti-Semitism[65] the Jews were not valued for their monotheist tradition. The *rojos* were villianized as infidels and replaced the *moros*, who were now allies, as antagonists. A newspaper from Navarre clearly stated: "If you observe the Moors of yesterday and today, it is proven that those from yesterday, against whom the Spaniards fought, are the Reds of today, just as the Reds of today are the destructive Moors of yesterday."[66] This new association was made at various levels in the rhetoric. A Catholic chaplain who served under the rebels praised the "religious spirit" of the Moroccan soldiers.[67] Queipo de Llano reported that Muslim soldiers had remarked, when confronted with a scene of destruction caused by the Republicans: "People who do such things want to civilize Morocco?"[68] In his speeches, Franco conjured the image of the

Civil War as a new crusade and depicted the causalities as a necessary sacrifice for a good cause:

> Our war is a religious war. All of us who are fighting, Christian or Muslim, are soldiers of God, fighting not against other people, but rather against atheism and materialism, against everything contrary to the dignity of mankind, which we want to exalt, cleanse, and ennoble.[69]

The war's religious dimension impacted the treatment of the Moroccans. When Republican troops bombed a ship which Franco had provided for a pilgrimage to Mecca on 20 January 1937, it was an opportunity to show solidarity with the "Muslim brothers": "They are insulting your most noble emotions, stamping upon your religion with their feet, and attacking you in the depths of your hearts," wrote the officer Tomás García Figueras in a special edition of the newspaper El Heraldo de Marruecos.[70] The pilgrims were able to travel despite it all; after their return, Franco received a delegation on 2 April, fittingly in Alcázar in Seville. In front of several generals, archbishops, and important representatives of the rebels, Franco professed ties to Islam, in a radical inversion of centuries-old stereotypes.

> Spain and Islam have always been two peoples [sic] who understood each other exceedingly well. . . . Russia's act aims to destroy the traditions, the mosques, everything that possesses a spiritual worth, [everything] that forms the foundation of Islam and the Muslim people. Your Highness, imperial vizier: the brotherly love of the Spaniards conveys the best feelings of the head of state and the Spanish population towards the Muslim people. And when the roses of victory bloom, we will give them the most beautiful flowers.[71]

However, such declarations by Franco and his followers proved to be empty promises. The Moroccan with the most significant career in Franco's regime was Muhammad Ben Mizzian (1897–1975). He was educated in the military academy in Toledo and served in many important battles of the war, rising through the ranks in the Civil War to the position of colonel. After the war he was made general. Franco first named him commanding officer in Ceuta, later capitán general in his native Galicia, and finally in the Canary Islands.[72] However, this was an isolated case. In reality the Moroccans served primarily in raiding troops and as cannon fodder on the front lines, as evidenced in the high number of casualties they suffered. The Spanish troops were thus spared these dangerous assignments.[73] For most of the troops from Morocco and for their families in Africa, there could be no talk of the roses of victory.

Appropriation: Discourses of brotherhood in early Francoism (1936–1956)

After the Civil War, the theme of "brotherhood" became an institution-alized part of the discourse in early Francoism. The initial appointment of officers who had served in Africa to important positions within the government brought the corresponding rhetoric directly into the ministries in Madrid. The British ambassador Samuel Hoare's description of Colonel Juan Beigbeder, who served as Franco's secretary of state from 1939 to 1940, reflects how this change in political leadership was perceived as remarkable:

> "We are all Moors," he [Beigbeder] once said to me, and certainly his dark, thin Quixotic figure was more in keeping with the Riff and the desert than with the small, stuffy room in which he sat in the Ministry of Foreign Affairs. From time to time the winds of Africa would break into the stifling heat of Madrid, and, in the middle of a discussion of high politics, he would start an Arabic chant from the illuminated Koran that always lay on his table.[74]

Ideologues who were loyal to the regime pointed to Morocco as the origin of a "national renewal." Franco repeatedly emphasized his affinity for Africa, which he considered his personal and political foundation: "My years in Africa live within me with indescribable force.... Without Africa, I can scarcely explain myself to myself, nor can I explain myself properly to my comrades in arms."[75] The Christian *caudillo* demonstrably surrounded himself with Moroccan bodyguards, which lent an exotic aura to his public appearances in the early years of the regime, when the most similarity is apparent to those cults of leadership which emerged in Italy and Germany (Plate 7).[76] At the same time this was an expression of Franco's claim to power in Morocco. His ideologues saw the Moorish bodyguards as further evidence of the historical roots which provided a supposed line of continuity from the Romans through Queen Isabella I and Cardinal Cisneros to Franco himself.[77] A similar function was served by academic institutions which were founded or expanded in the early phase of Francoism, especially the Instituto de Estudios Africanos (Institute for African Studies),[78] which was grounded in 1945 and became a mouthpiece for the *africanista* soldiers by offering them a platform to process their experiences via scholarship.[79] In addition to descriptions of Islam and information about interacting with Muslim soldiers or official guests,[80] the publications of the Instituto de Estudios Africanos expanded and continued the colonial and nationalist discourse which had already been initiated in the 1920s by the magazine *Africa*, among others. The ongoing discourse over the unity of Christians and Muslims, of Spain and

North Africa, a dialogue which had been taking place since the beginning of the colonial conquests in 1859 and which presupposed that the Spaniards' actions were ordained by God, became expressed in biological racism and geographical determinism. Geographic similarities between Spain and Morocco underlined the argumentation of Francoist ideologues along racial lines. The suggestion that there was "unity of blood and unity of territory" aimed to lend these political demands the authority of natural laws, just as in the beginnings of the expansion in 1859.[81]

The discourse over an affinity for Morocco corresponded to an aversion to the other great European powers. The *africanistas* held a grudge against Great Britain over Gibraltar; France was an ongoing rival in Morocco. Before and during World War II, Franco's sympathy for the regimes in Germany and Italy was obvious. Nevertheless, Hitler refused to assist Franco against France in Morocco, which was almost certainly one reason why Spain never entered the war on the side of the Axis powers.[82] Because Franco had been closely associated with the conquered dictatorships, however, the victors in Potsdam refused to admit Spain to the United Nations in 1945. Spain resorted to the discourse of brotherhood to appeal to the Arab world and avoid international isolation. Due to the support of Arab nations, Spain under Franco was finally permitted to join the U.N. in 1955.[83]

The discourse on brotherhood was limited in its political, colonial, and cultural dimensions: the relationships to the Arab states in 1955 were insufficiently old or deep to provide Spain the opportunity in the long term which they had hoped for of becoming a mediator between these world cultures.[84] At the political level, the colonial enterprise was an "empire which never existed"[85]: of the regions in the Gulf of Guinea, the Spanish Sahara, the tiny enclave Ifni, and the Rif mountains, Spain lost the largest and most important territory with the independence of Morocco in 1956. At the cultural level, in the perceptions of the population, it was difficult for the concept of an alliance with the *moros* to supplant the antagonistic stereotypes. In the school books of Franco's Spain, the old, anti-Muslim historical narrative prevailed.[86] The oft-cited personal friendship of the *caudillo* and the *moros* was likewise limited: except for a short visit to the Spanish Sahara in 1950, Franco never returned to Africa after he left Morocco in 1936.[87]

PORTUGAL: STRUGGLE TO MAINTAIN POWER (1890–1974)

Civilization: The idea of a Christian empire (1890–1945)

In Portuguese historiography, "Islam" was portrayed as only one of several opponents. This coincided with the perception—still common in the twentieth century—the the colonial Muslim population was one of various religious groups in an empire spread over four continents. What led to a particular view of Islam? What role did the medieval history play in the later perceptions and expectations?

The Muslims in Portuguese colonies in the nineteenth century were part of a discourse on civilization which transcended individual religions. This discussion was sparked by Portugal's colonial politics. For centuries, Brazil and the Far East were economically more lucrative than the colonies in Africa. As a result, at the end of the nineteenth century, only the coastal regions of Guinea, Angola, and Mozambique had been developed.[88] The competition of European nations in Africa at the end of the nineteenth century, however, forced Portugal to invest more in its African territories. The Portuguese vision was embodied in the Mapa cor-de-rosa (pink map) which the foreign minister, Henrique Barros Gomes presented in 1887; the region colored pink, "Portuguese South Africa," stretched across the continent, coast to coast, from Angola to Mozambique. This vision was abruptly ended by the British ultimatum on 11 January 1890, which demanded that Portugal retreat or face the withdrawal of English diplomats and military strikes. By the beginning of the twentieth century, the research and settlement of African territories had been largely taken over by the European governments. The private population had only limited interest in these areas, which attracted very few immigrants.[89]

As the interior of Africa was developed between 1890 and 1910, new strategies of colonization and dealing with the native population had to emerge. The question of missionary activity was one aspect of this, though within Portugal it was not only a religious consideration, but rather a reflection of the political events. In 1880 the Comissão de Estudo da Reforma da Missão Ultramarina (Commission for Reform of the Overseas Mission) had lamented the lack of personnel, educational opportunities, and means for the Portuguese mission: since there were too few Portuguese missionaries, foreigners were recruited to work in the Portuguese territories. These foreign missionaries were often not even Catholic, which, in the eyes of the commission, was contrary to Portugal's interests. The head of this commission, Luciano Cordeiro, further criticized the missionaries, whose education was often limited to theology. In his view, they should be "agents of civilization" with basic knowledge of not only theology, but also medicine, science, and trade.[90] In the republic, religious orders were banned for a short time until a decree by the colonial minister João Soares in 1919 allowed the establishment of lay and ecclesiastical missions as a necessary step to alleviate the personnel problem. In 1926 the Estatuto Orgânico das Missões Católicas Portuguesas (Statute of the Portuguese Catholic Missions) was passed in an attempt to repress the influence of foreign or non-Catholic missions.

In the Estado Novo, the concept of mission played a central role in the legitimization of the Portuguese empire, even though the infrastructure was hardly sufficient to support a widespread mission or sweeping Christianization.[91] The colonies were viewed as part of the Portuguese nation. The mission aimed on the one hand to integrate the colonies into the homeland, which is why the Estado Novo reversed some measures taken by the republic to grant the colonies more autonomy, and on the other hand to "civilize" the population of Africa.[92] The central colonial document of the early Estado Novo, the Acto Colonial of 8 July 1930, laid out quite confidently in article two the "historical function, to possess and colonize regions overseas and to civilize the native populations."[93] The Portuguese understanding of civilization was inseparable from the Christian religion: into the 1960s, the political and ecclesiastical policies were guided by the aim to promote "the spread of faith and the empire".[94]

Nevertheless the secularist tradition of the Portuguese republic, which had put religious freedom in the constitution in 1911, was evident, even during the Estado Novo under the Acto Colonial, which did not rescind that right. Article 23 guaranteed those in regions overseas "freedom of conscience and the free exercise of various beliefs, with the limitations necessary for the rights and sovereignty of Portugal."[95] This policy was continued in the Estatuto dos Indígenas (Statute for Natives) in 1954 for the colonial populations of Angola, Guinea, and Mozambique. The conditions under which an *indígena* could become a *cidadão português* (Portuguese citizen) did not include religious categories, although these were implied in the requirement that natives be sufficiently distant from indigenous traditions and customs.[96] The residents of Cape Verde, Goa, and Macao were not classified as *indígenas* but were granted citizen status at the outset.[97]

The Muslim population of the Portuguese empire lived in Mozambique (in the north and along the coast) and in Guinea. A text in the *Revista de Portugal* of 1890 can be seen as the beginning of an explicit discourse over Islam.[98] It portrayed Islam as Portugal's rival in the African expansion. During this decade, the policy of so-called "effective occupa- tion" of Portugal's African territories forced a closer consideration of the indigenous way of life. This in turn intensified the perception of a compe- tition with Islam. The colonial politician and later governor of Mozambique António Enes complained in a report to the government in 1893 that Christianity had to be propagated like an exotic plant while Islam spread like a weed.[99] Enes attributed this to the fact that Islam was a "simple religion" which was more compatible with the lifestyle and way of thinking of the *indígenas*: "A religion without dogma, without mysteries, without philosophy, without abstraction, without mysticism, without rigor, a religion for limited intelligence and for primitive peoples, which simplifies itself even more to gain acceptance from the

Africans—and thus they accept it."[100] Enes's position combines the stereotypes of a religiously inferior Islam with that of a culturally inferior Africa.

Opinions like his were no exception in the nineteenth and early twentieth century, but they were limited to a particular circle. For decades Islam had played no significant role in the efforts to integrate the provinces abroad. It did appear in anti-Western propaganda produced during World War I. The Portuguese leadership was almost certainly aware of this, and also of Spain's bloody entanglement in Morocco, but they paid little attention to Islam. Between the World Wars and during the Spanish Civil War, in which Salazar's government supported Franco's rebels with soldiers, weapons, and other shipments, Bolshevism was seen as a more present threat than Islam.[101]

Distrust: Islam as threat for the colonies (1945–1960)

The new world order after 1945 and the insecurity it evoked also deeply unsettled Portugal, which had remained neutral in the conflict. The sharpening divide between East and West, the process of decolonization, and the new self-confidence of former colonial territories, evidenced in the Bandung Conference in 1955, all led to Portugal's being more intensely concerned about Islam. It was now seen as a threat to the colonies and therefore an endangerment to an important pillar of Portuguese identity. Reports in the colonial press painted a bleak picture of a rapid Islamization:

> The Muslims, restless travelers and peddlers, invade the villages, peddling their knick-knacks or trading for goods. Their prayers are ostentatious, which pleases the chiefs with their pliable morality and convinces them to devote themselves to Allah. . . . [The natives] adjust to all the circumstances, and one fine day, without anyone having noticed, the entire village has been Islamicized."[102]

Authors like António da Silva Rego and Eduardo Dias read the situation along the same lines that António Enes had half a century earlier. Da Silva Rego viewed the Muslim traditions, especially polygamy and the exclusive right of the man to divorce his spouse, as a "continuous moral contradiction."[103] Dias viewed jihad as the "only original element of Islam." This position emphasized that Islam posed not only a moral, but an even more significant political danger.[104] As this foe was well known from the past, Dias called for increased caution: "We should . . . be aware that there are still *Moors* on Portuguese soil" [emphasis in original].[105] The governor of Guinea, Manoel Maria Sarmento Rodrigues, also drew this historical connection when he called Guinea an "open battlefield for our crusade of nationalization: to teach the language and to spread the religion."[106] For representatives of the Catholic Church like Sebastião de Resende, Bishop of Beira in Mozambique, the association with Islam was incompatible with membership in the national community: "Islamicized natives are quickly lost to the Church, and hopefully not also to Portugal. Those who follow foreign movements do not belong to it."[107]

In the years between 1950 and 1960, warnings of the Islamic threat became especially loud as the process of decolonization in Africa and the virulent phase of East-West opposition intensified and became entrenched. Already in 1946, Dias warned that the twenty-five million Muslims living in the Soviet empire could help spread communist propaganda.[108] His argument remained influential. Ten years later the idea that Islam could become an instrument of Bolshevism was one of Antonio de Sousa Franklin's greatest fears. He saw Islam as a means to the end of attacking the overseas' power of the European states. Furthermore, in his opinion, Islam harbored the potential to spark dangerous rebellions, as contemporary events proved: "No one can guarantee that the Fula, Mandinka, and other Islamicized peoples who behave like our good friends today will not be waving banners of revolt tomorrow and aiming their weapons at us. The example of that which is currently unfolding in Algeria speaks for itself."[109] Islam was feared as a vehicle for the expanding tendency to demand autonomy: "Every Muhammadan preacher uses a simple and widely acceptable argument: Christianity is a good religion for the white man, Islam for the black man."[110] Colonial politicians and missionaries were more wary of the political implications of Islam's spread than of the religious ones: "The progress of Islamicization in Guinea is not a religious problem, but it could nevertheless become a growing obstacle in the greater integration of the natives into the national society."[111] This horror vision of Islam as a "Russified Trojan Horse"[112] which had been smuggled into the colonial empire combined and thereby intensified two antagonists.

The countermeasure to these perceived threats at the end of the 1950s was Lusitanization, the attempt to encourage the adoption of Portuguese language and culture, which took place on several levels. Because the Portuguese system seemed increasingly anachronistic within the context of decolonization, the Acto Colonial was formally abolished in 1951, although it was essentially incorporated into the constitution, whereby the term "colonial empire" ("*império colonial*") was replaced by the less authoritarian sounding "overseas province" ("*Ultramar*" or "*províncias ultramarinas*").[113] Colonial politicians, experts, and missionaries made various recommendations about how to best achieve "*aportuguesamento*" on the ground in the colonies. José Júlio Gonçalves of the Instituto Superior de Estudos Ultramarinos (High Institute of Overseas Studies) composed a list of suggestions for the monitoring of the Islamic presence in Guinea in a study in 1958: the Catholic mission should be strengthened, the possible political consequences and contacts following the pilgrimages to Mecca closely observed, the expansion of Arabic should be restricted in favor of Creole languages and Portuguese. According to his argument, Islam was a "denationalizing," "anti-Portuguese," and, not least, "anti-European" force.[114] The study also called for an improved education of the missionaries. It recommended that they learn Arabic and that the preparations for their assignment should include an "exact study of Muslim ideas."[115] While the political context of this anti-Muslim rhetoric and argumentation were new, the underlying assumptions were rooted deep in the Portuguese past.

Integration: Towards a "Portuguese ecumenism" (1960–1974)

In the 1960s there was a marked shift in attitudes towards Islam. This was primarily due to the increasing pressure on the regime: a series of conspiracies challenged Salazar between 1959 and 1962, and the movements for African autonomy affected Portugal during this time, as well. This wave included the foundation of the Partido Africano de Independência da Guiné e Cabo Verde (African Party for the Independence of Guinea and Cape Verde) and the Movimento Popular de Libertação de Angola (People's Movement for the Liberation of Angola) in 1956 and the Frente de Libertação de Moçambique (Mozambique Liberation Front) in 1962; their resistance became increasingly violent.[116] Confronted with these threats, the authorities were forced to evoke the "single [Portuguese] nation" more urgently than before: "A black man from Angola, a native of Mozambique or Goa will never say that he is 'Angolan,' 'Mozambican,' or 'Goan.' He will simply say he is Portuguese. Portuguese from Luanda, Portuguese from Beira, Portuguese from India, or Portuguese from Trás-os-Montes, from Minho, or the Algarve," claimed an editorial in the *Diário de Notícias*, the most important newspaper of the Estado Novo, in 1960.[117] In 1961 Lisbon abolished the Estatuto dos Indígenas and granted all residents of Angola, Guinea, and Mozambique Portuguese citizenship, making all residents of the overseas territories formally equal. In reality, however, this act was of primarily symbolic importance, for a notation in the passport continued to identify the natives as *indígena*.[118]

This improvement in the position of the colonial population, although it was in many ways superficial, also had implications for the treatment of Islam. Given the undeniable symptoms of decline within the colonial empire, politicians and missionaries began viewing the Muslims as a stabilizing factor rather than a threat. The exact number of Muslims within the colonies is difficult to estimate. The founder of Portugal's first Muslim community, Suleiman Valy Mamede, claimed that there were two million Muslims within the colonial territories,[119] but this is certainly too high. Herculano Lopes de Oliveira wrote of 190,000 Muslims in Guinea, ten times the number of Catholics in this region, and of half a million Muslims in the Diocese of Nampula in northern Mozambique.[120] Albano Mendes Pedro's study includes a similar estimate of 600,000 Muslims in Mozambique,[121] and the *Atlas Missionário Português* of 1962 indicated that 800,000 had been Islamicized there.[122] Regardless of which estimate is most accurate, the Muslim population was certainly large enough to garner the colonial politicians' close attention. Although Islam had been perceived in the preceding decades as a political and religious threat to the nation, it now seemed important for precisely these reasons that it be integrated into the concept of the nation.[123]

The potential inherent in the medieval past unfolded: just as the historical animosity had been invoked to make the threat more present, the alliance could now be legitimized as well. Much in the vein of the scholarship of the first Portuguese professor for Arab studies, David Lopes, the scholar and colonial expert Francisco José Veloso spoke at a conference in 1965: "When the Portuguese, whose homeland had experienced five hundred years of intense Arab acculturation, encountered the Arabianized and Arabs [in the colonies], it was as though they encountered a part of themselves."[124] Here, too, Islam was portrayed as an old acquaintance, and a line was drawn directly from medieval Muslims to the colonial population of the twentieth century. In 1970, the magazine *Panorama*, which was published by the Secretariado do Estado da Informação e Turismo (Secretariat of Information and Tourism),[125] claimed: "Catholicism could identify with the general demeanor of the nation, in some epochs more vividly than in others, but it never constituted its essence by itself."[126] Compared to the clear Catholic discourse of the early Estado Novo, this represented an about-face.

The "nationalization of Islam" thus became one of the central tasks of the Portuguese governors in Africa in the late 1960s.[127] Portugal presented itself as a protector and preserver of the Muslim religion and culture in an effort to prevent religious differences from feeding political opposition. As part of the so-called "*acção psicologica*" (psychological action) in Mozambique, the government aimed to strengthen the bond of Muslim dignitaries to Portugal in hopes that their authority and influence over the population could in turn be used to repress the subversive influence of the movements for autonomy.[128] This had the most significant effects in cultural policies, which were meant to demonstrate the ties between Lisbon and the religion and traditions of the regions overseas. In Guinea a series of new mosques was built at public expense.[129] This was a good opportunity to convince Muslims that the Portuguese government was tolerant and even appreciative of Islam. When the new mosque in Bissau was officially opened in April 1966, Governor Arnaldo Schulz proclaimed to the colonial politicians and Muslim dignitaries assembled for the occasion that Portugal had long been a religiously and ethnically diverse nation:

> Indeed the Portuguese have and continue to practice the sound principles of freedom of religion and equality of the races. Portugal is made up of people of different races and religions who live in a perfect spirit of understanding and tolerance: black, white, yellow, and Hindu live together just as peacefully as Christians, Muslims, Buddhists, and even Animists, and combine their efforts to ensure the material, social, and political progress of the great Portuguese nation.[130]

Whereas pilgrimages to Mecca had once been viewed with skepticism, the government now explicitly facilitated the trip for those who were, as a Muslim dignitary in Guinea put it, "children of God, disciples of Muhammad, Portuguese under the law."[131] These trips brought the pilgrims through Lisbon to foster acquaintance with the capital city, according to the state-sponsored magazine *Panorama* (Plate 6). The same issue noted proudly that the number of Portuguese (*sic*) who were participating in pilgrimages to Mecca was continually rising.[132] The first Portuguese politician who explicitly addressed to the Muslims was the governor of Mozambique, Baltazar Rebello de Souza. On 17 December 1968 he delivered a radio address on Laylat al-Qadr, the "Night of Destiny," in which according to Muslim tradition the first revelations to Muhammad took place. It began with the national hymn followed by the opening sura of the Quran.[133] Rebello de Souza invoked the "common truths of faith" and assured the Muslims of Portuguese friendship.[134] Further signs of a cultural rapprochement were an official translation of the Quran into Portuguese commissioned by the Ministério do Ultramar (Overseas Ministry)[135] and the foundation of the first organized Muslim community within Portugal itself in Lisbon in 1968. As their first leader, Suleiman Valy Mamede from Mozambique, noted with pride, the congregation was open to both Sunni and Shia Muslims.[136] Valy Malmede called for the foundation of a mosque in Lisbon in 1969, arguing that all other European capitals had a mosque for the Muslim population and that Lisbon should be no exception. In a nutshell he was arguing for a mosque because it meant keeping pace with the rest of Europe.[137] It is indicative of the changed times that the Islamic Community now hoped to win over Portuguese leaders with a complete reversal of the older argument which had seen Islam as the antipode to Europe.

This transition in colonial policies was supported by at least two social developments: the growing acceptance of a theory of *luso-tropicalismo* in the 1950s and the Catholic Church's openness to ecumenism in the

1960s. The theory of *luso-tropicalismo* developed by the Brazilian anthro-
pologist Gilberto Freyre (1900–1987) credited Portugal with being
uniquely able to deal with "tropical" cultures due to the experience with
the Arabs in the Middle Ages.[138] The Portuguese had taken on the
Africans' "social flexibility," as evidenced in the biological mingling,
polygamous tendency,[139] and the ranking of faith over race. According to
this argument, Portuguese colonization had been "Christ-centered," in
contrast to the "ethnic-centered" ideas of Great Britain or Germany,
where racial and biological arguments had dominated.[140] Freyre's theses
are certainly controvertible and are not explicitly rooted in the colonial
discourse of the regime,[141] but elements of his thinking were increasingly
appropriated.[142] His theory suggests a symbiotic connection of Portugal
and Africa, which was in turn the result of Portugal's previous
"Africanization" by the North African Muslims. This argumentation
(that Africa is Portugal and Portugal is Africa) helped to legitimize the
Portuguese government's continued claims over their empire in the face
of mounting international pressure.

Even more important than the theory of *luso-tropicalismo* for the
Estado Novo—which although officially neutral was clearly influenced
by Catholicism[143]—was the revolution in the Catholic Church in the
1960s. The declaration on the relation of the church to non-Christian
religions passed by the Second Vatican Council on 28 October 1965,
Nostra Aetate, called upon Christians and Muslims, despite their historical animosity, "to forget the past and to work sincerely for mutual
understanding and to preserve as well as to promote together for the
benefit of all mankind social justice and moral welfare, as well as peace
and freedom."[144] However, a document from Rome could hardly banish
the antagonistic images which had been built up within the collective
imagination over centuries. Likewise, the regime could hardly abandon
its reservations towards Islam from one day to the next. The old fears
remained. In 1966, for example, a report of the secret police force PIDE
described Muhammad as a precursor of Karl Marx, both warriors against
imperialism and capitalism, which were equated with the goals of a
supposed "African-Asian cooperation" and its battle against colonialism.[145] Catholic missionaries also warned that Portugal would lose its
"Christian soul" by accommodating Muslims; they viewed the financing
of a mosque in Guinea as a "conscious denial" of Portuguese identity.[146]
Valy Mamede's activities, his travels throughout Muslim areas, and his
contacts there were closely observed by the PIDE.[147]

The regime thus remained internally skeptical of Islam, even as it
made a point of presenting itself as open to the religion when this seemed
to serve colonial interests. This fostered discourse on ecumenism. A good
example of this is the career of Eurico Dias Nogueira (1923–2014), who
became bishop of the Diocese of Vila Cabral (modern-day Lichinga) in

northern Mozambique. In 1966, nine months after the end of Vatican II, he penned a "Fraternal Letter to the Muslims"—apparently with Salazar's approval, albeit discrete[148]—which stressed the common elements of Islam and Christianity and assured Muslims of Portugal's benevolence towards them. This letter was read in mosques throughout the country. In a reflection of the ecumenical spirit of the age, it was translated into French, Arabic, and Italian.[149] The state magazine *Panorama* subsequently pointed to Dias Nogeira as the representative of a supposedly "continuous, ancient Portuguese ecumenism."[150] This "Portuguese Islam" could no longer be discounted in the political debates about the role of religion, which led to new constellations: Valy Mamede participated as president of the Muslim Community of Lisbon in a campaign to reintroduce the name of God into the constitution because it had been removed in the revisions of 1959.[151] General António de Spínola (1910–1996), who was the military governor of Guinea-Bissau removed from office a few weeks before the Carnation Revolution because of his open criticism of colonial policies, emphasized in an interview in 1971: "Because Portuguese culture displays relevant Islamic traits, we cannot view the Muslim religion as contrary to the perpetuation of the nation without denying part of our own heritage."[152]

The growing openness to the Muslim population, however, could not prevent and at most delayed the disintegration of the overseas empire. The empire, which was Portugal's most significant claim to power in the European context, was ultimately the undoing of the Estado Novo. The Revolution of 25 April 1974 was not the work of the democratic lay opposition but rather an uprising of the military against the colonial politics.[153] Thus the discourse about the religiously diverse colonial empire and the friendship with the "Portuguese Muslims" represents the swan song of the Estado Novo.[154] It is difficult to determine to what extent these attempts at rapprochement succeeded with the Muslim population because the official publications only cited those who were pro-Portuguese. Anecdotal evidence indicates that there was true affection and friendship beyond the officially sanctioned tactics: when Dias Nogueira was slated to be relocated to Angola after eight years in Vila Cabral, Muslim dignitaries in his diocese sent a letter to the pope in which they beseeched him not to send the bishop away. They further requested that if it should be absolutely necessary for Dias Nogueira to be posted elsewhere, the pope should please see that his successor be of similar character. Dias Nogueira was transferred, but Paul VI is reported to have mandated that this letter be carefully preserved in the papal archives: it was the first time in history that Muslims had asked the pope for a bishop.[155]

COMPARATIVE CONCLUSIONS

In many ways the discourses in Spain and Portugal surrounding colonization were comparable to that taking place within other European nations. The opposition negotiated between "civilization" and "barbarism," the description of the colonial population as "primitive," the negation of the worth of native culture, and the patriarchal mission of "education" were constant topics underlying the cultural foundations of the colonial policies of European societies. The discourse on the Iberian Peninsula was, however, unique in that Iberians considered themselves better acquainted with their colonial adversary because of their historical encounter. The Iberian states had been the early modern forerunners of colonization but had lost this advantage by the nineteenth century and were painfully aware of their own inferiority, especially in comparison to the British Empire. The medieval past offered the chance to make a cultural argument: no British, French, or German politician was able to claim that Indians, West Africans, or New Guineans had visited their homelands in previous centuries, resulting in a historical mission to civilize those exotic places. Iberian colonial politicians cultivated the perception that they knew their Muslim counterpart in the colonies especially well due to their common history. The memory of the medieval Muslim as preserved in historical accounts, scholarship, and everyday culture affected the way that the Moroccan farmer and the Guinean marabout were perceived; it colored both the concrete encounters of politicians and natives in the colonies and the politicians' abstract concept of the "natives" when they were sitting in Madrid or Lisbon. In this respect, the Muslim population of the Spanish and Portuguese colonies was not only an object of a general discourse on civilization but rather one which appeared to be legitimized by history. The equation of the historical and contemporary *moros* and *mouros*, and thus of the Islamicized Berber tribes of the eighth century with those of the North, West, and East African Muslims of the early twentieth century, repudiated any developmental potential of the Muslim counterpart and contributed an additional facet to the already negative discourse.

Despite these commonalities, some differences in the importance of the Muslim population for the Spanish and Portuguese nations are evident. Of Spain's colonial empire, only the Islamic regions in Africa remained in 1898, which exacerbated the transfer of the medieval antagonism into the colonies. The colonial opposition and especially the negative connotations were thus intensified by the historiographical discourse of animosity between Christianity and Islam. The erstwhile rival in the battle over Spain was now considered an especially stubborn adversary in the colonial ambitions. The old foe seemed to confront Spain at every step along the way.

In Portugal, Christianity was also central to the civilizing mission, and this during a period in which the European neighbors had already lost control over some or all of their colonies.[156] The territorial and cultural diversity the colonies brought with them thus had a longer effect on Portugal. As a result, less attention was paid to colonial Islam at first. Only after the 1940s did Islam emerge as an important topic. Discussions of the danger posed by Islam in the colonies developed in Portugal, similar to those in France and Belgium.[157] Islam was especially prominent in these concerns because of the potential for a network of fellow believers that extended beyond Africa. Legal measures taken in the colonies, however, show that this danger was viewed as more political than religious. In contrast to Spain, where the colonial rhetoric was often based on dualistic view of Christianity and Islam, in Portugal the emphasis was on the stylization of a single cultural identity without stressing the role of an opponent.

At the same time, within the colonial discourse there was a more marked shift towards positive perceptions and expectations of Islam than in other areas of politics and culture. Islam, as a multifunctional antagonist upon which all possible dangers to religion and state could be projected, morphed into a tactical instrument to work against the loss of power within the colonies. This became most evident under the dictators: Francoism discovered the "brothers from the other side of the strait" as allies in the battle against Republican atheism, while the cultural commonalities served as a source of political cohesion. The Estado Novo attempted at the outset of the movements for independence to forge bonds with the Islamic leaders, and in turn with the population, in order to reinforce loyalty to Lisbon and to undermine the movements themselves. The creation of a Portuguese ecumenism was a simultaneous attempt to accommodate the foreign critics of an anachronistic system of power and to present Portugal as a realization of ideas that had only begun to circulate. A condition for this acquiescence was certainly that Islam could no longer serve as the most powerful stereotypical antagonist. This role was inherited by communism. The multifaceted stereotype surrounding Islam was dissolved, but its function was transferred to another foe.

4

Islam as a National Lesson: Staging the Past

"However, when the sun began to go down in the direction of the sea
and touched the clear horizon, the voice of the muezzin could be heard
coming from the great mosque, calling out for the last time from on
high where he had taken refuge, *Allahu akbar*.
The Moors came out in goose pimples at the summons of Allah,
but the plea did not reach its end because a Christian soldier,
more zealous than most, or thinking one more casualty was needed to
conclude the war, went racing up the steps of the minaret
and with one blow from his sword beheaded the old man,
in whose blind eyes a light flickered at the moment of death."

José Saramago, *The History of the Siege of Lisbon* (1989)[1]

Within the realms of historical narratives, scholarship, and colonial politics, images of Islam emerged that circulated among far beyond an audience of elites. Islam served as the basis for a lesson for the nation, a lesson conveyed both in formal instruction and in reenactments of historical events. The following chapter examines depictions of Islam intended for a broader audience and the motivations behind their selection. School textbooks provide an indication of how the Muslim past was portrayed in the context of formal instruction, and the stagings of historical events as part of commemorative festivities likewise embodied certain didactic messages.

The respective chronologies necessitate a somewhat asymmetrical comparison: central anniversary celebrations of the so-called "*reconquista*"—like the anniversary of the Battles of Las Navas de Tolosa (1912) and Covadonga (1918)—took place in Spain in the age of the monarchy, while the anniversary of the Battle of Ourique (1940) and the conquest of Lisbon from the Moors (1947) are perfect examples of the celebratory culture under Salazar.[2] Despite the asymmetrical structures of government in Spain and Portugal in the examples chosen, the comparison of these commemorations does allow for some conclusions regarding the flashy reenactments of victories over the Muslim foe in the early twentieth century.

School books and anniversary celebrations might initially seem to be two very different historical genres. However, they shared a didactic purpose of disseminating historical narratives. To this aim, both simplify the portrayal of the historical Islam and perpetuate certain stereotypes. These accounts were aimed, in the case of school books, at children and youth, in the case of the anniversary celebrations, at the middle class within these regions.

The attempt to trace the methods of dissemination of popular accounts of Islam is limited in its methods and content: the high rate of illiteracy in the nineteenth century on the Iberian Peninsula and, in Portugal's case, even into the twentieth, meant that the population had limited access to written historical accounts. The target audience for school texts, but also for speeches and publications as part of commemorative events, belonged to the educated classes. These media aimed more to permeate certain circles with this historical knowledge than to expose the broad masses to it. In the end, however, the sources reveal only the intentions rather than the extent to which these efforts in fact succeeded. The analysis here concentrates therefore on the production of images of Islam and, to some extent, on their distribution, rather than on the actual reception, which is practically impossible to gauge.

ISLAM AS A LEADING ACTOR:
THE "MOORS OF OUR DAYS" IN SPAIN

History textbooks from the Spanish Restoration to Francoism

There are, as Rafael Valls Montés has convincingly illustrated, four phases in the institutional development of formal instruction of history in Spain from the nineteenth century to the present: the formation of a canon within the discipline in the mid-nineteenth century (1836–1880); the positivist reformation and implementation of important liberal educational goals in the Restoration period and the Second Republic (1880–1939); the Catholic-dominated phase during Franco's reign (1939–1970); and, finally, the search, which continues to the present day, for a new educational canon following the transition to democracy (1970–2006).[3] For most of this period, the Ley Moyano (Moyano Law),[4] passed in 1857 in an attempt to forge a compromise between ecclesiastical and state educational concepts, provided the legal foundation. The responsibility for personnel, curriculum, and instructional materials was therein delegated to the Ministerio de Fomento (Ministry of Development), although this legislation also recognized private educational institutions and granted the church the right to review the curriculum and the materials used in instruction. These goals reflected the liberal agenda of improving education to advance development in hopes of achieving parity with the other nations of Western Europe. However, many measures foreseen in the law, for example the obligatory elementary school attendance, were not universally implemented over many decades. Many factors were to blame: the continuous change at the helm of the Spanish government; the lack of support at the local level; the unwillingness of families, especially poor ones, to send their children to school; and the Catholic Church's mistrust of secular educational institutions.[5] The Ley Moyano—among Spain's longest surviving legislation—was first officially supplanted in 1970 with the passage of the Ley General de Educación.

In the course of the political struggle between liberals and conservatives, formal education became the focus of an ideological discussion. The church tried to influence social developments by founding schools of its own. The private school system was dominated by religious orders well into the twentieth century.[6] The progressives viewed the educational system as the foundation of a modern democratic society. The Institución Libre de la Enseñanza, founded in 1876, became a symbol of liberal secular education; it was committed to remaining independent of religious, political, and philosophical dogmas and endured vigorous criticism from the church. In its heyday the institution was attended by at most two hundred and fifty pupils per year, but its graduates and teachers nevertheless constituted an important leftist liberal network for over fifty years.[7] The worldview of the respective schools determined which schoolbooks were employed in instruction and which historiographical tendencies were taught, whether Catholic or secular, conservative or progressive, etc.

Compared to the rest of Western Europe, the social reach of such instruction within Spain was limited in the nineteenth and twentieth centuries for two primary reasons. First of all, the rate of illiteracy during the Restoration was considerable: in 1887 approximately sixty-five percent of Spaniards were illiterate, and this number had sunk only by half by 1930.[8] Second, even within the small class of potential readers, there was little widespread distribution of individual books. The textbooks produced in Madrid and Barcelona starting in 1880 by the first publishers specializing in school books were limited to editions of two to five hundred copies, and only a few of those would have been used simultaneously in around ten institutions.[9] Even today it is difficult to reach well founded conclusions about the extent of distribution, market share, or even editions of individual texts. Statistics which have been compiled for the nineteenth century and data contained within library catalogs do allow some analysis for the nineteenth century.[10] This information provides the basis for the selection of texts analyzed in this study.

1 *Top*: The magazine *África: Revista de tropas coloniales* did not deal exclusively with military themes; rather it portrayed the Spanish territory in Morocco and its native residents. These pictures depicted the *moros* as ethnically primitive, beautiful, and exotically fascinating. "Vulcano marroquí" (Moroccan blacksmith), in *África: Revista de tropas coloniales*, September 1927, p. 219 (Photograph: Lázaro). "Belleza marroquí" (a Moroccan beauty), in *África: Revista de tropas coloniales*, June 1927, p. 135 (Photograph: Lázaro). ©Biblioteca Nacional de España.

2 The façade of the former mosque Igreja Matriz de Mértola during renovations in 1948. The river Guadiana, visible in the background, was a connection to the Mediterranean which made the city an important trading post in ancient and medieval times. © Instituto da Habitação e da Reabilitação Urbana, Portugal. SIPA FOTO 0170377.

3 Granada's capitulation was a popular subject among Spanish historical painters at the end of the nineteenth century. Francisco Pradilla y Ortiz' depiction of this event became particularly well known, presumably due to its nearly photographic technique, and the image was reproduced often, for example, as here on a fan. Fan with image reproduced from original by Francisco Pradilla y Ortiz, "La rendición de Granada" (The Capitulation of Granada), after 1882, paper and ivory, 38 x 73 cm, Palacio Real de Aranjuéz. © Patrimonio Nacional de España.

4 Caricature from the magazine *L'Esquella de la Torratxa* of 28 August 1936 with the caption, "Moors and Christians: the savages have finally united." Especially at the beginning of the Civil War, republican caricatures and texts frequently mocked the participation of Moroccan soldiers in the insurgent army. Reproduced in Eloy Martín Corrales, *La imagen del magrebí en España: una perspectiva histórica siglos XVI-XX* (Barcelona, 2002), p. 155.

5 *Left:* The excavated mihrab (Muslim prayer niche) in the Igreja Matriz de Mértola in 1953. Here the altar is placed in front of the mihrab: after four hundred years on the northeast side of the church, the altar was returned to the place it had already occupied at one point after the conversion of the mosque into a church. © Instituto da Habitação e da Reabilitação Urbana, Portugal. SIPA FOTO 0170511.

6 *Right:* Guinean Muslims in front of the Torre de Belém in Lisbon. In the 1960s the Portuguese government facilitated both the pilgrimage of the colonial Muslim population to Mecca and their visits to Portugal. Such measures were intended to strengthen ties to Portugal and weaken the drive for autonomy. Reproduced in Rogério Seabra Cardoso, "Islamitas Portugueses: linhas de força de um passado; realidades de um presente; bases de um futuro," in *Panorama: Revista portuguesa de arte e turismo*, series IV, nrs. 33/34 (March/June 1970), pp. 49–62, p. 59. © Hemeroteca Municipal de Lisboa.

7 *Top:* Franco at the victory celebration in Madrid in May 1939 following the end of the Civil War. The *guardia mora* is visible in the foreground: these Moorish bodyguards became a standard part of Franco's military entourage in the years after this conflict. Title page of the newspaper *La Vanguardia Española* (Barcelona) from 21 May 1939. © Arxiu Històric de la Ciutat de Barcelona. Reproduced courtesy of La Vanguardia Ediciones, Barcelona.

8 The celebration of the 800th anniversary of the capture of Lisbon from the Moors: Honor guard in front of the statue of Afonso Henriques by the Castle of São Jorge in Lisbon, 1947. The celebrations were characterized by hero worship with no opponent, for, in most cases, Afonso's victory was glorified with no mention of the Moors. © Arquivo Municipal de Lisboa, Photograph: Claudino Madeira, PT/AMLSB/FDM/001388.

LA VANGUARDIA
ESPAÑOLA
NOTAS GRÁFICAS   Domingo, 21 de mayo de 1939 · Año de la Victoria   CUATRO PÁGINAS

LA HISTORICA FIESTA DE LA VICTORIA EN MADRID

9 In addition to the surrender of Granada and the Battle of Covadonga, the battle of Las Navas de Tolosa was a favored subject of historical paintings intended to portray mythic defeats of Islam. This painting uses the contrast of black and white to stress the differences between Moors and Christians, emphasizing the Moors' "blackness." Marceliano Santa Maria, "El triunfo de la Santa Cruz en la batalla de Las Navas de Tolosa" (The Triumph of the Holy Cross in the Battle of Las Navas de Tolosa), 1892, oil on canvas, 450 x 600 cm, Museo Marceliano Santa María, Burgos. © akg-images/Album/Oronoz.

10 The celebratory banners from Alcoy changed over the years to reflect evolving attitudes: the banner from 1907 features oriental stereotypes and emphasizes the exotic character of the festival; the republican banner from 1932 refrains from visual depictions and does not mention religious affiliations; the banner for the festival in 1940, the first one following the disruption of the Civil War, portrays a menacing *moro*, perhaps in response to the participation of Moroccan soldiers in the conflict; since the 1960s there has been an increasing tendency to present the adversaries as equals. © Asociación de San Jorge de Alcoy (Museu Alcoià de la Festa). Reproduced courtesy of the Museu Alcoià de la Festa and the municipality of Alcoy.

11 *Top:* The celebration of the 800th anniversary of the capture of Lisbon from the Moors: Arabs with drums in Rossio Square during a historical procession in Lisbon on 6 July 1947. Together with Africans, Indians, and other ethnic groups, the Arabs in the procession were intended to demonstrate the extent of the Portuguese empire and to lend an exotic flair to the proceedings; they were not ascribed any especial significance. © Arquivo Municipal de Lisboa, Photograph: Judah Benoliel, PT/AMLSB/JBN/003723.

12 The *capitán moro* (Moorish captain) of the *filà* "Marrakesh," 1924. The captains were – and are even today – among the most important and extravagantly costumed characters of the festival. Only the wealthiest citizens could shoulder the financial burden associated with these roles. © Asociación de San Jorge de Alcoy (Museu Alcoià de la Festa). Reproduced courtesy of the Museu Alcoià de la Festa and the municipality of Alcoy.

13 *This page:* "Ferrabrás," mid-twentieth century. In 1962, donations from the festival's supporters provided more elaborate and expensive costumes than in the preceding decades. This led to an increasingly exotic portrayal of the *turcos.* Photograph: Leandro Quintas Neves, reproduced in Alberto A. Abreu, *O Auto da Floripes e o imaginário minhoto* (Viana do Castelo, 2001), p. 82.

14 *Opposite top:* Books like this were intended to highlight Spain's architectural riches. Due to the intense interest of foreign travelers, the Alhambra, especially the Court of the Lions, became an icon of Spanish Muslim architecture. Francisco Javier Parcerisa, "Fuente de los Leones (The Fountain of Lions)," in ibid. and Francisco Pi y Margall, *Recuerdos y bellezas de España* (Madrid, 1850). © Patronato de la Alhambra y Generalife / Archivo / Colección de dibujos/D-00108.

15 *Opposite below:* Strangers were not allowed into the chambers of Muslim women, but these "forbidden spaces" inspired European fantasies and were a popular subject for Orientalist painters. The harem symbolized sensuousness, passion, and feminine submission. Marià Fortuny, "La odalisca" (The Odalisque), 1861, oil on cardboard, 56.9 x 81 cm, Museu Nacional d'Art de Catalunya, Barcelona. © 2014 Photo SCALA, Florence.

16 *Top:* The title page of this diocesan bulletin depicts the victorious commander Pelayo treading upon the corpse of a Moor. The drawing alludes iconographically to portrayals of the Virgin Mary in which she treads upon a serpent, a symbol of evil. To the left, the background includes the grotto fabled to have been where the battle occurred and accordingly venerated as the "Holy Cave." To the right is the basilica, completed in 1901, which was intended to bring new prominence to the long-forgotten pilgrimage site. Nicolás Soria, *Covadonga: Boletín de la Junta Diocesana para la Coronación Canónica de la Santísima Virgen*, 1917, title page. In *Covadonga – iconografía de una devoción* (Oviedo, 2001), p. 443.

17 The *turcos* "Balaão," "Ferrabrás," "Floripes," and "Brutamontes" in 1948. With their turbans and embroidered garments, the actors here appeared more exotic than their counterparts in 1930. Photograph: Leandro Quintas Neves, reproduced in Alberto A. Abreu, *O Auto da Floripes e o imaginário minhoto* (Viana do Castelo, 2001), p. 41.

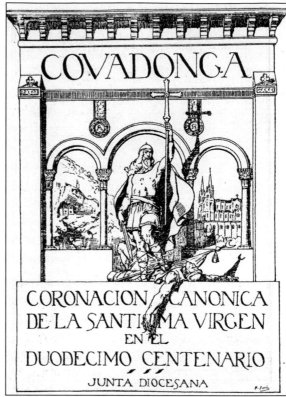

18 *Below:* Battle between *cristãos* and *turcos*, 1930-1931. The actors used hats and capes to lend an antiquated flair to their own rustic clothing. Some of these had been used for decades because the participants had little means to acquire new ones. Photograph: Alexandre Gigante, reproduced in Alberto A. Abreu, *O Auto da Floripes e o imaginário minhoto* (Viana do Castelo, 2001), p. 63.

Until 1900 history was taught only in secondary schools, at which point it was introduced at all levels of instruction intended to prepare pupils for university.[11] Some of the books for the secondary level were used for a remarkably long time: The accounts of Spanish history by Alejandro Gomez Ranera were published repeatedly for fifty-nine years, those by Manuel Ibo Alfaro for thirty-eight.[12] Both authors had begun their careers as teachers at preparatory school and then specialized as textbook authors[13] Their books survived several phases of the institutional development outlined above. Political turning points did not always have an immediate effect on instruction, which suggests that, in the nineteenth century, instruction in schools was not yet a medium for nationalization that transcended social class. In addition, this first generation of school books offered little to appeal to or influence young readers: books by the prominent textbook authors Joaquim Rubió y Ors and Eduardo Orodea y Ibarra[14] contained few if any graphics and were dominated by tedious, detailed textual accounts heavy on names and dates. Liberal republican authors like Orodea y Ibarra tended to ascribe certain qualities to the Arabs which, as already seen in Modesto Lafuente's account, were associated with negative assessments.[15] Taken as a whole, nineteenth-century textbooks reinforced the status quo and did little to strengthen national identity, lacking, as they were, both in distribution and in the appeal of their message.[16]

As the political landscape became progressively more fractured around the turn of the century, the competing groups became increasingly aware of the potential of educational institutions for propagating their social vision. The tendencies previously evident in academic scholarship were thus transferred into the textbooks. Whereas Catholic schools tended to closely link "Spanish" and "sacred" history, for example in the mythical account of Spain's founding by Noah's descendants Tubal und Tarshish,[17] they faced increasing competition from secular, liberal narratives. In addition to producing scholarship aimed at historians, traditionalist Catholic authors like Merry y Colón and liberals like Rafael Altamira wrote texts for schools and seminaries.[18] While the traditional interpretations stressing the Catholic essence of Spain were most influential in the texts used in religious schools, liberal accounts were more prevalent in public schools.

The evocative work of a prominent representative of the latter school, Rafael Ballester y Castell (1872–1931), drew an exceptionally wide audience. Ballester vacillated in his judgment of the Arabs just as Lafuente had a half a century earlier: "Ferocious, but generous and hospitable, open to poetry and rhetoric, lovers of freedom—their character is a unique mixture of barbarism and nobility."[19] There is a discernable influence of Lafuente's ambivalent position,[20] which was an important reference for the textbook authors, as was the more negative position of Padre

Mariana.[21] Other scholars shared this ambivalent position in regard to the Arabs.[22] Ballester's explicit praise of the caliphate's economic and cultural success—"one of the wealthiest and most populous countries of Europe"[23]—became especially significant during the end phase of the Restoration, considering Spain's marginalization within Europe. At the same time, just as in the historiography, the position of politically liberal authors or those more open to new pedagogical methods was not automatically more positive towards Muslims or Moors. Pedro Aguado Bleye (1884–1954), an influential textbook author from Bilbao, viewed the explusion of the *moriscos* in 1609 as a just punishment, unlike Altamira or Ballester, who viewed this event as an expression of the religious fanaticism of the age. In this respect Aguado Bleye's interpretation resembles that of the Catholic traditionalists.[24]

There are thus several similarities between the traditional Catholic and liberal progressive interpretations despite their differing perceptions of the Muslim past: the traditional focus on Castile and the Castilian tongue; the conviction that there is *one* collective Spanish spirit; and the Catholic dimension of its religious character.[25] The republic was too short-lived to supplant the religious images which had dominated textbooks with secular ones, so the former remained a significant constant into the age of Francoism.

Under Franco the situation changed quickly in the 1940s: both the differences in content between books and the limited distribution of individual titles were eliminated. In an attempt to eradicate preceding liberal interpretations of history, the regime instituted a previously unknown level of control over personnel and the materials used in instruction, including history texts: after 1939 disfavored teachers were gradually replaced with instructors who endorsed Franco's ideologies. This was combined with a strengthening of the Catholic Church as a pillar of the educational system: in addition to being approved by the Ministerio de Educación Nacional, textbooks were reviewed by representatives of the church who granted the status of *nihil obstat*. Older texts which did not meet these criteria disappeared from school libraries.[26]

Historical accounts which strengthened Spain's Catholic identity did not have to be reinvented by authors serving under Franco. Thanks to nineteenth-century Catholic historians, these were already available. The frequent condemnation of the historical Muslim adversary, however, did contradict Franco's claims of benevolence and even friendship towards the Moroccans. During the Civil War this discourse had been limited to the troops stationed in Africa, but after the rebels' victory it became an official element of the colonial policies and was used to reinforce Spanish claims to Morocco.[27] In 1938, during the Civil War, corresponding changes in the historical narrative were made in respect to Islam in two new textbooks produced for primary schools. The author of the second book was one of the most important ideologues in Franco's Spain, José María Pemán (1898–1981), whose text was structured around a teleological concept of history. The past was presented as a kind of crescendo along the lines of Franco's motto: "*España una*"—from prehistory to the Catholic monarchs; "*España grande*" —from the fall of Granada to the reign of Charles II, the last Habsburg ruler; "*España libre*" —from the first Bourbon ruler Philip V to Alfons XIII; and, finally, ending in the chapter "*Arriba España*" — which ended with the description of Franco's coup. All the significant events of Spanish history were presented as advances along the way to Francoism. The same was true for the Middle Ages: Pemán dwelled on the Cid's mercenary military service under the Muslims, which the conservative Catholic authors had tended to ignore in their portrayal of a Christian hero. Pemán not only interpreted the Cid as a link between Christians and Muslims, but as a role model for Franco. Beyond the seemingly friendly attitude towards the Moors, however, the hierarchical, paternalist character of the discourse of "brotherhood" reveals a certain cynicism:

> The Cid was the first leader of the *regulares* [i.e., of the Moroccan soldiers]. In his experience with the Moors, his knowledge of their language, and his respect for their customs, he resembles Franco or Varela,[28] who have become sort of contemporary saints for the Moors, whom they love and in whose service they happily perish.[29]

The Instituto de España sought to spread this discourse on brotherhood[30] into schools and to incorporate it into universal textbooks, but these attempts failed due to the resistance of the Catholic Church and the publishers of such books.[31] Though the book was revived by other companies later, it did not come to dominate the textbook market under Franco as the Instituto de España had hoped.

History classes became an established part of the primary school curriculum and played an important role in the early phase of the dictatorship by helping to assert a monolithic concept of history. The books by Agustín Serrano de Haro (1898–1982) became true classics: the inspector for primary school education in Jaén influenced an entire generation of pupils with the numerous texts he produced for history and religion classes in primary schools. Two of his titles, *Yo soy español* (I am a Spaniard) and *España es así* (This is Spain), were issued in around twenty-five editions between the 1940s and 1960s. They combined Islamophobia and anti-Semitism—for example, in the claim that a Jewish-Muslim conspiracy was responsible for the events of 711[32]—with praise of the Muslims' cultural achievements, which were possible "thanks to our environment, our sun, and our soil."[33] This simplified account for children drew together nearly all currents of the historiography up to this point. Serrano de Haro wove the degradation of the Islamic religion and the acquisition of Muslim civilization tightly together. Anti-Muslim judgments were paired with appreciation of their cultural accomplishments, at times from one sentence to the next:

> The Moors liked neither our Lord Jesus Christ nor the Virgin. The Moors believed in a man named Muhammad. Muhammad said: "Kill your enemies, wherever you find them." The Moors' churches are called mosques. The grandest mosque that the Moors built is the one in Córdoba, which has a thousand pillars. The palaces of the Moorish kings had fountains, gardens, and numerous beautiful pillars with many colorful decorations. The most beautiful palace built by the Moors is the Alhambra in Granada. The Moors had many wives. The place where the wives lived was called a "harem." Many Moors liked to bathe. And they played the guitar and sang songs just like in the villages of Andalusia. The Moorish children went to schools that were in the mosques and wrote with reed pens on wooden slates. And they had to memorize several very, very, very long books.[34]

The last sentence shows that Serrano de Haro attempted to use these opportunities to influence the children reading the texts and to convince them of their good fortune of being Christians. This pedagogical goal became even clearer in the suggestive questions for class discussions, which presented Islam as a less attractive religion: "Which families are happier, those of the Moors or of the Christians? Would you feel comfortable at home if there were many women telling you what to do?"[35] The descriptions of the *moros* in Serrano de Haro's accounts, however, were limited to the past. Contemporary North African *moros* or even the discourse of brotherhood were not mentioned. Instead Serrano de Haro adopted elements of the topos of "Spanish Islam": he credited the cultural achievements which could not be overlooked in his homeland, Andalusia, to the "Spanish Muslims." The illustrations more frequently featured Christian heroes and portrayed them more accurately: Muhammad and Abd-ar-Rahman III were depicted with flowing robes in nearly two-dimensional sketches while the scenes showing Saint James, Pelayo, or the Christian kings seemed more realistic due to the details of their armor and helmets.

Similar prejudices are evident in other texts like *El Libro de España* (The Book of Spain), which reads more like a story book than a history text and was published over and over again until the late 1950s.[36] In the style of a novella, it tells the story of two brothers who travel with their uncle through Spain: the text and abundant illustrations are meant to introduce young readers to the beauty and historical significance of their country. While the coat of arms of Francoist Spain on the title page clearly declares the book's loyalties, value judgments subtly pervade even the most innocent-seeming dialogue: It is no coincidence that the older, more reasonable of the brothers, Antonio, describes the cathedral in Toledo—seat of the primate of Spain and thus symbol of Spanish Catholicism—as the most beautiful structure in Spain, while the younger, more playful Gonzalo praises the mosque in Córdoba:

> [Gonzalo said:] "I was completely fascinated by this pavilion, which looks like a fine silk tapestry. It was a delight to see this filigree, these arches, these patterns and colors. . . . This mosque is one of my nicest memories." "You said that well," answered Antonio, "but Toledo has more depth." "Toledo," interjected Don Gabriel, "also shows much Moorish influence, even if only in its narrow, windy alleyways and the beautiful chapel of Cristo de la Luz. However, the grand historical artworks of Toledo are Christian." "Even if I contradict Gonzalo," insisted Antonio, "the cathedral in Toledo satisfies me more deeply than the mosque in Córdoba. . . . The magnificence of the nave, the towers, the portals, the rose windows fascinated me, [as did] the richness of the paintings and sculptures. . . . And then these countless chapels with their screens, paintings, and statues, from which we can follow the entire history of Spanish art in two of our grandest centuries, the fifteenth and sixteenth."[37]

This hierarchization is not only evident in the ordering of the structures according to the age of the children and in the emphasis on Spain's "grandest centuries," which correspond to the expansion of power within the colonies and the Catholic Church; it continues in the association of certain attributes to each structure. In their debates over a national architectural style, nineteenth-century scholars had already assigned certain characteristics to the respective religions: depth, sobriety, and grandeur on the one hand, decorativeness, sensuality, and delicacy on the other.[38] The fact that these judgments reached a whole new audience a century later via a children's book is testimony to the longevity of these underlying expectations.

The textbook authors who worked under Franco did not have to invent new historical concepts; they simply put the pieces of an existing puzzle together differently. While Islam as a religion was clearly seen to rank below Catholicism, the Islamic cultural heritage was interpreted through a Spanish lens to become another glorious chapter of the nation's history. The seemingly benevolent, but in fact paternalistic discourse towards the Moors, present in the colonial context until Morocco's independence in 1956, was absent from the school books used during Franco's reign.[39] Thus the evolution of the colonial conception of

Islam during and after the Civil War remained limited to diplomacy and the military.

The reasons for this have to do with the relationship of the church, state, and colonies. First of all, the Catholic Church and the Falange party shared to some extent their understanding of history and educational goals. At the same time, conservative Catholics and the Falangists were rivals for control of the educational system.[40] The Catholic Church might have withdrawn its support for the regime if classroom instruction had been seen as overly sympathetic to the Falangists' interpretation of history. On the other hand, the discourse of fraternity was a tactical method of reinforcing power rather than a foreshadowing of the ecumenical discourse on tolerance of the Second Vatican Council. The interest in the Moroccan Muslims was politically motivated and did not reflect any wider shift in collective attitudes. Following the coexistence of traditional and liberal concepts of Islam in the early twentieth century, Franco's Spain presented itself as a clearly Catholic nation decorated with the cultural achievements of a few Muslim Spaniards. This identity changed only slowly following the demise of that regime.[41]

Commemorations during the Restoration (1912–1918)

Commemorative celebrations were especially important in the last years of the Restoration because they offered an opportunity for strengthening identities in this period of extraordinary political and social division. The interpretations of El Greco,[42] Don Quixote,[43] and the Battles of Covadonga[44] and Las Navas de Tolosa[45] on the occasions of their respective anniversaries intensified the discussion over the *ser de España* which had played a central role in the historiography. Unlike those academic debates, however, the accounts produced for anniversary celebrations were not confined to books or scholarly circles. They determined the art and nature of such festivities, which were often planned years in advance and lasted for several days.

The anniversary of two important medieval battles fell in the end phase of the Restoration: 1912 marked seven hundred years since the Battle of Las Navas de Tolosa, in which an alliance of the kingdoms of Castile, Aragon, Navarre, and Portugal had defeated the Almohads and, due to the strategic importance of this place, permanently barred the route into the center of the peninsula. Six years later, Spain celebrated the thirteen hundredth anniversary of the mythical Battle of Covadonga,[46] in which the nobleman Pelayo defeated the Muslim troops as they were pressing north: it was not a particularly consequential battle but was portrayed in the commemorative events as the beginning of a supposed *reconquista*.

In addition to these particular anniversaries, there were annual *ofrendas* (donations) of the king to Saint James (Santiago), a tradition started by Philip IV in 1643. In the myth which had surrounded the Apostle James since the Middle Ages, religious conviction, legends, proven medieval forgeries, and political motives were all intertwined.[47] There were three common iconographical depictions of the saint: as apostle, pilgrim, and militant *matamoros* (Moor slayer).[48] Following the reign of Ferdinand of Aragon and Isabella of Castile, the latter became an icon in the struggle against Islam. It did not achieve its widest dissemination during the actual conflict with Muslim rulers in the High Middle Ages, but rather in an era during which the *moros* posed no real threat. The myth of the *matamoros* was well suited to the inquisitorial atmosphere and was transformed in the American colonies to live on in the figure of the *mataindios* (Indian slayer).[49] As a subject of painting it was only of marginal interest in the eighteenth and nineteenth centuries. As a symbol of religious unity, the Visigoth king Reccared supplanted Saint James, and, as a Christian soldier, Pelayo did the same.[50] However, Saint James the Moor Slayer incorporated the mythological concept of a Catholic Spain at war with enemies of the faith, a concept which was certainly still active. Instead of fading into obscurity, the contents of the myth were reincarnated in regionally specific images. This became evident in the celebrations surrounding the anniversaries of Las Navas de Tolosa and Covadonga.

Las Navas de Tolosa's anniversary was celebrated in the Andalusian town of La Carolina near the site of the battle and in the provincial seat of Jaén. A significantly more influential celebration, however, was staged in Pamplona, the capital of Navarre. Here the battle appeared not—as it did in Jaén—as a fixed, historical event, but rather as a sort of foundational moment in the history of Navarre, a moment in which the hero of the battle, King Sancho VII, played a central role. His legendary trophies of victory had become symbols of the region: the king supposedly laid claim to the golden chains which had surrounded the tent of the Almohad ruler Muhammad al-Nasir and incorporated these into his coat of arms. Over the centuries, this royal coat of arms came to symbolize Navarre. In 1910, two years before the anniversary of the battle, the provincial government of Navarre officially adopted a similar coat of arms featuring golden chains and a crown against a red background. Modern scholarship has shown that this symbolism was mistaken and that the incorporation of the chains into the royal coat of arms does not correspond with the battle.[51] Nevertheless, 1912 was seen as an occasion to celebrate the heroic king as a foundational character of the region, the new coat of arms as a symbol of their collective identity, and the historical significance of the erstwhile kingdom.

Covadonga symbolized the royal and religious Asturias. A small, unassuming local sanctuary—possibly dating from the eighth century—was supposedly erected by Alfons I out of gratitude for Pelayo's victory, which, according to legend, was the result of the Virgin Mary's intervention.[52] Starting in 1872, Benito Sanz y Forés, the bishop of Oviedo, rediscovered this location and recognized its potential to revitalize the Christian tradition. He subsequently began developing this geographically removed sanctuary, entirely forgotten beyond the region, into a symbol for the "cradle of the *reconquista*."[53] Sanz y Forés's successors continued this process, which culminated in the anniversary celebrations, by improving the streets, improving infrastructure for pilgrims, and constructing a new basilica.

Both battles were known long before the jubilees as central events within the *reconquista* myth, within both the historiography and the genre of triumphant historical painting. After 1879 a painting of the Battle of Las Navas—painted by Francisco de Paula von Halen in 1864— hung in the Spanish Senate.[54] In this scene depicting a chaotic battle, the Christian knights, in their shining armor and white robes, overshadow the Moors, in their distinctive colorful turbans and clothing. An even stronger dualist tendency is evident in an image depicting the "Triumph of the Holy Cross in the Battle of Las Navas de Tolosa" (Plate 9), which was completed by Marceliano Santa María in 1892 and displayed at the Chicago World's Fair in 1893. It shows the Castilian knight Alvar Núñez de Lara as he broke through the Moorish ranks.[55] The Moors are portrayed as a dark, amorphous mass of scantily clad black Africans, who cower under the hooves of a white horse carrying a knight dressed in white who brandishes a banner with a cross symbolizing the order of Saint James. The metaphorical use of color and body language outlines a clear dualism which assumes both a cultural and religious hierarchy. Elements typical in the depiction of Covadonga were Pelayo with a cross raised against the enemy, as well as the staggering, helpless Moors, who fell from the rocky crags or were swept away by the river.[56] The physical weakness was meant to symbolize the weakness of their religion.

The images created for the anniversary of the battle showed different visions of Islam as either a political or religious opponent, though these certainly cannot be separated from each other and typically went hand in hand. In Jaén, the senator José del Prado Palácio, a member of the Partido Liberal-Conservador, commissioned the sculptor Jacinto Higueras to create a monument to the two significant battles in the province: Las Navas de Tolosa against the Moors in 1212 and Bailén against the French in 1808. Elements of antiquity dominated Higueras's design: the goddess of victory stands atop a high stone pillar, flanked at the base by allegorical depictions of the warriors in both battles. The inscription by the poet Bernardo López on the Dos de Mayo (1808) placed the aspect of national defense and the campaign for independence in the foreground.[57] The monument in La Carolina—which is no longer extant—combined such ancient elements with religious symbolism. The unadorned monolith was crowned by the legendary iron chains of the Muslim ruler. A bronze plaque quoted the legend of the Battle of the Milvian Bridge, "*In hoc signo vinces*," a reference to the Christian character of the victory.[58] In Covadonga, a frequent pilgrimage destination, the religious dimension was disproportionally significant: Pelayo, the cross, and the Virgin Mary were central elements of the iconography there. The Muslim adversaries were continually shown in an inferior state of being unable to defend themselves, for example, on the cover of the diocesan bulletin in 1917. That depiction of Pelayo treading upon a Moor recalls both the iconographical tradition of Saint James the Moor Slayer as well as portrayals of the Virgin Mary treading upon a serpent meant to represent the devil (Plate 16).[59]

In addition to the iconographical depictions, which in principle could have reached a wider audience, concepts of Islam were disseminated for a more limited audience in speeches, sermons, and lectures. The clergy strove to motivate their supporters and call them to solidarity. During a *semana social* (social week[60]) parallel to the anniversary of the battle of Las Navas, the bishop of Jaca, Antolín López Peláez (1866–1918), compared the historical conflict with Islam to the contemporary struggle against socialism and called upon fellow believers to take up the fight against the "new Moors": "Just like the socialist leaders, Muhammad gained followers by preaching a doctrine which paid homage to sensuality, which let passions run full course, and which aroused feelings of hate and revenge in all those tormented and discontent."[61] His speech aimed to create feelings of solidarity within his own camp. The founder of the Acción Católica[62] and director of the Real Academia Española, Alejándro Pidal y Mon, delivered a celebratory lecture to local elites in the theater in Burgos, a city which had been the capital of ancient Castile and the final resting place of the Cid, and which Pidal y Mon thus considered "the heart of the Spanish nation and the soul of its glorious history."[63] He credited the "holy triumph of the cross" over Islam to divine historical intervention.[64] The recurring theme in these speeches of Spain's having been divinely favored is also reflected in other genres— prayers, hymns, and poems honoring the Virgin of Covadonga—all of which celebrated the "liberation of Castile [*sic*] from the scimitar" and the "Pelayo's awakening of Spain."[65] The history of the battle and the sanctuary had been disseminated in travel guides and popular history books since the construction of the new basilica in Covadonga in the late nineteenth century and the improvements to the infrastructure to accomodate pilgrims and tourists. The location of the grotto on the river Deva, in which, according to legend, the Muslim troops drowned, made Covadonga the "Red Sea" and "New Jordan" of Spain.[66] In these guide books and works of popular history, especially, the Muslim foe was typically described in caricatured terms and secondary to Pelayo's glorification.

The planning of the actual anniversary celebration in Covadonga stirred up intense debates about the content of the festivities, which in the end was a question about the local identity being feted. The clergy and traditional Catholics advocated an overtly religious celebration to emphasize parallels between the defensive struggles against the "old" and "new" Moors; in 1917 they founded their own magazine to report on the preparations and support this cause, for example, by calling for donations to provide a crown for a statue of the Virgin Mary in Covadonga.[67] The liberal elite of Asturias, on the other hand, viewed the anniversary as an opportunity to celebrate their national freedom and unity. The former rector of the University of Oviedo, Fermín Canella y Secades (1849–1924), made the case before the Spanish Senate in 1916 for festivities which might become "a ceasefire for our daily political strife, uniting all Spaniards in love and peace," and thus serve as the starting point for a "national renewal."[68] Such liberal agendas refrained from a detailed description of Islam, focused as they were instead on national unity. By more or less ignoring the Islamic enemies, they did nothing to reinvent a liberal concept of Islam, unlike the corresponding historiography, in which it was at least acknowledged as an aspect of Iberian civilization.

The efforts of the liberals to provide alternative interpretations were thwarted by the resistance of the traditionalists. The commemorative stagings followed the classic pattern, unifying throne, altar, and military: the celebrations surrounding the Battle of Las Navas de Tolosa began in Roncesvalles, near the mountain pass where, according to legend, the rearguard of Charlemagne's army under Roland's command had been defeated by the Basques as they returned from a campaign against the Moors. As part of the celebrations, the mortal remains of King Sancho VII and his wife were moved to a new sepulcher within the royal collegiate church. On the anniversary of the battle, 16 July 1912, King Alfons XIII participated in a Te Deum in the cathedral which was followed by a procession of the provincial communities and church congregations bearing their banners and crucifixes. The participants in the procession met up with the military for an outdoor mass, and the day ended with a festive military ceremony.[69] These events were complimented by other elements meant to illustrate the contemporary state of the province, for example, an agricultural exhibition or a week-long air show. The official interpretations of the battle did not see beyond the conventional topoi of "two irreconcilable civilizations" and the victory against Islam which sealed "Europe's fate."[70] Similar elements were included in the celebration in Covadonga six years later: the monarchs, the archbishop of Toledo as primate of Spain, and numerous representatives of the nobility, military, and the church all participated in the ceremonial crowning of the Virgin meant to celebrate her divine protection against the Islamic enemy.[71] The population of Asturias and Navarre were thus exposed primarily to these religious images of the Muslim adversary: a religious and political foe which was hopelessly inferior to Spanish Christianity.

The predominance of conservative interpretations at the anniversary celebrations of Las Navas de Tolosa and Covadonga were not isolated cases but rather publicly effective examples of the dominance of conservative over liberal forces at the beginning of the twentieth century. Their success was so significant that even within the context of these commemorative celebrations, the conservative interpretations co-opted these protagonists once seen as liberal heroes.[72] The traditionalists' strength after 1900 was partly because the reinstatement of ecclesiastical privileges during the Restoration remained unchallenged after 1898 and the young King Alfons XIII was favorably disposed towards the church.[73] Furthermore, the traditionalists benefited from the weaknesses of their competitors. Identifying with the national concept was problematic at a time when the nation was mired in such difficulties. The ongoing war in Morocco, which also intensified the concept of the brutal *moros*, made the concept of the "new *moros*" more appealing. Conservatives could point to a clear, active antagonist. Liberal nationalists—concerned as they were with the unity of Spain and the integration of various interests—could not. In an age of political unrest, in which quickly changing governments were confronted with growing discontent within the military and with work stoppages organized by unions in the most important centers of industry, an ideological return to the "tried-and-true" was especially attractive. Both moderate liberals and advocates of a humanist, tolerant Catholicism were practically helpless against this radicalization.

As a result, the more nuanced understandings of Islam and of the Muslim past as found in the contemporary historiography were not incorporated into the reenactments of historical events planned for these festive anniversaries. The insistence within traditionalist circles on portraying Islam as the archenemy of Spain and the tendency to disregard liberal interpretations of this history resulted in the continuation and intensification of traditional, Islamophobic stereotypes.

ISLAM AS A SUPPORTING ACTOR: HEROES WITHOUT ENEMIES IN PORTUGAL

History textbooks from the Monarchy to the Estado Novo

In Portugal, Jaime Moniz (1837–1917), a lawyer, politician, and pedagogue, implemented reforms in 1895 that mark the beginning of modern secondary-school instruction. These improvements in teacher selection and education, along with a revision of the curriculum, were a response to Portuguese intellectuals' intense criticism of the school system.[74] Unlike earlier reforms, they emphasized intellectual and ethnic goals within which history lessons were to foster the "development of intelligence and memory."[75] Like their Spanish neighbors, the citizens of monarchical Portugal were less well educated than their Western European counterparts: in 1900 around seventy-five percent of the Portuguese were illiterate, and only one in five school-aged children attended primary school.[76] While the literacy rate was especially low in more rural areas like Beja, Portalegre, Castelo Branco and on Madeira, it was distinctly higher in Lisbon and Porto.[77] Schoolbooks were thus read primarily by a small class of urban elites.

The changes to the school system in the wake of Moniz's reforms had the consistent goal of fostering a national identity, although it often remained unclear exactly what this should mean.[78] The abrupt political transitions—monarchy, republic, military dictatorship, and Estado Novo—did not necessarily correspond to breaks in the instructional materials. This is especially evident in the *Compendio de Historia de Portugal* by Arsénio Augusto Torres de Mascarenhas (1847–?), who, like most of the textbook authors in Portugal in the early twentieth century, held a degree in legal studies from the University of Coimbra.[79] The book he wrote became one of the longest-lived in the history of Portuguese school books. The first edition was used during the monarchy[80] and an edition which had been "revised and expanded in accordance with the principles of the pedagogical orientation of the Estado Novo" saw several printings up to 1944.[81] The amendments to the latter edition contained no significant changes to the section on the Middle Ages. Within the small segment of society with access to advanced schooling, Mascarenhas was one of the most widely read textbook authors of the early twentieth century.

Mascarenhas differentiated between Arabian religion and culture: the religion itself, "with all the inherent mistakes of the Semitic race, [with] the polygamy permitted by the religion, [with] the laws and traditions and the fixed fatalism of the Quran, had exercised little significant moral influence on the peninsula."[82] He thus perpetuated the stereotypical Catholic judgments of Islam as a religion. Nevertheless he credited the Arabs with having been highly civilized and having accordingly enriched the Iberian Peninsula:

> However, even if the Goths surpassed the Muslims in terms of moral doctrines—the daughters of a more flawless religion, in political institutions, and in chivalrous honor—the Arabs, who were intellectually superior until the end of the twelfth century, brought advantages in the culture of letters, craftsmanship, luxury, and also in their financial system. . . . This influenced Christians, as well, in turn. Among these

the Saracen language became overwhelmingly dominant; all were taken with Arab science and poetry; [and] clothing, manners, and customs were all Saracen. In the end the frequent intermarriages between followers of the two races would have paved the way to a complete mingling of the two, if the differences of faith had not been an obstacle.[83]

The influence of Catholicism was palpable in Mascarenhas's writing, evidence of the church's ongoing role as a source of mortality and religion in nineteenth-century textbooks.[84] Nevertheless Portugal's historical heroes did have their critics: António Cândido de Figueiredo (1846–1925), a school inspector and author of numerous textbooks, portrayed the campaign of the first Portuguese king, Afonso Henriques, against the Moors as a bloodbath rather than a heroic struggle. Figueiredo, who had originally intended to become a priest,[85] contradicted the dominant Catholic perspective of the age by criticizing not only the monarch but also the behavior of the Crusaders:

> Afonso Henriques, whom the Moors called the *"tyrant from Coimbra,"* and who more than once displayed extraordinary valor and generous emotions, conquered Santarém in a traitorous manner and caused such carnage within the population as does no honor to the memory of our first king. The capturing of Lisbon was no less brutal, though there the violent excesses were perpetrated mostly by those foreigners who helped the Portuguese in this conquest. These foreigners were the so-called *Crusaders*, who had set out for the Holy Land, where they intended to wrest Christ's grave from the hands of the infidels, and, on the way through our ports, quenched their thirst for gold and vice here in Portuguese territory and against the Moors of Hispania.[86] [Emphases in original.]

Figueiredo is no exception. Altogether, Afonso Henriques and other medieval heroes were portrayed ambivalently. In the latter nineteenth century, authors appraised historical epochs as least in part based on social progress, and in this respect the Middle Ages lagged.[87] This set a distinct contrast to the later wholehearted glorification of these same Portuguese heroes during the Estado Novo.

The political break of the Republic had repercussions for the educational system. Church and state were officially separated by law on 20 April 1911: Roman Catholicism was no longer an official state religion, and freedom of conscience was recognized for all.[88] The republicans blamed the Jesuits for having fostered Portuguese decadence and banished them from Portugal for the third time (after 1759 and 1854). Their schools were disbanded. The republican reformers strove to establish secular schools and counter the widespread illiteracy, but realizing these important goals was difficult in face of the political instability.[89]

The shift from monarchy to republic, however, did little to change the contents of the books used in Portuguese schools. The texts by Mascarenhas and Figueiredo were reprinted during the era of the republic, and both authors produced new texts in accordance with the republican reforms.[90] Here, too, the concepts of Islam varied. An examination of three republican books intended for primary instruction covers a broad spectrum of descriptions and appraisals: Sezinado Chagas Franco (?–1944), a trained soldier, teacher, and journalist, describes Islam as a "religion of brutality and war": "Muslims devoutly believe that they will win [a place in] paradise by cutting off the heads of Christians. It is enough for them to show these to Allah after their death."[91] António de Matos Faria Artur (1881–1971), a close associate of the nationalist Catholic organization Cruzada Nacional D. Nuno Álvarez Pereira,[92] held a contrary view:

> Do not think, my children, that these peoples were wild. Much to the contrary, they were highly cultivated. So much so that we have them to thank for the introduction of many of our foodstuffs like rice, saffron, oranges, peaches, melons . . . ; they are also credited with the invention or at least the propagation of the numeric system, and, as they were exceptional architects, the architectural structures, which they built remain even today the object of much admiration.[93]

A book approved by the provisional government in the first months of the Republic, on the other hand, contrasted the behavior of the Muslims with that of the Christians:

> While the Arab invasion improved conditions for the slaves under the Visigoths, the Christian reconquest was most terrible for those who did not share their religious faith: Jews or Moors who did not fall victim to the brutal attack were thrown into the harshest slavery; they were treated once again as *things* (and not as humans) with which one could do anything one pleased—[they were] given away, sold, maimed, and killed. Alfons VI of Léon and Castile, however, made the situation less painful for them, by allowing them to enter contracts and even marriages with the Christians, and he himself married, in the Moorish fashion, Zaida, the daughter of the emir of Seville. Alfons VI's tolerance set an example which was followed by many; Christian princes after him treated the Moors and Jews whom they seized on the battlefield humanely.[94] [Emphasis in original.]

These three examples illustrate how diverse the images of Islam in the

Republican school books were, mirroring the spectrum present in the general historiography. The positive implications of Arab civilization for medieval Hispania were just as present as the rejection of Islam as a religion or appreciation of its role in insuring religious tolerance—each of these were abbreviated derivations of the most prominent historical master narratives. Among these, religion did not enjoy any special treatment.

Under the authoritarian regime of the Estado Novo, school was seen as an instrument of social control and national instruction. On 7 April 1932, the minister of education, Gustavo Cordeiro Ramos, declared: "Everything which has been done in the eight centuries of Portuguese history to strengthen . . . fundamental factors of social life . . . should be justified and glorified."[95] This included idolization of national heroes and their feats, especially the explorers; the emphasis on Portugal's Christian character; and Salazar's rigorous austerity as a symbol of a down-to-earth, honest working population and their traditions. As a famous poster, *A lição de Salazar* (Salazar's Lesson) suggested, "*Deus, Pátria, Família*" (God, Fatherland, Family) served as the pillars of education.[96] Nevertheless, the changes were more of an ideological adjustment than a systematic restructuring. They were concerned mostly with controlling rather than replacing structures taken over from the Republic.[97] Furthermore, the Estado Novo refrained from reversing many of the secular revisions of the Republic. Private schools which had been formally recognized were permitted to offer religious instruction. Much to the church's dismay, however, it had no influence over the curriculum for public schools, although the clergy's protests led to a constitutional stipulation in 1935 that the public school curriculum be oriented on Christian principles.[98]

The conflict with Islam was regarded in the Estado Novo as significant, but not as the most important national endeavor. The portrayal of the time between Portugal's foundation and the Age of Exploration changed very little between the Republic and the Estado Novo. There was much more dissent regarding the reasons for the crisis and Portugal's decadence.[99] As befitting the Catholic influence, Christian topoi were given more weight under the Estado Novo than in the secular Republic. Tomás de Barros (1892–1948) was the author of the most widely read textbooks of the early Estado Novo, including the *Sumário de História de Portugal*, which had been printed around fifty times by the 1950s. His description of the Miracle of Ourique reinforced the oft repeated legend and used it to interpret the Portuguese coat of arms. The victory against the Moors was thus elevated iconographically as a trophy:

The shield, red and white, has at its center five blue shields, which represent the five Moorish kings defeated by Afonso Henriques. The five white points on each shield stand for Christ's five wounds. The seven gold castles on the red part of the shield symbolize the seven castles that Alfons III captured from the Moors—[namely, those in] Albufeira, Aljezur, Cacela, Castro Marim, Estômbar, Paderne and Sagres.[100]

The Crusade also played an important conceptual role in the history text-books produced under the Estado Novo. The *Compêndio de História de Portugal* by the influential author António Gonçalves Matoso (1895–1975) emphasized the "centuries-long struggle with no ceasefire" between Christianity and Islam and described the capture of Granada as the collapse of the "last bastion of the infidels."[101] Simultaneously the book praised the "Muslim civilization," even though this had been, in Matoso's opinion, "no distinct or original [one]."[102] Matoso was familiar with the scholarship of the first academic Arabist in Portugal, David Lopes,[103] and cited both his definition of the term *mouro* and the appeal to God in the first lines of the Quran.[104] In addition, Matoso credited the Arabs for their architectural influence, which had led to the development of the extravagant Manueline style.[105] Famous structures in this style, the Jerónimos Monastery and the Tower of Belém, had embodied Portugal's grandeur for centuries and belonged to the country's most important architectural icons. Matoso did not view the recognition of this Muslim heritage as an "element of national disintegration," which Gustavo Ramos decreed to be the object of necessary censure.[106]

Despite the tendency of official historical scholarship under the Estado Novo to ascribe little importance to the Islamic influence, there were a few instances of positive appraisal. The greatness of the Portuguese nation was seen to be not only the result of the victory over Islam but also of the selective incorporation of elements of Islamic culture. The colonial discourse of the age claimed a civilizing mission for Portugal towards other peoples. It did not damage the national identity, however, to refer to civilizing influences in the past from groups not generally seen as Portuguese.

The textbooks of the Estado Novo were an important tool for education, but their sphere of influence was rather limited when compared with the general population. Salazar was not interested in solving the problem of illiteracy although it had been widely decried in the Republic. The indoctrination of elites was more important to him than the education of the masses.[107] To cultivate a sense of national identity and convey the corresponding lessons of history to a wider public, Salazar employed primarily visual symbols in festivities, monuments, statues, and other everyday objects.[108] Under Salazar the most important and influential historical accounts were related thus not in the classroom but rather as part of commemorative festivities in the early Estado Novo.

Commemorations in the Estado Novo (1939–1947)

The anniversary of two medieval battles against the Moors fell within a highly sensitive phase for Portugal and Europe as a whole. The eight hundredth anniversary of the Battle of Ourique in 1939 and the Conquest of Lisbon from the Moors in 1947 were prominent examples within a series of similar events in this volatile decade.[109] They responded to the young Estado Novo's need to position itself in a long national success story. These were tumultuous times: civil war had laid waste to neighboring Spain and the largest nations of Europe were in engaged first in a bloody world war and then the subsequent recovery. In this context, a celebration of historical continuity provided the ideologues of the Estado Novo with the perfect opportunity for historical propaganda aiming to reinforce feelings of solidarity with the regime and expand its ideological clout.

The myth of the Battle of Ourique, in which Afonso Henriques defeated the Moors and took an important step towards the independence of the county from León, has been considered Portugal's foundational moment since the fifteenth century. It had little effect for the stylization of the event that Alexandre Herculano and other historians after him had deconstructed the religious background of the myth and portrayed the battle itself as a skirmish.[110] In light of the radically changing political landscape in Europe and the rest of the world in the 1930s, Salazar saw Ourique as evidence of the miracle of Portuguese independence. He referred symbolically to this in a speech given on 14 August 1936 at Batalha, the monastery built in memory of the victory against Spain at Aljubarrota: "On the western edge of the peninsula, wedged between powerful neighbors and the vast ocean, we are condemned to live the drama of our lives in every moment, but under the benevolent face of Providence we look back upon eight centuries of work, suffering, battles, and freedom, and if this always represents the same danger, it is also always the same miracle."[111]

By making divine providence responsible for the course of Portuguese history, Salazar aimed to legitimize the Estado Novo. As a result, he was closely involved in the preparations for the anniversary in Ourique, which was celebrated together in 1940 with the three hundredth anniversary of Portuguese independence from Spain. The two events, a "double centenary," provided the basis for festivities stretching over several months to glorify the foundation of Portugal. For the head of the authoritarian regime, the celebration had ideological and economic aims: it was intended to fortify the "joy and confidence" of the Portuguese people and also to "increase the rhythm of activity of public and private services."[112] The latter may well have been the more important argument in the eyes of the former economics professor, for he was generally uninterested in cultural topics. Unlike Hitler, Mussolini, and Franco, Salazar avoided every kind of personal cult, but he recognized the potential of such grand experiences. Instead of choreographing human masses like the fascist dicators in Germany and Italy, he preferred to relegate the population to the role of a passive audience bombarded by historical performances, ceremonies, exhibitions, and conferences.[113] The committee responsible for the planning of the celebration accordingly included influential writers and journalists like Júlio Dantas (1876–1962), Augusto de Castro (1833–1970), and António Ferro (1895–1956). The latter, as head of the Secretariado de Propaganda Nacional (Secretariat for National Propaganda, SPN), founded the Revista dos Centenários, a magazine especially for the anniversaries falling in the years 1939 and 1940. It contained monthly information about the preparations and the schedule for the festivities as well as essays about Portuguese culture and history and press reports on related topics from home and abroad.

In addition to the many smaller exhibitions, concerts, lectures, and commemorative publications, the center of the festitives and the main attraction was the Exposição do Mundo Português (Exhibition of the Portuguese World) from 23 June to 2 December 1940.[114] This typical example of the Estado Novo's portrayal of history traced a distinct line from 1140 through 1640 to 1940. The exhibition was programmatically housed in the symbolic center of Portugal's early modern empire, in front of the Jerónimos Monastery and along the waterfront in Belém, the very place where Vasco da Gama, Ferdinand Magellan, and Pedro Álvares Cabral had set off on their explorations. The leading architect, José Ângelo Cottinelli Telmo, and his team of architects, sculptors, and painters created a monumental representation of the nation's past that covered 138 acres. Different pavilions, each with multiple rooms, displayed the epochs of Portuguese history, among others "foundation," "formation and conquest," "independence," "exploration," "Brazil," "Lisbon," and "colonization." The Christian character of Portugal was illustrated in the "House of Saint Anthony," Lisbon's patron saint, while another pavilion presented Portuguese folk life. More refined elements of Portuguese culture were featured in the "Poets' Garden."[115] On the banks of the Tagus, a stylized caravel was built with figures representing all the major Portuguese explorers and rulers who had presided over the colonial expansion. This Padrão dos Descobrimentos (Monument to the Discoveries) was initially intended only as part of the temporary exhibit, but it was subsequently installed permanently in concrete.[116] In six months, the exhibition attracted around three million visitors.[117]

As a historical adversary, Islam was featured within this depiction of Portuguese history in the "Pavilion on the Foundation of Portugal." Nevertheless, the only objects on display symbolized Christianity: Afonso Henriques's sword and a replica of the font in which Afonso Henriques had been baptized; statues of Afonso Henriques and other important warriors of this age including Geraldo sem Pavor (literally, Gerald the Fearless); the document in which Afonso Henriques had first been named king; and the papal bull officially recognizing him as sovereign.[118] There were no objects related to Islam. The foundation of Portugal was thus related as a story of victory in which the preceding struggle played no apparent role.[119]

The absence of the Muslim adversary was even more apparent in 1947 in the celebrations of the eight hundredth anniversary of the Conquest of Lisbon, an iniative of the city which was supported by the central government. It commemorated the siege of the important bay and commercial center which stretched over months and provided strategic support for the advance of the Christian troops into the Islamic territory south of the Tagus river. With the help of Anglo-Norman, Flemish, and North Rhinelander Crusaders on their way to the Holy Land, Afonso Henriques successfully stormed the Moors' fortress.[120] This anniversary fell within a period of crisis for the Estado Novo, during which the first serious opposition to the regime was emerging, plans for a coup were discovered, and shortages within the economy exacerbated internal tensions.[121] The festivities were that much more welcome as an attempt to demonstrate the strength of the Portuguese nation and the regime via the hero worship surrounding the first king and conqueror of Lisbon, Afonso Henriques (Plate 8), who combined "Christ's cross and the warrior's sword" according to an article by the "most Salazarist of all Portuguese historians,"[122] João Ameal (1902–1982), in the daily newspaper *Diario da Manhã*.[123] These symbols dominated the public celebrations: on 13 May 1947, after a Te Deum in the cathedral in Porto, Afonso Henriques's sword was escorted to Lisbon, where it was brought to São Jorge Castle, the Moorish fortress which Afonso had famously stormed. Just before midnight the battle was reenacted, followed by the projection above the fortress of a giant cross of light and the ringing of bells to mark the beginning of the anniversary months. The third pillar of the Estado Novo after the church and state, the military, staged an impressive parade to mark the conclusion of the celebrations on 25 October, the anniversary of the victory.[124]

Symbols and speeches during the festivities were permeated with the metaphorical language of victory and the Crusades stemming from the eyewitness account of the medieval siege *De expugnatione Lyxbonensi* (*The Conquest of Lisbon*).[125] The patriarch of Lisbon, Manuel Gonçalves Cerejeira, a close friend of Salazar's from university, marked the occasion with a speech in which he called this a day of joy for "the true Catholic, because the conquest gave this city to the church of Christ; [for] the patriotic Portuguese, because it delivered the city to Portugal; and [for] modern mankind, because it brought this city to civilization and progress."[126] Júlio Dantas, at the time president of the Academia das Ciências (Academy of Sciences) of Lisbon, interpreted the victory as a "universal event" and a precursor to the later conquests.[127] Spain's ambassador, Nicolas Franco Bahamonde, the Spanish dictator's brother, provided "Hispanic praise" in memory of the "Day of Splendor" when Christian hands tore Lisbon out of the Moorish hands."[128] The conquest of Lisbon was celebrated as the date of its true birth: "Muslim burnouses and Hebrew robes hunker down and in exchange life grows, disbelief is shaken off, and the mosques purified."[129] In addition, the anniversary provided an occasion for action in the present. The battle of 1947 was, as the politician Luís de Pina put it in a speech in the national theater, an "endless battle" against the new Moors: "the bad ideas, the bad deeds of contempt, and harm to our homeland."[130] In light of the "new advance of the infidels Barbars from the Orient,"[131] the lesson of 1147 was more pressing.

Nevertheless the festivities in 1947, just as those in 1939–1940, hardly mentioned the Moors, despite the impression perhaps given here by focusing on the few relevant passages of the speeches and texts for citation. The Arabists admittedly had a minor role in the celebrations and described the Arab settlements, literature, and arts within the context of outlining the history of Lisbon.[132] In the majority of the official texts, however, the mention of the Moors hardly went beyond the standard references to the "conquest of Lisbon from the Moors." The conquest itself appeared as a fait accompli: press releases, speeches, or other official texts made little if any effort to outline or analyze the events or to depict the Moors in an especially negative way. In his award-winning account, João Ameal portrayed the conquest as a precursor to the voyages of exploration, which the Estado Novo revered as the most important accomplishment of the nation:

> When Portugal acquired the Algarve it became complete—complete on the map of Europe; complete in its predestination as a land of adventurous sailors, challenged by visions of adventure and the call of the distant [unknown]; complete also in a spiritual sense in its apostolic mission. Al-Gharb—the Occident. In history Portugal will go down as the finest expression, the mightiest bulwark on the edge of the European West.[133]

In the historical parade on 6 July 1947, a "living lesson on the history of the fatherland,"[134] there were actors in Arab costume: veiled women balancing ceramic pots on their heads, Arab soldiers on camelback or with drums, and slaves carrying the baldachin of King Alfons V (Plate 11). They served a purpose similar to that of the Indian princes riding on elephants, the Africans clad in animal skins, and the medieval Christian knights. These figures were namely little more than trophies collected along the path of national development and evidence of the long tradition and geographical expanse of the Portuguese empire. In addition, they lent the festivities an exotic decorative air.[135] The Moor appeared here in no especially significant role.

In effect the Estado Novo planned the anniversary celebrations around Portuguese heroes who were worshipped without acknowledging their foes. Islam was neither stylized as a heroic adversary to emphasize the Portuguese valor, nor was it defamed or transposed on the present situtation. There are two possible explanations for this: Islam was alternately forgotten and repressed. On the one hand, Islam appeared to have been definitively conquered, meaning that the concept of *mouros* could only with difficulty be projected onto contemporary adversaries of the nation. Certainly within the collective conscience there was an awareness that the Moors had been their historical adversary, but this seemed insufficiently important to have consequences on their perception of the present.[136] On the other hand, the national identity under the Estado Novo was focused on homogenization and continuity. The heritage of those peoples and cultures which predated Portugal's emergence as a historical subject—i.e. in the prehistorical era, the age of the Roman Empire, or the Muslim rule—aroused little interest.[137] The ideologues of the Estado Novo were thus accordingly not interested in stressing the Muslim heritage, as evident in this interpretation produced for the festivities:

> After the conquest there were only a few vestiges left behind by the Arabs or Berbers. We never had a problem here with the *mouriscos* like that which so long afflicted the Castilian monarchy.... Thus to imagine that the Berber and Semites belong to the ethnic elements which formed Portugal and gave it its shape, is to construct a historical work of fiction which, given the proven facts, contains little truth.[138] [Emphasis in original.]

This attitude is also evident in the Estado Novo's lack of interest in Arab studies.[139] Both attempts at explanation can be to some extent combined: the Islamic foe was not consciously repressed or denied, for it was seen as too unimportant to warrant this. It was admittedly present in the collective memory, but there was little interest in moving it into the foreground as a prominent adversary. To the contrary, its role was marginalized for the occasion of these historical commemorations of events which which it was inextricably intertwined.

COMPARATIVE CONCLUSIONS

The attempts to convey historical lessons via formal instruction were more limited by circumstances on the Iberian Peninsula in the nineteenth and twentieth centuries than in other parts of Western Europe. The tendencies evident within the textbooks evolved similarly to the historical lessons directed at adults: in Spain the educational system was founded in the second half of the nineteenth century and reflected diverse historical portrayals of Islam which conveyed a relatively weak nationalism or other ideology. Such agendas emerged first in the phase between the turn of the century and the Second Republic, in which the political parties increasingly employed the educational system to propagate their understanding of history. Liberal authors in particular increasingly addressed Arab culture and religion in their texts. Under the control mechanisms of Franco's regime, the concepts of Islam in these contexts became homogenized. The regime favored the conservative narrative in which Spain was intrinsically Catholic and incorporated into this the cultural acheivements of Islam. A similar development took place in Portugal, where the heterogeneity of the accounts can be traced through the diverse forms of government from the monarchy to the republic. Textbook authors in the Estado Novo stressed the Catholic character of the country and recognized, if not most prominently, the contributions of the Muslim epochs.

A critical turning point was linked to the literacy of the general population: in Spain it was only in the 1920s, in Portugal not until the 1940s, that more than half of the adult population was able to read and write.[140] Thus the commemorative festivities played an especially important role in conveying historical knowledge, because they did so in a visual language accessible to the uneducated. Such visual representations—like pictorial language—were more evocative and emotionally moving. The rhetorical reference to the Moorish danger was reflected in the iconographical portrayal of the Moor as a dangerous, often amorphous adversary. Attributes like the scimitar, turban, and crescent emphasized both the dangerous and exotic nature of this foe.

In rhetorical and visual reenactments in Spain, Islam assumed the role of primary actor: continual references to the *moros* by authorities of the church evoked the danger of this historical adversary. The old image was projected onto new enemies like socialists, atheists, or republicans. As with any political myth, the actual focus was a call for action in the present. The reference to this historical defense was meant to incite the audience to defend the church against the perceived threats of secularism and anticlericalism. Under Francoism, the political and colonial discourse evolved so that the front was no longer between Christianity and Islam but rather between religion and atheism; it had little effect on

general concepts and interpretations of Islam. The strength of conservative images antagonistic towards Islam thus resulted from two factors:
first, those who fell on the liberal end of the spectrum did little to correct
this portrayal of Islam—even basically adopting it themselves; second,
under Franco the competing interpretations were suppressed and the
more traditional reading became dominant.

Conservative Catholic interpretations of Islam were also intentionally
propagated in Portugal. There, however, Islam played only an ancillary
role in the political mythos. This is partially due to the the weaker role of
Catholicism. The majority of educated elites there, especially the urban
middle class of the nineteenth and early twentieth centuries, shared
republican and often secular sympathies. As producers and distributors
of knowledge, they contributed to the eclipsing of Islam by other historical epochs that seemed more relevant to the contemporary political
situation: The Ages of the Inquisition or the Enlightenment could be
more easily appropriated to instruct and convey Republican ideals like
equality before the law or freedom of conscience than could medieval
battles against an obscure adversary. However, the cultural achievements
of Islam were included among the distinctive influences on Portugal's
development, as the examination of textbooks revealed.

This lack of awareness continued under the Catholic Salazar.
Although the church was a moral and ideological pillar of the state in the
early phase of the Estado Novo, Salazar was so concerned with the
balance of power that he carefully avoided giving the church too much
clout. For that reason the freedom of religion and the separation of
church and state which had been introduced in the Republic were maintained under the regime of the Estado Novo. A further difference can be
traced to the historical myth itself. Because the voyages of exploration
presented a better opportunity to parade the heroic deeds of the
Portuguese, there was little increase in the attention given to Islam. In
contrast to Spain, Portugal still held colonies during this phase. The
largest loss of territory, the independence of Brazil in 1822, was blood-
less. Because the son of the Portuguese king became the first emperor of
Brazil, the country remained, so to speak, in the family. The Estado Novo
boasted of Brazil as the "nation of our creation." Portugal thus had other
possibilities to display its national grandeur. For example, a well-known
map produced by the Secretariado de Propaganda Nacional entitled
Portugal não é um pais pequeno (Portugal is not a small country)
compared the area covered by the Portuguese colonies with that of
Europe.

The mechanisms with which concepts of Islam were propagated via
instruction and historical reenactment reinforced the tendencies which
had emerged within Arab studies and the colonial discourse. The lessons
which were linked thereby with Islam can be summarized in the simple

formulas "Spain is Catholic" and "Portugal is grand." The former could only be established in juxtaposition to a Muslim adversary. In the latter case, there were numerous alternatives—the fight against Spain, the voyages of exploration, or the dissemination of civilization and culture—with which to argue for this grandeur: Islam was reduced to an at most ancillary role.

5

Islam as Folkloristic Invention: Popular Festivals and Regional Identity

"What is the Moor other than a Muslim Spaniard?
And how many Spaniards do we see who are Moors in Christian disguise? . . .
Nothing is easier than that a Moor comes here, quickly learns the language,
and soon passes himself off as a born-and-bred Spaniard."[1]

Benito Pérez Galdós, *Aita Tettauen* (1905)

Staging a battle against *moros* or *turcos* is a part of ritual celebration in many regions in Mediterranean Europe, including southern France, Corsica, and Sicily,[2] but such events are most common and renowned in Spain. The Spanish festivals of Moors and Christians are a "bricolage"[3] of diverse traditions associated with patron saint celebrations, playful battle reenactments, popular dramatic plays, and elements related to these like parades, processions, show fighting, and dancing. They normally represent the battle between two adversaries over a symbol of the village or town: a fortress, a territory, or an icon. The *autos populares*[4] or *mouriscas*[5] festivals celebrated in Portugal contain similar elements: theatrical performances set to music, dance, and, to varying degrees, dialogue. The central element of these performances is a ritual battle against *turcos, mouros, pagãos* or *infiéis*—terms used practically interchangeably to refer to the "Other." Examples from the festivities in Neves in the Portuguese district of Viana do Castelo and in Alcoy in the Spanish province of Alicante in southern Valencia illustrate two contrasting portrayals of an adversary associated with Islam.[6] The question emerges as to how these adversaries served to stabilize local identities, and, furthermore, how and to what extent these local identities subsequently became integrated into the respective national identities. Although some of these festivals claim to be based on historical events, they cannot be viewed as actual reenactments. Instead they embody popular folklore surrounding the "Other."[7] For this reason their historical anachronisms must be examined and interpreted independently. Analyzing these celebrations sheds light on the concepts of Islam designed to influence the lower, uneducated classes. The worker in the textile factory in Alcoy and the farmer in Neves read neither Alexandre Herculano nor Modesto Lafuente. Once a year, however, they witnessed a symbolic battle in which actors donned colorful harem pants and turbans, engaged in shoot-outs, and, in the end, reached an outcome which was meant to harmoniously reconcile the two sides. In the regions examined, the audience for these performances transcended social class, whereas the same cannot be said of the academic literature produced in Madrid or Lisbon.

For a long time the festivals were part of a solely oral tradition, which makes it difficult to find definitive sources that predate the nineteenth century. Therefore, historians can often examine the performances based only on a few examples or most basic outlines. For Spain local studies of individual festivals[8] have processed records found in regional archives and newspapers.[9] More general academic studies have been completed by anthropologists and communication scientists which provide valuable insights and, to the extent possible address the historical aspects.[10] In Portugal the situation regarding sources is more difficult because the oral tradition was not recorded until the twentieth century. Here, too, there are anthropological and musicological studies available.[11] The state of the research allows for a contrast and comparison of Spanish and Portuguese portrayals of the Muslim Other as part of an interdisciplinary dialogue.

"MOORS AND CHRISTIANS": FESTIVALS IN SOUTHERN VALENCIA

Invention of tradition: Nationalization of the festivals in the nineteenth century

In the territory of the modern-day Valenican Community and in Andalusia, the centers of the festivals of Moors and Christians in Spain,[12] there was an especially significant Muslim historical presence. However, representations of the *moro* play a role in local festivals in other regions, too, like the Galician province of Ourense, especially as part of the celebrations of the Feast of Saint James.[13] The ritual festivities regularly claimed to be based on the historical conquest of the town by the Moors. A supposedly historical event became thus entrenched as legend and in turn presented an opportunity to strengthen local identities. As a result every town, every village even, had its own locally specific version of the *reconquista* myth.

As the festivals became established in the nineteenth century, a variety of older traditions were intertwined, including theatrical fighting between Muslims and Christians, which had been a common form of entertainment at medieval courts throughout Europe. On the Iberian Peninsula, one such event took place in Lleida as part of the celebrations surrounding the marriage of Count Ramón Berenguer IV of Barcelona to Petronilla of Aragón in 1150. Accounts of the festivities refer to a "dance of Moors and Christians with fierce fighting."[14] Apparently this was a symbolic celebration of victory, for the count had won the city back from the Moors only the previous year. In the thirteenth and fourteenth centuries there were similar elements within celebrations in important towns along the Mediterranean coast—Valencia, Barcelona, and Saragossa.[15]

In the sixteenth century a militaristic element was added: Philip II reformed the military and required the nobility to train local companies.[16] In the kingdom of Valencia, where in this period Barbary pirates often attacked the coast, choreographed fight simulations, the so-called *soldadescas*, served as a kind of training.[17] The soldiers also accompanied the icons in processions to celebrate and honor local patron saints, and the surrounding festivities were a highlight of early modern village life.[18] The festival in Alcoy, north of Alicante, served as a model for many other localities in that region. Between 1609 and 1688, long after the expulsion of the resident *moriscos*, the local population began regularly staging a battle between "Moors" and "Christians."[19] This festival was a regular occurrence by the seventeenth and eighteenth centuries, as evidenced by the record of its interruption during the War of the Spanish Succession (1706–1741) and due to a plague of locusts in 1756 and 1757.[20]

Despite this historical precedent for some of their religious, military, and dramatic elements, the basic characteristics of the modern festivals of Moors and Christians emerged only in the late eighteenth and early nineteenth centuries. A great deal suggests that they can be read as an "invention of tradition" in the sense that Eric Hobsbawm used the term: they were partly a rediscovery, partly a new creation or new combination of older or supposedly older elements. The Muslims' conquest of Alcoy in 1276 and the recovery of the territory by Aragón in the same year represented the historical occasion for the contemporary event, which annually threw the town into three days of excitement and upheaval that overshadowed the historical or legendary background.

The success of this new festival was related to economic and social developments in the nineteenth century. Alcoy benefited from its proximity to two rivers which could be harnessed for industry, and the city became a center of textile and paper manufacturing. This led to various changes in the town's social character, including the emergence of a wealthy middle class. In fact, during this period, Alcoy at times challenged Alicante's role as provincial capital.[21] This new middle class feted itself by supporting the festival and providing lavish costumes.[22] In the late eighteenth, and especially in the nineteenth century, as the festivities grew and became more elaborate, new *filás* (festival organizations) were founded to accommodate the growing number of participants.[23] As an industrial town, Alcoy was also the center of a broad labor movement, which drew international attention to itself with the Petroleum Revolution in July 1873: rebellious workers assassinated the mayor and took control of the city for a few days before the rebellion could be suppressed—an event about which Karl Marx subsequently wrote an essay.[24] Within this context, it is certainly feasible that the festival itself created a space in which real class conflict was played out at a symbolic level,[25] but the sources available speak little to this issue.

The festivities in Alcoy were organized by the elites who controlled the commission formed for that purpose together with the municipal government. The growing local confidence found iconographic expression in the evolution of the appearance of the urban patron, Sant Jordi (Saint George). Portrayed throughout the Christian tradition as a dragon slayer, in Alcoy Saint George became a slayer of Moors and bore an undeniable similarity to Saint James the Moor Slayer: this Saint George carried an arrow in his hand with which he was poised to pierce the *moros* at his feet.[26] The national symbol of Saint James was thus transposed for the local context, certainly in an attempt to improve the local status by associating the town with these grand myths.

In 1853 José Antonio Llobet y Vall-Llosera, a member of the Academia de Buenas Letras é Historia in Barcelona, described the standard procedure that had developed for the celebration:[27] the festivities began on 22 April with the *entrada*, when first the Christians and then the Moorish troops entered the town. They were led by their *capitáns*, who changed each year. The feast of Saint George on 23 April began with the *diana*, the reveille at dawn. This was the most overtly religious day of the celebration, as the icon was accompanied by *cristianos* and *moros* in a procession through the town. The third day, the *dia del alardo* (Day of the Soldiers' Inspection), was devoted to the conflict between the two parties: an *embajador* (ambassador) of the Moorish ruler appeared before the Christians' fortifications and called upon the Christians to surrender the palace. When they refused, a battle involving a great deal of gunpowder ensued, and the Moors took control of the fortress and symbolically hoisted a flag bearing the crescent. In the afternoon, the scene was repeated with the roles reversed, and the Christians succeeded in taking back the fortress when the Moors surrendered. Basically, the festival is still celebrated today along these lines.

Llobet y Vall-Llosera went to great effort to record all the historical anachronisms in the costumes, texts, and weapons used. He did not mince words when criticizing the "thousand ridiculous scenes which could be eliminated." However, he enthusiastically endorsed the "original and national principle which outshines it all."[28] It was this combination of ritual and comedic elements which no doubt attracted the audience. According to Llobet y Vall-Llosera, it was not only locals, but also "many strangers who were attracted by such a grand spectacle."[29] The central elements of the festivities in Alcoy, like the *entradas* of the participants, became more elaborate and lengthy over time, and the procession and the battle for control of the fortress—whether real or made of cardboard—were adopted by other towns in different areas of the former Valencian kingdom.They grew up out of the local legends concerning the Muslim presence and the local patron saints. Such celebrations provided an ideal opportunity for local elites to develop their own local histories and thus their regional identities. At the same time, the emerging concept of a Spanish nation was becoming increasingly important and regional and national identities developed along parallel lines, at times becoming entwined or even reciprocally reinforcing each other. This tendency can also be observed within the festivals.

The *embajadas*, the verbal disputes between Moors and Christians which preceded each party's respective conquest of the fortress, provided the best opportunities for conveying lessons in local and national history. Earlier versions of such staged battles from the eighteenth century, which had been based on early modern comedies, were increasingly replaced or expanded with new texts after the mid-nineteenth century.[30] The use of Castilian in these texts supports the reading of them as an expression of elite control: while the Valencian form of Catalan was the dominant language in the region for unofficial occasions, Castilian was the language used in public, especially in the press, schools, and the church.[31] It was possible to identify with Valencia and use Castilian, for the Valencian language was not viewed as a critical element of identity.[32] Castilian *embajadas* thus emphasized the elitist, but even more so, the public nature of the festival.[33]

Formulaic elements of the *embajadas* included mutual insults, confirmation of faith in God and Allah, and, in the case of the *cristianos*, an evocation of the national heroes. In these texts, local poets adapted political myths like Numantia[34] or local variations of the *reconquista* myth, for example, in the *embajada* of Castalla, a town south of Alcoy:

If it is true that the living flame of Iberian enthusiasm was extinguished in Guadalete,[35] then Castalla will once again inflame the ashes as a new Numantia. . . . If there were . . . Goths who avoided a hundred battles, we will not follow such a contemptible example.[36]

The *embajada* of Castalla thereby alluded to Castilian myths. This was not a given. In fact, the nineteenth-century *embajadas* evoked both Aragonese heroes like King James I, "the Conquerer"[37] (1208–1276), and Castilian heroes like the Cid.[38] Apparently the two were interchangeable, or at least not mutually exclusive: Llobet y Vall-Llosera noted for Alcoy that the battle cry of the Aragonese Christians should have been "Long live Aragon!" rather than the "Long live Spain!" which they actually called out as part of the *embajada*.[39]

In their role in the *embajadas,* the *moros* invoked Muhammad, the kings of Granada, or anonymous caliphs. Their portrayal was infused with the Oriental clichés of the nineteenth century, for example when they taunted the Christians by saying, "Their war banner will serve as our rug, their fortress as a harem."[40] In many towns the battle ended with the *moros'* declaration of regret for their atrocities: they surrendered to the "grandsons of Pelayo"[41] and genuflected before the cross or the Virgin Mary.[42] The Christians responded by generously forgiving the *moros* and accepting them into their society, effectively dissolving the opposing parties and marking the beginning of the ensuing celebration.

No doubt much of the text which was inserted into the *embajadas* with nationalist, religious, didactic, or simply dramatic intent was eclipsed by the comedic or spectacular elements which made a greater impact on the audience. Precisely the last lines of the *embajadas* may have been routinely drowned out by the smoke and noise of the final volleys, which seem to have been the real highlight for the participants and much more important than the text which was spoken. Nevertheless, the texts were a central element of the ritualization of these festivals and an allusion to supposedly ancient traditions and customs. These ritual celebrations bred local identities which, as the *embajadas* show, could be reinterpreted at the national level. The festivals could be read as a playful sphere in which to battle for the nation, even though they were not always perceived this way in practice. For despite all this, the real attraction of this diversion was the incorporation of Oriental elements, for example, the elaborate costumes with which one could be transformed into an exotic *moro* (Plate 12). The celebratory banners bear witness to this fascination, for they frequently portrayed the *moros* more prominently than their Christian counterparts: wild *moros* and gentle *moras* in the art deco style (Plate 10) reinforced the image of a Mardi Gras-like period, which remained, however, closely tied to the classical images and narratives of the national history.

Prohibition, fraternization, reservation: The festivals as a reflection of twentieth-century politics

Within the festivities as they were staged in the nineteenth century, religious elements like the procession and the mass were combined with secular elements like the *entrada* and the battle itself. There is reason to believe that these latter elements were the most popular part, as they attracted a growing number of participants with increasingly lavish costumes and accoutrements. Nevertheless, the festivals retained enough of their religious meaning to incur the criticism of secular politicians in the Second Republic. This is shown in the example of Alcoy: at the festival in 1931, only a few days after the proclamation of the Republic, members of the city council did not participate in the religious elements at all, and the Marseillaise was played to commence the festivities.[43] The next year, the town council banned the religious elements completely, upon which the Associación de San Jorge (Saint George's Association), which had organized the festival since the 1880s, withdrew from the preparations in protest. The banner for the festival advertised it only as the "festival and popular fair, April 1932." Unlike in previous years, it made no mention of *moros* or *cristianos*, and it featured the colors of the Republic (Plate 10).[44] In November 1936, the center of Republican government was transferred to the city of Valencia from Madrid, which had become the scene of intense fighting in the Civil War. In Alcoy and in most if not all of the towns with a tradition of festivals of Moors and Christians, there were no regular festivals in the ensuing period.

This lack of interest in the festivals of Moors and Christians on the part of the Republic was followed by a surge of interest in the first years under Franco. The playful encounter of *moros* and *cristianos* could be reinter-preted as evidence of a relationship spanning centuries and incorporated into the discourse of brotherhood propagated by the regime. A key figure in this reinterpretation of the festivals under Franco was Tomás García Figueras (1892–1981), an officer stationed in Morocco who published numerous texts concerning the Spanish colonies of Africa. Even before the Civil War, García Figueras had reported in the magazine *África* on the revival of the festival in Benamahoma (Cádiz), which had been discontinued in 1890. He emphasized how the experience of former soldiers in Morocco had influenced the dramatic portrayals at the festival. For example, the actor portraying the *capitán moro* allowed his beard to grow in order to trim it in the Moroccan style. In the revised battle scene, there were a few words of Arabic.[45] Immediately following the Civil War, García Figueras published several descriptions of festivals of Moors and Christians for the newly founded Instituto General Franco de Estudios e Investigación Hispano-Árabe (General Franco's Institute for Hispano-Arab Study and Research). He interpreted them in accordance with the regime's stance as evidence of established amiable ties between Spain and North Africa:

The Movimiento Nacional [under Franco], which has directed the attention of scholars to the wonderful phenomenon of the Moroccan contribution to Spain's mission, . . . daily sheds new light on the topic of the *reconquista* and dispels many shadows and prejudices which have prevailed between the one and the other continent. The actual battles between Moors and Christians in the *reconquista* and in both countries up to the beginning of the nineteenth century were primarily of a political nature and significance; these circumstances having been resolved, there is nothing left which stands in the way of the two peoples' heartfelt and productive coexistence.[46]

In this reading, the festivals became a symbol of the fraternity of Christianity and Islam propagated under Franco. The events of the Civil War led to changes in the dialogue. In Laroles in the Alpujarra near Granada, the historical Christian hero Guzmán el Bueno ("the good man") became directly affiliated with General Moscardó, who had defended the castle in Toledo and become a protagonist in one of the most important Francoist narratives of the Civil War.[47] Franco appeared in the *embajada* of Benadalid (Málaga) as a generous and forgiving hero, who "does not like to see kings and monarchs defeated, no matter how perfidious and tyrannical they may be; he only wants them to obey his weapons."[48] Franco's opponents in the Civil War certainly would have contested the veracity of this claim, but it illustrates how the festivals became one of many methods employed to demonstrate the supposed historical friendship of the Moors and the Christians.

At the end of the twentieth century, the festivals were confronted with new challenges: on the one hand, they became better known as a result of the growing tourism in the 1960s. At the same time, beginning in the 1980s, the growing population of immigrants from North Africa and especially from Morocco heightened sensitivity within Spain for that which was being staged each year. The Valencian Community is one of the regions with a high number of Moroccans. According to a census from 2001, there were 18,655 Moroccans living there, which amounts to four tenths of one percent of the population.[49] There was a noticeable tendency towards harmony in the banners for the festivals, for they increasingly portrayed both parties more equally: this was evident in Alcoy as early as the 1960s, when the symbols of the crescent and the cross were portrayed in a balanced manner or even intertwined (Plate 10).[50] In a similar and complementary vein, the notion of a medieval *convivencia* of the three cultures and religions historically present on the Iberian Peninsula was increasingly being used and fostered in the tourist sector, for example, in Andalusia and Toledo.

After the terrorist attacks of 2001 and 2004, reservations about the festivals grew, and the question was repeatedly raised as to whether it was appropriate or politically correct to dramatize the battle of a war between Christianity and Islam in this ritual. The chairman of the Federación

Española de Entidades Religiosas Islámicas (Spanish Federation of Islamic Religious Entities), Félix Herrero, demanded in 2006 that the festivals be banned because they were incongruent with a democratic Spain.[51] In many places the ritual was adapted. The giant doll called "La Mahoma" (Muhammad), for example, which was carried through the streets in many towns, was still destroyed, but its head was no longer made to explode and it was renamed the more neutral "*la efigie*" (figure).[52] In the Cathedral of Santiago, the Moors at the feet of Saint James the Moor Slayer were decorated with flowers, a custom which was likewise adopted for those at the feet of Saint George in Alcoy.[53] When the actors from the festival in Alcoy were invited to New York in 2006 for a parade on the Hispanic Day, only groups representing *cristianos* participated; the *moros* stayed home.[54]

Despite the changes outlined here, the function of the *moro* has remained essentially the same since the nineteenth century: he represents an interruption of everyday life which is the central feature of such festivals. The festivities begin with the symbolic entrance of the Moors and end with their defeat, which can be read as evidence that during the festival, the *moros* are in power.[55] They embody the exceptional circumstances which underline the social order that prevailed for the rest of the year. As a poem from 1924 put it: "I plead for God's forgiveness: as a good citizen of Alcoy, I am a Christian the whole year through, but during the festival, I am a Moor."[56] The *moro* is the Spanish "Other" par excellence, and this Otherness is transferred onto the entire festival period, giving it the sense of being "outside of time."

BUGIOS, TURCOS AND CHARLEMAGNE: FESTIVALS IN NORTHERN PORTUGAL

The *mouro*: His historical and mythical significance

The term *mouro* as used in Portugal refers not only to the Muslim Berbers and the Arab peoples of North Africa. In the northwestern corner of the Iberian Peninsula, especially in Galicia and northern Portugal, it refers to mythical, fanciful creatures at the center of many legends. They are credited with building dolmen, menhirs, or ancient fortresses and even thought responsible for mysterious stone formations and numinous springs.[57] The *mouros* guard over hidden treasures, and the stunningly beautiful *mouras encantadas* with their long blond hair are reputed to be irresistibly seductive. A central characteristic of the *mouros* is their opposition to the native population. In the folk tradition, they represent everything "different," which is evidenced by their contradictory behavior: some legends stress that they are not Christians, and that they sleep during the day to roam around at night.[58]

In a traditional turn of phrase, referring to something as coming from the *tempo dos mouros* (time of the Moors) means that it has an ancient, indefinable origin.[59]

These mythical creatures, however, are linguistically linked to the historical *mouros* by the shared terminology. In an essay in 1891, the Portuguese archaeologist, ethnologist, and author, Francisco Martins Sarmento (1833–1899) asked how the *mouros* could possibly be credited with the construction of fortresses and structures which predated the Arab rule on the peninsula or even in areas where they had never or just briefly been present. He thus suggested that the attribute "heathen," which had been used during the period of Christianization as a polemical term against the pre-Christian folk religions, had, with the introduction of Arab rule, become fused with the attribute "Moorish":

> "Heathen" was, as we know, Christians' preferred term for the followers of those religions which they had dethroned. This name was now not only used in the period of the Arab invasion, but rather transferred together with the term "Moor" onto the Arabs. . . . The terms "Moor" and "heathen" became synonymous, and, as in nearly all cases of overlapping synonyms, the term won out which had an objective reality. The abstract term "heathen" faded away, the ethnic term "Moor" remained and supplanted it in all uses, including absurdly anachronistic ones.[60]

It is difficult to assess the historical accuracy of Martins Sarmento's thesis. Ethnologists have at least gathered practical evidence which supports the theory. In the 1930s, the British scholar Rodney Gallop reached a similar conclusion in his studies of the Portuguese *mourisca* (morris dance): according to him, this shift in meaning is not an exclusively Portuguese phenomenon, for there is also an established tradition of such fantastic characters being referred to in this way is in the Basque Country.[61] Modern scholars assume a similar shift in the meaning of the historical term *mouros* as a synonym for pre-Christian groups.[62] It is not entirely clear why there is a discrepancy with numerous legends in precisely those areas with a weak historical presence of Muslims or Mozarabs. For the region Tras-os-Montes, the argument has been made that the proximity to Santiago de Compostela and the Camino raised awareness of the term *mouros* and led to its being used as a synonym for "the Other." At the same time, the actual Muslim presence was so insignificant that the oral legends and fantasies could flourish unchecked by reality, whereas in the southern regions of the peninsula the Moors were present and even dominant over centuries, which left less room for the collective imagination to run wild.[63]

Representations of otherness

This comingling of the mythical and historical with the *mouros* rooted firmly in a specific time is also evident in the *autos populares* and the *mouriscas*. Some of those were nonverbal, being performed only through dance and music. Other *autos* combined elements of spoken drama and dance. These pieces follow similar patterns. In many cases, their plots were inspired by the legends surrounding Charlemagne and his knights, central subjects in the medieval *chansons de geste*, which influenced many subsequent literary genres into the early modern era.[64] The *mouriscas* and *autos* can be found throughout the entire country including the islands, but are more common in the north. The connotations of "*mouros*" are numerous and cannot always be traced back to a historical encounter. This is illustrated by the fact that the *autos* have been exported internationally into regions where there is no historical basis for them and adapted to local circumstances there. In Brazil the *mouros* appear as "infidel [i.e. Protestant] Dutchmen"—maybe an allusion to the colonial conflict of the mid-seventeenth century.[65] In such pieces, the figure of Charlemagne has been transposed into the contexts of America and Africa, where the historical emperor never set foot.[66]

One of these pieces is the *Auto da Floripes* in Neves near Viana de Castelo. Although its origins are obscure, it is possible that it was performed already in the eighteenth century.[67] There are records of the event in 1860 and 1875, but the descriptions are exceedingly brief and vague on the question of the *turcos*.[68] In the era of the First Republic and the search for symbols of a national identity, interest grew in such local and regional traditions. Rural customs were seen as proof of the diversity and authenticity of Portuguese folk culture, and they were publicized as a way of increasing ties to the region and in turn to the Portuguese nation.[69] Quite often, interested local elites who were educated in other fields compiled the first studies of such festivities and traditions. Claudio Basto (1886–1945), for example, was a doctor and hobby ethnologist, who described the staging of the *Auto da Floripes* in 1910 as simple and hermetic; the local residents were suspicious of strangers, resented any attempt to make light of their ritual, and performed the piece in such an affected way as to make the text nearly unintelligible.[70] Basto was supposedly only able to note parts of the text due to the help of an elderly woman. Especially interesting in his description is that in this performance the Christians were played by older actors and the *turcos* by younger. A young man was assigned the central female role, a tradition that survived well into the twentieth century. Generally the characters were portrayed by the same actors, who passed these down to their heirs. The older residents of the village complained about the decline of the piece as the older, more experienced actors became gradually unavailable due to death or illness.[71] These details may reveal Basto's own agenda, as he sought to stress the insularity and seemingly archaic elements of the ritual drama.[72]

The text was first recorded in its entirety under the Estado Novo, which maintained the ethnographical interest of the Republic in a quest to shore up popular Portuguese identity.[73] The pharmacist Leandro Quintas Neves (1895–1972) had the actors recite the text from memory over and over again so that he could record it. This text came into the possession of the regional authorities of the Secretariado Nacional de Informação (Secretariat of National Information) in Porto and was printed in 1963.[74]

According to this edition,[75] the plot revolves around a duel between Olivares, one of Charlemagne's knights, and Ferrabrás, the king of Alexandria and son of Balaão the "King of the Turks." Each fights in the name of his ruler. Each of the main figures is captured by the opposing camp. While Ferrabrás asks to be baptized, his sister Floripes frees Olivares in hopes of being led to the Christian knight Guy of Burgundy, with whom she has fallen in love. There is an ensuing battle of the two kings in which the Turks finally surrender. Then the two parties are reconciled and sing a song praising Nossa Senhora das Neves (Our Lady of the Snows), the patron saint of Neves and "spiritual protagonist" of the *Auto da Floripes* on whose feast day, 5 August, the performance traditionally took and still takes place.[76]

The plot and texts include a variety of anachronisms. Ferrabrás prided himself on the atrocities committed against Christians, which must by no means be associated only with the historical Muslims but in general with other religions, too: "I am he who destroyed Rome, killed the apostles, and stole the relics. . . . I possess Jerusalem and the tomb in which your God was interred."[77] His father, the king of the Turks, underlines: "Our gods of Muhammad were always merciful."[78] Muhammad is considered a god and stereotypes of pre-Christian polytheism are projected onto Islam. This represents a textual overlap of the concepts of "heathen" and "Islamic" typical for Portuguese mythology. The portrayal of the *turco* Ferrabrás is not purely negative. In an allusion to the Bible, Ferrabrás offers repeatedly to anoint the wounded Olivares with healing balm, the same "with which your god was embalmed when he was taken from the cross and placed in the grave."[79] Olivares recognizes his "chivalry and nobility."[80]

In his description of the performance in 1932, the ethnologist Gallop emphasized the colorful extravagant costumes of the *turcos* and the clear division of the stage: on one side, a white flag with a red cross, on the other, a red flag with white crescent.[81] In 1931 Floripes wore a flowery dress with a pearl necklace and hat, just as contemporary Portuguese women did for special occasions. By 1948 the character wore an ankle-length dress with a cape and fanciful crown (Plate 17), while Charlemagne wore a long embroidered robe and a golden crown.[82] Over time, the costumes became more exotic and resplendent thanks to the financial support of sponsors. From the mid-twentieth century on, the *turcos* were portrayed with flowing robes, turbans, and crescents (Plate 13)—in other words, they were clearly defined with Oriental attributes. At the same time there were signs of contemporary influences: in a similar *auto* in Portela Susã near Neves, the Christian soldiers wore retired uniforms from the Portuguese army.[83]

The comingling of *turcos, mouros*, and *pagãos* in Neves is no isolated case, as the example of the *Turquia* in Crasto (Viana do Castelo) shows. This play also has roots in the Carolingian epics which were fashionable in the late fifteenth and early sixteenth centuries. The individual phases of development and revision cannot be traced in this case. *Turquia* (Turkey) is presented as the homeland of the "infidels," the sultan refers to himself as "Lord of Alexandria," and his delegate is called an "ambassador of Africa."[84] The geographic incongruence can be explained by the vague notions and reports which made their way into the northern Portuguese province, but they were never corrected or transformed for didactic reasons. Particularly interesting in regards to this text is that the *cristãos* spoke Portuguese, while the *turcos* spoke a bastardized Castilian which would have been just barely intelligible for the audience. This served to underline their Otherness, but it also added a comedic element meant to make the adversary seem ridiculous.[85]

These anachronisms prove that within the oral tradition of these performances, regardless of their actual meaning, the terms *mouro* or *turco* could be used for anyone who was thought to be the "Other" or an "enemy." Conversely, this means that the audience defined their "own" identity via Christianity and religion, but this connotation was similarly vague. The figure of the "Other" becomes even more ambiguous in nonverbal contexts, like, for example the Festa da Bugiada which is held in Sobrado (Porto) on the Feast Day of Saint John the Baptist (24 June): in this dance performance, Christian *bugios* ("monkeys"[86]) and *mourisqueiros* fight over an icon.[87] The dance of the *mourisqueiros* follows a prescribed choreography which is carefully practiced and committed to memory. The actors are young, unmarried men chosen in a selection process, and participation as a *mourisqueiros* is seen as a sort of ritual of initiation. This is opposed to the anarchic, wild behavior of the *bugios*. Anyone who wants to may participate in that capacity.[88] The *mourisqueiros* are the "Other," but they can hardly be construed as infidels. Their militaristic costumes underscore the exact choreography of their dances; these costumes have no similarity to Muslim turbans or sabers. Unlike the *bugios*, they do not wear masks. They are defeated primarily by a magic snake and not due to the intervention of a saint.

The many meanings of the *mouros* and *turcos* at Portuguese festivals give this a more abstract, legendary character open to interpretation rather than one grounded in history. Memories of the Islamic presence on the Iberian Peninsula apparently offered the backdrop for a legend which could be exploited for dramaturgical reasons. The connection of the festivals with the historic presence on the peninsula, however, is vague at best. Neither in the nineteenth century nor under the Estado Novo was there an attempt to make these antagonistic stereotypes more concrete or ideological. The festivities were not explicitly linked to the contemporary social situation beyond their role in strengthening local identities. As far as can be inferred from the sources, the opponents were neither nationalized nor modernized. There seems to have been little direction by the elites for didactic purposes. Even beyond the context of the *mouro*, this can be explained by the disinterest or lack of necessity of such an adversary for nationalization within Portugal. Typical for the national movements, on the other hand, is the reconstruction of "folkloric" traditions and the interest of an educated upper class in village legends and customs, which were advanced as evidence of the existence of a "national soul" and maturity.

COMPARATIVE CONCLUSIONS

Festivities fulfill a basic need for a break from everyday life. The details of food and drink, music and dance, games and diversions which characterize such occasions vary depending on the season and from region to region, religion to religion, and culture to culture. Their contents are interchangeable but their common function transcends these. However, the occasions for such festivities are not random. As long as a ritual survives, it must be expressing some underlying need. Changes are therefore testament to an evolution of these needs, but also of the potential to adapt as the circumstances warrant. At the same time, these celebrations have an effect on everyday life by offering a certain distance and opportunity to reflect critically on it. In the examples of such universal rituals outlined here for the Iberian context, the struggle with the folkloric concept of Islam presented the specific narrative frame adapted to the level of the village or town. *Moros* and *mouros* are vehicles through which ordinary time becomes extraordinary, everyday life is transformed into a celebration, and the negative space between "Us" and "Them" (i.e. "Ourselves" and the "Other") is renegotiated. The reconciliation with the adversary in the end celebrates the bridging of this gulf. By referencing the town itself or a local patron saint, these rituals have the potential to stabilize local identities.

In Spain the festivals of Moors and Christians are rooted in the regions in which the *moriscos* were historically significant—Valencia and Andalusia. In the nineteenth century the business and intellectual elites combined elements of older traditions to basically invent a new festival tradition with a didactic and in turn nationalist purpose: it alluded to historical legends which seemed to reflect historical facts, and, in many cases, stylized the local struggle as representative for Spain as a whole. This didactic appropriation was, however, not as politically charged as the anniversary celebrations had been: instead of focusing on the patriotic defense against a fearsome adversary, the fascination with the festivals of Moors and Christians was the Otherness of the *moro*. This exotic connotation made the event something extraordinary and distinguished it from everyday life. The festivals became a tourist attraction and drew attention from beyond the local sphere: political developments influenced their nature and interpretation, meaning that questions about how society should deal with the Other were also visible in the festivals.

In Portugal such festivals are a tradition primarily in regions where Islam never had a significant historical presence.[89] Here, too, they are a result of varied influences. They were not even transformed along didactic lines when ethnologists began recording and describing them in the twentieth century. Instead the festivals were seen as elements of an authentic Portuguese custom. The figures which represented the Other in these celebrations remained quite abstract and thus open to interpretation. The terms used to refer to them were interchangeable and the corresponding connotations evolved over time. The intended audience was decidedly local, and the message remained locally targeted rather than being extended to envision a Portuguese nation.

The contrast between the Spanish omnipresence and the Portuguese decline of an Other associated with Islam is evident in the statistics. The majority of the three hundred such festivals which are still held around the world are to be found in Spain.[90] An association for their coordination, the Unión Nacional de Entidades Festeras de Moros y Cristianos, was founded in 1976 and soon grew beyond the original twenty-five members. In addition, many villages and towns host such festivals without joining this organization. The number of localities which celebrate festivals similar to those in Alcoy and other towns is rising. Due to current political circumstances, their popular appeal is greater than ever; they attract many visitors including foreign tourists.[91] The actors, especially the *capitáns*, invest significant sums in the equipment and costumes.[92] Within Portugal, on the other hand, the traditional *mouriscas* are disappearing. While the Auto da Floripes and the Bugiada still exist, a recent study found nineteen that had been discontinued, six which took place only irregularly, and only eight such festivals which were being organized on a regular basis.[93]

Folkloric images of Islam influence, and are influenced by, the historiography compiled by elites. They are not entirely independent of each other, but are rather connected, even though these connections are often no longer apparent. The omnipresence of the Spanish *moro* in that nation's historiography is reflected in the rich tradition of these festivals, whereas the more open character of the Portuguese *mouro* has also found a place in the historical scholarship of that nation.

Conclusion

"Soon we will search in the margins of your history, in distant countries,
for what was once *our* history.
And in the end we will ask ourselves: Was Andalusia here or there?
On the land . . . or in the poem?"[1]

Mahmoud Darwish, *Eleven Stars Over Andalusia* (1992)

The concept of "Islam" was used on the Iberian Peninsula in a variety of contexts and had no clear-cut, consistent meaning. The term provided opportunities for projection just as diverse as those presented elsewhere by "Europe" or "Occident,"[2] and this projection was determined by the varied and evolving political, cultural, and social interests of the actors. To make sense of these, it is necessary to develop a model of periodization for the years included in this study and to systemically compare the situation in Spain and Portugal. Based on the conclusions reached here, the question is asked once again as to what extent the Iberian Peninsula can be regarded as a single historical region, especially when compared to the Balkan Peninsula as a historical zone of contact.

In the nineteenth and twentieth centuries, very diverse concepts of Islam and memories of the medieval Muslim presence were present on the Iberian Peninsula. These concepts, expectations, and judgments fell all along a spectrum from defense and marginalization to appropriation and exaggeration. These processes, however, did not occur along clear lines from one pole to the other. The continuities and caesuras in the way the crescent was remembered, judged, and connoted were influenced by intertwined cultural and political processes. In the periodization of such processes there are coincidental "clusters of intensified change"[3] which result from various overlapping structures of time. From this perspective, three phases of development of the concept of "Islam" on the Iberian Peninsula can be posited: 1) a phase in which historical narratives were formed in the latter half of the nineteenth century; 2) a phase in the first third of the twentieth century in which such concepts became more widespread in Spain and were marginalized in Portugal; and 3) a phase between World War II and the end of the dictatorships during which older negative stereotypes were partially revised.

The first phase began with the emergence of liberal historiography.

Authors like Modesto Lafuente and Alexandre Herculano, for example, placed the Iberian nations themselves, rather than the monarchies, in the center of their historical narratives. To tell this story, they had to assign the medieval Muslim past a particular role. They appropriated older concepts and placed these in a new historiographical context. Their scholarship must be read within the context of the rivalry between liberalism and conservatism as an attempt to cultivate and promote certain readings of their respective national histories. The struggle to define their society's contemporary structure was reflected in the competition of diverse historical understandings, which in turn led to differences in the concepts of Islam: affirmative, pejorative, or ambivalent. In Spain, especially, there were several factors which influenced the debate. Academic Arabists provided new models for interpreting the Islamic past, and *africanistas* and other colonial actors incorporated historical Islamophobic stereotypes and Oriental fantasies into their contemporary publications.

In the second phase—decades in which the political environment changed rapidly, as the monarchies were abolished and republics created only to collapse and give rise to dictatorships—the preexisting notions of Islam became entrenched. Due to the basic differences in the concepts of Islam that dominated within Spain and Portugal, it was in this phase that their development diverged most significantly.

In the final phase of the Spanish Restoration, the political camps intensified their debates about the *ser de España*, which, in turn, led to a broader spectrum of attitudes towards Islam. While liberal authors sought to secularize the Islamic past and primarily addressed its civilizing role, conservative Catholic authors emphasized the religious implications of the campaign against the "new Moors." During the Spanish Civil War these competing perspectives became especially clear, as the propaganda of the warring parties employed very different depictions of the Moroccans involved in the conflict. Whereas Islam had been stylized during the colonial wars as a foreign opponent of Spain, the two sides in the Civil War strategically appropriated the concept to portray each other as "un-Spanish."

In contrast, in Portugal there was an increasing tendency to marginalize the Islamic past. The creation of academic institutions for the study of Arab topics was less the result of a specific interest in this facet of the nation's history than it was part of an effort to better position Portugal within Western Europe by raising educational standards and emulating foreign universities by adding academic disciplines. The Estado Novo touted the unity of continental Europe and Portugal's Atlantic expansion. Portugal's multiculturalism as part of the greater Mediterranean region was potentially damaging to the image of a unified nation. For that reason, it was largely ignored.

Attempts to enforce ideological conformity under the dictatorships led to the consolidation of conceptions of history along lines in keeping with the respective regime's agenda. An intellectual discourse over the role of Islam as had existed in the preceding phrases was no longer possible. The most fervent historiographical debate in this period was that between Américo Castro and Claudio Sánchez-Albornoz, which tellingly took place from exile. Given the conservative bent of the dictatorial regimes, traditional historical narratives became entrenched, and the Catholic character of the nation was given a central role.

Despite this seeming stasis, the concept of Islam and the related understanding of the nation's past did gradually evolve: Islam was increasingly appraised positively, not only at a cultural level, but also as a religion. The underlying political motivation—namely, the retention of power over the noticeably anachronistic colonial empire—combined with the historical cultural legitimation: ideologues under Franco interpreted the Strait of Gibraltar as a connector and the Middle Ages less as a period of religious conflict than of contact. This interpretation proved useful even after Moroccan independence, for it allowed Spain to cultivate international contacts to the West via the Arab world. Colonial politicians in the Estado Novo, who practically ignored the Muslims in their colonies for decades, adopted the vocabulary of the revolution within the Catholic Church in the 1960s and began developing the concept of a "Portuguese ecumenism." Within both regimes, the changes were limited for the most part to political rhetoric. They did little to banish the negative stereotypes of Islam which were perpetuated, for example, in textbooks.

These mechanisms followed transformations of the political culture and the thematization of Islam that went along with them. Changes in the political system provided the framework within which certain concepts and notions could come to the forefront at different times. The discourse over Islam could survive from the age of the monarchies into that of the dictatorships. The sympathetic stance toward the Moors under Franco was not new but drew upon the preexisting narratives of the Arabists and *africanistas*. Whereas these had existed within a niche in the nineteenth and early twentieth centuries, they ascended to the political stage when they became politically useful under Franco in this updated form. The Republican rule, on the other hand, was too short to suggest an alternative concept of the Muslim past. Political structures and political notions did not always rise and fall together, but they could be superimposed on each other. Thus, political events and upheaval can be appraised less as the fundamental driving force of the evolution of the concept of Islam than as a catalyst. These events favored or marginalized particular concepts, and created or hemmed certain dynamics. However, the parallel existence of varied and competing cultural notions within the semantic spectrum of "Islam" did not abolish these.

This study has used the methods of cultural history and applied them to examine the subject from multiple angles to trace parallel and divergent developments within the given chronological and geographical parameters. These methods increase sensitivity to certain shared and intersecting aspects of these concepts and heighten awareness for parallel processes that are neither identical nor simultaneous. Cultural historical research on nationalism has examined the historical conditions which lead to changes in the construction of "Ourselves" and the "Other." By examining this object and the related transformations from multiple perspectives, it becomes easier to make sense of the "clusters of intensified change" mentioned above.

At the same time, this approach imposes a certain inherent structure on the results: especially in the nineteenth century, national ideas were explicitly or implicitly based on concepts of inclusion and exclusion. In the context of politically charged objects like wartime propaganda or objects produced for didactic purposes like school books, the negative connotation of the Other are especially apparent. A study based on such sources might conclude that the historical relationship with Islam was primarily antagonistic. On the other hand, an approach based more on aesthetic patterns and literary motives would result in the impression of a society significantly more sympathetic to the Moors. This is more readily accessible in artistic expressions than in political contexts, although art and politics do mutually influence each other in subtle ways. In order to navigate between these extremes of the seemingly omnipresent Islamophobia and the harmonious sympathy towards the Moors and determine the actual relationship, it is necessary to consider the context and conditions in which these attitudes were expressed.

Sociological, anthropological, or political research on the modern-day Muslim population on the Iberian Peninsula offers another perspective on Islam and nation as an object of study. It focuses on the formation of new Muslim communities, processes of integration, and Muslim identity in Spain and Portugal. However, this physical presence is preceded by the abstract presence in the collective imagination. The analysis of this historical fantasy in regards to Islam, which was more or less physically absent from the peninsula prior to 1975, thus helps to pinpoint the origins and mechanisms of the collective attitudes which still play a role in Iberian society and relations to the Muslim population there today. In attempting to investigate two parallel societies, the present study risks overseeing nuances within the individual societies. In exchange, the comparison sheds new light on the individual objects by examining them from a new, wider perspective.

The processes by which concepts of Islam on the Iberian Peninsula were rejected and accepted must be differentiated along qualitative and quantitative lines. The roots of the developments in the nineteenth and twentieth centuries stretch back into the Middle Ages. This study aims to contribute to a better understanding of several of these factors. Asking why the Spanish *moro* was much more prominent than the Portuguese *mouro* reveals basic differences in the historical development within these Iberian neighbors.

First of all, there are differences in the nation-building processes: Spain—with its strong regional identities linked to varied languages and independent traditions—needed a common Other to foster national solidarity. The emphasis on Islam as a primarily religious adversary was in accord with early modern attitudes which equated religion, ethnicity, and sovereignty, attitudes which manifested themselves in forced baptisms and the expulsion of religious minorities. In Spain the church served to bind together what had formerly been independent kingdoms, a function that became especially important after Castile and Aragón were united.[4] Indeed, even Portugal's statehood as a "historical coincidence"[5] bothered Spanish conservatives like Menéndez y Pelayo who cultivated the concept of a steadfast cohesiveness among the Christian kingdoms of the peninsula.[6] In the social disarray of the nineteenth century, the political myth of the *reconquista* reinforced the association of religion and sovereignty. Due to the colonial focus in North Africa, this historical enmity could be prolonged into the present. The *moro* was the most plausible antagonistic stereotype because old clichés could be projected onto a current adversary. Portugal had less need of a Muslim Other because the nation was not plagued by these internal tensions, the church and its master narrative had less influence, and the Portuguese colonies were so heterogeneous that it would have been overly limiting to focus on Islam.

Furthermore, there was a divergent selection of national myths: the repertoire of myths of all European nations prominently feature exaggerations of military conflicts. In many cases the religious differences of the adversaries heighten the sense of political opposition, and this is reflected in the national myths. This is especially true for myths surrounding the Crusades and the Ottoman Empire. In early modern Spain, Catholicism, political power, and ethnicity were interlaced, which logically led to the placement of the struggle against Islam at the center of the national myth. Attempts at explanation which suggest that religious difference encourage mythical stylization prove true in many cases. The Portuguese example shows, however, that historical conflicts with Islam do not necessarily lead to Islam's being portrayed as a central Other in the period of nation formation. In Portugal, national myths also played a central role in defining mechanisms of inclusion and exclusion, but these became evident primarily in other contexts: in the turning to the Atlantic and in the delimitation of Spain. These factors proved to be more significant in the emergence of the national concept than Islam. The smaller Portugal had not only managed to assert itself against its powerful neighbor in the Middle Ages, but is had also managed to extricate itself from Spain's control after the sixty-year interregnum period in the early modern era (1580–1640). Given the relatively stable colonial empire that persisted into the 1960s, the Age of Exploration could be incorporated into a larger, geographically more ambitious mythological narrative of victory than the medieval victory over Islam.

The disparate lengths of the medieval Muslim rule, which ended in the territory which later became Portugal nearly two and a half centuries earlier than within the later Spanish territories, cannot entirely explain the differences in how these myths developed. Real and mythical presence do not necessarily correspond. Events of which there is no historical evidence often play a significant role in national myths. The fact that the end of the Muslim reign in Portugal in 1249 was hardly mythologized whereas the Spanish parallel in 1492 is featured as a key moment in that nation's national myth can also be attributed to their chronological proximity to other mythologized events: the so-called "discovery" of America and the publication of the *Grammatica Antonii Nebrissensis*, the first grammar of the Castilian language, by Antonio de Nebrija. Comparing these similar events and the vastly different myths that resulted from them reveals once again how mechanisms of selection shape national myths.

Third, the Spaniards and the Portuguese have very different understandings of the relationship between religious and national identities: within the process of nation formation, political and cultural elements are often inextricably intertwined. Nevertheless, the emphasis on the religious within the Spanish national identity resulted in an intense rejection of Islam as a religion. In Portugal, on the other hand, where the process of nation formation was influenced in the nineteenth century by republican and anticlerical intellectuals, the nation was understood to have secular roots and Muslims were seen foremost as political and only secondarily as religious adversaries. It was possible to wage war against them or make peace without salvific historical implications. An indicator in the constitutional history illustrates how secularism on the one hand and Catholicism on the other were anchored within the larger political and social sphere: the Portuguese Constitution of 1911 established the separation of church and state and was not abolished under the Estado Novo. In Spain, on the other hand, after the interlude of the Second Republic and legislation passed under Franco in 1967 regarding the freedom of religion, the constitution was only amended to include separation of church and state in 1978.[7]

How can examining the concepts of Islam shed light on the question as to whether the Iberian Peninsula can be considered a single historical region?[8] First of all, it confirms the conclusions which other studies of the region have reached: similarities in political and structural developments, but also cultural factors like the medieval past and the interpretation of this in the modern age are indications of the existence of a region which can be seen as a unified historical region. At the same time, there are striking differences in the details and conflicts related to these processes.[9] There are overlaps in their perceptions of Islam, similar narratives of *reconquista* and *convivencia*, of their being a chosen people, fighting for European salvation. However, these were clearly not entirely congruent. The common experience with Islam in the Middle Ages and its subsequent incorporation into the culture of the two neighboring societies did little to really connect them, and generally speaking the efforts at finding commonalities were minimal. The idea of employing the common struggle against Islam in the Middle Ages to motivate Spanish–Portuguese cooperation was not unheard of, but it was rarely implemented. The different cultures of memory correspond to the heterogeneity of the Iberian Peninsula.

Within nineteenth- and twentieth-century Spain and Portugal, the attitudes towards Islam provide a revealing indicator of national identities. Behind the seemingly stable collective identity which the sources ascribe to the nation, there was a continuous search for identity(s), driven by uncertainty and the need to adapt to changing realities. Processes of political, religious, ethnic, or cultural demarcation directed at Islam and their changes were a significant expression of this transformation. Beyond that, the changes in the notions surrounding Islam display the volatility and mutability of constructions of identity.

These mechanisms can be reconstructed based on other historical zones of contact with the Islamic world, as well. Only a few examples can be addressed here: The celebrations in Vienna of the victory over the Ottoman empire in 1683 featured varied historical antagonistic stereotypes of Islam. The hundredth anniversary of the battle—celebrated during the Enlightenment under Joseph II—offered more than anything an opportunity to praise the valor of the Viennese; their opponents were not demonized.[10] On the other hand, one hundred years later, when the Ottoman Empire was signficantly weaker, the two hundredth anniversary portrayed the event as a triumph over Islam for which Christian Europe should be credited. The historian Joseph Alexander von Helfert (1820–1910) claimed on this occasion: "The Turk alone has remained Asian on the Balkan Peninsula to the present day, just as in his time, the Moor, despite centuries of being present and at home on the Pyrenean [*sic*] Peninsula, remained African; .. neither the Moor of yesterday nor the Turk of today has entered the circle of European peoples."[11] In Croatia, the legend surrounding the Christian leader Nikola Šubić Zrinski, who perished in battle against the Ottomans during the siege of the fortress Szigetvár in 1566, developed into a myth around this "bastion of Christianity." These attributions were so flexible that Croatia, as a part of the Habsburg Empire, was alternatively seen as a bulwark and bridge.[12] The most famous example of how a myth surrounding a historical event could influence contemporary politics is the (first) Battle of Kosovo between the Serbian prince Lazar Hrebeljanović and the Ottoman sultan Murad I: the outcome of the battle is unknown and it was certainly no historical turning point. It was this battle, however, which was mythologized and sacralized for centuries.[13] The myth played a role in the ideological motivation for the bloody conflict between Orthodox Serbs and Muslim Albanians into the nineteenth and twentieth centuries, even as recently as 1989: a month after his election as president of Serbia-Montenegro, Slobodan Milošević, in a pompously staged appearance on the anniversary of the battle held a speech in which he posited that this myth was of central importance for contemporary Serbia and drew conclusions for the present: "Today, six centuries later, . . . we are again at war and faced with war. It is not conducted with arms, although that cannot be ruled out."[14] Given the events that ensued, the last clause must be read as a dismal prophecy of the wars that plagued in Yugoslavia in the decade following.

In the Balkans and on the Iberian Peninsula, there were many shared metaphors used to define national identities: a "bulwark" against the Islamic adversaries, the "battle for the salvation of Europe, " and, in less militaristic contexts, the "bridge to other cultures. " In a universal sense, these metaphors are a response to their specific situation. In a concrete situation which could sometimes be confusing, they offered sweeping statements about the past and the present. Concepts and stereotypes of Islam served to orient and shape the thought patterns of the nation, and to determine courses of action.[15] They were used as necessary to frame the contact with Islam either as a story of triumph or as a heroic defeat,[16] either of which could reinforce a sense of social solidarity and establish the idea of a nation as an imagined community among members sharing a common destiny. They also served to regulate the cultural proximity to "Europe" as these societies understood it.[17] Nations which sought to approach Europe—for example, Bulgaria after it became independent of the Ottoman Empire in 1878[18]—abnegated ties to Islam. If the intention, however, was to stress the cultural richness of these outlying regions as opposed to the material wealth of northern and central Europe—for example, during the period of Spanish Romanticism in the nineteenth century—Islamic and Jewish influences were often cited as evidence of these cultural riches.

The similarities of metaphorical language, however, belie the important differences in the situation within the historical zones of contact in Iberia and the Balkans in the nineteenth and twentieth centuries. The significant Muslim presence in the Balkan region meant that contemporary conflicts could become ethnically, religiously, and mythologically charged. The Balkan Wars in 1912 and 1913 and the collapse of Yugoslavia served to ingrain prejudices against the Balkans into Europeans' "mental map." It was seen as backwards, chaotic, and hopelessly complicated in regards to the constellations of ethnicity and religion, according to Maria Todorova's response to Edward Said's Orientalism thesis. [19] In addition, the demise of Yugoslavia allowed for the emergence of Islam as a significant political player on European soil for the first time since the end of the Ottoman Empire. [20]

The most recent military conflicts in the Balkans refreshed the collective memory of the historical struggle in south-eastern Europe between Christianity and Islam; this "hot memory" [21] is thus still actively present in the collective memory of Europe. In contrast, at least beyond Spain itself, the encounter of Christians and Muslim on the Iberian Peninsula has largely been consigned to the realm of "cold memory": the antagonistic stereotype of Islam was projected into the contemporary context even though there was no actual contemporary Muslim presence there. In reference to Oriental or Balkan stereotypes, actual conflicts seem to be extensions of historical ones. This happened because Islam was a useful code to suggest that a contemporary opponent was a fundamental Other and give this Otherness a historical basis.

Reactions to contemporary events rather than historical automatisms made Islam one of the most prominent Others in European national myths. As examples taken from contemporary Spain show, the mythical, dualistic categories of *reconquista* und *convivencia* have seen an increase in usage. In the context of the wave of immigrants from Maghreb, Spain's foreign policy position in the early twenty-first century, and the Islamist attack in Madrid on 11 March 2004, polemical disputes once again flared up along the lines of that between Américo Castro and Claudio Sánchez-Albornoz. [22] In Andalusia and Toledo, especially, the tourist industry actively promotes a positive portrayal of the medieval Al-Andalus and advertises its cultural grandeur. There is, of course, a financial incentive to do so. [23] The medieval coexistence of Judaism, Christianity, and Islam should inspire the search for new paths for religions and cultures to coexist today. At times it is forgotten that the medieval concept of tolerance had little to do with acceptance and legal equality, but was first and foremost the restraint from violent expulsion or forced conversion. [24] The Arabist Serafín Fanjul deconstructs the myth of a harmonious Al-Andalus, in opposition to Castro. [25]

Furthermore, the term *reconquista*, which had fallen out of favor in the scholarship, has seen a resurgence of popular usage since the terrorist attacks of 11 September 2001 and 11 March 2004, which inflamed public opinion. It is found in the proclamations of the Islamist terrorists, who aim for nothing less than the "reconquest of Al-Andalus," claiming a historical motivation but presumably rather oblivious to the intricacies of the centuries-long relationships on the Iberian Peninsula. Remarkably, the former prime minister, José María Aznar responded to this six months after the attacks in Madrid, also declaring: "The problem Spain has with al-Qaeda and Islamic terrorism did not begin with the Iraq crisis. In fact, it has nothing to do with government decisions. You must go back no less than 1300 years, to the early eighth century, when a Spain recently invaded by the Moors refused to become just another piece in the Islamic world and began a long battle to recover its identity."[26] A similar phenomenon is evident in popular bestselling literature, which draws an ahistorical connection to create a continuity of Spanish-Muslim opposition stretching from "Muhammad to bin Laden."[27]

Compared to their counterparts in the media and universities of other European countries, journalists and scholars in Portugal had paid relatively little attention to the Muslims who began immigrating there in the mid-twentieth century, mostly from the former colonies of Mozambique and Guinea-Bissau. [28] Since 11 September 2001, Muslims within Portugal have also garnered more attention.[29] Muslim communities have since then been confronted with increased curiosity and occasionally polemical rhetoric, but representatives of Islam stress that Portuguese Muslims are well integrated into the society.[30]

The demographic reality of our day is that Muslims are part of the population in most of Europe, either as recent immigrants or as descendants of earlier immigrants, which has affected and at the same time transformed old questions about identity. This has led to a renewed discussion whether and how "Europe" and "Islam" are compatible, and to the attempt to define "Ourselves"—depending on the context and the circles in which the question is debated, as "European," "secular," or "Christian"—against an Islamic "Other." Beyond this lies the even more complex question of how to deal with religion as such in a secular society. This is reflected in the debates about placing limits on immigration, measures to facilitate integration, the banning of headscarves, the height of minarets, non-Christian religious instruction, or crucifixes in schools. Quite often, the clichéd depictions of the Islamic Other utilize the repertoire developed within the historical zones of contact. [31] They thereby run the risk of haphazardly choosing interpretations out of this historical arsenal. An ill-considered projection onto the contemporary situation reveals the potential for controversy within these historical notions. The conditions of modern coexistence are unlike those in the historical zones of contact, but there are just as many preconceived notions and varied projections related to Islam and those who practice the religion today as there were in the past. For this reason, examining these historical precedents must be seen as an opportunity to better understand the mechanisms of segregation and integration.

The historical encounter with Islam left many traces on Europe; that was a supposition of this study. It has sought to demonstrate how this encounter has been held onto in collective memories and historical interpretation, and how the contours of Ourselves were determined via an Other which existed primarily in the imagination. The Palestinian writer Mahmud Darwish (1941–2008) combined these mechanisms in a literary cycle over Al-Andalus. The poem "On our last evening on this land" suggests that fantasies are a potent reality: "on the land . . . or in the poem?" The phrase "soon we will search in the margins of your history . . . for what was once our history" seems to suggest softly that the composition of historical research itself determines the framing of the question about the relationship and perception of "our" and "your" history. The heritage of these historical encounters, and the concepts of Europe and Islam which resulted, are part of a daily reality which must be understood in the context of history and shaped in our contemporary society.

NOTES

Introduction

1 Luís Vaz de Camões, *The Lusíads* (canto four, stanza 100), trans. by Landeg White (Oxford and New York, 1997), p. 97. Unless otherwise indicated, the translator has translated quoted passages into English from the author's original translation into German.

2 Miguel de Cervantes Saavedra, *The Ingenious Hidalgo Don Quixote de la Mancha*, trans. by John Rutherford (New York, 2003), p. 75.

3 The term "Islam" is used in this text in a collective sense to include the multifaceted and often contradictory images and conceptions which this study seeks to detail.

4 Maxime Rodinson, *Die Faszination des Islam* (Munich, 1985), pp. 21–22; Norman Daniel, *Islam and the West: The Making of an Image* (Oxford, 1993). First edition 1960.

5 "Images" refers both here and throughout the text to all conceptions and portrayals of Islam, not (only) visual representations.

6 Monika Flacke (ed.), *Mythen der Nationen: Ein europäisches Panorama*, 2nd ed. (Munich and Berlin, 1998). The exhibition took place at the German Historical Museum in Berlin from Oct. 2004 to Feb. 2005.

7 On the myth of "the Islamic danger" especially in the early modern period, see Étienne François, "Le 'mythe du péril islamique' au miroir de l'histoire," in Hamit Bozarslan (ed.), *Regards et miroirs: Melanges Rémy Leveau* (Leipzig, 1997), pp. 89–99: here, p. 92.

8 Gereon Sievernich and Hendrik Budde (eds.), *Europa und der Orient 800–1900* (Gütersloh and Munich, 1989); Petra Kappert, "Europa und der Orient," in Jochen Hippler and Andrea Lueg (eds.), *Feindbild Islam* (Hamburg, 1993), pp. 44–76.

9 On the topic of "Turkish fashion" and the stylization of the "Turks" after the battle in 1683, see the exhibition catalog: *Die Türken vor Wien. Europa und die Entscheidung an der Donau 1683*, 2nd ed. (Vienna, 1983); on Mozart's opera, ibid., pp. 269 and 281.

10 On the cultural reception of Napoleon's campaign, compare the exhibition catalog: *Bonaparte et l'Egypte: feu et lumières* (Paris, 2008).

11 Richard Francis Burton, *Personal Narrative of a Pilgrimage to Mecca and Medina* (Leipzig, 1874). First edition 1855–1856.

12 On the deconstruction of the concepts "Orient" and "Occident," see, among others, Marshall G. S. Hodgson, *L'islam dans l'histoire mondiale* (Paris, 1998), p. 23.

13 The most well-known work is still Edward W. Said, *Orientalism* (London, 1995). First edition 1978. For an overview of the many scholarly responses to Said, see Stefan F. Hauser, "Orientalismus," in *Der neue Pauly*, vol. 15/1 (Stuttgart and Weimar, 2001), columns 1234–1243; Daniel Martin Varisco,

Reading Orientalism: Said and the Unsaid (Seattle and London, 2007); Reinhard Schulze, "Orientalism: Zum Diskurs zwischen Orient und Okzident," in Iman Attia (ed.), *Orient- und Islambilder: Interdisziplinäre Beiträge zu Orientalismus und antimuslimischem Rassismus* (Münster, 2007), pp. 45–68; Jürgen Osterhammel, "Edward W. Said und die 'Orientalismus'-Debatte: Ein Rückblick," in *Asien Afrika Lateinamerika* 25 (1997), pp. 597–607. On the more recent studies of antagonistic stereotypes see Christoph Weller, "Feindbilder – zwischen politischen Absichten und wissenschaftlichen Einsichten," in *Neue politische Literatur* 54, no. 1 (2009), pp. 87–103. On the topic of Islam as an antagonistic stereotype in Western society, see Hippler and Lueg, *Feindbild Islam.*

14   On the general concept and terminology of "frontier," see Christoph Marx, "Grenzfälle: Zu Geschichte und Potential des Frontierbegriffs," in *Saeculum* 54, no. 1 (2003), pp. 123–143; on the nineteeth century, see Jürgen Osterhammel, *The Transformation of the World: A Global History of the Nineteenth Century*, trans. by Patrick Camiller (Princeton, 2014), pp. 322–391.

15   Mario Apostolov, *The Christian–Muslim Frontier: A Zone of Contact, Conflict or Cooperation* (London and New York, 2004), p. 1.

16   For a comparison between Spain and Sicily, see Deborah Puccio-Den, *Les Théâtres de "Maures et Chrétiens": Conflits politiques et dispositifs de recon-ciliation: Espagne, Sicile, XVIIe–XXIe siècles* (Turnhout, 2009); Gabriella d'Agostino, "Moros y cristianos en la cultura tradicional siciliana," in Marlène Albert-Llorca and José Antonio González Alcantud (eds.), *Moros y cristianos: representaciones del otro en las fiestas del Mediterráneo occidental* (Toulouse, 2003), pp. 163–176.

17   On the mezzogiorno, see Martin Baumeister, "Diesseits von Afrika? Konzepte des europäischen Südens," in Frithjof Benjamin Schenk and Martina Winkler (eds.), *Der Süden: Neue Perspektiven auf eine europäische Geschichtsregion* (Frankfurt am Main, 2007), pp. 23–47: here, pp. 34–38.

18   For an overview, see for example on politics: Ludwig Vones, *Geschichte der Iberischen Halbinsel im Mittelalter 711–1480* (Sigmaringen, 1993); André Clot, *Al-Andalus: Das maurische Spanien* (Düsseldorf and Zurich, 2002); on culture: Arnold Hottinger, *Die Mauren: Arabische Kultur in Spanien* (Munich, 1995); Georg Bossong, *Das maurische Spanien: Geschichte und Kultur* (Munich, 2007).

19   Joaquim Chorão Lavajo, "Islão e christianismo, entre a tolerância e a guerra santa," in *História religiosa de Portugal*, vol. 1: *Formação e limites da cristan-dade* (Lisbon, 2000), pp. 127–133: here, pp. 127–28.

20   On the expulsion of the *moriscos* from Spain, see Ron Barkai (ed.), *Chrétiens, musulmans et juifs dans l'Espagne médiévale : De la convergence à l'expulsion* (Paris, 1994); Mikel de Epalza, *Los moriscos antes y después de la expulsion* (Madrid, 1992); Antonio Dominguez Ortíz and Bernard Vincent, *Historia de los moriscos: Vida y tragedia de una minoría* (Madrid, 1978); Mercedes García-Arenal, *La diáspora de los andalusíes* (Barcelona, 2003); Raphaël Carrasco, *La monarchie catholique et les Morisques (1520–1620): Études franco-espagnoles* (Montpellier, 2005); León Poliakov, *Geschichte des Antisemitismus*, vol. IV: *Die Marranen im Schatten der Inquisition, mit einem Anhang: Die Morisken und ihre Vertreibung* (Worms, 1981); Isabel M. R.

Mendes Drumond Braga, "A questão mourisca em Portugal," in Nuria Martínez de Castilla and Rodolfo Gil Benumeya Grimau (eds.), *De Cervantes y el islam* (Madrid, 2006), pp. 161–178.

21   For an overview on the concepts of memory from Maurice Halbwachs to our day, see: Astrid Erll, *Kollektives Gedächtnis und Erinnerungskulturen: eine Einführung* (Stuttgart, 2005); Franziska Metzger, *Geschichtsschreibung und Geschichtsdenken im 19. und 20. Jahrhundert* (Bern, Stuttgart, and Vienna, 2011), pp. 42–59. Aleida Assman used the German concept of education to illustrate the connection between nation and memory: Aleida Assmann, *Arbeit am nationalen Gedächtnis: Eine Geschichte der deutschen Bildungsidee* (Frankfurt am Main, 1993). In this work I will refrain from using the term *"lieux de mémoire,"* as coined by Pierre Nora; my intention thereby is to emphasize the dynamic character of the memory of Islam and the related mechanisms of inclusion and exclusion. Historians have already begun to apply Nora's concept in the Spanish context, for example in the literary aesthetic approach in Ulrich Winter (ed.), *Lugares de memoria de la guerra civil y del franquismo: representaciones literarias y visuales* (Madrid, 2006) as well as at the conference *Spanische Erinnerungsorte,* Institut für Europäische Geschichte Mainz, 25 March 2010. There is still no explicit study of *"lieux de mémoire"* within Portugal.

22   On the concept of cultural memory, see the definition of Jan Assmann, "Kollektives Gedächtnis und kulturelle Identität," in ibid. and Tonio Hölscher (eds.), *Kultur und Gedächtnis* (Frankfurt am Main, 1988), pp. 9– 19.

23   The connotations of the English word "Moor" are much less complex than those of the expressions in Spanish and Portuguese. For this reason, the original terms are used throughout this text, except when citing the contemporary literature.

24   For the multi-layered use of the term and its history, it is helpful to consult the *Diccionario de la lengua española* of the Real Academia Española and the so-called *Enciclopedia Espasa* from the beginning of the twentieth century: *"Moro,"* in *Enciclopedia universal ilustrada europeo-americana,* vol. 36, (Madrid, 1918), p. 1132. More recent dictionaries like María Moliner (ed.), *Diccionario de uso del español,* 2nd ed. (Madrid, 1998) and Julio Casares (ed.), *Diccionario ideológico de la lengua española* (Barcelona, 1999) adopt them as well.

25   Epalza, *Los moriscos antes y después de la expulsión,* p. 17.

26   Maria Rosa de Madariaga, "Imagen del moro en la memoria colectiva del pueblo español y retorno del moro en la Guerra Civil de 1936," in *Revista internacional de sociología* 46, no. 4 (1988), pp. 575–599: here, p. 580.

27   Ekkehart Rotter, *Abendland und Sarazenen: Das okzidentale Araberbild und seine Entstehung im Frühmittelalter* (Berlin and New York, 1986), pp. 68–77: here, p. 75.

28   Epalza, *Los moriscos antes y después de la expulsión,* p. 16.

29   "Moors on the coast."

30   "Like Moors without a leader."

31   "There are Moors and Christians."

32   "To descend to the Moor."

33 See the article under "Moro" in the supplement of the *Enciclopedia Espasa* of 2005.

34 José Serrão, "Mouro," *Dicionário de História de Portugal,* vol. IV (Porto, 1984), p. 352; "Mouro," *Dicionario de História Religiosa de Portugal,* vol. 3 (Lisbon, 2001), p. 279.

35 "A Moor is walking on the coast."

36 "To work like a Moor."

37 See the article under "Mouro" in *Grande Enciclopedia portuguesa e brasileira* (Lisbon and Rio de Janeiro, 1945ff.); Antonio de Morais Silva, *Novo Dicionário compacto da língua portuguesa,* 7th ed. (Lisbon, 1992).

38 "The bewitched female Moor."

39 "Time of the Moors."

40 Alexandre Parafita, *A Mitologia dos Mouros: Lendas, mitos, serpentes, tesouros* (Canelas, 2006), p. 191; on Galicia, Mar Llinares García, *Os mouros no imaxinario popular galego* (Santiago de Compostela, 1990).

41 On the different concepts of *moriscos* und *mouriscos* see Rogério de Oliveira Ribas, "Filhos de Mafoma: Mouriscos, cripto-islamismo e inquisição no Portugal quinhentista," 2 vols., Ph.D. thesis, Universidade de Lisboa, 2004, pp. 73–74.; Braga, *A questão mourisca em Portugal,* p. 165.

42 For an overview, see Maria Soledad Carrasco Urgoiti, *El moro de Granada en la literatura* (Granada, 1989).

43 The sermon of the Old Man is in Canto Four of the Lusíads, stanza 94–104: here stanza 95. Camões, *Lusíads,* p. 96.

44 Cervantes Saavedra, *The Ingenious Hidalgo Don Quixote de la Mancha,* p. 854.

45 Claudio Sánchez-Albornoz, *España, un enigma histórico,* vol. 1 (Barcelona, 1973), p. 191. First edition 1956.

46 Alan Freeland, "The People and the Poet: Portuguese National Identity and the Camões Tercentenary," in Clare Mar-Molinero and Angel Smith (eds.), *Nationalism and the Nation in the Iberian Peninsula: Competing and Conflicting Identities* (Oxford, 1996), pp. 53–67; Eric Storm, "El tercer centenario dcl Don Quijote en 1905 y el nacionalismo español," in *Hispania* 58, no. 199 (1998), pp. 625–654.

47 See Gerald M. Moser, "What Did the Old Man of the Restelo Mean?," in *Luso-Brazilian Studies* 17, no. 2 (1980), p. 139–151; André Stoll, "Woher kommt Dulcinea, und was schreibt Cide Hamete Benengeli? Cervantes' Erkundung der semitischen Zwischenwelten Kastiliens," in Christoph Strosetzki (ed.), *Miguel de Cervantes' Don Quijote: Explizite und implizite Diskurse im Don Quijote* (Berlin, 2005), pp. 99–135; Georges Güntert, "Der Diskurs der Minderheiten: Sancho und der Moriske Ricote," in Strosetzki (ed.), *Miguel de Cervantes' Don Quijote,* pp. 83–97; Mariano Delgado, "Dem 'christlichen Beruf' treu geblieben? Zu den expliziten und impliziten religiösen Diskursen im Quijote," in Strosetzki (ed.), *Miguel de Cervantes' Don Quijote,* pp. 59–81.

48 For a definition of historical myths, see for example Frank Becker, "Begriff und Bedeutung des politischen Mythos," in Barbara Stollberg-Rilinger (ed.), *Was heißt Kulturgeschichte des Politischen?* (Berlin, 2005), pp. 129–148; Heidi Hein-Kircher, "Überlegungen zu einer Typologisierung von politi-

schen Mythen aus historiographischer Sicht – ein Versuch," in ibid. and Hans Hennig Hahn (eds.), *Politische Mythen im 19. und 20. Jahrhundert in Mittel- und Osteuropa* (Marburg 2006), pp. 407–424; Yves Bizeul, "Politische Mythen, Ideologien und Utopien: Ein Definitionsversuch," in *Mythos, no. 2: Politische Mythen* (Würzburg, 2006), pp. 10–29.

49 M. Rainer Lepsius, "The Nation and Nationalism in Germany," trans. by Jean A. Campbell, in *Social Research: An International Quarterly* 71, no. 3 (2004), pp. 481–500: here, p. 481.

50 For an overview of national myths in Europe, see Siegfried Weichlein, *Nationalbewegungen und Nationalismus in Europa* (Darmstadt, 2006), pp. 112–141.

51 See Paul Noltenius, *Dichterfeiern in Deutschland: Rezeptionsgeschichte als Sozialgeschichte am Beispiel der Schiller- und Freiligrath-Feiern* (Munich, 1984); ibid., "Die Nation und Schiller," in Helmut Scheuer (ed.), *Dichter und ihre Nation* (Frankfurt am Main, 1993), pp. 151–175; Ute Gerhard, "Schiller im 19. Jahrhundert," in Helmut Koopmann (ed.), *Schiller-Handbuch* (Stuttgart, 1998), pp. 759–772; Thies Schulze, *Dante Alighieri als nationales Symbol Italiens 1793–1915* (Tübingen, 2005).

52 On Olivença/Olivenza see Xosé Manoel Núñez Seixas, "The Iberian Peninsula: Real and Imagined Overlaps," in Tibor Frank and Frank Hadler (eds.), *Disputed Territories and Shared Pasts: Overlapping National Histories in Modern Europe* (Basingstoke, 2010), pp. 329–348: here, pp. 330–334.

53 José Álvarez Junco, "El nacionalismo español como mito movilizador: Cuatro guerras," in Rafael Cruz (ed.), *Cultura y movilización en la España contemporánea* (Madrid, 1997), pp. 35–67.

54 On Portugal, see Maria Isabel João, *Memória e Império: Comemorações em Portugal 1880–1960* (Lisbon, 2002). On Spain, see Eric Storm, "Las conmemoraciones de héroes nacionales en la España de la Restauración: El centenario de El Greco de 1914," in *Historia y Política* 12 (2004), pp. 79–104, ibid., "El tercer centenario del Don Quijote."

55 José Álvarez Junco, *Mater dolorosa: La idea de España en el siglo XIX* (Madrid, 2001).

56 Eva Maria von Kemnitz, "Envoys, Princesses, Seamen and Captives: The Muslim Presence in Portugal in the 18th and 19th Centuries," in *Lusotopie* 14, no. 1 (2007), pp. 105–113.

57 Gonzalo Álvarez Chillida, *El Antisemitismo en España: La imagen del judío 1812–2002* (Madrid, 2002).

58 On the conceptual history of the reconquista myth, see Martin F. Ríos Saloma, "La Reconquista: una invención historiográfica (siglos XVI–XIX)," in Daniel Baloup and Philippe Josserand (eds.), *Regards croisés sur la Guerre Sainte: Guerre, idéologie et religion dans l'espace méditerranéen latin (XIe–XIIIe siécle): Actes du Colloque international tenu à la Casa de Velázques (Madrid) du 11 au 13 avril 2005* (Toulouse, 2006), pp. 413–429; ibid: "De la Restauración a la Reconquista: la construcción de un mito nacional: Una revisión historiográfica: Siglos XVI–XIX," in *En la España Medieval* 28 (2005), pp. 379–414. See also Alexander Pierre Bronisch, *Reconquista und Heiliger Krieg: Die Deutung des Krieges im christlichen Spanien von den Westgoten bis ins frühe 12. Jahrhundert* (Münster, 1998), pp. 1–14.

59 Mariano Delgado, "Europa und der Islam in der Frühen Neuzeit:

Exklusions- und Inklusionstypen zwischen 1453 und 1798," in Kerstin Armborst-Weihs and Judith Becker (eds.), *Toleranz und Identität: Geschichtsschreibung und Geschichtsbewusstsein zwischen religiösem Anspruch und historischer Erfahrung* (Göttingen, 2010), pp. 53–77; Ludolf Pelizaeus, "Die Konstruktion eines Islambildes in Spanien und Portugal als iberischer Integrationsfaktor," in Gabriele Haug-Moritz and Ludolf Pelizaeus (eds.), *Repräsentationen der islamischen Welt im Europa der Frühen Neuzeit* (Münster, 2010), pp. 177–205.

60 See for example Michael Werner and Bénédicte Zimmermann, "Vergleich, Transfer, Verflechtung: Der Ansatz der Histoire croisée und die Herausforderung des Transnationalen," in *Geschichte und Gesellschaft* 28 (2002), pp. 607–637.

61 See Hartmut Kaelble, "Die interdisziplinären Debatten über Vergleich und Transfer," in ibid. and Jürgen Schriewer (eds.), *Vergleich und Transfer: Komparatistik in den Sozial-, Geschichts- und Kulturwissenschaften* (Frankfurt am Main, 2003), pp. 469–493: here, p. 477.

62 An investigation of processes of transfer concerning Islam on the Iberian Peninsula would only make sense if there had been some sort of actual contact, whether that of contemporaries or chronologically offset literary influence. Such processes can be observed within Iberianism or the dictatorships, for example, but hardly for the conceptions of Islam.

63 On the question of selection of the objects for comparison and the related difficulties, see generally Hartmut Kaelble, *Der historische Vergleich: Eine Einführung zum 19. und 20. Jahrhundert* (Frankfurt am Main and New York, 1999); on the offset chronology, see esp. ibid., pp. 14–16.

64 On assymetries in contrasting comparisons, see also Heinz-Gerhard Haupt and Jürgen Kocka, "Historischer Vergleich: Methoden, Aufgaben, Probleme: Eine Einleitung," in ibid. (eds.), *Geschichte und Vergleich: Ansätze und Ergebnisse international vergleichender Geschichtsschreibung* (Frankfurt am Main and New York, 1996), pp. 9–45: here: p. 15 and pp. 24–25.

65 A. H. de Oliveira Marques, *Geschichte Portugals und des portugiesischen Weltreichs* (Stuttgart, 2001), p. 397.

66 Sérgio Campos Matos, "Iberismo e identidade nacional (1851–1910)," in *Clio: Revista do Centro de História da Universidade de Lisboa* 14 (2006), pp. 349–400; ibid., "Conceitos de iberismo em Portugal," in *Revista de História das Ideias* 28 (2007), pp. 169–193; ibid., "Was Iberism a Nationalism? Conceptions of Iberism in Portugal in the Nineteenth and Twentieth Centuries," in *Portuguese Studies* 25, no. 2 (2009), pp. 215–229; José António Rocamora, *El nacionalismo ibérico 1792–1936* (Valladolid, 1994).

67 Matos, "Iberismo e identidade nacional," p. 361.

68 Xosé Manoel Núñez Seixas, "History of Civilization: Transnational or Post-Imperial? Some Iberian Perspectives (1870–1930)," in Stefan Berger and Chris Lorenz (eds.), *Nationalizing the Past: Historians as Nation-Builders* (Basingstoke, 2010), pp. 384–403.

69 Matos, "Iberismo e identidade nacional," p. 358.

70 For an overview of the term "historical region" as a geographical entity larger than a country and smaller than a continent which displays numerous social, economic, cultural, and political similarities, see Stefan Troebst,

"Introduction: What's in a Historical Region? A Teutonic Perspective," in *European Review of History* 10, no. 2 (2003), pp. 173–188. On the Iberian Peninsula as a historical region, see Antonio Sáez-Arance, "Constructing Iberia: National Traditions and the Problem(s) of a Peninsular History," in *European Review of History* 10, no. 2 (2003), pp. 189–202: here p. 197–198.

71 A representative sample of the many works on Spanish nationalism: Jean-Louis Guereña (ed.), *Les nationalismes dans l'Espagne contemporaine: Idéologies, mouvements, symboles* (Paris, 2001); Carlos Taibo (ed.), *Nacionalismo español: Esencias, memoria e instituciones* (Madrid, 2007); Javier Moreno Luzón (ed.), *Construir España: Nacionalismo español y procesos de nacionalización* (Madrid, 2007); Javier Moreno Luzón and Xosé Manoel Núñez Seixas, *Ser españoles: Imaginarios nacionalistas en el siglo XX* (Barcelona, 2013). On the time of the *transición*, see Sebastian Balfour and Alejandro Quiroga, *The Reinvention of Spain: Nation and Identity since Democracy* (Oxford, 2007); Xosé Manoel Núñez Seixas, *Patriotas y demócratas: El discurso nacionalista español después de Franco* (Madrid, 2010).

72 On the concept of peripheral nationalism in Spain, see Xosé Manoel Núñez Seixas, "The Region as Essence of the Fatherland: Regionalist Variants of Spanish Nationalism (1840–1936)," in *European History Quarterly* 31 (2001), pp. 483–518.

73 José Manuel Sobral, "O Norte, o Sul, a raça, a nação – representações da identidade nacional portuguesa (séculos XIX–XX)," in *Análise social* 39 (2004), pp. 255–284: here, p. 280.

74 Ibid., p. 277.

75 See José Mattoso, *A identidade nacional* (Lisbon, 1991).

76 See José Manuel Sobral's study of the Portuguese case, in which he applies and analyzes important theories of nation formation, including those of Gellner, Anderson, Hastings, and Smith: ibid., "A formação das nações e o nacionalismo: os paradigmas explicativos e o caso português," in *Análise social* 37 (2003), pp. 1093–1126.

77 Almut Höfert, "Alteritätsdiskurse: Analyseparameter historischer Antagonismusnarrative und ihre historiographischen Folgen," in Haug-Moritz and Pelizaeus (eds.), *Repräsentationen der islamischen Welt im Europa der Frühen Neuzeit*, pp. 21–40: here, p. 22.

78 For an overview on recent scholarship, see Siegfried Weichlein, "Nationalismus und Nationalstaat in Deutschland und Europa: Ein Forschungsüberblick," in *Neue politische Literatur* 51, no. 2/3 (2006), pp. 265–351.

79 For a critical analysis of Hobsbawm, Gellner, and Anderson's theories of nationalism and their theses explaining the lack of nationalist thought and action in the Middle Ages and early modern era, see Caspar Hirschi, *Wettkampf der Nationen: Konstruktionen einer deutschen Ehrgemeinschaft an der Wende vom Mittelalter zur Neuzeit* (Göttingen, 2005), pp. 24–44.

80 Ernest Renan, "What is a Nation?" in Geoff Eley and Ronald Grigor Suny (eds.), *Becoming National: A Reader* (Oxford, 1996), pp. 42–55: here, p. 45.

81 On the interaction between ideas and discourses on the one hand and social situations and manners on the other hand, see Lutz Raphael, "Ideen als gesellschaftliche Gestaltungskraft im Europa der Neuzeit," in ibid. and

Heinz-Elmar Tenorth (eds.), *Ideen als gesellschaftliche Gestaltungskraft im Europa der Neuzeit: Beiträge für eine erneuerte Geistesgeschichte* (Munich, 2006), pp. 11–27: here, p. 12–13.

82 Weichlein, "Nationalismus und Nationalstaat in Deutschland und Europa," p. 351.

83 This study adopts a pragmatic understanding of the term "discourse," similar to the approach of William H. Sewell, Jr., who spoke of a "set of inter-related texts": William H. Sewell, Jr., *Work and Revolution in France: The Language of Labor from the Old Regime to 1848* (Cambridge, 1980), p. 11. Discourses are understood as a collection of statements on a specific topic. Based on the "constructed character of sociocultural realities" (Achim Landwehr), this study seeks to define the conditions under which these are constructed. See also Achim Landwehr, "Diskurs und Diskursgeschichte: Version 1.0," in *Docupedia-Zeitgeschichte*, 11 Feb. 2010, http://docupedia.de/zg/Diskurs_und_Diskursgeschichte?oldid= 75508 (accessed 17 Nov. 2010).

84 Eloy Martín Corrales, "El cine en el protectorado español de Marruecos (1909–1939)," in *Cuadernos del Archivo Municipal de Ceuta* 10 (1996), pp. 227–240; Alberto Elena, "Romancero Marroquí: Africanismo y cine bajo el franquismo," in *Secuencias: Revista de Historia del Cine* 4 (1996), pp. 83–118; Susan Martin-Márquez, *Disorientations: Spanish Colonialism in Africa and the Performance of Identity* (New Haven and London, 2008), pp. 220–299.

85 Maria Soledad Carrasco Urgoiti, *The Moorish Novel* (Boston, 1976); ibid., *El moro retador y el moro amigo* (Granada, 1996).

86 Carrasco Urgoiti, *El moro de Granada en la literatura*.

87 For an overview, see Norbert Rehrmann, *Das schwierige Erbe von Sefarad: Juden und Mauren in der spanischen Literatur: Von der Romantik bis zur Mitte des 20. Jahrhunderts* (Frankfurt am Main, 2002).

88 On Portugal, especially on Alexandre Herculano und Almeida Garrett, see Ana Maria Ramalhete, "Ficcionalização de Contactos Culturais e Especifidade Nacional: Olhares Românicos sobre Modelos, Cristãos e Mouros," in Margarida L. Losa, Isménia de Sousa, and Gonçalo Vilas-Boas (eds.), *Literatura Comparada: Os Novos Paradigmas* (Porto, 1996), pp. 67–74.

89 Pedro Antonio de Alarcón, *Diario de un testigo de la Guerra de África* (Seville, 2005). English translation: Pedro Antonio de Alarcón, *Diary of a Witness to the War in Africa*, trans. by Bern Keating (Memphis 1988).

90 Antonio M. Carrasco González, *La novela colonial hispanoafricana: Las colonias africanas de España a través de la historia de la novela* (Madrid, 2000).

91 For a recent analysis of this work in the context of Spanish-Moorish identity, see Fabian Sevilla, *Die "Drei Kulturen" und die spanische Identität: ein Konflikt bei Américo Castro und in der spanischsprachigen Narrativik der Moderne* (Tübingen 2014), pp. 172–192.

92 On Goytisolo's novels, see Luce López-Baralt, *Islam in Spanish Literature: From the Middle Ages to the Present* (Leiden, 1992), pp. 259–299. First edition Madrid, 1985; Friederike Heitsch, *Imagologie des Islam in der neueren und neuesten spanischen Literatur* (Kassel, 1998), Sevilla, *Die "Drei Kulturen" und die spanische Identität*, pp. 193–283.

93 Juan Goytisolo, "Cara y cruz del moro en nuestra literatura," in *Revista internacional de sociología* 46, no. 4 (1988), pp. 601–615.

94 English translation: Juan Goytisolo, *Count Julian*, trans. by Helen Lane (London 1989).

95 See Oliver Zimmer, "Nation und Religion: Von der Imagination des Nationalen zur Verarbeitung von Nationalisierungsprozessen," in *Historische Zeitschrift* 283 (2006), pp. 617–656: here pp. 618–620.

96 Friedrich Wilhelm Graf, "Die Nation – von Gott 'erfunden'?" in ibid., *Die Wiederkehr der Götter: Religion in der modernen Kultur* (Munich, 2004), pp. 102–132.

97 Hartmut Lehmann (ed.), *Säkularisierung, Dechristianisierung, Rechristianisierung im neuzeitlichen Europa* (Göttingen, 1997); José Casanova, *Public Religions in the Modern World* (Chicago, 1994).

98 Heinz-Gerhard Haupt and Dieter Langewiesche (eds.), *Nation und Religion in Europa: Mehrkonfessionelle Gesellschaften im 19. und 20. Jahrhundert* (Frankfurt am Main, 2004); Martin Schulze Wessel (ed.), *Nationalisierung der Religion und Sakralisierung der Nation im östlichen Europa* (Stuttgart, 2006); Alois Mosser (ed.), *"Gottes auserwählte Völker": Erwählungsvorstellungen und kollektive Selbstfindung in der Geschichte* (Frankfurt am Main, 2001); Graf, "Die Nation – von Gott 'erfunden'?"; Adrian Hastings, *The Construction of Nationhood* (Cambridge, 1997).

99 Gerd Krumeich and Hartmut Lehmann (eds.), *"Gott mit uns": Nation, Religion und Gewalt im 19. und frühen 20. Jahrhundert* (Göttingen, 2000); Gerd Krumeich and Susanne Brandt (eds.), *Schlachtenmythen: Ereignis – Erzählung – Erinnerung* (Cologne, 2003); Nikolaus Buschmann and Dieter Langewiesche (eds.), *Der Krieg in den Gründungsmythen europäischer Nationen und der USA* (Frankfurt am Main, 2003).

100 Dieter Langewiesche, "Nation und Religion in Europa," in ibid., *Reich, Nation, Föderation: Deutschland und Europa* (Munich, 2008), pp. 68–92: here, p. 91.

101 Langewiesche, "Nation und Religion in Europa," pp. 74–84; Peter Haber, Erik Petry, and Daniel Wildmann, *Jüdische Identität und Nation: Fallbeispiele aus Mitteleuropa* (Cologne, Weimar, and Vienna, 2006).

102 Among the abundant studies: Haug-Moritz and Pelizaeus (eds.), *Repräsentationen der islamischen Welt im Europa der Frühen Neuzeit*; Almut Höfert, *Den Feind beschreiben: "Türkengefahr" und europäisches Wissen über das Osmanische Reich 1450–1600* (Frankfurt am Main, 2003).

103 For an overview, see Maria Todorova, "The Ottoman Legacy in the Balkans," in Leon Carl Brown (ed.), *Imperial Legacy: The Ottoman Imprint on the Balkans and the Middle East* (New York, 1996), pp. 45–77; Gunnar Hering, "Die Osmanenzeit im Selbstverständnis der Völker Südosteuropas," in Hans Georg Majer (ed.), *Die Staaten Südosteuropas und die Osmanen* (Munich, 1989), pp. 355–380; Marco Dogo, "The Balkan Nation-States and the Muslim Question," in Stefano Bianchini and Marco Dogo (eds.), *The Balkans: National Identities in a Historical Perspective* (Ravenna, 1998), pp. 61–74; Nathalie Clayer, "Der Balkan, Europa und der Islam," in *Enzyklopädie des europäischen Ostens (EEO)*, 2006, pp. 303–328; http://wwwg.uni-klu.ac.at/eeo/Clayer_Balkan (1 Sept. 2010); on Bosnia, Xavier Bougarel, "L'héritage ottoman dans les recompositions de l'identité

bochniaque," in Sylvie Gangloff (ed.), *La perception de l'héritage ottoman dans les Balkans* (Paris, 2005), pp. 63–94, on Bulgaria, Marina Liakova, "'Europa' und 'der Islam' als Mythen in den öffentlichen Diskursen in Bulgarien," in Hein-Kircher and Hahn (eds.), *Politische Mythen im 19. und 20. Jahrhundert in Mittel- und Osteuropa*, pp. 225–242, on Croatia, Ivo Žanić, "The Symbolic Identity of Croatia in the Triangle Crossroads-Bulkwark-Bridge," in Pål Kolstø (ed.), *Myths and Boundaries in South-Eastern Europe* (London, 2005), pp. 35–76; on Bulgaria, Maria Todorova: "Die Osmanenzeit in der bulgarischen Geschichtsschreibung seit der Unabhängigkeit," in Majer (ed.), *Die Staaten Südosteuropas und die Osmanen*, pp. 127–161.

104 Martin Baumeister, "Atraso de España – Las dos Españas," in Joachim Born et al. (eds.), *Handbuch Spanisch: Sprache, Literatur, Kultur, Geschichte in Spanien und Hispanoamerika: Für Studium, Lehre, Praxis* (Berlin, 2011), pp. 556–561: here, p. 558.

105 Antonio Machado, *Times Alone: Selected Poems of Antonio Machado*, trans. by Robert Bly (Middletown, Connecticut, 1983), p. 113.

106 Mariano Delgado, "Religion und Nation in den 'zwei Spanien': Der Kampf um die nationale Identität 1812–1980," in Urs Altermatt and Franziska Metzger (eds.), *Religion und Nation: Katholizismen im Europa des 19. und 20. Jahrhunderts* (Stuttgart, 2007), pp. 51–68.

107 On the relation of church and state prior to the founding of the Portuguese republic, see António Matos Ferreira, "A constitucionalização da religião," in *História religiosa de Portugal*, vol. III: *Religião e Sécularização* (Lisbon, 2002), pp. 37–59; Ana Isabel Marques Guedes, *Algumas considerações sobre a "questão religiosa" em Portugal (meados do séc XIX a início do séc. XX): O anticlericalismo e o espírito republicano* (Porto, 1990); Vítor Neto, *O Estado, a Igreja e a sociedade em Portugal 1831–1911* (Lisbon, 1998); Steffen Dix, "As esferas seculares e religiosas na sociedade portuguesa," in *Análise social 45*, no. 194 (2010), pp. 5–27.

108 Stanley G. Payne, *A History of Spain and Portugal*, 2 vols. (Madison, 1973).

109 Sáez-Arance, "Constructing Iberia," p. 192.

110 See, for example, this collection of essays: Carlos Serrano (ed.), *Nations en quête de passé: La péninsule ibérique XIXe–XXe siécles* (Paris, 2000). It includes twelve essays about Spain (including Galicia, Catalonia, and the Basque region), and only one about Portugal.

111 Xosé Manoel Núñez Seixas and António Costa Pinto, "Portugal and Spain," in Roger Eatwell (ed.), *European Political Cultures? Conflict or Convergence?* (London and New York, 1997), pp. 172–192.

112 Mar-Molinero and Smith (eds.), *Nationalism and the Nation in the Iberian Peninsula*.

113 Richard Herr and John H. R. Polt (eds.), *Iberian Identity: Essays on the Nature of Identity in Portugal and Spain* (Berkeley, 1989).

114 Hipólito de la Torre Gómez (ed.), *Portugal y España contemporâneos* (Madrid, 2000).

115 Hipólito de la Torre Gómez and António José Telo (eds.), *La mirada del otro: Percepctiones luso-españolas desde la historia* (Mérida, 2001).

116 Hipólito de la Torre Gómez and António José Telo, *Portugal e Espanha nos sistemas internacionais contemporâneos* (Lisbon, 2000).

117   Sérgio Campos Matos and David Mota Álvarez, "Portuguese and Spanish Historiography: Distance and Proximity," in Stefan Berger and Chris Lorenz (eds.), *The Contested Nation: Ethnicity, Class, Religion and Gender in National Histories* (London, 2008), pp. 339–365; Núñez Seixas, "The Iberian Peninsula: Real and Imagined Overlaps."

118   Hedwig Herold-Schmidt, "Die Feste der iberischen Diktaturen: Portugal und Spanien in den 1940er Jahren," in Michael Maurer (ed.), *Festkulturen im Vergleich: Inszenierungen des Religiösen und Politischen* (Cologne, Weimar, and Vienna, 2010), pp. 291–319.

119   On the two scholars and on the context of the debate, see Baumeister, "Diesseits von Afrika?," p. 23–29.

120   On the debate see: José Luis Gómez-Martínez, *Américo Castro y el origen de los españoles: Historia de una polémica* (Madrid, 1975), pp. 34–59.

121   Américo Castro, *The Structure of Spanish History*, trans. by Edmund L. King (Princeton, 1954), p. 96.

122   English translation: Claudio Sánchez-Albornoz, *Spain, a Historical Enigma*, trans. by Colette Joly Dees and David Sven Reher (Madrid, 1975).

123   Sánchez-Albornoz, *España, un enigma histórico*, vol. 1, p. 199.

124   Claudio Sánchez-Albornoz, "España y el islam," in ibid., *De la invasión islamica al estado continental: entre la creación y el ensayo* (Seville, 1974), pp. 15–40: here, p. 36. First publication: *Revista de Occidente* 24, no. 57 (1929).

125   Vones, *Geschichte der Iberischen Halbinsel im Mittelalter 711–1480*, p. 21.

126   For example in claims like "Castro darkened our past more than anyone had ever done." Sánchez-Albornoz, *España, un enigma histórico*, vol. 2, p. 68.

127   Eloy Martín Corrales, "El 'moro', decano de los enemigos exteriores de España: Una larga enemistad (VIII–XXI)," in Xosé Manoel Núñez Seixas and Francisco Sevillano (eds.), *Los enemigos de España: Imagen del otro, conflictos bélicos y disputas nacionales, siglos XVI–XX* (Madrid, 2010), pp. 165–182.

128   Eloy Martín Corrales, *La imagen del magrebí en España: Una perspectiva histórica siglos XVI–XX* (Barcelona, 2002).

129   David Parra Monserrat, "A Bridge between 'East' and 'West'? The View of the Muslim Past in 19th and 20th Century Spain," in Haug-Moritz and Pelizaeus (eds.), *Repräsentationen der islamischen Welt im Europa der Frühen Neuzeit*, pp. 269–277; ibid., "La Narrativa del Africanismo Franquista: Génesis y Prácticas Socio-Educativas," Ph.D. thesis, Universidad de Valencia, 2012; Rafael Valls Montés, "La imagen del islam en los actuales manuales escolares españoles de historia," in Luigi Cajani (ed.), *Conociendo al otro: El islam y Europa en sus manuales de historia* (Madrid, 2008), pp. 73–122. For a discussion of pictures of Islam in history textbooks, see Michael Wobring, "The Picturing of Islam in European History Textbooks (1970–2010)," in *Jahrbuch der Internationalen Gesellschaft für Geschichtsdidaktik/Yearbook of the International Society of History Didactics* 10 (2014), pp. 229–252.

130   Bernabé López García, "Arabismo y Orientalismo en España: Radiografía y diagnóstico de un gremio escaso y apartadizo," in *Awraq*, supplement to vol. 11 (1990), pp. 35–69; ibid., "La cruz y la espada," in ibid., "*Marruecos y España: Una historia contra toda lógica* (Seville, 2007), pp. 139–162; Eduardo Manzano Moreno, "La creación de un esencialismo: la historia de al-

Andalus en la visión del arabismo español," in Gonzalo Fernández Parrilla and Manuel C. Feria García (eds.), *Orientalismo, exotismo y traducción* (Cuenca, 2000), pp. 23–37; James Monroe, *Islam and the Arabs in Spanish Scholarship: Sixteenth Century to the Present* (Leiden, 1970).

131 Sebastian Balfour, *Deadly Embrace: Morocco and the Road to the Spanish Civil War* (Oxford, 2002), especially pp. 184–202; Josep Lluís Mateo Dieste, *El "moro" entre los primitivos: El caso del Protectorado español en Marruecos* (Barcelona, 2003); Martin-Márquez, *Disorientations*; Alfonso Iglesias Amorín, "La memoria de las guerras de Marruecos en España 1859–1936," Ph.D. thesis, Universidade de Santiago de Compostela, 2014.

132 Eloy Martín Corrales, "Entre el 'moro' violador y el 'moro' seductor: la imagen de los marroquíes en la guerra civil según las fuerzas republicanas," in Ángeles Ramírez (ed.), *Antropología y antropólogos en Marruecos: Homenaje a David M. Hart* (Barcelona, 2002), pp. 221–236; Madariaga, "Imagen del moro en la memoria colectiva del pueblo español y retorno del moro en la Guerra Civil de 1936"; ibid., *Los moros que trajo Franco: La intervención de tropas coloniales en la Guerra Civil* (Barcelona, 2002); Francisco Sánchez Ruano, *Islam y Guerra Civil española: moros con Franco y con la república* (Barcelona, 2004); José Antonio González Alcantud (ed.), *Marroquíes en la Guerra Civil española: Campos equívocos* (Barcelona, 2003).

133 Aurora Rivière Gómez, *Orientalismo y nacionalismo español: Estudios árabes y hebreos en la universidad de Madrid 1843–1868* (Madrid, 2000).

134 Margarita Díaz-Andreu, "Islamic Archaeology and the Origin of the Spanish Nation," in ibid. and Timothy Champion (eds.), *Nationalism and Archaeology in Europe* (London, 1996), pp. 68–89.

135 Carolyn P. Boyd, "The Second Battle of Covadonga: The Politics of Commemoration in Modern Spain," in *History and Memory* 1, no. 2 (2002), pp. 37–64; ibid., "Covadonga y el regionalismo asturiano," in *Ayer* 64, no. 4 (2006), pp. 149–178.

136 Xosé Manoel Núñes Seixas, *¡Fuera el Invasor! Nacionalismos y movilización bélica durante la Guerra Civil española* (Madrid, 2006), especially pp. 124–45 and pp. 261–270.

137 José Antonio González Alcantud, *Lo moro: Las lógicas de la derrota y la formación del estereotipo islámico* (Barcelona, 2002).

138 Christiane Stallaert, *Etnogénesis y etnicidad: Una aproximación histórico-antropológica al casticismo* (Barcelona, 1998).

139 Demetrio E. Brisset Martín, *Representaciones rituales hispanicas de conquista* (Madrid, 1988); ibid., "Fiestas hispanas de moros y cristianos: Historia y significados," in *Gazeta de Antropología* 17 (2001), http://www.ugr.es/~pwlac/G17_03DemetrioE_Brisset_Martin.html (accessed 13 Apr. 2008); Albert-Llorca and González Alcantud (eds.), *Moros y cristianos*.

140 Anna Menny and Britta Voß (eds.), *Die Drei Kulturen und spanische Identitäten: Geschichts- und literaturwissenschaftliche Beiträge zu einem Paradigma der iberischen Moderne* (Gütersloh, 2011); on the "three cultures" in Spanish literature Sevilla, *Die "Drei Kulturen" und die spanische Identität*; especially on Judaism in this context Anna Lena Menny, *Spanien und Sepharad: Über den offiziellen Umgang mit dem Judentum im Franquismus und in der Demokratie* (Göttingen, 2013).

141 Eduardo Lourenço, *Portugal como destino: Dramaturgia cultural portuguesa* (São Paulo, 1999), pp. 92–94.

142 Eduardo Lourenço, "O imaginário português e o Islão," unpublished manuscript of a lecture delievered at the closing ceremony of the celebration of the thirtieth anniversary of the foundation of the Muslim Community at the central mosque of Lisbon, 21 Nov 1998, as quoted in AbdoolKarim Vakil, "Questões inacabadas: Colonialismo, Islão e Portugalidade," in Margarida Calafate Ribeiro and Ana Paula Ferreira (eds.), *Fantasmas e fantasias imperiais no imaginário português contemporâneo* (Porto, 2003), pp. 255–294: here, p. 292.

143 João Medina, *Portuguesismo(s) acerca da identidade nacional* (Lisbon, 2006).

144 Not only the Muslim community but also the non-confessional Academia de Altos Estudos Ibero-Árabes protested this omission. See João Lopes Marques, "'Mouros forros' esquecidos," in *Público*, 10 Dec. 1996, p. 9, and on the context, Nina Clara Tiesler, "Muçulmanos na margem: a nova presença islámica em Portugal," in *Sociologia: Problemas e práticas* 34 (2000), pp. 117–144, especially p. 132.

145 AbdoolKarim Vakil, "Questões inacabadas"; ibid., "The Crusader Heritage: Portugal and Islam from Colonial to Postcolonial Identities," in Robert Shannan Peckham (ed.), *Rethinking Heritage: Cultures and Politics in Europe* (London, 2003), pp. 29–44. On Mozambique see Lorenzo Macagno, *Outros Muçulmanos: Islão e narrativas coloniais* (Lisbon, 2006); Mário Artur Machaqueiro, "The Islamic Policy of Portuguese Colonial Mozambique, 1960–1973," in *The Historical Journal* 55, no. 4 (2012), pp. 1097–1116. For an overview, see Mário Artur Machaqueiro, "Islão transnacional e os fantasmas do colonialismo português," in *Relações Internacionais: Revista do Instituto Portguês de Relações Internacionais da Universidad Nova de Lisboa*, June 2011, no. 30, pp. 71–82; on the former president of the Islamic Community in Lisbon, ibid., "Estratégias, rivalidades e conflictos de poder identitário: Valy Mamede e a disputa pelo controlo das comunidades muçulmanas," http://run.unl.pt/bitstream/10362/2727/1/Valy%20Mamede%20e%20a%2 0disputa%20pelas%20comunidades%20isl%C3%A2micas.pdf (accessed 26 Jun. 2011).

146 Maria Cardeira da Silva, "O sentido dos árabes no nosso sentido: Dos estudos sobre árabes e sobre muçulmanos em Portugal," in *Análise social* 39, no. 173 (2005), pp. 781–806; Eva Maria von Kemnitz, "International Contacts of the Portuguese Arabists (XVIIIth and XIXth centuries)," in Barbara Michalak-Pikulska and Andrzej Pikulski (eds.), *Authority, Privacy and Public Order in Islam: Proceedings of the 22nd Congress of L'Union Européenne des Arabisants et Islamisants* (Leuven and Paris and Dudley, 2006), pp. 369–386, ibid., *Portugal e o Magrebe (séculos XVIII/XIX): Pragmatismo, inovação e conhecimento nas relações diplomáticas* (Lisbon, 2010), pp. 323–510.

147 See Eva Maria von Kemnitz, "Muslims as Seen by the Portuguese Press 1974–1999," in Wasif Shadid and Pieter S. van Koningsveld (eds.), *Religious Freedom and the Neutrality of the State: The Position of Islam in the European Union* (Leuven, 2002), pp. 7–26; Nina Clara Tiesler, "Novidades no terreno: muçulmanos na Europa e o caso português," in *Análise social* 39, no. 173

(2005), pp. 827–849; ibid., "Muçulmanos na margem"; Luis Bernardo, "The accommodation of Islam in Portugal and the Republic of Ireland: A Comparative Case Study," Master's thesis, Universidade Nova de Lisboa, 2009,
http://www.academia.edu/195450/The_accommodation_of_Islam_in_Por
tugal_and_the_Republic_of_Ireland_A_comparative_case_study
(accessed 8 Feb. 2015).

1 Islam as a Historical Enemy: The Middle Ages as Portrayed in the Historiography

1   Alexandre Herculano, *O Monge de Cistér ou a Epocha de João I*, ed. by David Lopes (Lisbon, n. d.), p. 6.

2   The political factions within Spain in the second half of the nineteenth century were internally heterogeneous. This makes it difficult to classify them. "Conservative" cannot automatically be understood as a synonym for members of the Partido (Liberal-)Conservador founded by Cánovas del Castillo, but also refers to opposition groups like Integrists or Carlists. On these groups along the conservative spectrum in Spain, see Maria Victoria López-Cordón Cortezo, "La mentalidad conservadora durante la Restauración," in José Luis Garcia Delgado (ed.), *La España de la Restauración: Politica, Economia, Legislación y Cultura* (Madrid, 1985), pp. 71–109: here, pp. 71–72.

3   Juan de Mariana, *Historia General de España,* vol. 1 (Madrid, 1855), p. 194 and p. 200. First edition 1592.

4   Delgado, "Europa und der Islam in der Frühen Neuzeit," p. 60.

5   Eduardo Manzano Moreno, "La construcción histórica del pasado nacional," in Juan Sisinio Pérez Garzón (ed.), *La gestión de la memória: la historia de España al servicio del poder* (Barcelona, 2000), pp. 33–62.

6   Julio Caro Baroja, *Razas, Pueblos y Linajes* (Madrid, 1957), p. 147. For an overview, see also: Stallaert, *Etnogénesis y etnicidad.*

7   The question of whether "we perhaps are these Muslims," which was present in this critical phase for the nation, motivated the Spanish historians in their search for relevant answers. Manzano Moreno, "La creación de un esencialismo," pp. 52–53.

8   On the conceptual history: Ríos Saloma, "La Reconquista: una invención historiográfica,"pp. 413–429: here, p. 423.

9   Ríos Saloma, "De la Restauración a la Reconquista," pp. 413–414.

10 For example, in the work of Modesto Lafuente, which led to the term's wider acceptance. Compare the comprehensive analysis of the Lafuente's texts in Ríos Saloma, "De la Restauración a la Reconquista,"pp. 403–413.

11 Ríos Saloma, "La Reconquista: una invención historiográfica,"pp. 421–427

12 Ríos Saloma, "De la Restauración a la Reconquista," p. 405.

13 On religion in this concept, see Bronisch, *Reconquista und Heiliger Krieg,* pp. 3–7.

14 For a time, the battle was thought to have taken place in 718, but it actually may have been several years later. Compare Boyd, "The Second Battle of Covadonga," p. 59, note 1.

15 For a general analysis of the expulsion of the *moriscos* in the historiography:

Miguel Ángel de Bunes Ibarra, *Los moriscos en el pensamiento histórico: Historiografía de un grupo marginado* (Madrid, 1983).

16   Mariano Esteban de Vega, "Castilla y España en la Historia general de Modesto Lafuente," in Antonio Morales Moya and Mariano Esteban de Vega (ed.), *¿Alma de España? Castilla en las interpretaciones del pasado español* (Madrid, 2005), pp. 87–140: here, p. 87–88.

17   On Lafuente, see the introduction of Juan Sisinio Pérez Garzón in Modesto Lafuente y Zamalloa, *Historia general de España desde los tiempos más remotos hasta nuestros días: Discurso preliminar*, ed. by Juan-Sisinio Pérez Garzón (Pamplona, 2002), p. LIV.

18   Modesto Lafuente y Zamalloa, *Historia general de España desde los tiempos más remotos hasta nuestros dias,* vol. 2, (Madrid, 1850ff.), p. 464–465.

19   Lafuente y Zamalloa, *Historia general de España: Discurso preliminar*, p. 36.

20   Lafuente y Zamalloa, *Historia general de España*, vol. 3, p. 250.

21   Ibid., p. 257.

22   Esteban de Vega, "Castilla y España," p. 121.

23   Lafuente y Zamalloa, *Historia general de España: Discurso preliminar*, p. 7071.

24   Lafuente y Zamalloa, *Historia general de España*, vol. 15, p. 394.

25   See the chapter on Menendez y Pelayo below.

26   Stanley G. Payne, *El catolicismo español* (Barcelona, 1984), p. 150.

27   Antonio Santoveña Setién, *Marcelino Menéndez Pelayo: revisión crítico-biográfica de un pensador católico* (Santander, 1994), p. 195.

28   Ibid., p. 192.

29   Ibid., p. 27.

30   English translation: Marcelino Menéndez y Pelayo, *A History of the Spanish Heterodox*, trans. by Eladia Gomez-Posthill (London, 2009).

31   Compare Álvarez Junco, *Mater dolorosa*, p. 457.

32   Marcelino Menéndez y Pelayo, *Historia de los Heterodoxos Españoles*, vol. 2 (Madrid, 1956), pp. 1192–1193. First edition 1880–1882.

33   Rehrmann, *Das schwierige Erbe von Sefarad*, pp. 276–299.

34   Menéndez y Pelayo, *Historia de los Heterodoxos Españoles*, vol. 1, p. 348.

35   Menéndez Pelayo refers here to the so-called *rebelión de las Germanías* (in Catalan: *revolta de les Germanies*, an insurgency of the local artisan guilds against the nobility. The rebellion had a strong anti-Muslim tendency, the so-called Agermanados (Catalan: Agermanats) attacked the Muslim population and forced them to convert or face death.

36   Menéndez y Pelayo, *Historia de los Heterodoxos Españoles*, vol. 2, p. 279.

37   Ibid., p. 282.

38   Ibid., p. 279.

39   On Merry y Colón, see Carolyn P. Boyd, *Historia Patria: Politics, History, and National Identity in Spain, 1875–1975* (Princeton, 1997), pp. 108–111; López-Cordón Cortezo, "La mentalidad conservadora durante la Restauración," pp. 85–91.

40   Manuel Merry y Colón and Antonio Merry y Villalba, *Compendio de la historia de España* (Seville, 1889), p. 42.

41   Boyd, *Historia Patria*, p. 109.

42   Merry y Colón and Merry y Villalba, *Compendio de la historia de España*, p. 42.

43　On the discussion concerning the actual location, see the commentary by José Eduardo López Pereira in his edition: *Continuatio Isidoriana Hispana: Crónica mozárabe de 754: Estudio, edición crítica y traducción José Eduardo López Pereira*, León 2009, pp. 55–59.

44　Merry's model was either the edition by Teófilo Escobar from 1870 or by Henrique Flórez in volume 8 of the España Sagrada. Both were accredited to "Isidoro Pacense," Isidore of Beja. *Continuatio Isidoriana Hispana*, p. 170.

45　Merry y Colón and Merry y Villalba, *Compendio de la historia de España*, p. 43.

46　Ibid., p. 45.

47　English translation: Rafael Altamira, *A History of Spanish Civilization*, trans. by P. Volkov (London, 1930).

48　Rafael Altamira, *Historia de España y de la civilizacion española*, vol. 1 (Barcelona, 2001), pp. 159. First edition 1900.

49　Compare Rafael Altamira, *Histoire d'Espagne* (Paris, 1931), p. 90.

50　Rafael Altamira, *Los elementos de la civilización y del carácter españoles* (Buenos Aires, 1950), p. 278.

51　Boyd, *Historia Patria*, p. 143.

52　See, for example: Ángel Ganivet and Miguel de Unamuno, *El porvenir de España* (Madrid, 2005). First edition 1898; Miguel de Unamuno, "Sobre la europeización," in ibid., *Obras completas*, ed. by Ricardo Senabre, vol. 8: *Ensayos* (Madrid, 2007), pp. 999–1016; José Ortega y Gasset, *España invertebrada* (Madrid, 1922); Ramiro de Maeztu, *Defensa de la Hispanidad* (Madrid, 1946). First edition 1943.

53　Ramón Menéndez Pidal, "España, eslabón entre cristiandad e islam," in ibid., *Islam y cristianidad: España entre las dos culturas*, ed. by Álvaro Galmés de Fuentes, vol. 1 (Malaga, 2001), pp. 33–36. First published in *Philologisch-Philosophische Studien: Festschrift für Eduard Wechssler* (Jena and Leipzig 1929), pp. 111–114.

54　Ibid., p. 34.

55　Ibid., p. 35.

56　See also an expanded form from 1952: Ramón Menéndez Pidal, "España como eslabón entre el cristianismo y el islam," in ibid., *Islam y cristianidad*, vol. 1, pp. 37–75. (Conferencia inaugural del Instituto Egipcio de Estudios Islámicos en Madrid, el 19 de febrero de 1952, published in the *Revista del Instituto Egipcio de Estudios Islámicos* (1953), pp. 1–20). See also Monroe, *Islam and the Arabs*, pp. 251–256.

57　Claudio Sánchez-Albornoz, "España y el islam," in ibid., *De la invasión islamica al estado continental: entre la creación y el ensayo* (Seville, 1974), pp. 15–40. First published in *Revista de Occidente* 24, no. 57 (1929).

58　In the preface to his *España – un enigma historico*, publishsed in 1977, Sánchez-Albornoz points to the earlier essay "España y el islam" as a synthesis of his thoughts on this topic. Sánchez-Albornoz, *España, un enigma histórico*, vol. 1, p. III.

59　Sánchez-Albornoz, "España y el islam," p. 36.

60　Ibid., p. 32.

61　Ibid., p. 38–39.

62　Alvarez Junco, *Mater dolorosa*, pp. 404, 426, 431

63　See also Boyd, *Historia Patria*, p. 285.

64   See chapter 2.

65   To distinguish themselves from the rest of Spain, Catalan and Galician nationalists used the argument that there had been a relatively small or even nonexistent Muslim population there during the Middle Ages. A systematic examination of this aspect of the historiography is lacking. On Catalonia and the contacts with the Islamic world from the Middle Ages to the early modern era, compare the following collection: Josep Giralt (ed.), *El Islám y Cataluña* (Barcelona and Granada, 1998).

66   Carlos Collado Seidel, *Die Basken: Ein historisches Porträt* (Munich, 2010), pp. 54–56.

67   On the ethnic aspect of Arana's nationalism see Stallaert, *Etnogénesis y etnicidad*, p. 76; Collado Seidel, *Die Basken*, pp. 196–197.

68   Javier Corcuera Atienza, *La patria de los vascos: Orígenes, ideología y organización del nacionalismo vasco 1876–1903* (Madrid, 2001), p. 42.

69   The term, which originated in Bilbao, refers to "the one who comes from beyond." Compare Antonio Elorza, *Un pueblo escogido: Génesis, definición y desarrollo del nacionalismo vasco* (Barcelona, 2001), p. 183.

70   Corcuera Atienza, *La patria de los vascos*, p. 426; Stallaert, *Etnogénesis y etnicidad*, p. 81.

71   Sabino Arana Goiri, "¿Somos Españoles?," in ibid., *Obras escogidas: antologia política* (San Sebastián, 1978), pp. 152–157: here, p. 155.

72   Sabino Arana Goiri, "Nuestros moros," in ibid., *Obras escogidas*, pp. 183–184: here, p. 183.

73   Ibid.

74   Corcuera Atienza, *La patria de los vascos*, p. 430.

75   Estanislao de Labayru y Goicoechea, *Historia General del señorío de Bizcaya* (Bilbao, 1967), pp. 269–272. First edition 1895.

76   Bernardo Estornés Lasa, *Historia del pais basko* (Zarauz, 1933), p. 26 and p. 73.

77   Gregorio de Balparda, *Historica crítica de Vizcaya y de sus fueros*, vol. 1 (Madrid, 1924), p. 157–158.

78   See chapter 3.

79   Maria Rosa de Madariaga, "Le nationalisme basque et le nationalisme catalan face au problème colonial au Maroc," in *Pluriel débat* 13 (1978), pp. 31–54: here, p. 37.

80   Ibid., p. 47–48.

81   See Albert Garcia Balanà, "Patria, plebe y política en la España isabelina: la guerra de África en Cataluña 1859–1860," in Eloy Martín Corrales (ed.), *Marruecos y el colonialismo español (1859–1912): De la Guerra de África a la penetración pacífica* (Barcelona, 2002), pp. 13–77.

82   Eloy Martín Corrales, "El catalanismo y el andalucismo ante la aventura colonial en Marruecos," in *Actas del Tercer Congreso de Historia Catalano-Andaluza: Cataluña y Andalucía, 1898–1939* (Barcelona, 2003), pp. 155–191: here, pp. 163–165; ibid.," El nacionalismo catalán y la expansión colonial española en Marruecos: de la guerra de África a la entrada en vigor del Protectorado (1860–1912)," in ibid. (ed.), *Marruecos y el colonialismo español*, pp. 167–215.

83   Especially Alexandre Herculano, see: Sérgio Campos Matos, *Historiografia*

e Memória Nacional no Portugal do Séc. XIX 1846–1898 (Lisbon, 1998), pp. 319–320.

84 Compare the research which views Herculano's work as a epochal and analytical caesura: *A historiografia portuguesa anterior a Herculano: Actas do coloquio* (Lisbon, 1977); *A historiografia portuguesa de Herculano a 1950: Actas do colóquio* (Lisbon, 1978).

85 Alexandre Herculano, *Historia de Portugal: Desde o começo da monarquia até o fim do reinado de Afonso III*, vol. 1 (Lisbon, 1980), p. 42. First edition 1846–1851.

86 Ibid., p. 81–82.

87 Fernando Catroga, "Alexandre Herculano e o Historicismo Romantico," in ibid., Luís Reis Torgal, and José Maria Amado Mendes, *História da História em Portugal séculos XIX–XX*. 2 vols., 2nd ed. (n. p., 1998), pp. 44–98: here, p. 82; Matos, *Historiografia e Memória Nacional*, p. 315.

88 Alfons VII of León recognized Portugal as a kingdom and Afonso Henriques as king in 1143; in 1179 Pope Alexander III followed suit.

89 Herculano, *Historia de Portugal*, vol. 1., p. 83.

90 Vítor Neto, *O Estado, a Igreja e a sociedade em Portugal 1831–1911* (Lisbon, 1998), p. 327.

91 Vasco Pulido Valente, *Uma Educação Burguesa: Notas sobre a Ideologia do Ensino no Século XIX* (Lisbon, 1974), p. 18.

92 For the medieval development of this legend, see: Luís Filipe Lindley Cintra, *Sobre a formação e evolução da lenda de Ourique* (Lisbon, 1957); Monica Blöcker-Walter, *Alfons I. von Portugal: Studien zu Geschichte und Sage des Begründers der portugiesischen Unabhängigkeit* (Zurich, 1966); Luis Carmelo, *O milagre de Ourique ou um mito nacional de sobrevivência*, http://www.bocc.ubi.pt/pag/carmelo-luis-Ourique.pdf (acccessed 19 Jan. 2009).

93 Matos, *Historiografia e Memória Nacional*, p. 316.

94 Herculano, *Historia de Portugal*, vol. 1, p. 436.

95 Ana Isabel Carvalhão Buescu, *O Milagre de Ourique e a Historia de Portugal de Alexandre Herculaneo: Uma polémica oitocentista* (Lisbon, 1987). On the debate, see ibid., pp. 18–32.

96 Herculano, *Historia de Portugal*, vol. 3, p. 227.

97 António Dias Farinha, "A civilização árabe na obra de Herculano," in *Alexandre Herculano à luz do nosso tempo*, ed. by the Academia Portuguesa da História (Lisbon, 1977), pp. 323–340: here, p. 338.

98 David Lopes, Portugal's first academic Arabist, later extended Herculano's explanations about Islam and Muslims. See chapter 2.

99 Fernando Catroga, "História e Ciências Sociais em Oliveira Martins," in ibid., Torgal and Mendes, *História da História em Portugal*, vol. 1, pp. 136–185: here, p. 163.

100 Joaquim Pedro Oliveira Martins, *História de Portugal* (Lisbon, 1988), p. 78. First edition 1879.

101 Matos, *Historiografia e Memória Nacional*, p. 334.

102 English translation: Joaquim Pedro Oliveira Martins, A History of Iberian Civilization, trans. by Aubrey FitzGerald Bell (London, 1930).

103 Joaquim Pedro Oliveira Martins, "Os povos peninsulares e a civilização

moderna," in ibid., *Política e história*, vol. 1 (Lisbon, 1957), pp. 217–246: here, p. 221.

104 Ibid., p. 221–222.

105 Joaquim Pedro Oliveira Martins, *História da civilização ibérica* (Lisbon, 1984), p. 108–109.

106 Ibid., p.118.

107 See Núñez Seixas, *History of Civilization*.

108 Braga assumed a broader "Mozarab" term, which included "not only the Christian population [under Muslim rule], but also those Berber and Moorish colonies brought from Africa." Teófilo Braga, *A Pátria Portuguesa: o Território e a Raça* (Porto, 1894), p. 293.

109 Ibid., pp. 280–281.

110 Ibid., p. 285.

111 Teófilo Braga, *História da litteratura portugueza* (Porto, 1870), p. 50.

112 Ibid., p. 64.

113 Braga, A Pátria Portuguesa, p. 290.

114 Joaquim Pedro Oliveira Martins, *A teoria do mosarabismo de Teófilo Braga* (Coimbra, 1953), p. 44. (Separata of *Biblos*, vol. 28.). The criticism was published posthumously.

115 José de Sousa Amado, *Historia da Egreja Catholica em Portugal, no Brasil e nas possessões portuguezas*, vol. 2: *Desde Flavio Recaredo até ao Conde D. Henrique* (Lisbon, 1871), p. V.

116 Sérgio Campos Matos, "A historiografia religiosa contemporânea: uma perspectiva," in ibid., *Consciência histórica e nacionalismo, Portugal, séc XIX e XX* (Lisbon, 2008), pp. 85–94: here, p. 89.

117 Amado, *Historia da Egreja Catholica em Portugal*, vol. 2, p. VII.

118 Matos, "A historiografia religiosa contemporânea," p. 91.

119 Fortunato de Almeida, *História de Portugal* (Lisbon, 2003), p. 67. First edition 1922–1928.

120 Joaquim Reis Alves Lopes, *A Villa de Vallongo* (Porto, 1904), p. 97.

121 Ibid., p. 97, note 2.

122 Matos and Mota Álvarez, "Portuguese and Spanish Historiography," p. 366.

123 The conception of a "Spanish Islam" was one possible solution to this interpretative dilemma: see chapter 2.

124 See chapter 3.

125 Compare thoroughly Matos, "Iberismo e identidade nacional;" ibid., "Conceitos de iberismo em Portugal;" ibid., "Was Iberism a Nationalism?"

126 Matos and Mota Álvarez, "Portuguese and Spanish Historiography," p. 366.

127 This was the name of the painting by Acácio Lino which the Assembleia da República, the Portuguese parliament, commissioned in 1922. It was also used as the frontispiece in the so-called História "de Barcelos": Damião Peres (ed.), *História de Portugal*, vol. 1 (Barcelos, 1928).

128 Admittedly, the foundation of a second important monastery, Alcobaça, was related to the Moors' conquest of Santarém and Lisbon. Its foundation was unlikely the result of a purely religious motivation, though according to legend Afonso Henriques vowed to erect a monastery if he should emerge as victor. Instead the strategic need to defend the newly conquered territories probably played a role. Compare Alberto Gusmão, *A real abadia de Alcobaça: Estudio Histórico-Arquelógico* (Lisbon, 1948), pp. 24–26.

129 This emerging "national Catholicism" extended into Franco's reign, during which Menéndez y Pelayo was considered one of the most important Spanish intellectuals. On this term, see, among others: Alfonso Botti, *Cielo y dinero: El nacionalcatolicismo en España 1881–1975* (Madrid, 2008), pp. 23–25.

130 See also chapter 4 on textbooks.

2 Islam as an Object of Research: Integration of the Islamic Cultural Heritage

1 António Maria de Oliveira Parreira, *Os luso-arabes: Scenas da vida mussulmana no nosso pais*, vol. 2 (Lisbon, 1898), p. 229.

2 Said, *Orientalism*, p. 3.

3 See for example the discussions in Osterhammel, "Edward Said und die 'Orientalismus'-Debatte." Also, Schulze, "Orientalism," and Hauser, "Orientalismus."

4 Manuela Marín, "Arabistas en España: Un asunto de familia," in *Al-Qantara* 13, no. 2 (1992), pp. 379–393: here, p. 381; ibid., "Orientalismo en España: Estudios árabes y acción colonial en Marruecos (1894–1943)," in *Hispania* 69, no. 231 (2009), pp. 117–146: here, p. 118.

5 López García, "Arabismo y Orientalismo en España," p. 35.

6 Ibid., pp. 40–50.

7 See Marín, "Orientalismo en España," pp. 122–123 and p. 146.

8 See chapter 3.

9 Victor Morales Lezcano, "El norte de África, estrella del orientalismo español," in *Awraq*, supplement to vol. 11 (1990), pp. 17–34: here, pp. 29–34; ibid., "Orientalismo marroquista vs. Africanismo español (1859–1860 en adelante)," in José Antonio González Alcantud (ed.), *El orientalismo desde el Sur* (Barcelona, 2006), pp. 217–228; Miguel Ángel de Bunes Ibarra, "El orientalismo español de la edad moderna, la fijación de los mitos descriptivos," in González Alcantud (ed.), *El orientalismo desde el Sur*, pp. 37–53: here, p. 52.

10 Manzano Moreno, "La creación de un esencialismo," pp. 24–25.

11 Ibid., p. 27.

12 Monroe, *Islam and the Arabs*, p. 13 and p. 32.

13 Rivière Gómez, *Orientalismo y nacionalismo español*, pp. 57–58.

14 Monroe, *Islam and the Arabs*, pp. 23–26.

15 Ibid., pp. 49–83.

16 English translation: José Antonio Conde, *History of the Dominion of the Arabs in Spain*, trans. by Mrs. Jonathan Foster (London, 1854–1855).

17 José Antonio Conde, *Historia de la dominación de los árabes en España, sacado de varios manuscritos y memorias arabigas* (Paris, 1840), p. VII. First edition 1820–1821.

18 Ibid., p. V.

19 For example, Conde's periodization of the Muslim era is still used by modern researchers. Monroe, *Islam and the Arabs*, p. 52.

20 This privilege was set down in the Ley Moyano from 1857 in article 129. See also, Christophe Charle, "Grundlagen," in Walter Rüegg (ed.), *Geschichte*

der Universität in Europa, vol. 3: *Vom 19. Jahrhundert zum Zweiten Weltkrieg 1800–1945* (Munich, 2004), pp. 43–82: here, pp. 46–47.

21   Rivière Gómez, *Orientalismo y nacionalismo español,* p. 61–62; Díaz-Andreu, "Islamic Archaeology," p. 72.

22   See chapters 2 (below), 3, and 4.

23   Real Orden from 5 Oct. 1843, quoted in Rivière Gómez, *Orientalismo y nacionalismo español,* p. 61.

24   Ibid., p. 132.

25   Miguel Asín Palacios and Emilio García Gómez, "Nota Preliminar," in *Al-Andalus* 1, no. 1 (1933), pp. 1–5: here, p. 3.

26   Rivière Gómez, *Orientalismo y nacionalismo español,* pp. 71–81.

27   The text in quotation marks is taken from James Monroe, *Islam and the Arabs,* p. 86.

28   For a bibliography of Simonet, see Bernabé López García, "Origen, Gestión y Divulgación de la Historia de los Mozárabes de Francisco Javier Simonet (con una bibliografía del Simonet publicista)," in *Awraq* 22 (2001–2005), pp. 183–211.

29   Francisco Javier Simonet, *Discurso leido ante el claustro de la Universidad Central por D. Francisco Javier Simonet en el solemne acto de recibir la investidura de Doctor en Filosofia y Letras* (Granada, 1867), p. 55.

30   The text in quotation marks is taken from James Monroe, *Islam and the Arabs,* p. 88.

31   López García, "Origen, Gestión y Divulgación de la Historia de los Mozárabes," p. 190.

32   Francisco Javier Simonet, *Historia de los mozarabes de España* (Madrid, 1897; reprint, Valladolid, 2005), p. VII.

33   José Antonio González Alcantud relates this anecdote in: "El cronotopo de todos los vientos," in ibid. and Antonio Malpica Cuello (eds.), *Pensar la Alhambra* (Barcelona and Granada, 2001), pp. 7–20: here, pp. 11–12.

34   Rivière Gómez, *Orientalismo y nacionalismo español,* p. 87.

35   Quoted in ibid., p. 81.

36   Manzano Moreno, "La creación de un esencialismo," p. 27.

37   Rivière Gómez, *Orientalismo y nacionalismo español,* p. 81.

38   Ibid., p. 82.

39   Marín, "Arabistas en España," pp. 386–387.

40   Monroe, *Islam and the Arabs,* pp. 153–154.

41   Julián Ribera y Tarragó, "El arabista español," in ibid., *Disertaciones y opúsculos 1887–1927,* vol. 1 (Madrid, 1928), pp. 457–488: here, p. 468.

42   *Discursos leídos ante la Real Academia de la Historia en la recepción pública de don Francisco Codera y Zaidín el día 20 de abril de 1879* (Madrid, 1879), pp. 87–88, quoted in López García, "Arabismo y Orientalismo en España," p. 43.

43   Ibid., p. 44.

44   On the Centro de Estudios Históricos see José María López Sánchez, "Im Dienste der Wissenschaft: Der Centro de estudios históricos und die Begründung eines liberalen Nationalbewußtseins in Spanien," in *Berichte zur Wissenschaftsgeschichte* 29, no. 2 (2006), pp. 121–136, on Arabic studies, p. 127.

45   Ibid., p. 127; López García, "Arabismo y Orientalismo en España," pp. 47–48.

46   Manzano Moreno, "La creación de un esencialismo," p. 31.

47   See chapter 3.

48   Marín, "Arabistas en España," p. 387, note 31.

49   López García, "Arabismo y Orientalismo en España," p. 55.

50   See chapter 3.

51   López García, "Arabismo y Orientalismo en España," p. 56.

52   Miguel Asín Palacios, "Por qué lucharon a nuestro lado los musulmanes marroquíes?," in *Revista de la Universidad de Madrid* 1 (1940), pp. 143–167: here, p. 147.

53   Manzano Moreno, "La creación de un esencialismo," p. 34. See also Abdelamjid Benjelloum, "Las causas de la participación de marroquíes en la Guerra Civil española," in José Antonio González Alcantud (ed.), *Marroquíes en la Guerra Civil española: Campos equívocos* (Barcelona, 2003), pp. 42–57.

54   Asín Palacios, "Por qué lucharon . . . ," p. 144.

55   Ibid., p. 152.

56   See chapter 3.

57   Asín Palacios, "Por qué lucharon . . . ," p. 160.

58   Ibid., p. 157. This is a direct contrast to the Portuguese Arabist David Lopes, who highlighted the fact that this context had been forgotten, and called this, only half in jest, "sacrilegious." David Lopes, *Portugal contra os mouros* (Lisbon, n. d.), pp. 37–38.

59   For the connection between nationalism, archaeology, and Islam, see Díaz-Andreu, "Islamic Archaeology." For an overview on Europe, see ibid., *A World History of Nineteenth-Century Archaeology: Nationalism, Colonialism and the Past* (Oxford, 2007).

60   Isabel Ordieres Díez, *La formación de la conciencia patrimonial: Legislación e instituciones en la historia de la restauración arquitectónica en España* (Madrid, 1998), p. 14.

61   Alfonso Muñoz Cosme, *La conservación del patrimonio arquitectonico español* (Madrid, 1989), p. 22.

62   Margarita Díaz-Andreu, "The Past in the Present. The Search for Roots in Cultural Nationalism: The Spanish Case," in Justo G. Beramendi, Ramón Maiz, and Xosé M. Núñez Seixas (eds.), *Nationalism in Europe: Past and Present*, vol. 1 (Santiago de Compostela, 1994), pp. 199–218: here, p. 205.

63   Aurora Rivière Gómez, "Arqueólogos y arqueología en el processo de construcción del Estado-nacional español (1834–1868)," in Gloria Mora and Margarita Díaz-Andreu (eds.), *La cristalización del pasado: Génesis y desarrollo del marco institucional de la arqueología en España* (Málaga, 1997), pp. 133–139: here, p. 136.

64   Muñoz Cosme, *La conservación del patrimonio arquitectonico español*, p. 22.

65   Javier Blas, "Monumentos arquitectónicos de España, la representación científica de la Arquitectura," in *Anticuaria y arqueología: Imágenes de la España Antigua 1757–1877* (Madrid, 1997), pp. 51–60: here, p. 52.

66   Ibid., p. 54.

67   Juan Facundo Riaño, *Palacio árabe de la Alhambra* (Madrid, 1856), p. 1.

68   Díaz-Andreu, "Islamic Archaeology," p. 74.

69   This concern is evident, for example, in the petition of the Real Academia de Bellas Artes de San Fernando, which called for this official recognition of the Islamic palatial complex Madinat al-Zahra near Córdoba for precisely this reason: "Informe sobre declaración de Monumento nacional de los restos de la ciudad y palacio de Medina-Az-Zahara, situado en el lugar conocido por Córdoba la Vieja," in *Boletin de la Real Academia de Bellas Artes de San Fernando* V, no. 17 (1885), pp. 33–34.

70   See the article under "Monumento Nacional" in Margarita Díaz-Andreu and Gloria Mora and Jordi Cortadella (eds.), *Diccionario Histórico de la Arqueología en España, siglos XV–XX* (Madrid, 2009), pp. 444–445.

71   See the digitalized documents at the Real Academia de la Historia: http://www.cervantesvirtual.com/FichaObra.html?portal=124&Ref=30567 2 (Alhambra), http://www.cervantesvirtual.com/servlet/SirveObras/ rahis/01305064225029173190802/p0000001.htm (Cristo de la Luz) (8 July 2010). On the Mosque of Córdoba, see Francine Giese, "Die Grosse Moschee von Córdoba zwischen Christianisierung und Re-Islamisierung," in *Bauforschung online*, Aug. 2007, www. bauforschungonline.ch (8 July 2010).

72   José Amador de los Ríos y Serrano, *Primeros Monumentos del arte mahometano en Toledo: Mezquitas llamadas del Santo Cristo de la Luz y de las Tornería* (Madrid, 1877), p. 10.

73   Rodrigo Amador de los Ríos y Fernández-Villalta, *La Ermita del Santo Cristo de la Luz en Toled: Estudio arqueológico motivado por los últimos descubrimientos de febrero de 1899* (Madrid, 1899), p. 41.

74   José Amador de los Ríos y Serrano, *Toledo Pintoresca* (Madrid, 1845; reprint, Valladolid, 2006), p. 216.

75   Díaz-Andreu, "Islamic Archaeology," p. 73.

76   Zur Baugeschichte u.a. Hottinger, *Die Mauren*, pp. 321–328.

77   José Oliver Hurtado and Manuel Oliver Hurtado, *Granada y sus monumentos árabes* (Malaga, 1875), p. VIII; Isabel Ordieres Díez, *Historia de la restauración monumental en España, 1835–1936* (Madrid, 1995), p. 160.

78   Hottinger, *Die Mauren*, p. 321.

79   José Manuel Rodríguez Domingo, "La Alhambra arqueológica (1847–1907): Origen y evolución de un modelo anticuario," in Mora and Díaz-Andreu (eds.), *La cristalización del pasado*, pp. 341–350: here, p. 343.

80   On the enthusiasm of foreigners for Andalusia and its interplay with remnants of the Black Legend, see Baumeister, "Diesseits von Afrika?," pp. 38–41.

81   Tonia Raquejo, *El palacio encantado: La Alhambra en el arte británico* (Madrid, 1989), p. 16. On the Romantic interest in the Alhambra, see Cristina Viñes Millet, *La Alhambra que fascinó a los románticos* (Granada, 2007).

82   Rodríguez Domingo, "La Alhambra arqueológica," p. 343.

83   See Stefan Koppelkamm, *Der imaginäre Orient: Exotische Bauten des achtzehnten und neunzehnten Jahrhunderts in Europa* (Berlin, 1987), especially pp. 61–76.

84   This meant that he was especially responsible for the stucco decorations in the building. See also Francine Giese, "Sein und Schein in der spanisch-islamischen Architektur. Die Arkaturen der Capilla de Villaviciosa und des

Patio de los Leones," in *Miradas: Elektronische Zeitschrift für Iberische und Ibero-amerikanische Kunstgeschichte* 1 (2014), pp. 3–14: here, p. 10.

85 Nieves Panadero Peropadre, "Recuerdos de la Alhambra: Rafael Contreras y el Gabinete Árabe del Palacio Real de Aranjuez," in *Reales Sitios: Revista del Patrimonio Nacional* 31, no. 122 (1994), pp. 33–40.

86 On the Contreras family, see Rodríguez Domingo, "La Alhambra arqueológica," pp. 344–347; Luis Seco de Lucena Escalada, *La Alhambra – cómo fué y cómo es* (Granada, 1935), pp. 367–368.

87 On the biographies, see the articles "Gómez-Moreno Gónzalez" and "Gómez-Moreno Martínez" in Díaz-Andreu and Mora and Cortadella (eds.), *Diccionario Histórico de la Arqueología en España*, pp. 304–307 and "Seco de Lucena Escalada" and "Seco de Lucena Paredes, " ibid., pp. 605–606.

88 Díaz-Andreu, "Islamic Archaeology,"pp. 76–80.

89 Rafael Contreras, *Estudio descriptivo de los monumentos arabes de Granada, Sevilla y Cordoba* (Saragossa, 1993), p. 12 and p. 15. First edition 1878.

90 Manuel Gómez-Moreno González, *Guía de Granada*, vol. 1 (Granada, 1892; reprint, Granada, 1994), p. 6.

91 Ibid., p. 12.

92 Contreras, *Estudio descriptivo*, p. 15.

93 Ibid., p. 197.

94 Gómez-Moreno González, *Guía de Granada*, vol. 1, p. 5.

95 Sören Brinkmann, "Spanien. Für Freiheit, Gott und König," in Flacke (ed.), *Mythen der Nationen*, pp. 476–501: here, p. 489; Carlos Reyero, *Imagen histórica de España, 1850–1900* (Madrid, 1987), p. 253.

96 Compare the media campaign for its preservation described in Seco de Lucena Escalada, *La Alhambra*, pp. 370–380.

97 Ibid., pp. 361–362.

98 See chapter 1.

99 Stallaert, *Etnogénesis y etnicidad*, p. 91.

100 On the lay forerunners of Arab studies and the linguistic contact between Portugal and the Arabic-speaking world, see José Pedro Machado, "Os estudos arábicos em Portugal," in ibid., *Ensaios arabico-portugueses* (Lisbon, 1997), pp. 109–144: here, pp. 111–125.

101 Kemnitz, *Portugal e o Magrebe*, p. 498.

102 Machado, "Os estudos arábicos em Portugal," p. 126; Adel Sidarus, "Os estudos árabes de Portugal (1772–1962)," in ibid. (ed.), *Islão e Arabismo na Península Ibérica: Actas do XI Congresso da Uniao Europeia de Arabistas e Islamólogos* (Évora, 1986), pp. 37–54: here, pp. 38–39.

103 On Cenáculo and Abrantes, see Kemnitz, *Portugal e o Magrebe*, pp. 133–151 and pp. 333–342.

104 See Machado, "Os estudos arábicos em Portugal," pp. 128–129.

105 Kemnitz, "International contacts," p. 374.

106 On de Sousa's activities as professor, see Kemnitz, *Portugal e o Magrebe*, pp. 343–358; on his works, pp. 441–453; and on his literary remains, pp. 474–479.

107 Kemnitz, "International Contacts," p. 383.

108 Sidarus, "Os estudos árabes de Portugal," p. 44.

109   On Colaço and his works, see Kemnitz, *Portugal e o Magrebe*, pp. 313–314, p. 508, pp. 535–536.

110   Ibid., pp. 506–507.

111   *Diário do Governo*, 24 Mar. 1911 and 22 Apr. 1911. See also Marques, *Geschichte Portugals*, p. 547.

112   On Herculano, see chapter 1.

113   Sidarus, "Os estudos árabes de Portugal," p. 46.

114   António Dias Farinha, "Os estudos árabes na historiografia posterior a Herculano," in *A historiografia portuguesa de Herculano a 1950: Actas do colóquio* (Lisbon, 1978), pp. 293–304: here, p. 294.

115   David Lopes, *Os Arabes nas obras de Alexandre Herculano* (Lisbon, 1911).

116   On the conceptual history of "mouro," see the introduction.

117   Lopes, *Portugal contra os mouros*, pp. 3–4. The book was published in 1917 according to Sidarus, "Os estudos árabes de Portugal,"p. 48.

118   In 1954 and 1981 the series added a volume on the history of the republic and the Estado Novo, so that it currently includes ten volumes.

119   On Ameal, see chapter 4. Luís Reis Torgal, "A história em tempo de 'ditadura,'" in Fernando Catroga, Luís Reis Torgal, and José Maria Amado Mendes, *História da História em Portugal séculos XIX–XX*, vol. 1, 2nd ed. (n. p., 1998), pp. 272–310: here, p. 305.

120   This is Torgal's judgment in ibid, p. 306.

121   Ibid., pp. 304–305.

122   David Lopes, "O domínio árabe," in Damião Peres (ed.), *História de Portugal*, vol. 1 (Barcelos, 1928), pp. 389–431: here, pp. 405–406.

123   Lopes, *Portugal contra os mouros*, p. 37.

124   Lopes, "O domínio árabe," p. 422.

125   Sidarus, "Os estudos árabes de Portugal," p. 51.

126   In the late 1960s, Machado translated the Quran into Portuguese—a project which was by no means uncontroversial. See chapter 3 and Machaqueiro, *Estratégias, rivalidades e conflictos de poder identitário*, pp. 48–49.

127   See the list of Arabist works after Lopes's death in 1942 up to 1958 in José Domingo Garcia Domingues, "Os estudos arábicos em Portugal depois de David Lopes," in *Revista de Portugal* 24 (1959), pp. 23–35: here, pp. 32–35.

128   José Domingo Garcia Domingues, "Presença Árabe no Algarve," in Sidarus, *Islão e Arabismo na Península Ibérica*, pp. 113–130: here, p. 131.

129   Domingues, "Os estudos arábicos em Portugal," pp. 29–30. On Dias, see chapter 3.

130   See chapter 3.

131   See chapter 4.

132   Carlos Fabião, "Archeology and Nationalism: The Portuguese Case," in Díaz-Andreu and Champion (eds.), *Nationalism and Archaeology in Europe*, pp. 90–107: here, p. 104.

133   António Borges Coelho, *Portugal na Espanha Árabe*, vol. 1 (Lisbon, 1989), pp. 24–25. First edition 1971.

134   Santiago Macias, "Entrevista a António Borges Coelho," in ibid. (ed.), *Historiador em discurso directo: António Borges Coelho* (Mértola, 2003), pp. 15–42: here, p. 38.

135   Regina Anacleto, "A Reinvenção do Mourisco na Arte Portuguesa de

Oitocentos," in Rosa Maria Perez (ed.), *Memórias Árabo-Islâmicas em Portugal* (Lisbon, 1998), pp. 129–142.

136 Jorge Custódio, "Salvaguarda do Património – Antecedentes Históricos," in *Dar futuro ao passado*, ed. by the Instituto Português do Património Arquitectónico e Arqueológico (Lisbon, 1993), pp. 33–71: here, p. 43.

137 Ibid., pp. 51–54.

138 The list was published in the *Diário do Governo*, 23 June 1910.

139 Carlos Fabião, "Para a história da arqueologia em Portugal," in *Penélope 2* (1989), pp. 10–26: here, p. 12.

140 Eva Maria von Kemnitz, "O panorama das colecções museológicas islâmicas de Portugal," in Santiago Macias and Cláudio Torres (eds.), *Portugal Islâmico: Os Últimos Sinais do Mediterrâneo* (Lisbon, 1998), pp. 307–319: here, p. 308–309. This includes an overview of the inventory of medieval Muslim objects in Portuguese museums.

141 Sebastião Philippes Martins Estácio da Veiga, *Memórias das antiguidades de Mértola* (Lisbon, 1880; reprint, Lisbon, 1983), p. 137.

142 See Fabião, "Archeology and Nationalism," p. 102.

143 Vakil, "The Crusader Heritage," p. 29.

144 See chapter 4.

145 Damião Peres, *A gloriosa história dos mais belos castelos de Portugal* (Barcelos, 1969).

146 José Domingo Garcia Domingues, *Silves – Guia turístico* (Silves, 1958); Pedro P. Mascarenhas Júdice, *A Sé e o Castelo de Silves* (Gaia, 1934).

147 *Igreja Matriz de Mértola. Boletim da Direcção-Geral dos Edifícios e Monumentos Nacionais* (1953), quoted in Joaquim Manuel Ferreira Boiça and Maria de Fátima Rombouts de Barros, "A Igreja Matriz de Mértola," in Santiago Macias et al. (eds.), *Mesquita Igreja de Mértola* (Mértola, 2011), pp. 33–87: here, p. 85.

148 For a comprehensive description of the renovations, see ibid., pp. 83–86.

149 Kemnitz, "O panorama das colecções museológicas islâmicas," p. 312.

150 Cláudio Torres, "A arqueologia medieval e a historiografia portuguesa nos últimos anos," in *Actas do IV Congresso Internacional "A cerâmica medieval no mediterrâneo ocidental" organizado pelo Campo Arqueológico de Mértola, na Fundação Calouste Gulbenkian em Lisboa, 16–22 Novembro 1987* (Mértola, 1991), pp. 15–17: here, p. 15.

151 On the project and its beginnings, see Cláudio Torres, "Dignidad regional y desarollo," in *Jornadas andaluzas sobre: La función de la cultura en el desarollo local* (Córdoba, 1993), pp. 15–20, ibid., "A arqueologia, o território e o desenvolvimento local," in *Efeitos sociais do património à escala local* (Mértola, 2001), pp. 21–26.

152 Cláudio Torres and Santiago Macias, *O legado islâmico em Portugal* (Lisbon, 1998); ibid. (eds.), *Portugal Islâmico*; Cláudio Torres, "O Islão no ocidente ibérico," in Guilhermina Mota (ed.), *Minorias étnicas y religiosas em Portugal: História e actualidade: Actas do Curso de Inverno 2002* (Coimbra, 2003), pp. 91–100; Cláudio Torres and Santiago Macias, *Museum von Mértola – islamische Kunst* (Mértola, 2003).

153 See, for example, Valdemar Coutinho, *Centros históricos de influência Islâmica* (Portimão, 2001); Helena Catarino, *O Algarve Islâmico: Roteiro por*

Faro, Loulé, Silves e Tavira (Faro, 2002); Maria da Conceição Amaral, *Caminhos do Gharb: Estratégia de interpretação do património islâmico no Algarve: o caso de Faro e de Silves* (n. p., 2002).

154 See for example Alberto Alves, *Portugal: Ecos de um Pasado Árabe* (Lisbon, 1989); ibid., *Portugal e o Islão: Escritos do crescente* (Lisbon, 1989); ibid., *O meu coração é árabe*, 3rd ed. (Lisbon, 1989).

155 Silva, "O sentido dos árabes no nosso sentido,"pp. 796–797.

156 Ibid., p. 801.

157 Vakil, "The Crusader Heritage," p. 41.

158 Rómulo de Carvalho, *Historia do ensino de Portugal*, 2nd ed. (Lisbon, 1996), p. 728.

3 Islam as a "Colonial Other": The Iberian Dictatorships

1   Ramón J. Sender, *Imán* (Barcelona, 2003), p. 200. The text cited here is an original translation. There is an extant English translation by James Cleugh; it was published under two separate titles: Ramón J. Sender, *Earmarked for Hell*, trans. by James Cleugh (London, 1934); and Ramón J. Sender, trans. by James Cleugh, *Pro Patria* (Boston, 1935).

2   C. Richard Pennell, *Morocco since 1830: A History* (London, 2001), pp. 64–66.

3   See for example Garcia Balanà, "Patria, plebe y política;" Collado Seidel, *Die Basken*, p. 89.

4   See López García, " La cruz y la espada," p. 140.

5   Jürgen Osterhammel, *Kolonialismus: Geschichte, Formen, Folgen*, 6th ed. (Munich, 2009), pp. 115–116.

6   *La Correspondencia*, 10 Oct. 1859, quoted in Marie Claude Lécuyer and Carlos Serrano, *La Guerre d'Afrique et ses répercussions en Espagne 1859–1904* (Paris, 1976), p. 40.

7   Emilio Castelar, "La política española," in *La Discusión*, 20 Oct. 1859, quoted in López García, "La cruz y la espada," pp. 140–141.

8   See chapter 2.

9   Álvarez Junco, "El nacionalismo español como mito movilizador," p. 47.

10   Ibid., p. 48.

11   Pennell, *Morocco since 1830*, p. 105.

12   Letter to Juan Valera, 2 Nov. 1893, in Marcelino Menéndez y Pelayo, *Antología General: Recopilación orgánica de su doctrina*, ed. by Ángel Herrera Oria (Madrid, 1956), p. 223.

13   Luís Royo Villanova, "La Guerra del Moro," in *Blanco y negro*, 21 Oct.1893, pp. 2–3: here, p. 2.

14   Eneas, "La Guerra de África," in *El Correo Español*, 3 Oct. 1893, p. 1.

15   *El Liberal*, 5 Oct. 1893, p. 1.

16   Adolfo Llanos Alcaraz, *La campaña de Melilla de 1893–1894* (Madrid, 1894; reprint, Málaga and Melilla, 1994), p. 318.

17   Ibid., pp. 318–319.

18   Martín Corrales, *La imagen del magrebí*, pp. 99–124.

19   Llanos Alcaraz, *La campaña de Melilla de 1893–1894*, p. 320.

20   Madariaga, "Imagen del moro," p. 582.

21   Ibid., p. 589.

22   Balfour, *Deadly embrace*, p. 197.

23   Fernando de Urquijo, *La campaña del Rif en 1909: Juicios de un testigo* (Madrid, 1910), pp. 17–19. The English translation is taken from Sebastian Balfour, *Deadly Embrace*, p. 198.

24   See the interpretation in Martin-Márquez, *Disorientations*, pp. 130–131, and pp. 136–137.

25   Quoted in Martín Corrales, *La imagen del magrebí*, p. 115. There are also examples of photos.

26   See Martin-Márquez, *Disorientations*, pp. 186–187.

27   Francisco Franco Bahamonde, *Diario de una bandera* (Seville, 1939), p. 133. Translated into English as *Francisco Franco's Moroccan War Diary 1920–1922: Critical Analysis and Translation, Biographical and Topographical notes*, trans. by Paul Sothern (Bromley, 2007). I (PH) would like to thank Jesus Albert for directing me to this passage in Franco's diary.

28   Illustrations reprinted in Martín Corrales, *La imagen del magrebí*, pp. 118–120.

29   Balfour, *Deadly embrace*, p. 201.

30   Ibid.

31   See chapter 1.

32   Madariaga, "Imagen del moro," p. 582.

33   See Rudibert Kunz and Rolf-Dieter Müller, *Giftgas gegen Abd el Krim: Deutschland, Spanien und der Gaskrieg in Spanisch-Marokko 1922–1927* (Freiburg im Breisgau, 1990).

34   Quoted in Angel Flores Morales (ed.), *Africa a traves del pensamiento español: De Isabel la Católica a Franco* (Madrid, 1949), p. 28.

35   On the testament and its reception see Bernabé López García, "Expansión colonial e ideología religiosa. Un caso típico: El Africanismo y Arabismo de la segunda mitad del siglo XIX español," in ibid. (ed.), *Marruecos y España*, pp. 49–60: here, p. 51–54.

36   Bernabé López García, "España en África: Génesis y significación de la decana de la prensa africanista del siglo XX," in ibid. (ed.), *Marruecos y España*, pp. 61–84: here, p. 69.

37   Geoffrey Jensen, "Toward the 'Moral Conquest' of Morocco: Hispano-Arabic Education in Early Twentieth Century North Africa," in *European History Quarterly* 31, no. 2 (2001), pp. 205–229: here, p. 213. See also ibid., "The Peculiarities of 'Spanish Morocco': Imperial Ideology and Economic Development," in *Mediterranean Historical Review* 20, no. 1 (2005), pp. 81–102: here, pp. 84–85.

38   Gustau Nerín and Alfred Bosch, *El imperio que nunca existió: La aventura colonial discutida en Hendaya* (Barcelona, 2001), pp. 31–32.

39   For an overview, see Victoriano Darias de las Heras, "El africanismo español y la labor comunicadora del Instituto de Estudios Africanos," in *Revista Latina de Comunicación Social* 46 (2002), http://www.ull.es/ publicaciones/latina/2002/latina46enero/4601darias.htm (accessed 4 Jun. 2010).

40   Paul Preston, *Franco: A Biography* (London, 1993), p. 43.

41   José Asensio Torrado, "Los ejercitos coloniales," in *Africa: Revista de tropas coloniales* no. 4 (1931), pp. 83–90 and no. 5 (1931), pp. 95–100.

42   Emilio L. López, "Tetuán por dentro: Una casa mora es así," in *Africa: Revista de tropas coloniales*, no. 4 (1931), pp. 81–82: here, p. 82.

43   Ignácio Bauer y Landauer, "El factor musulmán en la cultura española," in *Africa: Revista de tropas coloniales*, no. 12 (1933), pp. 234–236: here, p. 234.
44   Ibid.
45   Ibid., pp. 234–235.
46   Luis Oleaga, "Aproximación cristiano-musulmana," in *Africa: Revista de tropas coloniales*, no. 6 (1930), pp. 263–264: here, p. 263.
47   Ibid., p. 264.
48   On violence in the Spanish Civil War see Martin Baumeister and Stefanie Schüler-Springorum (eds.), *"If you tolerate this . . ."*: *The Spanish Civil War in the Age of Total War* (Frankfurt am Main, 2008).
49   On the European dimension of the Civil War see Carlos Collado Seidel, *Der Spanische Bürgerkrieg: Geschichte eines europäischen Konflikts* (Munich, 2006), p. 91.
50   For the statistics, see José María Garate Cordoba, "Las tropas de Africa en la Guerra Civil española," in *Revista de historia militar* 70 (1991), pp. 9–62: here, pp. 58–61; see also the further statistics included in Francisco Sánchez Ruano, *Islam y Guerra Civil española: Moros con Franco y con la republica* (Barcelona, 2004), pp. 249–252.
51   Balfour, *Deadly embrace*, p. 278.
52   There is extensive analysis of the motivations for their participation in Benjelloum, "Las causas."
53   Members of the *Tercio de Estranjeros*, the Spanish counterpart of the French Foreign Legion.
54   Members of the *Fuerzas Regulares Indígenas*, the Moroccans under the rebels' command.
55   Quoted in Guillermo Cabanellas, *Cuatro Generales*, vol. 2: *Lucha por el poder* (Barcelona, 1977), p. 55. A somewhat different version of the remark cited is included in Martín Corrales, "Entre el 'moro' violador y el 'moro' seductor," p. 225.
56   See the interpretation of Martín Corrales, ibid.
57   Michail Koltsov, *Diario de la Guerra de España* (Paris, 1963), p. 96, quoted in Martín Corrales, "Entre el 'moro' violador y el 'moro' seductor," p. 225.
58   Balfour, *Deadly embrace*, p. 292; Madariaga, *Los moros que trajo Franco*, p. 316.
59   *L'Esquella de la Torratxa*, 3 Sept. 1936, reprinted in Martín Corrales, *La imagen del magrebí*, p. 154.
60   *Diario de Barcelona*, 25 Oct. 1936, reprinted in Martín Corrales, *La imagen del magrebí*, p. 155.
61   Quoted in Sánchez Ruano, *Islam y Guerra Civil española*, p. 259.
62   Sánchez Ruano, *Islam y Guerra Civil española*, p. 269. On Sidqi and Ossidhoum, see also Abdelatif Ben Salem, "La participación de los voluntarios árabes en las brigadas internacionales: Una memoria rescatada," in José Antonio González Alcantud (ed.), *Marroquíes en la Guerra Civil española*, pp. 111–129.
63   Sánchez Ruano, *Islam y Guerra Civil española*, p. 256.
64   El Tebib Arrumi, "Nuestros amigos los moros," 30 Nov. 1937, quoted in Núñes Seixas, *¡Fuera el Invasor!*, p. 263.
65   On Franco's anti-Semitism in this period, see also Menny, *Spanien und Sepharad*, pp. 68–69.

66 *El Pensamiento Navarro*, 1 Mar. 1937, quoted in Núñes Seixas, *¡Fuera el Invasor!*, pp. 266–267.

67 José Caballero, *Diario de campaña de un capellán legionario* (Madrid, 1976), p. 269.

68 *La Unión*, 21 Aug. 1936, pp. 8–9, quoted in Ian Gibson, *Queipo de Llano: Sevilla, verano de 1936* (Barcelona, 1986), p. 18.

69 *L'Echo de Paris*, 16 Nov. 1937, quoted in Francisco Franco Bahamonde, *Franco ha dicho: Recopilación de las más importantes declaraciones del caudillo desde la iniciación del alzamiento nacional hasta el 31 de diciembre de 1946* (Madrid, 1946), pp. 8–9.

70 Quoted in Madariaga, *Los moros que trajo Franco*, p. 348.

71 Quoted in ibid., p. 352.

72 Ibid., p. 276.

73 Balfour, *Deadly embrace*, p. 312.

74 Samuel Hoare, *Ambassador on Special Mission* (London, 1946), p. 50.

75 Quoted in Preston, *Franco*, p. 16.

76 See Walther L. Bernecker and Sören Brinkmann, *Kampf der Erinnerungen: Der Spanische Bürgerkrieg in Politk und Gesellschaft 1936–2006* (Nettersheim, 2006), pp. 155–163; Toni Morant i Ariño, "'Der Caudillo wird nur durch seinen eigenen Willen begrenzt.' Der Franco-Mythos in Spanien, 1936–1945," in Benno Ennker and Heidi Hein-Kircher (eds.), *Der Führer im Europa des 20. Jahrhunderts* (Marburg, 2010), pp. 157–180.

77 Juan Priego López, *Escoltas y guardias moras de los jefes de Estado españoles* (Madrid, 1952), pp. 29–34.

78 Luis Beltrán, "African Studies in Spain," in *African Studies Bulletin* 11, no. 3 (1968), pp. 316–325: here, pp. 318–324.

79 Nerín and Bosch, *El imperio que nunca existió*, pp. 264–265.

80 For example, Ángel Doménech Lafuente, *Del Islam* (Madrid, 1950); and, ibid., *Un oficial entre moros* (Larache, 1948).

81 Tomás Borrás, *La España completa* (Madrid, 1950), pp. 11–12.

82 Nerín and Bosch, *El imperio que nunca existió*, pp. 284–285.

83 See María Dolores Algora Weber, *Las relaciones hispano-árabes durante el régimen de Franco: la ruptura del aislamiento internacional, 1946–1950* (Madrid, 1995), here pp. 34–36.

84 Ibid., p. 308.

85 See the main argument in Nerín and Bosch, *El imperio que nunca existió*.

86 See chapter 4.

87 Xavier Casals Meseguer, "Franco 'El Africano'," in *Journal of Spanish Cultural Studies* 7, no. 3 (2006), pp. 207–224: here, p. 219.

88 Marques, *Geschichte Portugals*, p. 455.

89 Ibid., pp. 456–457.

90 Nuno da Silva Gonçalves, "A dimensão missionária do catolicismo português," in *História religiosa de Portugal*, vol. 3: *Religião e Sécularização* (Lisbon, 2002), pp. 353–397: here, p. 356.

91 Marques, *Geschichte Portugals*, p. 626.

92 Malyn Newitt, *Portugal in Africa: The Last Hundred Years* (London, 1981), pp. 184–187.

93 Article two of the *Acto Colonial*, (Lisbon, 1933), p. 35.

94 Gonçalves, "A dimensão missionária," p. 388.

95 *Acto Colonial*, Art. 23.

96 Macagno, *Outros Muçulmanos*, pp. 44–45.

97 Marques, *Geschichte Portugals*, p. 610.

98 See the interpretation of Vakil, "Questões inacabadas," pp. 258–259.

99 António Enes, *Moçambique: Relatório apresentado ao Govêrno*, 3rd ed. (n. p., 1946), p. 212. First edition 1893.

100 Ibid., p. 214.

101 Vakil, "Questões inacabadas," pp. 259–260.

102 "O perigo do Islão em África," in *Boletim Geral do Ultramar* 378 (1956), pp. 104–106, here: p. 104.

103 António da Silva Rego, *O Oriente e o Ocidente: Ensaios* (Lisbon, 1939), p. 47 and p. 51.

104 Eduardo Dias, "Um Problema: o Islamismo e a sua penetração na África Negra," in *Rumo: Revista da cultura portuguesa* 6 (1946), pp. 232–243: here, p. 228. See also the interpretation of Vakil, "Questões inacabadas," pp. 260–261.

105 Dias, "Um Problema," p. 243.

106 Manoel Maria Sarmento Rodrigues, "Os maometanos no futuro da Guiné," in *Boletim Cultural da Guiné Portuguesa* 3, no. 9 (1948), pp. 219–231: here, p. 229.

107 Sebastião Soares de Resende, *Falsos e verdadeiros caminhos da vida* (Lourenço Marques, 1948), p. 51.

108 Dias, "Um Problema," p. 239.

109 António George C. de Sousa Franklin, *A Ameaça Islâmica na Guiné Portuguesa* (Lisbon, 1956), pp. 24–25. See also Joaquim Correia da Costa, "A Ameaça Afro-Asiatica," in *Diario de Lisboa*, 2 Oct. 1956, pp. 12–13.

110 Albano Mendes Pedro, "Islamismo e Catolicismo em Moçambique," in *Volumus: Revista trimestral de formação missionária* 11, no. 4 (1959), pp. 170–212: here, p. 206.

111 Teixera da Mota, *Guiné Portuguesa*, vol. 1 (Lisbon, 1954), p. 256, quoted in Vakil, "Questões inacabadas," p. 272.

112 Lobiano do Rego [Padre Albino da Silva Pereira], *A "Declaração sobre a Liberdade religiosa" no Tempo e Espaço da Nação Portuguesa* (Braga, 1966), p. 79, quoted in Machaqueiro, "Estratégias, rivalidades e conflictos de poder identitário," p. 15.

113 Marques, *Geschichte Portugals*, p. 611.

114 José Júlio Gonçalves, *O Mundo Árabo-Islâmico e o Ultramar Português* (Lisbon, 1958), p. 169 and p. 238.

115 Frederico José Peirone, "A importância do estudo da língua e da cultura árabe para a missionação dos indígenas islamizados de Moçambique," in *Garcia da Orta: Revista da Junta das Missões Geográficas e de Investigações do Ultramar* 6, no. 3 (1956), pp. 371–381: here, p. 380.

116 Wolfgang Reinhard, *Geschichte der europäischen Expansion*, vol. 4: *Dritte Welt Afrika* (Stuttgart, 1990), p. 158.

117 Augusto de Castro, "A Nação inteira!," in *Diario de Noticias*, 18 Oct. 1960, p. 1.

118 Macagno, *Outros Muçulmanos*, p. 52.

119 Suleiman Valy Mamede, *O Islão no espaço português* (Braga, 1970), p. 5.

120 Herculano Lopes de Oliveira, "Aspectos actuais do problema missionário

no Ultramar Português," in *Volumus: Revista trimestral de formação missionária* 8, no. 3/4 (1956), pp. 136–148: here, p. 148.

121 Pedro, "Islamismo e Catolicismo em Moçambique," p. 205.

122 Macagno, *Outros Muçulmanos*, p. 81.

123 Vakil, "Questões inacabadas," p. 272.

124 Francisco José Veloso, "Portugal, os árabes e os muçulmanos," in *Cultura islâmica e cultura árabe: Estudos em honra de David Lopes* (Lisbon, 1969), pp. 89–95, p. 92.

125 This institution had evolved from the earlier *Secretariado de Propaganda Nacional* (Department of National Propaganda) in the Estado Novo.

126 Rogério Seabra Cardoso, "Islamitas Portugueses: Linhas de força de um passado; Realidades de um presente; Bases de um futuro," in *Panorama. Revista portuguesa de arte e turismo* series IV, nrs. 33/34 (March/June 1970), pp. 49–62: here, p. 49.

127 Vakil, "Questões inacabadas," p. 279.

128 Fernando Amaro Monteiro, "Moçambique 1964–1974: As comunidades islâmicas, o Poder e a Guerra," in *Africana* 5 (1989), pp. 81–124: here, p. 84.

129 Cardoso, "Islamitas Portugueses," p. 60.

130 "Inauguração da mesquita," in *Boletim Cultural da Guiné Portuguesa* 21, no. 83 (1966), pp. 376–381: here, pp. 379–380.

131 Ibid., p. 378.

132 Cardoso, "Islamitas Portugueses," p. 60.

133 Monteiro, "Moçambique 1964–1974," p. 85.

134 Reprinted in ibid., pp. 117–119 and also in Fernando Amaro Monteiro, "O Islão, o poder e a Guerra: Moçambique 1964–1974," Ph.D. thesis, Universidade Técnica de Lisboa, 1992, pp. 494–496, quote on p. 495.

135 Suleiman Valy Mamede, "No XIV centenário do Alcorão," in *Cultura islâmica e cultura árabe: Estudos em honra de David Lopes* (Lisbon, 1969), pp. 81–88.

136 Mamede, *O Islão no espaço português*, p. 10.

137 Machaqueiro, "Estrategias, rivalidades e conflictos de poder identitário," p. 7.

138 Macagno, *Outros Muçulmanos*, p. 61–77.

139 The "polygamy" to which Freyre referred was the sexual contact of Brazilian land owners with their slaves.

140 Gilberto Freyre, *Um brasileiro em terras portuguêsas* (Lisbon, 1955), pp. 63–65.

141 Macagno, *Outros Muçulmanos*, p. 77.

142 Valentim Alexandre, "A África no imaginário político português (séculos XIX–XX)," in *Penélope* 15 (1995), pp. 39–52: here, p. 49.

143 See Dix, "As esferas seculares," pp. 16–17.

144 *Nostra aetate*, quoted in http://www.vatican.va/archive/ hist_councils/ ii_vatican_council/documents/vat-ii_decl_19651028_nostra-aetate_en .html (accessed 15 Jan. 2015).

145 Quoted in Machaqueiro, "Islão transnacional e os fantasmas do colonial-ismo português," p. 75.

146 Pedro, "Islamismo e Catolicismo em Moçambique," p. 206.

147 See Machaqueiro, "Estrategias, rivalidades e conflictos de poder identitário."

148 Machaqueiro, "Islão transnacional e os fantasmas do colonialismo português," p. 77.
149 Eurico Dias Nogueira, *Episódios da Minha Missão em África* (Braga, 1995), p. 34.
150 Cardoso, "Islamitas Portugueses," p. 52.
151 See Vakil, "Questões inacabadas," p. 289.
152 Quoted in ibid., p. 287.
153 Marques, *Geschichte Portugals*, p. 646; António Reis, "Revolution und Demokratisierung," in Fernando Rosas (ed.), *Vom Ständestaat zur Demokratie: Portugal im 20. Jahrhundert* (Munich, 1997), pp. 89–106: here, p. 89.
154 The young republic also emphasized the historical relationship with Islam. At a meeting of the Arab League in Rabat in 1974, the second republican president, General Francisco da Gosta Gomes (1914–2001), remarked: "Portugal in its centuries long history received from the Arab civilization a precious legacy of knowledge and experience incorporated and assimilated by its own culture. The blood of its Arab brethren irrigates the veins and soul of the Portuguese people." The text in quotation marks is taken from Kemnitz, "Muslims as seen by the Portuguese press 1974–1999," p. 13.
155 See the documents in Nogueira, *Episódios da Minha Missão em África*, pp. 38–41.
156 See for example a statement of the Portuguese bishops during their general assembly in 1961: "At this hour in which the West seems to have lost its own conscience, . . . [given the] disdain for Christian values and the disregard for their defense, Portugal is aware of its mission to evangelize and civilize." Quoted in Alexandre, "A África no imaginário político português," pp. 49–50.
157 Articles about Islam in magazines produced by the Portuguese missions included many references to French sources, which are similarly comprehensive on these topics, especially the Maghreb. See for example the description of a connection between "paganism" and Islam in Africa in Hubert Deschamps, *Les religions de l'Afrique Noire* (Paris, 1954), pp. 93–96.

4 Islam as a National Lesson: Staging the Past

1 José Saramago, *The History of the Siege of Lisbon*, trans. by Giovanni Pontiero (New York, San Diego, and London, 1996), p. 312.
2 A good Spanish counterpart of the festivals under Salazar in terms of commemorations of the Iberian dictatorships would be the Día de la Raza, the commemoration of the "discovery" of America and the feast of the Virgin of del Pilar in Saragossa, as these occurred in similar periods and under similar governments. However, because the Día de la Raza celebrated the connection of Catholicism and the Nation, there was no Muslim adversary in the foreground, and therefore it provides no possibility to analyze the Moorish "Other." For a comparison of the Dia de la Raza and the commemorations under Salazar, see Herold-Schmidt, "Die Feste der iberischen Diktaturen."
3 See Rafael Valls Montés, *Historiografía escolar española: Siglos XIX–XXI* (Madrid, 2007), pp. 55–65.

4   Named after their author, the liberal politician Claudio Moyano (1809–1890).
5   On the Ley Moyano and its critics see Boyd, *Historia Patria*, pp. 4–9.
6   Valls Montés, *Historiografía escolar española*, p. 106.
7   Boyd, *Historia Patria*, pp. 35–36.
8   The illiteracy rate was highest in the southern rural areas like Murcia, Pais Valenciano, and Andalusia, and it was higher among women than among men. For statistics, see Mercedes Vilanova Ribas and Xavier Moreno Juliá, *Atlas de la evolución del analfabetismo en España de 1887 a 1981* (Madrid, 1992), p. 166 and p. 412.
9   Valls Montés, *Historiografía escolar española*, p. 78.
10 Compare the statistics on the distribution of textbooks in the nineteenth century in Ignacio Peiro, "La difusión del libro de texto: autores y manuales de historia en los institutos del siglo XIX," in *Didáctica de las Ciencias Experimentales y Sociales* 7 (1993), pp. 39–57, and in Valls Montés, *Historiografía escolar española*, pp. 109–110.
11 Valls Montés, *Historiografía escolar española*, p. 56.
12 Alejandro Gómez Ranera, *Compendio de la Historia de España desde su origen hasta el reinado de doña Isabel II y el año 1843*, 3rd ed. (Madrid, 1844); Manuel Ibo Alfaro, *Compendio de la Historia de España* (Madrid, 1895).
13 Peiro, "La difusión del libro de texto," p. 44 and p. 46.
14 Valls Montés, *Historiografía escolar española*, pp. 109–110.
15 According to Orodea y Ibarra, the Arabs displayed "the most contradictory characteristics, a mixture of enthusiasm for plunder and chivalrous generosity." Eduardo Orodea y Ibarra, *Curso de lecciones de Historia de España ó estudio crítico-filosófico de todas las épocas más notables de nuestra historia nacional desde los más remotos tiempos hasta el presente siglo . . .*, 9th ed. (Ávila, 1886), p. 145.
16 Boyd, *Historia Patria*, pp. 88–91.
17 On this relationship, see Pilar Maestro González, "La idea de España en la historiografia escolar del siglo XIX," in Morales Moya and Esteban de Vega (eds.), *¿Alma de España?*, pp. 141–194: here, p. 160.
18 On Merry y Colón and Altamira, see chapter 1.
19 Rafael Ballester, *Curso de Historia de España* (Gerona, 1917), p. 61.
20 On Lafuente, see chapter 1.
21 Maestro González, "La idea de España," p. 177.
22 For example, the Catalan teacher and textbook author Juan Bosch Cusi (1866–1939), whose books were published in multiple editions between the the time of the Second Republic and Franco's reign: "The Arab is lethargic and melancholic, but he has an impressive and inflamed fantasy, at times discouraged by the smallest vexation, at times undertaking the most formidable task with determination and courage." Juan Bosch Cusi, *Historia de España: Grado medio: Libro del alumno* (Gerona, 1930), p. 39.
23 Ballester, *Curso de Historia de España*, p. 72.
24 On Bleye see David Parra Monserrat, "Islam e identidad en la escuela franquista: Imágenes y tópicos a través de los manuales," in *Didáctica de las Ciencias Experimentales y Sociales* 21 (2007), pp. 15–32: here, pp. 22–23.
25 Ramón Lopez Facal, "La Historia enseñada en España," in Taibo (ed.), *Nacionalismo español*, pp. 329–350: here, pp. 337–338.

26   Valls Montés, *Historiografía escolar española*, p. 92.
27   See chapter 3.
28   General José Enrique Varela (1891–1951) was one of those who led the coup in July 1936. In 1945 he was named high commissioner of Morocco.
29   Instituto de España [José María Pemán], *Manual de Historia de España: Segundo grado* (Santander, 1939), p. 80.
30   See also Pemán's justification of the "friendly Moor" with related references to the Middle Ages: José María Pemán, "Los moros amigos," in ibid., *Obras completas*, vol. 5: *Doctrina y Oratoria* (Madrid, 1953), pp. 486–489.
31   Valls Montés, *Historiografía escolar española*, p. 91. Pemán's book appeared under his name and the title *La história de España contada con sencillez* in various editions in the following decades.
32   Agustín Serrano de Haro, *Yo soy español: El libro de primer grado de Historia* (Madrid, 1943), p. 36.
33   Agustín Serrano de Haro, *España es así* (Madrid, 1960), p. 82.
34   Serrano de Haro, *Yo soy español*, pp. 40–42.
35   Ibid., p. 42.
36   In 2007 the publishers RBA and Altaya reissued the *Libro de España* unchanged, i.e. with the coat of arms of Franco's Spain on the title page and without additional introductory material. While Altaya at least noted that it was a reprint of the edition published by Vives in 1958, the status of the RBA edition must be deduced from the ISBN hidden on the last page.
37   *El Libro de España* (Saragossa, 1944), p. 300.
38   See chapter 2.
39   See the analysis of Parra Monserrat, "Islam e identidad," pp. 15–32.
40   Boyd, *Historia Patria*, p. 236–237.
41   On the textbooks after Franco, see Valls Montés, "La imagen del islam."
42   Storm, "Las conmemoraciones de héroes nacionales."
43   Storm, "El tercer centenario del Don Quijote."
44   Boyd, "The Second Battle of Covadonga;" ibid., "Covadonga y el regionalismo asturiano."
45   Patricia Hertel, "Reconquista Reenacted: National Myths in the Spanish Restoration (1898–1918)," in: Franziska Metzger (ed.), *Trans-national Perspectives on Nationalism – Methodological Approaches and Case Studies* (Berlin, forthcoming).
46   The battle was dated to 718 at the time, but may have actually taken place several years later. Boyd, "The Second Battle of Covadonga," p. 59, note 1.
47   The vast literature includes: Ofelia Rey Castelao, *Los mitos del apóstol Santiago* (Vigo, 2006); Klaus Herbers, "Der Apostel Jakobus: Vom spanischen zum europäischen Mythos," in Inge Milfull and Michael Neumann (eds.), *Mythen Europas: Schlüsselfiguren der Imagination: Mittelalter* (Regensburg, 2004), pp. 48–66; Francisco Márquez Villanueva, *Santiago: Trayectoria de un mito* (Barcelona, 2004); Raphaela Averkorn, "Der Jakobus-Mythos: Die Entwicklung eines Mythos vom Mittelalter bis zur Gegenwart," in: Ulrich Müller and Werner Wunderlich (eds.), *Herrscher, Helden, Heilige*, 2nd ed. (St. Gallen, 2001), pp. 252–541.
48   Averkorn, "Der Jakobus-Mythos," p. 531.
49   Márquez Villanueva, *Santiago*, p. 192.

50 Nicolas Ciezar, *Santiago Matamoros: Historia y imagen* (Málaga, 2004), p. 197.

51 María Dolores Rosado Llamas and Manuel Gabriel López Payer, *La Batalla de Las Navas de Tolosa* (Madrid, 2002), pp. 160–161.

52 For an overview, see Francisco Crabiffosse Cuesta, "Evocación y memoria del Santuario de Covadonga," in *Covadonga – iconografía de una devoción: exposición conmemorativa del centenario de la dedicación de la Basílica de Covadonga 1901–2001* (Oviedo, 2001), pp. 95–107.

53 Boyd, "The Second Battle of Covadonga," p. 45.

54 Reyero, *Imagen histórica*, p. 122.

55 Ibid., pp. 124–125.

56 For example in the paintings of Luis de Madrazo, "Don Pelayo en Covadonga" (1856), reproduced in Reyero, *Imagen histórica de España*, p. 68; Francisco de Paula van Halen, "Alzamiento de Pelayo" (1852), reproduced in *Covadonga – iconografía de una devoción*, p. 181; Antonio Roca, "Defensa de Covadonga" (1872), reproduced ibid., p. 183.

57 Rosario Anguita Herrador, *Jacinto Higueras: El artista y su obra* (Jaén, 1995), p. 44.

58 Reproductions of the monument in Rosado Llamas and López Payer, *La Batalla de Las Navas de Tolosa*, pp. 12–14.

59 Nicolás Soria, title page of the bulletin *Covadonga: Boletín de la Junta Diocesana para la Coronación Canónica de la Santísima Virgen en el Duodécimo Centenário*, reproduced in: *Covadonga – iconografía de una devoción*, p. 443.

60 These had been planned starting in 1906 by the Spanish episcopacy, along the examples set in Germany and France, to develop and spread the social ideals of the church.

61 Antolín López Peláez, *La batalla de las Navas de Tolosa y la batalla contra el socialismo: Conferencia del Obispo de Jaca en la Semana Social celebrada para conmemorar el centenario de las Navas* (Saragossa, 1912), p. 11. There are similar images and comparisons related to Covadonga, for example in a sermon of the bishop of Oviedo, Ramón Martínez Vigil: "The Moors of our day don't brandish the scimitar . . . instead, they brandish the book, the pamphlet and the newspaper . . . in order to poison hearts and pervert the consciences of nations, to rip out their faith in Christ and their devotion to Most Holy Mary, and to transform people that believe, pray and work into victims of unparalleled ambition and greed." Ramón Martínez Vigil, "El santuario de Covadonga (9 de septiembre de 1884)," in ibid., *Pastorales del Rmo. P. Martínez Vigil de la Orden de Predicadores, Obispo de Oviedo, conde de Noreña etc.*, vol. 1 (Madrid, 1898), pp. 45–60: here, pp. 48–49. The text quoted here is taken from the translation in Boyd, "The Second Battle of Covadonga," p. 48.

62 The Acción Católica strove to unify nationalist ideals with Catholicism. Pidal y Mon, like his friend Menéndez y Pelayo, became affiliated with the Partido Liberal-Conservador of Cánovas de Castillo, which displeased the integralists. See Álvarez Junco, *Mater dolorosa*, pp. 445–446; Santoveña Setién, *Marcelino Menéndez Pelayo*, pp. 188–189.

63 Alejandro Pidal y Mon, *Discurso sobre la batalla de Las Navas de Tolosa: Leído*

por D. Alejandro Pidal y Mon en la veladas celebrada en el Teatro de Burgos la Noche del Dia 16 de julio 1912 (Madrid, 1912), p. 3.

64   Ibid., p. 15.

65   Fernando Fernández Rosete, *Pelayo y Covadonga* (Arriondas, 1909), p. 46 and p. 69.

66   Acácio Cáceres Prat, *Covadonga: Tradiciones, Historias y Leyendas,* 2nd ed. (Madrid, 1890), pp. 49–50.

67   Boyd, "The Second Battle of Covadonga," pp. 54–55.

68   Fermin Canella y Secades, *De Covadonga: Contribuición al XII centenario* (Madrid, 1918), pp. 226–227.

69   *Séptimo centenario de la batalla de Las Navas de Tolosa y de la adopción del actual escudo de Navarra* (Madrid, 1912), pp. 12–15. This includes an extensive description of the schedule of festivities.

70   Ibid., p. 5.

71   Boyd, "The Second Battle of Covadonga," p. 56.

72   See also the analysis of this process in Storm, "Las conmemoraciones de héroes nacionales," p. 81.

73   Payne, *El catolicismo español,* p. 159.

74   For example Joaquim de Oliveira Martins: "The greatest weakness of the formal instruction in Portugal is that the books are bad and the teachers are worse, and the curriculum . . . would in some cases be brilliant if they were something other than pure bureaucratic suppositions." Quoted in Sérgio Campos Matos, *História, mitologia, imaginário nacional: A História no Curso dos Liceus 1895–1939* (Lisbon, 1990), p. 15.

75   Ibid., pp. 25–26.

76   The numbers are taken from: António Nóvoa, *Le Temps des Professeurs: Analyse socio-historique de la profession enseignante au Portugal (XVIIIe–XXe siècle),* vol. 2 (Lisbon, 1987), p. 569 and p. 575.

77   Ibid., p. 571.

78   On the reforms, see Matos, *História, mitologia, imaginário nacional,* pp. 24–38.

79   See the biographies in ibid., pp. 210–224.

80   Arsenio Augusto Torres de Mascarenhas, *Compendio de História de Portugal: Aprovado pelo governo para uso dos alumnos da 5.a classe dos lyceus,* 2nd ed. (Lisbon, 1901).

81   Arsenio Augusto Torres de Mascarenhas, *História de Portugal: Remodelada e ampliada de harmonia com os princípios de orientação educativa do Estado Novo por João Afonso de Miranda,* 4th ed. (Lisbon, 1944).

82   Mascarenhas, *Compendio de História de Portugal,* p. 33.

83   Ibid.

84   Luís Reis Torgal, "Ensino da história," in Catroga, Torgal and Mendes, *História da História em Portugal,* vol. 2, pp. 84–152: here, pp. 88–89.

85   "Figueiredo, António Cândido de," in António Nóvoa (ed.), *Dicionario de Educadores Portugueses* (Porto, 2003), n. pag.

86   António Cândido de Figueiredo, *Historia de Portugal: Resumida e organisada para uso do povo e das escolas,* 3rd ed. (Lisbon, 1888), p. 30.

87   Matos, *História, mitologia, imaginário nacional,* pp. 135–137.

88   See Vítor Neto, *O Estado, a Igreja e a sociedade em Portugal 1831–1911* (Lisbon, 1998), pp. 266–273.

89 Nóvoa, *Le Temps des Professeurs*, vol. 2, p. 529.

90 Arsenio Augusto Torres de Mascarenhas, *Resumo da História de Portugal: Aprovado pelo Govêrno Provisório da República em portaria de 6 de Dezembro de 1910* (Lisbon, 1910); António Cândido de Figueiredo, *História de Portugal sumariada para uso do povo e das escolas*, 5th ed. (Lisbon, 1913).

91 Sezinado Chagas Franco and Anibal Magno, *Primeiros esboços da História de Portugal: Aprovado pelo governo da republica para as escolas primárias em 1910 e novamente aprovados pela comissão revisora dos livros de ensino em 1913* (Lisbon, 1914), pp. 17–18.

92 See Ernesto Castro Leal, *Nação e nacionalismos: A Cruzada Nacional D. Nuno Álvares Pereira e as origens do Estado Novo 1918–1938* (Lisbon, 1999); ibid., "Nacionalismos portugueses: cultura e política no século XX," in *Revista da Faculdade de Letras de Lisboa* 26 (2002), pp. 29–39.

93 António de Matos Faria Artur, *História de Portugal organizada em lições* (Paris and Lisbon, n. d. [after 1921]), p. 20.

94 José Nunes da Graça and Fortunato Correia Pinto, *Resumo de História Pátria para as escolas d' instrução primária* (Lisbon, 1911), p. 10.

95 The text is reproduced in João Medina, *Historia Contemporanea de Portugal: Das invasões francesas aos nossos dias*, vol. 5 (n. p., 1990), pp. 45–47.

96 Ibid.

97 António Costa Pinto, "Twentieth Century Portugal: An Introduction," in ibid. (ed.), *Contemporary Portugal: Politics, Society and Culture* (New York, 2003), pp. 1–46: here, p. 39.

98 Manuel Braga da Cruz "Der Estado Novo und die katholische Kirche," in Rosas (ed.), *Vom Ständestaat zur Demokratie*, pp. 49–64: here, p. 52.

99 Torgal, "Ensino da história," p. 108.

100 Tomás de Barros, *Sumário de História de Portugal: Com narrativa dos factos principais de cada reinado, recapitulação em questionário e variado exercícios para a 4a classe do Ensino Primário e admissão aos Liceus* (Porto, 1940), p. 174. The castles were first listed by name in the editions after 1945.

101 Antonio Gonçalves Matoso and Antonino Henriques, *Compêndio de História Geral e Pátria*, vol. 1: *Antiguidade e Idade Média: Ensino Técnico Profissional*, 2nd ed. (Lisbon, 1937), p. 184.

102 Ibid., p. 185.

103 See chapter 2.

104 Matoso and Henriques, *Compêndio de História Geral e Pátria*, p. 188.

105 Antonio Gonçalves Matoso, *Compêndio de História de Portugal: Aprovado oficialmente como texto único para o 6.o ano dos liceus*, 3rd ed. (Lisbon, 1940), p. 29.

106 Quoted in Medina, *Historia Contemporanea de Portugal*, vol. 5, p. 47.

107 On illiteracy in the Estado Novo see Maria Filomena Mónica, *Educação e sociedade no Portugal de Salazar* (Porto, 1978), pp. 109–129.

108 Matos, *História, mitologia, imaginário nacional*, p. 173.

109 See the list in David Corkill and José Carlos Pina Almeida, "Commemoration and Propaganda in Salazar's Portugal: The Mundo Português Exposition of 1940," in *Journal of Contemporary History* 44, no. 3 (2009), pp. 381–399: here, p. 383.

110 See chapter 1.

111 António de Oliveira Salazar, "Sempre o mesmo milagre," in ibid., *Discursos*

e notas políticas, vol. 2: *1935–1937* (Coimbra, 1937), pp. 175–179: here, p. 176.

112 António de Oliveira Salazar, "Comemorações centenárias," in, ibid., *Discursos e notas políticas,* vol. 3: *1938–1943* (Coimbra, 1943), pp. 41–58: here, pp. 42–43. This official statement was published in the Portuguese newspapers on 27 Mar. 1938.

113 Corkill and Almeida, "Commemoration and Propaganda in Salazar's Portugal," p. 384. For an overview of Salazar's government, see Filipo Ribero de Meneses, *Salazar: A Political Biography* (New York, 2010).

114 See João, *Memória e Império*; ibid., "Public Memory and Power in Portugal (1880–1960)," in *Portuguese Studies* 18 (2002), pp. 96–120; Margarida Acciaiuoli, *Exposições do Estado Novo 1934–1940* (Lisbon, 1998); especially on architecture, José-Augusto França, "Exposição do Mundo Português," in *Colóquio Artes* 45 (1980), pp. 34–47; Rui Afonso Santos, "Comemorações/Festas oficiais," in Fernando Rosas and José Maria Brandão Brito (eds.), *Dicionário da História do Estado Novo* (Lisbon, 1996), pp. 162–167.

115 See the official guide: *Guia oficial da Exposição do mundo português* (Lisbon, 1940).

116 Today it is one of Lisbon's most recognized landmarks.

117 Júlia Leitão de Barros, "Exposição do Mundo Português," in Rosas and Brito (eds.), *Dicionário da História do Estado Novo,* pp. 325–327: here, p. 326.

118 See the descriptions and photos in: "Exposição do mundo português," in *Revista dos Centenários,* no. 7/8 (1940), pp. 17–35: here, pp. 18–19; Acciaiuoli, *Exposições do Estado Novo 1934–1940,* pp. 136–143.

119 Also, another article which appeared in the *Revista dos Centenários* about Portugal's obtainment of political autonomy briefly outlined the history of the Age of Exploration, but the Muslim Moorish opponent is hardly mentioned: José de Oliveira Boléo, "Como conseguiu Portugal a sua autonomia política? Segunda parte" in *Revista dos Centenários,* no. 12 (1939), pp. 41–44.

120 The Portuguese Nobel Prize winner José Saramago wrote a book, *The History of the Siege of Lisbon,* in which an editor ponders what would have happened if the Crusaders had not aided the Portuguese.

121 On the background of the celebrations, see Ernesto Castro Leal, "Poder, Memória e Glória," in *Revista Portuguesa de História* 36, no. 2 (2002–2003), pp. 313–334: here, pp. 316–322.

122 Luís Reis Torgal, "A história em tempo de 'ditadura'," in Catroga, Torgal, and Mendes, *História da História em Portugal,* vol. 1, pp. 272–310: here, p. 279. João Ameal is a pseudonym for João Francisco de Barbosa Azevedo de Sande Aires de Campos. His history of Portugal is representative of the historiography sympathetic to the regime produced under the Estado Novo.

123 João Ameal, "A Cruz e a Espada," in *Diario da Manhã,* 17 May 1947.

124 *Programa oficial das comemorações do VIII. centenário da tomada de Lisboa* (Lisbon, 1947); Leal, "Poder, Memória e Glória," pp. 326–327.

125 The authorship of this account has been unclear for a long time: some scholars have attributed it to an Anglo-Norman crusader called Osbern. These included a Portuguese scholar whose translation of the text provided a reference for the commemoration in 1947: *Conquista de Lisboa aos Mouros*

(1147): *Narrada pelo Cruzado Osberno, testemunha presencial*, trans. by José Augusto de Oliveira (Lisbon, 1935). Recent scholarship has identified Osbern as the addressee rather than the author and has attributed the text to a Frank or Anglo-Norman priest named Raol. See Harold Livermore, "The 'Conquest of Lisbon' and its author," in *Portuguese Studies* 6 (1990), pp 1–16, here: p. 2 and p. 6. For an English translation, see *De expugnatione Lyxbonensi – The Conquest of Lisbon*, trans. by Charles Wendell David, with a new foreword and bibliography by Jonathan Phillips (New York, 2001).

126 These words were quoted on the title page of the *Diario da Manhã* from 16 May 1947, the complete speech on p. 6.

127 The speech was quoted in the article "Sessão solene nos paços do Concelho," in *Revista municipal de Lisboa* 33, no. 2 (1947), pp. 17–23: here, p. 20.

128 The welcoming addresses were printed in: *Programa oficial das comemorações do VIII centenário da tomada de Lisboa*, n. pag.

129 Gustavo de Matos Sequeira "Biografia de Lisboa," in *Programa oficial das comemorações do VIII centenário da tomada de Lisboa*, n. pag.

130 Luís de Pina, "Regresso a Deus: batalha sem fim: Do Porto cristão à Lisboa mourisca," in *Boletim Cultural da Câmara Municipal do Porto* 10 (1947), pp. 5–26: here, p. 6. The speech was delivered on 26 Oct. 1947 in the Teatro Nacional to conclude the festivities.

131 Ibid., p. 24.

132 José Domingo Garcia Domingues, "Arabes e moiros," in Gustavo de Matos Sequeira (ed.), *Lisboa, oito séculos de história* (Lisbon, 1947), pp. 84–119. On Garcia Domingues see chapter 2.

133 João Ameal, *História de Portugal* (Porto, 1940), p. 99.

134 "O cortejo do mundo português: Uma lição viva de História Pátria," in *Revista dos Centenários* no. 4 (1939), pp. 5–10.

135 Photos are reproduced in the *Revista Municipal de Lisboa* 32 (1947), n. pag.

136 María Isabel João speaks of a "residual concept," which, however, was not fed by any particular animosity towards Muslims or by any conflict with Muslim peoples or states. João, *Memória e Império*, p. 675.

137 This thesis is posited in the studies on nationalism and archealogy by Fabião, "Archeology and nationalism," p. 90.

138 A. Marques Guedes, "Portugal é uma Nação (Part 3)," in *Revista dos Centenários* no. 3 (1940), pp. 6–10: here, p. 9.

139 See chapter 2.

140 Vilanova Ribas and Moreno Juliá, *Atlas de la evolución del analfabetismo*, p. 166; Nóvoa, *Le Temps des Professeurs*, vol. 2, p. 569.

5 Islam as a Folkloristic Invention: Popular Festivals and Regional Identity

1 Benito Pérez Galdós, *Aita Tettauen* (Madrid, 1976), p. 1062. First edition 1905.

2 See Brisset Martín, *Representaciones rituales hispanicas de conquista*. For a comparison between Sicily and Spain, see Puccio-Den: *Les Théâtres de Maures et Chrétiens*. On Sicily d'Agostino, "Moros y cristianos en la cultura tradicional siciliana."

3   On the concept of the festivals, see Marlène Albert-Llorca and José Antonio González Alcantud, "Metáforas y laberintos de la alteridad," in ibid. (eds.), *Moros y cristianos*, pp. 9–21: here, p. 10.

4   Paulo Raposo defines the *auto popular* as a "hybrid of poetic and theatrical representations which emerged from the popular distribution of ancient medieval romances or militant epic songs, in which the original learned tradition mixed with the popular versions, leading to the loss of the original version over the course of time." Paulo Raposo, "O Auto da Floripes: 'Cultura popular', etnógrafos, intelectuais e artistas," in *Etnografia* 2, no. 2 (1998), pp. 189–219 : here, p. 189, note 2.

5   Barbara Alge describes the *mourisca* as a "dramatic, usually ritual, often processional dance of an exotic nature and with partially militaristic elements." Barbara Alge, *Die Performance des* Mouro *in Nordportugal: Eine Studien von Tanzdramen in religiösen Kontexten* (Berlin, 2010), p. 205.

6   See Patricia Hertel, "Moros y cristianos: Inszenierungen des 'Wir' und des 'Anderen' als erfundene Tradition im Spanien des 19. Jahrhunderts," in David Luginbühl et al. (eds.), *Religiöse Grenzziehungen im öffentlichen Raum: Mechanismen und Strategien von Inklusion und Exklusion im 19. und 20. Jahrhundert* (Stuttgart, 2011), pp. 213–229.

7   The rightly criticized term "folklore" is used here in the sense of Jan Harold Brunvand and the subsequent revision of Hermann Bausinger to emphasize the following aspects of the concept of Islam as described in this chapter: the passing down of an oral tradition from one person to another over multiple generations (including the evolution of traditions), a formulaic character both within the performance of a particular locality as well as among several localities, varied versions within this basic formula, and the anonymity or low profile of the author. For the festivals studied here, these criteria can be assessed to varying degrees depending on the chronology. For example, in nineteenth-century Alcoy there was such a transformation that it can no longer be considered an oral tradition, while the formulaic character and the variations within localities suggested by this model are still present. In Neves the oral tradition persisted into the twentieth century. Variations within a particular type can be observed in the evolution in particular localities and regions of the Earth. The term "folklore" serves in this chapter primarily to describe the conditions under which the popular concepts of Islam emerged which are described here and to define these in contrast to those presented in the previous chapters. On the term and the discussion of it, see Hermann Bausinger, "Folklore, Folkloristik"in *Enzyklopädie des Märchens: Handwörterbuch zur historischen und vergleichenden Erzählforschung*, ed. by Kurt Ranke, vol. 4 (Berlin and New York, 1975ff.), column 1397–1403.

8   On Alcoy, see Julio Berenguer Barceló, *Historia de los Moros y Cristianos de Alcoy* (Alcoy, 1974); José Luis Mansanet Ribes, *La Fiesta de Moros y Cristianos de Alcoy y su Historia* (Alcoy, 1991); Rafael Coloma, *Libro de la fiesta de moros y cristianos de Alcoy* (Alcoy, 1962); Adrián Espí Valdés, *De las embajadas y los embajadores de los moros y cristianos de Alcoy* (Alcoy, 1989); ibid., *El Arte en las Fiestas de Moros y Cristianos de Alcoy* (Alcoy, 1976). For an overview, see *Tercer Congreso Nacional de fiestas de moros y cristianos* (Murcia, 2002).

9   These include many historical facts, although it must be considered that they often aimed to provide evidence for the long tradition and the significance of the local festival.

10   See Albert-Llorca and González Alcantud (eds.), *Moros y cristianos*; Brisset Martín, *Representaciones rituales hispanicas de conquista.*

11   Raposo, "O Auto da Floripes"; Alge, *Die Performance des* Mouro *in Nordportugal.*

12   Within Spain, the modern festivals held in the Valencian Community and Andalusia take somewhat different forms. The accoutrements in Valencia are much more luxurious, which led to a preference for the exotic *moros* role. The *moros* in the Andalusian festivals are portrayed as being more chaotic, which makes them attractive to young people. At the same time, the *moros* have less dialogue and are accorded less social prestige than in the Valencian cases. On the differences between Alcoy in the Valencian Community and Válor in Andalusia, see Sina Lucia Kottmann, "Moros y Cristianos in Südspanien: Fiesta zwischen Spiel und Ernst," Master's thesis, Eberhard Karls Universität, Tübingen, 2004.

13   Xaquín Rodríguez Campos, "As festas patronais e a identidade en Galícia," in: *Galicia: Antropoloxía,* vol. 27: *Relixión. Crenzas. Festas* (A Coruña, 1997), pp. 354–375; Xesus Taboada Chivite, "Moros y cristianos en tierras de Laza (Orense)," in ibid., *Ritos y creencias gallegas* (A Coruña, 1980), pp. 59–77. First published in *Revista de dialectología y tradiciones populares* 11, no. 3 (1955).

14   Max Harris "Muhammed and the Virgin: Folk Dramatizations of Battles Between Moors and Christians in Modern Spain," in *The Drama Review* 38, no. 1 (1994), pp. 45–61: here, p. 46; Brisset Martín, "Fiestas hispanas de moros y cristianos."

15   Brisset Martín, *Representaciones rituales hispanicas de conquista,* pp. 403–407.

16   Brisset Martín, "Fiestas hispanas de moros y cristianos," n. pag.

17   See the introduction of Juan A. Grima Cervantes in the book: Ramon de Cala y Lopez and Miguel Flores González-Grano de Oro, *La fiesta de Moros y Cristianos en la Villa de Carboneras precedida de una noticia histórica* (Cuevas, 1918; reprint, Carboneras and Almería, 1993), p. XXIIIf.

18   Harris, "Muhammed and the Virgin,"p. 46.

19   This was the assumption for Alcoy in: Mansanet Ribes, *La Fiesta de Moros y Cristianos de Alcoy,* p. 24. For the year 1688 there are records of a fight to mark the occasion of the feast of the patron, Saint George, on 23 April.

20   Ibid., p. 83.

21   Jesús Millán, "El País Valencià en l'inici de l'Estat centralista del vuit-cents: Una aproximació," in *L'Estat-nació i el conflicte regional: Joan Mañé i Flaquer, un cas paradigmàtic* (Barcelona, 2004), pp. 63–90: here, p. 78.

22   José Fernando Domene Verdú, "Síntesis histórica de las Fiestas de Moros y Cristianos," in *Tercer Congreso Nacional de fiestas de moros y cristianos,* pp. 353–376: here, p. 365.

23   Mansanet Ribes, *La Fiesta de Moros y Cristianos de Alcoy,* p. 43.

24   Karl Marx, "Die Bakunisten an der Arbeit: Denkschrift über den Aufstand in Spanien im Sommer 1873," in: ibid. and Friedrich Engels, *Werke,* vol. 18 (Berlin, 1973), pp. 476–493.

25   See the interpretation of José Fernando Domene Verdú and Antonio Sempere Bernal, *Las fiestas de Moros y Cristianos de Villena* (Alcoy, 1989), p. 206 and p. 209.

26   Such a figure was first commissioned in 1810 and completed by the Valencian artist José Pérez Broquer. See Mansanet Ribes, *La Fiesta de Moros y Cristianos de Alcoy*, p. 191. This was in a period when there were hardly any new depictions of Saint James the Moor Slayer. See Ciezar, *Santiago Matamoros*, pp. 191–210.

27   José Antonio Llobet y Vall-Llosera, *Apuntes históricos acerca de las fiestas que celebra cada año la ciudad de Alcoy a su Patrón San Jorge con referencias a la historia antigua de la misma ciudad en los tiempos de la reconquista sobre los árabes* (Alcoy, 1853; reprint, Alcoy, 1998), pp. 5–8.

28   Ibid., p. 8.

29   Ibid., p. 3.

30   See the introduction of the edition of the *embajadas* in José Fernando Domene Verdú and Maria Mercedes Molina Berenguer (eds.), *Textos de las embajadas de la fiesta de moros y cristianos* (Alicante, 2003), pp. 8–9.

31   On the complex diglossia, especially on the language used in the mass, see: Vicent Pitarch, "La llengua de l'administració eclesiàstica (País Valencià, segles XVII–XVIII)," in *L'espill* 6–7 (1980), pp. 41–76; on the nineteenth century, see Brauli Montoya Abat, *Alacant: La llengua interrompuda* (Valencia, 1996); on the language and nation, see Ferran Archilés and Manuel Martínez, "La construccción de la Nación española durante el siglo XIX: logros y límites de la asimliación en el caso valenciano," in *Ayer* 35 (1999), pp. 171–190: here, pp. 175–179; Millán, "El País Valencià en l'inici de l'Estat centralista del vuit-cents," p. 85–86.

32   Millán, "El País Valencià en l'inici de l'Estat centralista del vuit-cents," p. 86.

33   Even today the *embajadas* are predominately performed in Castilian, not Valencian. After the centralization of language under Franco and the ensuing revitalization of regional languages when democracy was reinstated, there was a failed movement to return to the Valencian texts in Alcoy in 1985. Espí Valdés, *De las embajadas y los embajadores de los moros y cristianos*, pp. 16–17.

34   Numantia was a Celtiberian *oppidum*, which had passionately resisted the Roman conquest and been razed by Scipio Aemilianus in 133 B.C. Numantia was mythologized as a symbol of "Spanish" resistance against invading peoples. See Brinkmann, "Spanien, " pp. 478–481.

35   A reference to the defeat of the Goths against Tariq in the Battle of Guadalete in 711.

36   Eduardo Infantes y Olivares, "Embajada de Castalla (1879)," in Domene Verdú and Molina Berenguer (eds.), *Textos de las embajadas*, pp. 141–145: here, p. 142.

37   For example in Juan Baptista Pastor y Aycart, "Embajada de Beneixama (first performed in 1872, text edited in 1878)," in Domene Verdú and Molina Berenguer (eds.), *Textos de las embajadas*, pp. 93–102: here, p. 93; Infantes y Olivares, "Embajada de Castalla," p. 143.

38   For example in José Vicente Senabre Villaplana, "Embajada de Muro de l'Alcoi (1852)," in Domene Verdú and Molina Berenguer (eds.), *Textos de las embajadas*, pp. 263–268: here, p. 266; Juan Baptista Pastor y Aycart,

"Embajada de Fontanars dels Alforins," in Domene Verdú and Molina Berenguer (eds.), *Textos de las embajadas*, pp. 191–194: here, p. 192 and p. 194.

39   Llobet y Vall-Llosera, *Apuntes históricos*, p. 8.
40   Pastor y Aycart, "Embajada de Fontanars dels Alforins," p. 192.
41   Pastor y Aycart, "Embajada de Beneixama," p. 96.
42   Ibid., p. 102; Pastor y Aycart, "Embajada de Fontanars dels Alforins," p. 194.
43   Berenguer Barceló, *Historia de los Moros y Cristianos de Alcoy*, pp. 614–617.
44   See also ibid., p. 639.
45   Tomás García Figueras, "Folklore marroqui: La fiesta de 'moros y cristianos' en Benamahoma (Cádiz)," in *Africa: Revista de tropas coloniales*, no. 6 (1935), pp. 110–112.
46   Tomás García Figueras, *Notas sobre las fiestas de moros y cristianos en Benadalid (Málaga)* (Larache, 1939), p. 4f. For a similar interpretation, see ibid., *Notas sobre las fiestas de "moros y cristianos" en España*, vol 2: *Las fiestas de San Jorge, en Alcoy* (Tetuán, 1940), p. 2 of the introduction.
47   Roland Emerich Baumann, "'Moors, Demons and Arabs': The Changing Significance of 'Moros y Cristianos' Performances in the Alpujarra, Spain," in *Human mosaic* 25 (1991), pp. 66–73: here, p. 7.
48   García Figueras, *Notas sobre las fiestas de moros y cristianos en Benadalid*, p. 66.
49   Daniela Flesler and Adrián Pérez Melgosa, "Battles of Identity, or Playing 'Guest' and 'Host': the Festivals of Moors and Christians in the Context of Moroccan Immigration in Spain," in *Journal of Spanish Cultural Studies* 4, no. 2 (2003), pp. 151–168: here, p. 161. Generally on the problematic of the modern-day festivals in the context of immigration, see also Sina Lucia Kottmann, "Mocking and Miming the 'Moor': Staging of the 'Self' and 'Other' on Spain's borders with Morocco," in *Journal of Mediterranean Studies* 20, no. 1 (2011), pp. 107–136; ibid., "Moros en la Costa! – Mauren an christlichen Ufern: Abwehr und Inkorporation des Fremden im Süden Spaniens," in *Peripherie* 29, no. 114/15 (2009), pp. 282–303.
50   See ibid., pp. 161–163. Other depictions on Alcoy's banners showed the cross and crescent as feathers of a chicken (1962), arrows on a target (1965), petals of a flower (1967), leaves on a tree (1975), and playing cards (1980).
51   See "Las entidades islámicas contra las fiestas de Moros y Cristianos," in *El Mundo*, 5 Oct. 2006, http://www.elmundo.es/papel/2006/10/05/espana/2033704.html (accessed 20 Jan. 2008).
52   This change occurred in 2008, see Maria J. C. Krom, "Festivals of Moors and Christians: Performance, Commodity and Identity in Folk Celebrations in Southern Spain," in *Journal of Mediterranean Studies* 18, no. 1 (2008), pp. 119–138: here, pp. 125–126. and p. 136, note 4.
53   Flesler and Pérez Melgosa, "Battles of Identity," pp. 164–165.
54   Beatriz Santamarina Campos, "Moros y cristianos: De la batalla festiva a la discursiva," in *Gazeta de Antropologia* 24, no. 1 (2008), http://www.ugr.es/~pwlac/G24_16Beatriz_Santamarina_Campos.pdf (accessed 11 Feb. 2015).
55   Harris, "Muhammed and the Virgin," p. 47.
56   Quoted in Berenguer Barceló, *Historia de los Moros y Cristianos de Alcoy*, pp. 577–578.

57   This mythical connotation can be found as far away as the south of France, as shown by the example of the so-called Dolmen de la Balma del Moro in Laroque-des-Albères (Pyrénées-Orientales).

58   Llinares García, *Os mouros*, p. 16.

59   See, on this point, one of the first significant Portuguese ethnologists, José Leite de Vasconcelos: "As we know, the word *mouro* is used among our people not only to refer to houses which have fallen to ruin, but also ... those with a peculiar appearance. The Moors were the last powerful rulers on the peninsula and thus those who left the strongest mark, which is why this term is used so frequently." José Leite de Vasconcelos, *Portugal Pre-Historico* (Lisbon, 1885), p. 21.

60   Francisco Martins Sarmento, "O que podem ser os mouros da tradição popular," in *O Pantheon* 1 (1881), pp. 105–106 and pp. 121–124: here, p. 106.

61   Rodney Gallop, *The Origins of the Morris Dance* (n. p., 1935), p. 128.

62   Parafita, *A Mitologia dos Mouros*, p. 191.

63   Ibid., p. 35.

64   Raposo, "O Auto da Floripes," pp. 194–195. On Carolingian sagas in the Portuguese culture, see the following relatively brief articles published in the last phase of the Estado Novo: António Machado Guerreiro, "Floripes e os Pares de França no Teatro Popular," in *Vértice* 32 (1972), pp. 612–629; and Azinhal Abelho, "Teatro popular no Minho: Ciclo Carolíngio," in *Mensario das casas do Povo* 19, no. 2 (1970), pp. 9–11.

65   Luiz Antônio Barreto, "Cristãos e mouros na cultura brasileira," in Braulio do Nascimento (ed.), *Euro-América: Uma realidade comum?* (Rio de Janeiro, 1996), pp. 153–172: here, p. 170. See also Luís da Câmara Cascudo, *Mouros, Franceses e Judeus: Três Presenças no Brasil*, 3rd ed. (São Paulo, 2001), pp. 16–39.

66   Jerusa Pires Ferreira, "Um rei a resmas: Carlos Magno e a América," in Nascimento (ed.), *Euro-América*, pp. 133–151.

67   See Alberto A. Abreu, *As Neves, centro regional entre o Lima e o Neiva* (Neves, 2014), p. 110.

68   See the sources in Raposo, "O Auto da Floripes," pp. 196–197.

69   João Leal, *Etnografias Portuguesas (1870–1970): Cultura Popular e Identidade Nacional* (Lisbon, 2000), pp. 57–58.

70   Claudio Basto, "Falas e tradições de Viana do Castelo – Auto da Floripes," in *Revista Lusitana* 15, no. 1–4 (1912), pp. 71–102: here, pp. 93–94.

71   Ibid., p. 93.

72   See Raposo, "O Auto da Floripes," pp. 200–201.

73   Leal, *Etnografias Portuguesas*, p. 58.

74   Raposo, "O Auto da Floripes," p. 204, note 15.

75   *Auto da Floripes: Recolhida da tradição e anotado por Leandro Quintas Neves* (Porto, 1963). The text quoted here is taken from the edition that was considered "official" for a long time. For a critical edition of the text, including more recent versions, see Alberto A. Abreu, *O Auto da Floripes e o imaginário minhoto* (Viana do Castelo, 2001), pp.105–141.

76   On the cult of Our Lady of the Snows in Neves and the connection with the Auto da Floripes, see Abreu, *As Neves*, pp. 93–116, quote on p. 114.

77   *Auto da Floripes*, p. 18.

78 Ibid., p. 15.
79 Ibid., p. 19.
80 Ibid., p. 22.
81 Rodney Gallop, *Portugal – a Book of Folk-Ways* (Cambridge, 1936), p. 177.
82 See the photos in Abreu, *O Auto da Floripes e o imaginário minhoto*, pp. 40–55, and the text on p. 47.
83 Ibid., p. 29, photo on p. 31.
84 See the text in Claudio Basto, "A Batalha entre turcos e cristãos na Ribeira (Ponte-do-Lima)," in *Revista Lusa* 15–16 (1917), pp. 119–124.
85 This technique was used already by the early modern playwright Gil Vicente (ca. 1465–1536). See António P. de M. dos Reis, "Origem da 'Turquia' de Crasto," in *Almanaque de Ponte de Lima* (Ponte de Lima, 1980), pp. 143–148: here, pp. 146–147.
86 Alge, *Die Performance des* Mouro *in Nordportugal*, p. 147; Paula Costa Machado and Hélder Ferreira: *Bugiada Valongo* (Valongo, 2002), p. 38.
87 There are eyewitness reports of these dances from 1882. See José Leite de Vasconcelos, *Etnografia Portuguesa*, vol. 8 (Lisbon, 1997), p. 409. First edition 1933ff.
88 Manuel Pinto, *A Bugiada: festa, luta e comunicação*. Paper presented at the 4th Encontro Lusófono de Ciências da Comunicação in São Vicente, Brasil, 19–22 Apr. 2000, http://www.bocc.ubi.pt/pag/_texto.php? html2=pinto-manuel-bugiada.html (accessed 20 Jan. 2008).
89 In the Algarve, for example, the region within contemporary Portugal with the longest Muslim presence, there are many fewer such festivals associated with the *mouros*. There is a record of a *combate de mouros* in Santa Catarina da Fonte do Bispo (Faro) in the twentieth century to celebrate the Feast of the Patron Saint Nossa Senhora das Dores (Our Lady of Sorrows) on the third weekend of August. It ended with the Christians' victory and the burning of a symbolic fortress. This performance might be a distant allusion to the battle between Moorish troops and Paio Peres Correia, grandmaster of the Order of Santiago, which captured many cities in the Algarve from the Moors in the thirteenth century. See José Fernandes Mascarenhas, *Elementos históricos sobre a freguesia de Santa Catarina da Fonte do Bispo e a batalha do "Desbarato" entre mouros e cristãos* (Tavira, 1972), pp. 22–23. A possible historical predecessor was the spectacle with dance and fighting organized in 1575 in Tavira for King Dom Sebastião in which many participants wore costumes "*á mourisca*." See Damião Augusto de Brito Vasconcelos, *Notícias Históricas de Tavira 1242–1840* (Tavira, 1999), p. 68. First edition 1937. The modern festival in Santa Catarina is held every two years. My thanks to the Museu Municipal de Tavira for this information.
90 Number from Brisset Martín, "Fiestas hispanas de moros y cristianos," n. pag.
91 In 1980 the Spanish Ministry of Tourism declared the festival in Alcoy a "Fiesta de Interés Turístico Internacional" (Fiesta of International Tourist Interest).
92 The financing of the festivals varies. An example for the costs of a normal participant, not a *capitán*, can be found in Krom, "Festivals of Moors and Christians," p. 132.
93 See Alge, *Die Performance des* Mouro *in Nordportugal*, pp. 219–222.

Conclusion

1   Mahmoud Darwish, *Eleven Stars Over Andalusia*, trans. by Mona Anis and Nigel Ryan, with Aga Shahid Ali and Ahmad Dallal, in *Comparative Criticism* 18 (1996), pp. 213–223: here, p. 213.

2   See, for example, the results of a study on West German ideas of Europe: Vanessa Conze, *Das Europa der Deutschen: Ideen von Europa in Deutschland zwischen Reichstradition und Westorientierung 1920–1970* (Munich, 2005).

3   Osterhammel, *The Transformation of the World*, p. 66.

4   This process is even visible in the colonies themselves, where missions and colonial administration in the Spanish colonies of South America were more densely developed than in Brazil. The Portuguese missions were more secular in nature and more open to allowing prominent local landowners to assume authoritative positions. This contributed to the fact that Brazil seceded of its own accord in 1822 without violence and with the son of the former king as head of state.

5   Sánchez-Albornoz, *España, un enigma histórico*, vol. 2, p. 518.

6   Compare Marcelino Menéndez y Pelayo's reaction to a claim made by Teófilo Braga: "To the extent that Portugal is a *sterile and gloomy* nation, it is not the fault of the clerics, but rather because the Portuguese set out to establish a distinct nation and a distinct group while lacking the means and a truly inherent and powerful unity. . . . Compare the situation in Portugal and Catalonia and then say truthfully whether autonomy is more important for the life and culture of a small country or the straightforward and loyal connection to peoples of the same race and similar traditions, even when these have their own history and speak another language." [Emphasis in original.] Menéndez y Pelayo, *Historia de los Heterodoxos Españoles*, vol. 1, pp. 861–862.

7   See Delgado, "Religion und Nation in den 'zwei Spanien,'" pp. 63–68.

8   On the concept of "historical region," see the introduction, note 70.

9   See the similar results in Sáez-Arance, "Constructing Iberia."

10 Peter Rauscher, "Die Erinnerung an den Erbfeind: Die 'Zweite Türkenbelagerung' Wiens 1683 im öffentlichen Bewusstsein Österreichs im 19. und 20. Jahrhundert," in Haug-Moritz and Pelizaeus (eds.), *Repräsentationen der islamischen Welt im Europa der Frühen Neuzeit*, pp. 278–305: here, pp. 286–287.

11 Joseph Alexander Helfert, *Die weltgeschichtliche Bedeutung des Wiener Sieges von 1683* (Vienna, 1883), pp. 26–27. Quoted in Karl Vocelka, "Die zweite Wiener Türkenbelagerung von 1683 und ihr Reflex in der Wissenschaft, den Schulbüchern und Jubiläumsveranstaltungen," in *Studia Austro-Polonica* 3 (1983), pp. 359–379: here, p. 365. On the ambivalence towards the Ottoman Empire under the Habsburg monarchy during this period, see the extensive analysis in Maureen Healy, "In aller 'Freundschaft'? Österreichische 'Türkenbilder' zwischen Gegnerschaft und 'Freundschaft' vor und während des Ersten Weltkrieges," in Laurence Cole, Christa Hämmerle, and Martin Scheuz (eds.), *Glanz – Gewalt – Gehorsam: Militär und Gesellschaft in der Habsburgermonarchie 1800–1918* (Essen, 2011), pp. 269–291.

12 Žanić, "The symbolic identity," p. 49.

13 Holm Sundhaussen, "Kriegserinnerung als Gesamtkunstwerk und

Tatmotiv: Sechshundertzehn Jahre Kosovo-Krieg (1389–1999)," in Dietrich Beyrau (ed.), *Der Krieg in religiösen und nationalen Deutungen der Neuzeit* (Tübingen, 2001), pp. 11–40: here, pp. 18–20.

14   Quoted in Caroline Fetscher, "Der postmoderne Despot," in Thomas Großbölting and Rüdiger Schmidt (eds.), *Der Tod des Diktators: Ereignis und Erinnerung im 20. Jahrhundert* (Göttingen, 2011), pp. 251–276: here, p. 254, on this commemoration in general, see pp. 252–256.

15   See also Dieter Langewiesche, "Die Idee Nation als Handlungsorientierung," in: Raphael and Tenorth (eds.), *Ideen als gesellschaftliche Gestaltungskraft*, pp. 359–368: here, pp. 359–360.

16   On the topic of mythic defeats and their historical interpretations, see generally: Wolfgang Schivelbusch, *The Culture of Defeat: On National Trauma, Mourning, and Recovery* (London, 2004); Siegfried Weichlein, "Die Verlierer der Geschichte: Zu einem Theorem Carl Schmitts," in Christian Giordano, Jean-Luc Patry and François Rüegg (eds.), *Trugschlüsse und Umdeutungen: Multidisziplinäre Betrachtungen unbehaglicher Praktiken* (Berlin, 2009), pp. 147–165.

17   Beyond the Balkans and the Iberian Peninsula, a good example for this is the notion of Poland as an *antemurale christianitatis* and defender of European values, with shifting connotations throughout the centuries. See Małgorzata Morawiec, "Antemurale christianitatis: Polen als Vormauer des christlichen Europa," in *Jahrbuch für Europäische Geschichte* 2 (2001), pp. 249–260.

18   See Liakova, "'Europa' und 'der Islam.'"

19   Maria Todorova, *Imagining the Balkans* (New York and Oxford, 1997), especially pp. 3–20. See also Frithjof Benjamin Schenk, "Mental maps: Die Konstruktion von geographischen Räumen in Europa seit der Aufklärung," in *Geschichte und Gesellschaft* 28 (2002), pp. 493–514: here, p. 508.

20   See for example Sabine Riedel, "Die Politisierung islamischer Geschichte und Kultur am Beispiel Südosteuropas," in *Südost-Europa* 46, no. 1–2 (1997), pp. 539–561.

21   This draws on the terminology which Charles S. Maier developed for his comparison of the collective memory of fascism and communism: Charles S. Maier, "Hot Memory . . . Cold Memory: On the Political Half-Life of Fascist and Communist Memory," in *Transit: Tr@nsit online* 22 (2002), http://www.iwm.at/read-listen-watch/transit-online/hot-memory-cold-memory-on-the-political-half-life-of-fascist-and-communist-memory/ (accessed 28 Jan. 2015).

22   This is the conclusion reached in Ignacio Álvarez-Ossorio Alvariño, "El islam y la identidad española: De Al-Andalus al 11 M," in Taibo (ed.), *Nacionalismo español*, pp. 267–290: here, p. 267.

23   For example, the foundation El Legado Andalusí (The Andalusian Heritage), founded in 1993, works to develop tourist routes, exhibits, and additional cultural programs. Their work is controversial, however. See González Alcantud, *Lo moro*, pp. 193–194; Martin-Márquez, *Disorientations*, pp. 305–360.

24   Mariano Delgado, "Der Mythos 'Toledo': Zur Konvivenz der drei monotheistischen Religionen und Kulturen im mittelalterlichen Spanien," in Sabine Hering (ed.), *Toleranz – Weisheit, Liebe oder Kompromiss? Multikulturelle Diskurse und Orte* (Opladen, 2004), pp. 69–91: here, p. 83.

25 Serafín Fanjul, *Al-Andalus contra España: La forja del mito* (Madrid, 2000); ibid., *La quimera de Al-Andalus* (Madrid, 2005).

26 The original text of Aznar's speech, delivered in English, is quoted in: Hishaam D. Aidi, "The Interference of al-Andalus: Spain, Islam and the West," in *Social Text* 24, no. 2 (2006), pp. 67–88: here, p. 83.

27 César Vidal, *España frente al islam: de Mahoma a Ben Laden* (Madrid, 2004).

28 See Tiesler, "Muçulmanos na margem,"; and ibid., "Novidades no terreno."

29 This is especially true for young Muslims. See Nina Clara Tiesler and David Cairns, "Representing Islam and Lisbon Youth: Portuguese Muslims of Indian-Mozambican Origin," in *Lusotopie* 14, no. 1 (2007), pp. 223–238: here pp. 225–227.

30 Nina Clara Tiesler, "Portugal," in *Yearbook of Muslims in Europe* 2 (2010), pp 413–423: here, p. 421.

31 See also Wolfgang Benz, "Zur Genese und Tradition des Feindbildes Islam," in *Zeitschrift für Geschichtswissenschaft* 58, no. 7/8 (2010), pp. 585–590: here, pp. 585–586.

Bibliography

In the bibliography and the index, Spanish authors are listed under the first family name, Portuguese authors under the last family name.

Sources

Acto Colonial (Lisbon, 1933).

Alarcón, Pedro Antonio de, *Diario de un testigo de la Guerra de África* (Seville, 2005). English translation: Pedro Antonio de Alarcón, *Diary of a Witness to the War in Africa*, trans. by Bern Keating (Memphis 1988).

Almeida, Fortunato de, *História de Portugal* (Lisbon, 2003). First edition 1922–1928.

Altamira, Rafael, *Histoire d'Espagne* (Paris, 1931).

Altamira, Rafael, *Historia de España y de la civilizacion española*, 2 vols. (Barcelona, 2001). First edition 1900. English translation: Rafael Altamira, *A History of Spanish Civilization*, trans. by P. Volkov (London, 1930).

Altamira, Rafael, *Los elementos de la civilización y del carácter españoles* (Buenos Aires, 1950).

Amado, José de Sousa, *Historia da Egreja Catholica em Portugal, no Brasil e nas possessões portuguezas*, vol. 2: *Desde Flavio Recaredo até ao Conde D. Henrique* (Lisbon, 1871).

Amador de los Ríos y Fernández-Villalta, Rodrigo, *La Ermita del Santo Cristo de la Luz en Toledo: Estudio arqueológico motivado por los últimos descubrimientos de febrero de 1899* (Madrid, 1899).

Amador de los Ríos y Serrano, José, *Toledo Pintoresca* (Madrid, 1845; reprint, Valladolid, 2006).

Amador de los Ríos y Serrano, José, *Primeros Monumentos del arte mahometano en Toledo: Mezquitas llamadas del Santo Cristo de la Luz y de las Tornerías* (Madrid, 1877).

Ameal, João, "A Cruz e a Espada," in *Diario da Manhã*, 17 May 1947.

Ameal, João, *História de Portugal* (Porto, 1940).

Arana Goiri, Sabino, *Obras escogidas: antologia política* (San Sebastián, 1978).

Artur, António de Matos Faria, *História de Portugal organizada em lições* (Paris and Lisbon, n. d. [after 1921]).

Asensio Torrado, José, "Los ejercitos coloniales," in *Africa: Revista de tropas coloniales*, no. 4 (1931), pp. 83–90 and no. 5 (1931), pp. 95–100.

Asín Palacios, Miguel, "Por qué lucharon a nuestro lado los musulmanes marroquíes?," in *Revista de la Universidad de Madrid* 1 (1940), pp. 143–167.

Asín Palacios, Miguel, and Emilio García Gómez, "Nota Preliminar," in *Al-Andalus* 1, no. 1 (1933), pp. 1–5.

Auto da Floripes: Recolhida da tradição e anotado por Leandro Quintas Neves (Porto, 1963).

Ballester, Rafael, *Curso de Historia de España* (Gerona, 1917).

Balparda, Gregorio de, *Historica crítica de Vizcaya y de sus fueros* (Madrid, 1924).

Barros, Tomás de, *Sumário de História de Portugal: Com narrativa dos factos principais de cada reinado, recapitulação em questionário e variado exercícios para a 4a classe do Ensino Primário e admissão aos Liceus* (Porto, 1940).

Basto, Claudio, "A Batalha entre turcos e cristãos na Ribeira (Ponte-do-Lima)," in *Revista Lusa* 15–16 (1917), pp. 119–124.

Basto, Claudio, "Falas e tradições de Viana do Castelo – Auto da Floripes," in *Revista Lusitana* 15, no. 1–4 (1912), pp. 71–102.

Bauer y Landauer, Ignácio, "El factor musulmán en la cultura española," in *Africa: Revista de tropas coloniales*, no. 12 (1933), pp. 234–236.

Boléo, José de Oliveira, "Como conseguiu Portugal a sua autonomia política? Segunda parte" in *Revista dos Centenários*, no. 12 (1939), pp. 41–44.

Borges Coelho, António, *Portugal na Espanha Árabe*, 2 vols (Lisbon, 1989). First edition 1972–1975.

Borrás, Tomás, *La España completa* (Madrid, 1950).

Bosch Cusi, Juan, *Historia de España: Grado medio: Libro del alumno* (Gerona, 1930).

Braga, Teófilo, *A Pátria Portuguesa: o Território e a Raça* (Porto, 1894).

Braga, Teófilo, *História da litteratura portugueza* (Porto, 1870).

Burton, Richard Francis, *Personal Narrative of a Pilgrimage to Mecca and Medina* (Leipzig, 1874). First edition 1855–1856.

Caballero, José, *Diario de campaña de un capellán legionario* (Madrid, 1976).

Cáceres Prat, Acácio, *Covadonga: Tradiciones, Historias y Leyendas*, 2nd ed. (Madrid, 1890).

Cala y Lopez, Ramon de, and Miguel Flores González-Grano de Oro, *La fiesta de Moros y Cristianos en la Villa de Carboneras precedida de una noticia histórica* (Cuevas, 1918; reprint, Carboneras and Almería, 1993).

Camões, Luís Vaz de, *The Lusíads*, trans. by Landeg White (Oxford and New York, 1997).

Canella y Secades, Fermin, *De Covadonga: Contribuición al XII centenario* (Madrid, 1918).

Cardoso, Rogério Seabra, "Islamitas Portugueses: Linhas de força de um passado; Realidades de um presente; Bases de um futuro," in *Panorama. Revista portuguesa de arte e turismo* series IV, nrs. 33/34 (March/June 1970), pp. 49–62.

Castro, Américo, *The Structure of Spanish History*, trans. by Edmund L. King (Princeton, 1954).

Castro, Augusto de, "A Nação inteira!," in *Diario de Noticias*, 18 Oct. 1960, p. 1.

Cervantes Saavedra, Miguel de, *The Ingenious Hidalgo Don Quixote de la Mancha*, trans. by John Rutherford (New York, 2003).

Conde, José Antonio, *Historia de la dominación de los árabes en España, sacado de varios manuscritos y memorias arabigas* (Paris, 1840). First edition 1820–1821. English translation: José Antonio Conde, *History of the Dominion of the Arabs in Spain*, trans. by Mrs. Jonathan Foster (London, 1854–1855).

Conquista de Lisboa aos Mouros (1147): Narrada pelo Cruzado Osberno, testemunha presencial, trans. by José Augusto de Oliveira (Lisbon, 1935).

Continuatio Isidoriana Hispana: Crónica mozárabe de 754: Estudio, edición crítica y traducción José Eduardo López Pereira, León 2009.

Contreras, Rafael, *Estudio descriptivo de los monumentos arabes de Granada, Sevilla y Cordoba* (Saragossa, 1993). First edition 1878.

"O cortejo do mundo português: Uma lição viva de História Pátria," in *Revista dos Centenários* no. 4 (1939), pp. 5–10.

Costa, Joaquim Correia da, "A Ameaça Afro-Asiatica," in *Diario de Lisboa*, 2 Oct. 1956, pp. 12–13.

Darwish, Mahmoud, *Eleven Stars Over Andalusia*, trans. by Mona Anis and Nigel Ryan, with Aga Shahid Ali and Ahmad Dallal, in *Comparative Criticism* 18 (1996), pp. 213–223.

De expugnatione Lyxbonensi – The Conquest of Lisbon, trans. by Charles Wendell David, with a new foreword and bibliography by Jonathan Phillips (New York, 2001).

Deschamps, Hubert, *Les religions de l'Afrique Noire* (Paris, 1954).

Dias, Eduardo, "Um Problema: o Islamismo e a sua penetração na África Negra," in *Rumo: Revista da cultura portuguesa* 6 (1946), pp. 232–243.

Domene Verdú, José Fernando, and Maria Mercedes Molina Berenguer (eds.), *Textos de las embajadas de la fiesta de moros y cristianos* (Alicante, 2003).

Doménech Lafuente, Ángel, *Del Islam* (Madrid, 1950).

Doménech Lafuente, Ángel, *Un oficial entre moros* (Larache, 1948).

Domingues, José Domingo Garcia, "Arabes e moiros," in Gustavo de Matos Sequeira (ed.), *Lisboa, oito séculos de história* (Lisbon, 1947), pp. 84–119.

Domingues, José Domingo Garcia, "Os estudos arábicos em Portugal depois de David Lopes," in *Revista de Portugal* 24 (1959), pp. 23–35.

Domingues, José Domingo Garcia, "Presença Árabe no Algarve," in Adel Sidarus, *Islão e Arabismo na Península Ibérica: Actas do XI Congresso da Uniao Europeia de Arabistas e Islamólogos* (Évora, 1986), pp. 113–130.

Domingues, José Domingo Garcia, *Silves – Guia turístico* (Silves, 1958).

Eneas, "La Guerra de África," in *El Correo Español*, 3 Oct. 1893, p. 1.

Enes, António, *Moçambique: Relatório apresentado ao Govêrno*, 3rd ed. (n. p., 1946). First edition 1893.

"Las entidades islámicas contra las fiestas de Moros y Cristianos," in *El Mundo*, 5 Oct. 2006, http://www.elmundo.es/papel/2006/10/05/espana/2033704.html (accessed 20 Jan. 2008).

Estornés Lasa, Bernardo, *Historia del pais basko* (Zarauz, 1933).

"Exposição do mundo português," in *Revista dos Centenários*, no. 7/8 (1940), pp. 17–35.

Facundo Riaño, Juan, *Palacio árabe de la Alhambra* (Madrid, 1856).

Fernández Rosete, Fernando, *Pelayo y Covadonga* (Arriondas, 1909).

Figueiredo, António Cândido de, *História de Portugal sumariada para uso do povo e das escolas*, 5th ed. (Lisbon, 1913).

Figueiredo, António Cândido de, *Historia de Portugal: Resumida e organisada para uso do povo e das escolas*, 3rd ed. (Lisbon, 1888).

Flores Morales, Angel (ed.), *Africa a traves del pensamiento español: De Isabel la Católica a Franco* (Madrid, 1949).

Franco Bahamonde, Francisco, *Diario de una bandera* (Seville, 1939). English translation: *Francisco Franco's Moroccan War Diary 1920–1922: Critical Analysis and Translation, Biographical and Topographical notes*, trans. by Paul Sothern (Bromley, 2007).

Franco Bahamonde, Francisco, *Franco ha dicho: Recopilación de las más impor-*

tantes declaraciones del caudillo desde la iniciación del alzamiento nacional hasta el 31 de diciembre de 1946 (Madrid, 1946).

Franco, Sezinado Chagas, and Anibal Magno, *Primeiros esboços da História de Portugal: Aprovado pelo governo da republica para as escolas primárias em 1910 e novamente aprovados pela comissão revisora dos livros de ensino em 1913* (Lisbon, 1914).

Franklin, António George C. de Sousa, *A Ameaça Islâmica na Guiné Portuguesa* (Lisbon, 1956).

Freyre, Gilberto, *Um brasileiro em terras portuguêsas* (Lisbon, 1955).

Ganivet, Ángel, and Miguel de Unamuno, *El porvenir de España* (Madrid, 2005). First edition 1898.

García Figueras, Tomás, "Folklore marroqui: La fiesta de 'moros y cristianos' en Benamahoma (Cádiz)," in *Africa: Revista de tropas coloniales,* no. 6 (1935), pp. 110–112.

García Figueras, Tomás, *Notas sobre las fiestas de "moros y cristianos" en España,* vol. 2: *Las fiestas de San Jorge, en Alcoy* (Tetuán, 1940).

García Figueras, Tomás, *Notas sobre las fiestas de moros y cristianos en Benadalid (Málaga)* (Larache, 1939).

Gómez Ranera, Alejandro, *Compendio de la Historia de España desde su origen hasta el reinado de doña Isabel II y el año 1843,* 3rd ed. (Madrid, 1844).

Gómez-Moreno González, Manuel, *Guía de Granada,* 2 vols. (Granada, 1892; reprint, Granada, 1994).

Gonçalves, José Júlio, *O Mundo Árabo-Islâmico e o Ultramar Português* (Lisbon, 1958).

Graça, José Nunes da, and Fortunato Correia Pinto, *Resumo de História Pátria para as escolas d'instrução primária* (Lisbon, 1911).

Guedes, A. Marques, "Portugal é uma Nação (Part 3)," in *Revista dos Centenários* no. 3 (1940), pp. 6–10.

Guia oficial da Exposição do mundo português (Lisbon, 1940).

Herculano, Alexandre, *Historia de Portugal: Desde o começo da monarquia até o fim do reinado de Afonso III,* 4 vols. (Lisbon, 1980ff.). First edition 1846–1851.

Herculano, Alexandre, *O Monge de Cistér ou a Epocha de João I,* ed. by David Lopes (Lisbon, n. d.).

Hoare, Samuel, *Ambassador on Special Mission* (London, 1946).

Ibo Alfaro, Manuel, *Compendio de la Historia de España* (Madrid, 1895).

"Inauguração da mesquita," in *Boletim Cultural da Guiné Portuguesa* 21, no. 83 (1966), pp. 376–381.

Infantes y Olivares, Eduardo, "Embajada de Castalla (1879)," in José Fernando Domene Verdú and Maria Mercedes Molina Berenguer (eds.), *Textos de las embajadas de la fiesta de moros y cristianos* (Alicante, 2003), pp. 141–145.

"Informe sobre declaración de Monumento nacional de los restos de la ciudad y palacio de Medina-Az-Zahara, situado en el lugar conocido por Córdoba la Vieja," in *Boletin de la Real Academia de Bellas Artes de San Fernando* V, no. 17 (1885), pp. 33–34.

Instituto de España [José María Pemán], *Manual de Historia de España: Segundo grado* (Santander, 1939).

Júdice, Pedro P. Mascarenhas, *A Sé e o Castelo de Silves* (Gaia, 1934).

Labayru y Goicoechea, Estanislao de, *Historia General del señorío de Bizcaya* (Bilbao, 1967). First edition 1895.

Lafuente y Zamalloa, Modesto, *Historia general de España desde los tiempos más remotos hasta nuestros días: Discurso preliminar,* ed. by Juan Sisinio Pérez Garzón (Pamplona, 2002).

Lafuente y Zamalloa, Modesto, *Historia general de España desde los tiempos más remotos hasta nuestros dias* (Madrid, 1850ff.).

El Libro de España (Saragossa, 1944).

Llanos Alcaraz, Adolfo, *La campaña de Melilla de 1893–1894* (Madrid, 1894; reprint, Málaga and Melilla, 1994).

Llobet y Vall-Llosera, José Antonio, *Apuntes históricos acerca de las fiestas que celebra cada año la ciudad de Alcoy a su Patrón San Jorge con referencias a la historia antigua de la misma ciudad en los tiempos de la reconquista sobre los árabes* (Alcoy, 1853; reprint, Alcoy, 1998).

Lopes, David, "O domínio árabe," in Damião Peres (ed.), *História de Portugal,* vol. 1 (Barcelos, 1928), pp. 389–431.

Lopes, David, *Os Arabes nas obras de Alexandre Herculano* (Lisbon, 1911).

Lopes, David, *Portugal contra os mouros* (Lisbon, n. d.).

Lopes, Joaquim Reis Alves, *A Villa de Vallongo* (Porto, 1904).

López Peláez, Antolín, *La batalla de las Navas de Tolosa y la batalla contra el socialismo: Conferencia del Obispo de Jaca en la Semana Social celebrada para conmemorar el centenario de las Navas* (Saragossa, 1912).

López, Emilio L., "Tetuán por dentro: Una casa mora es así," in *Africa: Revista de tropas coloniales* no. 4 (1931), pp. 81–82.

Machado, Antonio, *Times Alone: Selected Poems of Antonio Machado,* trans. by Robert Bly (Middletown, Connecticut, 1983).

Maeztu, Ramiro de, *Defensa de la Hispanidad* (Madrid, 1946). First edition 1943.

Mamede, Suleiman Valy, "No XIV centenário do Alcorão," in *Cultura islâmica e cultura árabe: Estudos em honra de David Lopes* (Lisbon, 1969), pp. 81–88.

Mamede, Suleiman Valy, *O Islão no espaço português* (Braga, 1970).

Mariana, Juan de, *Historia General de España,* vol. 1 (Madrid, 1855). First edition 1592.

Marques, João Lopes, "'Mouros forros' esquecidos," in *Público,* 10 Dec. 1996, p. 9.

Martínez Vigil, Ramón, "El santuario de Covadonga (9 de septiembre de 1884)," in ibid., *Pastorales del Rmo. P. Martínez Vigil de la Orden de Predicadores, Obispo de Oviedo, conde de Noreña etc.,* vol. 1 (Madrid, 1898), pp. 45–60.

Martins, Joaquim Pedro Oliveira, "Os povos peninsulares e a civilização moderna," in ibid., *Política e história,* vol. 1 (Lisbon, 1957), pp. 217–246.

Martins, Joaquim Pedro Oliveira, *A teoria do mosarabismo de Teófilo Braga* (Coimbra, 1953).

Martins, Joaquim Pedro Oliveira, *História da civilização ibérica* (Lisbon, 1984). English translation: Joaquim Pedro Oliveira Martins, *A History of Iberian Civilization,* trans. by Aubrey FitzGerald Bell (London, 1930).

Martins, Joaquim Pedro Oliveira, *História de Portugal* (Lisbon, 1988). First edition 1879.

Marx, Karl, "Die Bakunisten an der Arbeit: Denkschrift über den Aufstand in Spanien im Sommer 1873," in: ibid. and Friedrich Engels, *Werke,* vol. 18 (Berlin, 1973), pp. 476–493.

Mascarenhas, Arsenio Augusto Torres de, *Compendio de História de Portugal: Aprovado pelo governo para uso dos alumnos da 5.a classe dos lyceus,* 2nd ed. (Lisbon, 1901).

Mascarenhas, Arsenio Augusto Torres de, *História de Portugal: Remodelada e ampliada de harmonia com os princípios de orientação educativa do Estado Novo por João Afonso de Miranda*, 4th ed. (Lisbon, 1944).

Mascarenhas, Arsenio Augusto Torres de, *Resumo da História de Portugal: Aprovado pelo Govêrno Provisório da República em portaria de 6 de Dezembro de 1910* (Lisbon, 1910).

Matoso, Antonio Gonçalves, and Antonino Henriques, *Compêndio de História Geral e Pátria*, vol. 1: *Antiguidade e Idade Média: Ensino Técnico Profissional*, 2nd ed. (Lisbon, 1937).

Matoso, Antonio Gonçalves, *Compêndio de História de Portugal: Aprovado oficialmente como texto único para o 6.o ano dos liceus*, 3rd ed. (Lisbon, 1940).

Menéndez Pidal, Ramón, *Islam y cristianidad: España entre las dos culturas*, ed. by Álvaro Galmés de Fuentes, 2 vols. (Malaga, 2001).

Menéndez y Pelayo, Marcelino, *Antología General: Recopilación orgánica de su doctrina*, ed. by Ángel Herrera Oria (Madrid, 1956).

Menéndez y Pelayo, Marcelino, *Historia de los Heterodoxos Españoles,* (Madrid, 1956). First edition 1880–1882. English translation: Marcelino Menéndez y Pelayo, *A History of the Spanish Heterodox*, trans. by Eladia Gomez-Posthill (London, 2009).

Merry y Colón, Manuel, and Antonio Merry y Villalba, *Compendio de la historia de España* (Seville, 1889).

Nogueira, Eurico Dias, *Episódios da Minha Missão em África* (Braga, 1995).

Nostra aetate, quoted in http://www.vatican.va/archive/hist_councils/ii_vatican_council/documents/vat-ii_decl_19651028_nostra-aetate_en.html (accessed 15 Jan. 2015).

Oleaga, Luis, "Aproximación cristiano-musulmana," in *Africa: Revista de tropas coloniales,* no. 6 (1930), pp. 263–264.

Oliveira, Herculano Lopes de, "Aspectos actuais do problema missionário no Ultramar Português," in *Volumus: Revista trimestral de formação missionária* 8, no. 3/4 (1956), pp. 136–148.

Oliver Hurtado, José, and Manuel Oliver Hurtado, *Granada y sus monumentos árabes* (Malaga, 1875).

Orodea y Ibarra, Eduardo, *Curso de lecciones de Historia de España ó estudio crítico-filosófico de todas las épocas más notables de nuestra historia nacional desde los más remotos tiempos hasta el presente siglo . . .* , 9th ed. (Ávila, 1886).

Ortega y Gasset, José, *España invertebrada* (Madrid, 1922).

Parreira, António Maria de Oliveira, *Os luso-arabes: Scenas da vida mussulmana no nosso pais*, 2 vols. (Lisbon, 1898).

Pastor y Aycart, Juan Baptista, "Embajada de Beneixama (first performed in 1872, text edited in 1878)," in José Fernando Domene Verdú and Maria Mercedes Molina Berenguer (eds.), *Textos de las embajadas de la fiesta de moros y cristianos* (Alicante, 2003), pp. 93–102.

Pastor y Aycart, Juan Baptista, "Embajada de Fontanars dels Alforins," in José Fernando Domene Verdú and Maria Mercedes Molina Berenguer (eds.), *Textos de las embajadas de la fiesta de moros y cristianos* (Alicante, 2003), pp. 191–194.

Pedro, Albano Mendes, "Islamismo e Catolicismo em Moçambique," in *Volumus: Revista trimestral de formação missionária* 11, no. 4 (1959), pp. 170–212.

Peirone, Frederico José, "A importância do estudo da língua e da cultura árabe para a missionação dos indígenas islamizados de Moçambique," in *Garcia da Orta: Revista da Junta das Missões Geográficas e de Investigações do Ultramar* 6, no. 3 (1956), pp. 371–381.

Pemán, José María, "Los moros amigos," in ibid., *Obras completas*, vol. 5: *Doctrina y Oratoria* (Madrid, 1953), pp. 486–489.

Peres, Damião (ed.), *História de Portugal* (Barcelos, 1928ff.).

Peres, Damião, *A gloriosa história dos mais belos castelos de Portugal* (Barcelos, 1969).

Pérez Galdós, Benito, *Aita Tettauen* (Madrid, 1976). First edition 1905.

"O perigo do Islão em África," in *Boletim Geral do Ultramar* 378 (1956), pp. 104–106.

Pidal y Mon, Alejandro, *Discurso sobre la batalla de Las Navas de Tolosa: Leído por D. Alejandro Pidal y Mon en la veladas celebrada en el Teatro de Burgos la Noche del Dia 16 de julio 1912* (Madrid, 1912).

Pina, Luís de, "Regresso a Deus: batalha sem fim: Do Porto cristão à Lisboa mourisca," in *Boletim Cultural da Câmara Municipal do Porto* 10 (1947), pp. 5–26.

Priego López, Juan, *Escoltas y guardias moras de los jefes de Estado españoles* (Madrid, 1952).

Programa oficial das comemorações do VIII. centenário da tomada de Lisboa (Lisbon, 1947).

Rego, António da Silva, *O Oriente e o Ocidente: Ensaios* (Lisbon, 1939).

Resende, Sebastião Soares de, *Falsos e verdadeiros caminhos da vida* (Lourenço Marques, 1948).

Ribera y Tarragó, Julián, "El arabista español," in ibid., *Disertaciones y opúsculos 1887–1927*, vol. 1 (Madrid, 1928), pp. 457–488.

Rodrigues, Manoel Maria Sarmento "Os maometanos no futuro da Guiné," in *Boletim Cultural da Guiné Portuguesa* 3, no. 9 (1948), pp. 219–231.

Royo Villanova, Luís, "La Guerra del Moro," in *Blanco y negro*, 21 Oct. 1893, pp. 2–3.

Salazar, António de Oliveira, *Discursos e notas políticas*, 6 vols. (Coimbra, 1935–1967).

Sánchez-Albornoz, Claudio, "España y el islam," in ibid., *De la invasión islamica al estado continental: entre la creación y el ensayo* (Seville, 1974), pp. 15–40. First publication: *Revista de Occidente* 24, no. 57 (1929).

Sánchez-Albornoz, Claudio, *España, un enigma histórico*, 2 vols. (Barcelona, 1973). First edition 1956. English translation: Claudio Sánchez-Albornoz, *Spain, a Historical Enigma*, trans. by Colette Joly Dees and David Sven Reher (Madrid, 1975).

Saramago, José, *The History of the Siege of Lisbon*, trans. by Giovanni Pontiero (New York, San Diego, and London, 1996).

Sarmento, Francisco Martins, "O que podem ser os mouros da tradição popular," in *O Pantheon* 1 (1881), pp. 105–106 and pp. 121–124.

Seco de Lucena Escalada, Luis, *La Alhambra – cómo fué y cómo es* (Granada, 1935).

Senabre Villaplana, José Vicente, "Embajada de Muro de l'Alcoi (1852)," in José Fernando Domene Verdú and Maria Mercedes Molina Berenguer (eds.), *Textos de las embajadas de la fiesta de moros y cristianos* (Alicante, 2003), pp. 263–268.

Sender, Ramón J., *Imán* (Barcelona, 2003). First edition 1930. English translation: Ramón J. Sender, *Earmarked for Hell*, trans. by James Cleugh (London, 1934), in the USA published under the title *Pro Patria* (Boston, 1935).

Séptimo centenario de la batalla de Las Navas de Tolosa y de la adopción del actual escudo de Navarra (Madrid, 1912).

Sequeira, Gustavo de Matos (ed.), *Lisboa, oito séculos de história* (Lisbon, 1947).

Sequeira, Gustavo de Matos, "Biografia de Lisboa," in *Programa oficial das comemorações do VIII. centenário da tomada de Lisboa* (Lisbon, 1947), n. pag.

Serrano de Haro, Agustín, *España es así* (Madrid, 1960).

Serrano de Haro, Agustín, *Yo soy español: El libro de primer grado de Historia* (Madrid, 1943).

"Sessão solene nos paços do Concelho," in *Revista municipal de Lisboa* 33, no. 2 (1947), pp. 17–23.

Simonet, Francisco Javier, *Discurso leido ante el claustro de la Universidad Central por D. Francisco Javier Simonet en el solemne acto de recibir la investidura de Doctor en Filosofia y Letras* (Granada, 1867).

Simonet, Francisco Javier, *Historia de los mozarabes de España* (Madrid, 1897; reprint, Valladolid, 2005).

Unamuno, Miguel de, "Sobre la europeización," in ibid., *Obras completas,* ed. by Ricardo Senabre, vol. 8: *Ensayos* (Madrid, 2007), pp. 999–1016.

Urquijo, Fernando de, *La campaña del Rif en 1909: Juicios de un testigo* (Madrid, 1910).

Vasconcelos, José Leite de, *Portugal Pre-Historico* (Lisbon, 1885).

Veiga, Sebastião Philippes Martins Estácio da, *Memórias das antiguidades de Mértola* (Lisbon, 1880; reprint, Lisbon, 1983).

Veloso, Francisco José, "Portugal, os árabes e os muçulmanos," in *Cultura islâmica e cultura árabe: Estudos em honra de David Lopes* (Lisbon, 1969), pp. 89–95.

Periodical Sources

The dates included in parentheses indicate the years of the periodical which were systematically examined for this study.

Africa: Revista de tropas coloniales, Ceuta (1926–1936).

Blanco y negro, Madrid (Oct.–Nov. 1893).

Diário da Manhã, Lisbon (May 1947).

El Correo Español, Madrid (Oct.–Nov. 1893).

El Heraldo de Madrid, Madrid (Oct.–Nov. 1893).

El Imparcial, Madrid (Oct.–Nov. 1893).

El Liberal, Madrid (Oct.–Nov. 1893).

Revista dos Centenários, Lisbon (1939–1940).

Revista Municipal de Lisboa, Lisbon (1947).

VII. Centenario de la Batalla de Las Navas de Tolosa. Periodico semanal dirigido por la Junta Local Organizadora de su celebración, La Carolina (1912).

Literature

Abelho, Azinhal, "Teatro popular no Minho: Ciclo Carolíngio," in *Mensario das casas do Povo* 19, no. 2 (1970), pp. 9–11.

Abreu, Alberto A., *As Neves, centro regional entre o Lima e o Neiva* (Neves, 2014).

Abreu, Alberto A., *O Auto da Floripes e o imaginário minhoto* (Viana do Castelo, 2001).

Acciaiuoli, Margarida, *Exposições do Estado Novo 1934–1940* (Lisbon, 1998).

Aidi, Hishaam D.,"The Interference of al-Andalus: Spain, Islam and the West," in *Social Text* 24, no. 2 (2006), pp. 67–88.

Albert-Llorca, Marlène, and José Antonio González Alcantud (eds.), *Moros y cristianos: representaciones del otro en las fiestas del Mediterráneo occidental* (Toulouse, 2003).

Albert-Llorca, Marlène, and José Antonio González Alcantud, "Metáforas y laberintos de la alteridad," in ibid. (eds.), *Moros y cristianos: representaciones del otro en las fiestas del Mediterráneo occidental* (Toulouse, 2003), pp. 9–21.

Alexandre, Valentim, "A África no imaginário político português (séculos XIX–XX)," in *Penélope* 15 (1995), pp. 39–52.

Alge, Barbara, *Die Performance des Mouro in Nordportugal: Eine Studien von Tanzdramen in religiösen Kontexten* (Berlin, 2010).

Algora Weber, María Dolores, *Las relaciones hispano-árabes durante el régimen de Franco: la ruptura del aislamiento internacional, 1946–1950* (Madrid, 1995).

Altermatt, Urs, and Franziska Metzger (eds.), *Religion und Nation: Katholizismen im Europa des 19. und 20. Jahrhunderts* (Stuttgart, 2007).

Álvarez Chillida, Gonzalo, *El Antisemitismo en España: La imagen del judío 1812–2002* (Madrid, 2002).

Álvarez Junco, José, "El nacionalismo español como mito movilizador: Cuatro guerras," in Rafael Cruz (ed.), *Cultura y movilización en la España contemporánea* (Madrid, 1997), pp. 35–67.

Álvarez Junco, José, *Mater dolorosa: La idea de España en el siglo XIX* (Madrid, 2001).

Álvarez-Ossorio Alvariño, Ignacio, "El islam y la identidad española: De Al-Andalus al 11 M," in Carlos Taibo (ed.), *Nacionalismo español: Esencias, memoria e instituciones* (Madrid, 2007), pp. 267–290.

Alves, Alberto, *O meu coração é árabe*, 3rd ed. (Lisbon, 1989).

Alves, Alberto, *Portugal e o Islão: Escritos do crescente* (Lisbon, 1989).

Alves, Alberto, *Portugal: Ecos de um Pasado Árabe* (Lisbon, 1989).

Amaral, Maria da Conceição, *Caminhos do Gharb: Estratégia de interpretação do património islâmico no Algarve: o caso de Faro e de Silves* (n. p., 2002).

Anacleto, Regina, "A Reinvenção do Mourisco na Arte Portuguesa de Oitocentos," in Rosa Maria Perez (ed.), *Memórias Árabo-Islâmicas em Portugal* (Lisbon, 1998), pp. 129–142.

Anderson, Benedict, *Imagined Communities: Reflections on the Origins and Spread of Nationalism*, 2nd rev. ed. (London, 2006). First edition 1983.

Anguita Herrador, Rosario, *Jacinto Higueras: El artista y su obra* (Jaén, 1995).

Apostolov, Mario, *The Christian–Muslim Frontier: A Zone of Contact, Conflict or Cooperation* (London and New York, 2004).

Archilés, Ferran, and Manuel Martínez, "La construccción de la Nación española durante el siglo XIX: logros y límites de la asimliación en el caso valenciano," in *Ayer* 35 (1999), pp. 171–190.

Assmann, Aleida, *Arbeit am nationalen Gedächtnis: Eine Geschichte der deutschen Bildungsidee* (Frankfurt am Main, 1993).

Assmann, Jan, "Kollektives Gedächtnis und kulturelle Identität," in ibid. and

Tonio Hölscher (eds.), *Kultur und Gedächtnis* (Frankfurt am Main, 1988), pp. 9–19.

Azevedo, Carlos A. Moreira (ed.), *Dicionário de História Religiosa de Portugal* (Lisbon, 2000ff.).

Balfour, Sebastian, and Alejandro Quiroga, *The Reinvention of Spain: Nation and Identity since Democracy* (Oxford, 2007).

Balfour, Sebastian, *Deadly Embrace: Morocco and the Road to the Spanish Civil War* (Oxford, 2002).

Barkai, Ron (ed.), *Chrétiens, musulmans et juifs dans l'Espagne médiévale: De la convergence à l'expulsion* (Paris, 1994).

Barreto, Luiz Antônio, "Cristãos e mouros na cultura brasileira," in Braulio do Nascimento (ed.), *Euro-América: Uma realidade comum?* (Rio de Janeiro, 1996), pp. 153–172.

Barros, Júlia Leitão de, "Exposição do Mundo Português," in Fernando Rosas and José Maria Brandão Brito (eds.), *Dicionário da História do Estado Novo* (Lisbon, 1996), pp. 325–327.

Baumann, Roland Emerich, "'Moors, Demons and Arabs': The Changing Significance of 'Moros y Cristianos' Performances in the Alpujarra, Spain," in *Human mosaic* 25 (1991), pp. 66–73.

Baumeister, Martin, "Atraso de España – Las dos Españas," in Joachim Born et al. (eds.), *Handbuch Spanisch: Sprache, Literatur, Kultur, Geschichte in Spanien und Hispanoamerika: Für Studium, Lehre, Praxis* (Berlin, 2011), pp. 556–561.

Baumeister, Martin, "Diesseits von Afrika? Konzepte des europäischen Südens," in Frithjof Benjamin Schenk and Martina Winkler (eds.), *Der Süden: Neue Perspektiven auf eine europäische Geschichtsregion* (Frankfurt am Main, 2007), pp. 23–47.

Baumeister, Martin, and Stefanie Schüler-Springorum (eds.), *"If you tolerate this . . . ": The Spanish Civil War in the Age of Total War* (Frankfurt am Main, 2008).

Bausinger, Hermann, "Folklore, Folkloristik" in *Enzyklopädie des Märchens: Handwörterbuch zur historischen und vergleichenden Erzählforschung*, ed. by Kurt Ranke, vol. 4 (Berlin and New York, 1975ff.), column 1397–1403.

Becker, Frank, "Begriff und Bedeutung des politischen Mythos," in Barbara Stollberg-Rilinger (ed.), *Was heißt Kulturgeschichte des Politischen?* (Berlin, 2005), pp. 129–148.

Beltrán, Luis, "African Studies in Spain," in *African Studies Bulletin* 11, no. 3 (1968), pp. 316–325.

Benjelloum, Abdelamjid, "Las causas de la participación de marroquíes en la Guerra Civil española," in José Antonio González Alcantud (ed.), *Marroquíes en la Guerra Civil española: Campos equívocos* (Barcelona, 2003), pp. 42–57.

Benz, Wolfgang, "Zur Genese und Tradition des Feindbildes Islam," in *Zeitschrift für Geschichtswissenschaft* 58, no. 7/8 (2010), pp. 585–590.

Beramendi, Justo G., Ramón Maiz, and Xosé M. Núñez Seixas (eds.), *Nationalism in Europe: Past and Present*, 2 vols. (Santiago de Compostela, 1994).

Berenguer Barceló, Julio, *Historia de los Moros y Cristianos de Alcoy* (Alcoy, 1974).

Bernardo, Luis, "The accommodation of Islam in Portugal and the Republic of

Ireland: A Comparative Case Study," Master's thesis, Universidade Nova de Lisboa, 2009, http://www.academia.edu/195450/The_accommodation _of_Islam_in_Portugal_and_the_Republic_of_Ireland_A_comparative_cas e_study (accessed 8 Feb. 2015).

Bernecker, Walther L., and Sören Brinkmann, *Kampf der Erinnerungen: Der Spanische Bürgerkrieg in Politk und Gesellschaft 1936–2006* (Nettersheim, 2006).

Bizeul, Yves, "Politische Mythen, Ideologien und Utopien: Ein Definitionsversuch," in *Mythos*, no. 2: *Politische Mythen* (Würzburg, 2006), pp. 10–29.

Blas, Javier "Monumentos arquitectónicos de España, la representación científica de la Arquitectura," in *Anticuaria y arqueología: Imágenes de la España Antigua 1757–1877* (Madrid, 1997), pp. 51–60.

Blöcker-Walter, Monica, *Alfons I. von Portugal: Studien zu Geschichte und Sage des Begründers der portugiesischen Unabhängigkeit* (Zurich, 1966).

Boiça, Joaquim Manuel Ferreira, and Maria de Fátima Rombouts de Barros, "A Igreja Matriz de Mértola," in Santiago Macias et al. (eds.), *Mesquita Igreja de Mértola* (Mértola, 2011), pp. 33–87.

Bonaparte et l'Egypte: feu et lumières (Paris, 2008).

Bossong, Georg, *Das maurische Spanien: Geschichte und Kultur* (Munich, 2007).

Botti, Alfonso, *Cielo y dinero: El nacionalcatolicismo en España 1881–1975* (Madrid, 2008).

Bougarel, Xavier, "L'héritage ottoman dans les recompositions de l'identité bochniaque," in Sylvie Gangloff (ed.), *La perception de l'héritage ottoman dans les Balkans* (Paris, 2005), pp. 63–94.

Boyd, Carolyn P., "Covadonga y el regionalismo asturiano," in *Ayer* 64, no. 4 (2006), pp. 149–178.

Boyd, Carolyn P., "The Second Battle of Covadonga: The Politics of Commemoration in Modern Spain," in *History and Memory* 1, no. 2 (2002), pp. 37–64.

Boyd, Carolyn P., *Historia Patria: Politics, History, and National Identity in Spain, 1875–1975* (Princeton, 1997).

Braga, Isabel M. R. Mendes Drumond, "A questão mourisca em Portugal," in Nuria Martínez de Castilla and Rodolfo Gil Benumeya Grimau (eds.), *De Cervantes y el islam* (Madrid, 2006), pp. 161–178.

Brinkmann, Sören, "Spanien. Für Freiheit, Gott und König," in Monika Flacke (ed.), *Mythen der Nationen: Ein europäisches Panorama*, 2nd ed. (Munich and Berlin, 1998), pp. 476–501.

Brisset Martín, Demetrio E., "Fiestas hispanas de moros y cristianos: Historia y significados," in *Gazeta de Antropología* 17 (2001), http://www.ugr.es/~pwlac/G17_03DemetrioE_Brisset_Martin.html (accessed 13 Apr 2008).

Brisset Martín, Demetrio E., *Representaciones rituales hispanicas de conquista* (Madrid, 1988).

Bronisch, Alexander Pierre, *Reconquista und Heiliger Krieg: Die Deutung des Krieges im christlichen Spanien von den Westgoten bis ins frühe 12. Jahrhundert* (Münster, 1998).

Buescu, Ana Isabel Carvalhão, *O Milagre de Ourique e a Historia de Portugal de Alexandre Herculaneo: Uma polémica oitocentista* (Lisbon, 1987).

Bunes Ibarra, Miguel Ángel de, "El orientalismo español de la edad moderna, la fijación de los mitos descriptivos," in José Antonio González Alcantud (ed.), *El orientalismo desde el Sur* (Barcelona, 2006), pp. 37–53.

Bunes Ibarra, Miguel Ángel de, *Los moriscos en el pensamiento histórico: Historiografía de un grupo marginado* (Madrid, 1983).

Buschmann, Nikolaus, and Dieter Langewiesche (eds.), *Der Krieg in den Gründungsmythen europäischer Nationen und der USA* (Frankfurt am Main, 2003).

Cabanellas, Guillermo, *Cuatro Generales*, vol. 2: *Lucha por el poder* (Barcelona, 1977).

Carmelo, Luis, *O milagre de Ourique ou um mito nacional de sobrevivência*, http://www.bocc.ubi.pt/pag/carmelo-luis-Ourique.pdf (accessed 19 Jan. 2009).

Caro Baroja, Julio, *Razas, Pueblos y Linajes* (Madrid, 1957).

Carrasco González, Antonio M., *La novela colonial hispanoafricana: Las colonias africanas de España a través de la historia de la novela* (Madrid, 2000).

Carrasco Urgoiti, Maria Soledad, *El moro de Granada en la literatura* (Granada, 1989).

Carrasco Urgoiti, Maria Soledad, *El moro retador y el moro amigo* (Granada, 1996).

Carrasco Urgoiti, Maria Soledad, *The Moorish Novel* (Boston, 1976).

Carrasco, Raphaël, *La monarchie catholique et les Morisques (1520–1620): Études franco-espagnoles* (Montpellier, 2005).

Carvalho, Rómulo de, *Historia do ensino de Portugal*, 2nd ed. (Lisbon, 1996).

Casals Meseguer, Xavier, "Franco 'El Africano'," in *Journal of Spanish Cultural Studies* 7, no. 3 (2006), pp. 207–224.

Casanova, José, *Public Religions in the Modern World* (Chicago, 1994).

Casares, Julio (ed.), *Diccionario ideológico de la lengua española* (Barcelona, 1999).

Cascudo, Luís da Câmara, *Mouros, Franceses e Judeus: Três Presenças no Brasil*, 3rd ed. (São Paulo, 2001).

Catarino, Helena, *O Algarve Islâmico: Roteiro por Faro, Loulé, Silves e Tavira* (Faro, 2002).

Catroga, Fernando, "Alexandre Herculano e o Historicismo Romantico," in ibid., Luís Reis Torgal, and José Maria Amado Mendes, *História da História em Portugal séculos XIX–XX*, vol. 1, 2nd ed. (n. p., 1998), pp. 44–98.

Catroga, Fernando, "História e Ciências Sociais em Oliveira Martins," in ibid., Luís Reis Torgal, and José Maria Amado Mendes, *História da História em Portugal séculos XIX–XX*, vol. 1, 2nd ed. (n. p., 1998), pp. 136–185.

Catroga, Fernando, Luís Reis Torgal, and José Maria Amado Mendes, *História da História em Portugal séculos XIX–XX*, 2 vols., 2nd ed. (n. p., 1998).

Charle, Christophe, "Grundlagen," in Walter Rüegg (ed.), *Geschichte der Universität in Europa*, vol. 3: *Vom 19. Jahrhundert zum Zweiten Weltkrieg 1800–1945* (Munich, 2004), pp. 43–82.

Ciezar, Nicolas, *Santiago Matamoros: Historia y imagen* (Málaga, 2004).

Cintra, Luís Filipe Lindley, *Sobre a formação e evolução da lenda de Ourique* (Lisbon, 1957).

Clayer, Nathalie, "Der Balkan, Europa und der Islam," in *Enzyklopädie des europäischen Ostens (EEO)*, 2006, pp. 303–328; http://wwwg.uni-klu.ac.at/eeo/Clayer_Balkan (accessed 1 Sept. 2010).

Clot, André, *Al-Andalus: Das maurische Spanien* (Düsseldorf and Zurich, 2002).

Collado Seidel, Carlos, *Der Spanische Bürgerkrieg: Geschichte eines europäischen Konflikts* (Munich, 2006).

Collado Seidel, Carlos, *Die Basken: Ein historisches Porträt* (Munich, 2010).

Coloma, Rafael, *Libro de la fiesta de moros y cristianos de Alcoy* (Alcoy, 1962).

Conze, Vanessa, *Das Europa der Deutschen: Ideen von Europa in Deutschland zwischen Reichstradition und Westorientierung 1920–1970* (Munich, 2005).

Corcuera Atienza, Javier, *La patria de los vascos: Orígenes, ideología y organización del nacionalismo vasco 1876–1903* (Madrid, 2001).

Corkill, David, and José Carlos Pina Almeida, "Commemoration and Propaganda in Salazar's Portugal: The Mundo Português Exposition of 1940," in *Journal of Contemporary History* 44, no. 3 (2009), pp. 381–399.

Coutinho, Valdemar, *Centros históricos de influência Islâmica* (Portimão, 2001).

Covadonga – iconografía de una devoción: exposición conmemorativa del centenario de la dedicación de la Basílica de Covadonga 1901–2001 (Oviedo, 2001).

Crabiffosse Cuesta, Francisco, "Evocación y memoria del Santuario de Covadonga," in *Covadonga – iconografía de una devoción: exposición conmemorativa del centenario de la dedicación de la Basílica de Covadonga 1901–2001* (Oviedo, 2001), pp. 95–107.

Cruz, Manuel Braga da, "Der Estado Novo und die katholische Kirche," in Fernando Rosas (ed.), *Vom Ständestaat zur Demokratie: Portugal im 20. Jahrhundert* (Munich, 1997), pp. 49–64.

Custódio, Jorge, "Salvaguarda do Património – Antecedentes Históricos," in *Dar futuro ao passado*, ed. by the Instituto Português do Património Arquitectónico e Arqueológico (Lisbon, 1993), pp. 33–71.

D'Agostino, Gabriella, "Moros y cristianos en la cultura tradicional siciliana," in Marlène Albert-Llorca and José Antonio González Alcantud (eds.), *Moros y cristianos: representaciones del otro en las fiestas del Mediterráneo occidental* (Toulouse, 2003), pp. 163–176.

Daniel, Norman, *Islam and the West: The Making of an Image* (Oxford, 1993). First edition 1960.

Darias de las Heras, Victoriano, "El africanismo español y la labor comunicadora del Instituto de Estudios Africanos," in *Revista Latina de Comunicación Social* 46 (2002), http://www.ull.es/publicaciones/latina/2002/latina46enero/4601darias.htm (accessed 4 Jun. 2010).

Delgado, Mariano, "Dem 'christlichen Beruf' treu geblieben? Zu den expliziten und impliziten religiösen Diskursen im Quijote," in Christoph Strosetzki (ed.), *Miguel de Cervantes' Don Quijote: Explizite und implizite Diskurse im Don Quijote* (Berlin, 2005), pp. 59–81.

Delgado, Mariano, "Der Mythos 'Toledo': Zur Konvivenz der drei monotheistischen Religionen und Kulturen im mittelalterlichen Spanien," in Sabine Hering (ed.), *Toleranz – Weisheit, Liebe oder Kompromiss? Multikulturelle Diskurse und Orte* (Opladen, 2004), pp. 69–91.

Delgado, Mariano, "Europa und der Islam in der Frühen Neuzeit: Exklusions- und Inklusionstypen zwischen 1453 und 1798," in Kerstin Armborst-Weihs and Judith Becker (eds.), *Toleranz und Identität: Geschichtsschreibung und*

Geschichtsbewusstsein zwischen religiösem Anspruch und historischer Erfahrung (Göttingen, 2010), pp. 53–77.

Delgado, Mariano, "Religion und Nation in den 'zwei Spanien': Der Kampf um die nationale Identität 1812–1980," in Urs Altermatt and Franziska Metzger (eds.), *Religion und Nation: Katholizismen im Europa des 19. und 20. Jahrhunderts* (Stuttgart, 2007), pp. 51–68.

Díaz-Andreu, Margarita, "Islamic Archaeology and the Origin of the Spanish Nation," in ibid. and Timothy Champion (eds.), *Nationalism and Archaeology in Europe* (London, 1996), pp. 68–89.

Díaz-Andreu, Margarita, "The Past in the Present. The Search for Roots in Cultural Nationalism: The Spanish Case," in Justo G. Beramendi, Ramón Maiz, and Xosé M. Núñez Seixas (eds.), *Nationalism in Europe: Past and Present*, vol. 1 (Santiago de Compostela, 1994), pp. 199–218.

Díaz-Andreu, Margarita, *A World History of Nineteenth-Century Archaeology: Nationalism, Colonialism and the Past* (Oxford, 2007).

Díaz-Andreu, Margarita, and Timothy Champion (eds.), *Nationalism and Archaeology in Europe* (London, 1996).

Díaz-Andreu, Margarita, Gloria Mora, and Jordi Cortadella (eds.), *Diccionario Histórico de la Arqueología en España, siglos XV–XX* (Madrid, 2009).

Dix, Steffen, "As esferas seculares e religiosas na sociedade portuguesa," in *Análise social* 45, no. 194 (2010), pp. 5–27.

Dogo, Marco, "The Balkan Nation-States and the Muslim Question," in Stefano Bianchini and Marco Dogo (eds.), *The Balkans: National Identities in a Historical Perspective* (Ravenna, 1998), pp. 61–74.

Domene Verdú, José Fernando, "Síntesis histórica de las Fiestas de Moros y Cristianos," in *Tercer Congreso Nacional de fiestas de moros y cristianos* (Murcia, 2002), pp. 353–376.

Domene Verdú, José Fernando, and Antonio Sempere Bernal, *Las fiestas de Moros y Cristianos de Villena* (Alcoy, 1989).

Dominguez Ortíz, Antonio, and Bernard Vincent, *Historia de los moriscos: Vida y tragedia de una minoría* (Madrid, 1978).

Elena, Alberto, "Romancero Marroquí: Africanismo y cine bajo el franquismo," in *Secuencias: Revista de Historia del Cine* 4 (1996), pp. 83–118.

Elorza, Antonio, *Un pueblo escogido: Génesis, definición y desarrollo del nacional-ismo vasco* (Barcelona, 2001).

Enciclopedia universal ilustrada europeo-americana (*Enciclopedia Espasa*) (Madrid, 1908ff.); supplement from 2005.

Epalza, Mikel de, *Los moriscos antes y después de la expulsion* (Madrid, 1992).

Erll, Astrid, *Kollektives Gedächtnis und Erinnerungskulturen: eine Einführung* (Stuttgart, 2005).

Espí Valdés, Adrián, *De las embajadas y los embajadores de los moros y cristianos de Alcoy* (Alcoy, 1989).

Espí Valdés, Adrián, *El Arte en las Fiestas de Moros y Cristianos de Alcoy* (Alcoy, 1976).

Esteban de Vega, Mariano, "Castilla y España en la Historia general de Modesto Lafuente," in Antonio Morales Moya and Mariano Esteban de Vega (eds.), *¿Alma de España? Castilla en las interpretaciones del pasado español* (Madrid, 2005), pp. 87–140: here, pp. 87–88.

Fabião, Carlos, "Archeology and Nationalism: The Portuguese Case," in

Margarita Díaz-Andreu and Timothy Champion (eds.), *Nationalism and Archaeology in Europe* (London, 1996), pp. 90–107.

Fabião, Carlos, "Para a história da arqueologia em Portugal," in *Penélope* 2 (1989), pp. 10–26.

Fanjul, Serafín, *Al-Andalus contra España: La forja del mito* (Madrid, 2000).

Fanjul, Serafín, *La quimera de Al-Andalus* (Madrid, 2005).

Farinha, António Dias, "A civilização árabe na obra de Herculano," in *Alexandre Herculano à luz do nosso tempo*, ed. by the Academia Portuguesa da História (Lisbon, 1977), pp. 323–340.

Farinha, António Dias, "Os estudos árabes na historiografia posterior a Herculano," in *A historiografia portuguesa de Herculano a 1950: Actas do colóquio* (Lisbon, 1978), pp. 293–304.

Ferreira, António Matos, "A constitucionalização da religião," in *História religiosa de Portugal*, vol. III: *Religião e Sécularização* (Lisbon, 2002), pp. 37–59.

Ferreira, Jerusa Pires, "Um rei a resmas: Carlos Magno e a América," in Braulio do Nascimento (ed.), *Euro-América: Uma realidade comum?* (Rio de Janeiro, 1996), pp. 133–151.

Fetscher, Caroline, "Der postmoderne Despot," in Thomas Großbölting and Rüdiger Schmidt (eds.), *Der Tod des Diktators: Ereignis und Erinnerung im 20. Jahrhundert* (Göttingen, 2011), pp. 251–276.

Flacke, Monika (ed.), *Mythen der Nationen: Ein europäisches Panorama*, 2nd ed. (Munich and Berlin, 1998).

Flesler, Daniela, and Adrián Pérez Melgosa, "Battles of Identity, or Playing 'Guest' and 'Host': the Festivals of Moors and Christians in the Context of Moroccan Immigration in Spain," in *Journal of Spanish Cultural Studies* 4, no. 2 (2003), pp. 151–168.

França, José-Augusto "Exposição do Mundo Português," in *Colóquio Artes* 45 (1980), pp. 34–47.

François, Étienne, "Le 'mythe du péril islamique' au miroir de l'histoire," in Hamit Bozarslan (ed.), *Regards et miroirs: Melanges Rémy Leveau* (Leipzig, 1997), pp. 89–99.

Freeland, Alan, "The People and the Poet: Portuguese National Identity and the Camões Tercentenary," in Clare Mar-Molinero and Angel Smith (eds.), *Nationalism and the Nation in the Iberian Peninsula: Competing and Conflicting Identities* (Oxford, 1996), pp. 53–67.

Gallop, Rodney, *Portugal – a Book of Folk-Ways* (Cambridge, 1936).

Gallop, Rodney, *The Origins of the Morris Dance* (n. p., 1935).

Garate Cordoba, José María, "Las tropas de Africa en la Guerra Civil española," in *Revista de historia militar* 70 (1991), pp. 9–62.

Garcia Balanà, Albert, "Patria, plebe y política en la España isabelina: la guerra de África en Cataluña 1859–1860," in Eloy Martín Corrales (ed.), *Marruecos y el colonialismo español (1859–1912): De la Guerra de África a la penetración pacífica* (Barcelona, 2002), pp. 13–77.

García-Arenal, Mercedes, *La diáspora de los andalusíes* (Barcelona, 2003).

Gellner, Ernest, *Nations and Nationalism* (Oxford, 1983).

Gerhard, Ute, "Schiller im 19. Jahrhundert," in Helmut Koopmann (ed.), *Schiller-Handbuch* (Stuttgart, 1998), pp. 759–772.

Gibson, Ian, *Queipo de Llano: Sevilla, verano de 1936* (Barcelona, 1986).

Giese, Francine, "Die Grosse Moschee von Córdoba zwischen Christianisierung und Re-Islamisierung," in *Bauforschung online*, Aug. 2007, www.bauforschungonline.ch (accessed 8 July 2010).

Giese, Francine, "Sein und Schein in der spanisch-islamischen Architektur. Die Arkaturen der Capilla de Villaviciosa und des Patio de los Leones," in *Miradas: Elektronische Zeitschrift für Iberische und Ibero-amerikanische Kunstgeschichte* 1 (2014), pp. 3–14.

Giralt, Josep (ed.), *El Islám y Cataluña* (Barcelona and Granada, 1998).

Gómez-Martínez, José Luis, *Américo Castro y el origen de los españoles: Historia de una polémica* (Madrid, 1975).

Gonçalves, Nuno da Silva, "A dimensão missionária do catolicismo português," in *História religiosa de Portugal*, vol. 3: *Religião e Sécularização* (Lisbon, 2002), pp. 353–397.

González Alcantud, José Antonio (ed.), *Marroquíes en la Guerra Civil española: Campos equívocos* (Barcelona, 2003).

González Alcantud, José Antonio, (ed.), *El orientalismo desde el Sur* (Barcelona, 2006).

González Alcantud, José Antonio, "El cronotopo de todos los vientos," in ibid. and Antonio Malpica Cuello (eds.), *Pensar la Alhambra* (Barcelona and Granada, 2001), pp. 7–20.

González Alcantud, José Antonio, *Lo moro: Las lógicas de la derrota y la formación del estereotipo islámico* (Barcelona, 2002).

Goytisolo, Juan, "Cara y cruz del moro en nuestra literatura," in *Revista internacional de sociología* 46, no. 4 (1988), pp. 601–615.

Graf, Friedrich Wilhelm, *Die Wiederkehr der Götter: Religion in der modernen Kultur* (Munich, 2004).

Grande Enciclopedia portuguesa e brasileira (Lisbon and Rio de Janeiro, 1945ff.).

Guedes, Ana Isabel Marques, *Algumas considerações sobre a "questão religiosa" em Portugal (meados do séc XIX a início do séc. XX): O anticlericalismo e o espírito republicano* (Porto, 1990).

Guereña, Jean-Louis (ed.), *Les nationalismes dans l'Espagne contemporaine: Idéologies, mouvements, symboles* (Paris, 2001).

Guerreiro, António Machado, "Floripes e os Pares de França no Teatro Popular," in *Vértice* 32 (1972), pp. 612–629.

Güntert, George, "Der Diskurs der Minderheiten: Sancho und der Moriske Ricote," in Christoph Strosetzki (ed.), *Miguel de Cervantes' Don Quijote: Explizite und implizite Diskurse im Don Quijote* (Berlin, 2005), pp. 83–97.

Gusmão, Alberto, *A real abadia de Alcobaça: Estudio Histórico-Arquelógico* (Lisbon, 1948).

Haber, Peter, Erik Petry, and Daniel Wildmann, *Jüdische Identität und Nation: Fallbeispiele aus Mitteleuropa* (Cologne, Weimar, and Vienna, 2006).

Harris, Max, "Muhammed and the Virgin: Folk Dramatizations of Battles Between Moors and Christians in Modern Spain," in *The Drama Review* 38, no. 1 (1994), pp. 45–61.

Hastings, Adrian, *The Construction of Nationhood* (Cambridge, 1997).

Haug-Moritz, Gabriele and Ludolf Pelizaeus (eds.), *Repräsentationen der islamischen Welt im Europa der Frühen Neuzeit* (Münster, 2010).

Haupt, Heinz-Gerhard, and Dieter Langewiesche (eds.), *Nation und Religion in*

Europa: Mehrkonfessionelle Gesellschaften im 19. und 20. Jahrhundert (Frankfurt am Main, 2004).

Haupt, Heinz-Gerhard, and Jürgen Kocka, "Historischer Vergleich: Methoden, Aufgaben, Probleme: Eine Einleitung," in ibid. (eds.), *Geschichte und Vergleich: Ansätze und Ergebnisse international vergleichender Geschichtsschreibung* (Frankfurt am Main and New York, 1996), pp. 9–45: here: p. 15 and pp. 24–25.

Hauser, Stefan F., "Orientalismus," in *Der neue Pauly*, vol. 15/1 (Stuttgart and Weimar, 2001), columns 1234–1243.

Healy, Maureen, "In aller 'Freundschaft'? Österreichische 'Türkenbilder' zwischen Gegnerschaft und 'Freundschaft' vor und während des Ersten Weltkrieges," in Laurence Cole, Christa Hämmerle, and Martin Scheuz (eds.), *Glanz – Gewalt – Gehorsam: Militär und Gesellschaft in der Habsburgermonarchie 1800–1918* (Essen, 2011), pp. 269–291.

Hein-Kircher, Heidi, "Überlegungen zu einer Typologisierung von politischen Mythen aus historiographischer Sicht – ein Versuch," in ibid. and Hans Hennig Hahn (eds.), *Politische Mythen im 19. und 20. Jahrhundert in Mittel- und Osteuropa* (Marburg 2006), pp. 407–424.

Hein-Kircher, Heidi, and Hans Henning Hahn (ed.), *Politische Mythen im 19. und 20. Jahrhundert in Mittel- und Osteuropa* (Marburg, 2006).

Heitsch, Friederike, *Imagologie des Islam in der neueren und neuesten spanischen Literatur* (Kassel, 1998).

Herbers, Klaus, "Der Apostel Jakobus: Vom spanischen zum europäischen Mythos," in Inge Milfull and Michael Neumann (eds.), *Mythen Europas: Schlüsselfiguren der Imagination: Mittelalter* (Regensburg, 2004), pp. 48–66.

Hering, Gunnar, "Die Osmanenzeit im Selbstverständnis der Völker Südosteuropas," in Hans Georg Majer (ed.), *Die Staaten Südosteuropas und die Osmanen* (Munich, 1989), pp. 355–380.

Herold-Schmidt, Hedwig, "Die Feste der iberischen Diktaturen: Portugal und Spanien in den 1940er Jahren," in Michael Maurer (ed.), *Festkulturen im Vergleich: Inszenierungen des Religiösen und Politischen* (Cologne, Weimar, and Vienna, 2010), pp. 291–319.

Herr, Richard, and John H. R. Polt (eds.), *Iberian Identity: Essays on the Nature of Identity in Portugal and Spain* (Berkeley, 1989).

Hertel, Patricia, "Moros y cristianos: Inszenierungen des 'Wir' und des 'Anderen' als erfundene Tradition im Spanien des 19. Jahrhunderts," in David Luginbühl et al. (eds.), *Religiöse Grenzziehungen im öffentlichen Raum: Mechanismen und Strategien von Inklusion und Exklusion im 19. und 20. Jahrhundert* (Stuttgart, 2011), pp. 213–229.

Hertel, Patricia, "Reconquista Reenacted: National Myths in the Spanish Restoration (1898–1918)," in: Franziska Metzger (ed.), *Trans-national Perspectives on Nationalism – Methodological Approaches and Case Studies* (Berlin, forthcoming).

Hirschi, Caspar, *Wettkampf der Nationen: Konstruktionen einer deutschen Ehrgemeinschaft an der Wende vom Mittelalter zur Neuzeit* (Göttingen, 2005).

História religiosa de Portugal, 3 vols. (Lisbon, 2000ff.)

A historiografia portuguesa anterior a Herculano: Actas do coloquio (Lisbon, 1977).

A historiografia portuguesa de Herculano a 1950: Actas do colóquio (Lisbon, 1978).

Hobsbawm, Eric and Terence Ranger (eds.), *The Invention of Tradition*, 23rd ed. (Cambridge, 2015). First edition 1983.

Hobsbawm, Eric, *Nations and Nationalism since 1780: Programme, Myth, Reality* (Cambridge, 1991).

Hodgson, Marshall G. S., *L'islam dans l'histoire mondiale* (Paris, 1998).

Höfert, Almut, "Alteritätsdiskurse: Analyseparameter historischer Antagonismusnarrative und ihre historiographischen Folgen," in Gabriele Haug-Moritz and Ludolf Pelizaeus (eds.), *Repräsentationen der islamischen Welt im Europa der Frühen Neuzeit* (Münster, 2010), pp. 21–40.

Höfert, Almut, *Den Feind beschreiben: "Türkengefahr" und europäisches Wissen über das Osmanische Reich 1450–1600* (Frankfurt am Main, 2003).

Hottinger, Arnold, *Die Mauren: Arabische Kultur in Spanien* (Munich, 1995).

Iglesias Amorín, Alfonso, "La memoria de las guerras de Marruecos en España 1859–1936," Ph.D. thesis, Universidade de Santiago de Compostela, 2014.

Jensen, Geoffrey, "The Peculiarities of 'Spanish Morocco': Imperial Ideology and Economic Development," in *Mediterranean Historical Review* 20, no. 1 (2005), pp. 81–102.

Jensen, Geoffrey, "Toward the 'Moral Conquest' of Morocco: Hispano-Arabic Education in Early Twentieth Century North Africa," in *European History Quarterly* 31, no. 2 (2001), pp. 205–229.

João, Maria Isabel, "Public Memory and Power in Portugal (1880–1960)," in *Portuguese Studies* 18 (2002), pp. 96–120.

João, Maria Isabel, *Memória e Império: Comemorações em Portugal 1880–1960* (Lisbon, 2002).

Kaelble, Hartmut, "Die interdisziplinären Debatten über Vergleich und Transfer," in ibid. and Jürgen Schriewer (eds.), *Vergleich und Transfer: Komparatistik in den Sozial-, Geschichts- und Kulturwissenschaften* (Frankfurt am Main, 2003), pp. 469–493.

Kaelble, Hartmut, *Der historische Vergleich: Eine Einführung zum 19. und 20. Jahrhundert* (Frankfurt am Main and New York, 1999).

Kappert, Petra, "Europa und der Orient," in Jochen Hippler and Andrea Lueg (eds.), *Feindbild Islam* (Hamburg, 1993), pp. 44–76.

Kemnitz, Eva Maria von, "Envoys, Princesses, Seamen and Captives: The Muslim Presence in Portugal in the 18th and 19th Centuries," in *Lusotopie* 14, no. 1 (2007), pp. 105–113.

Kemnitz, Eva Maria von, "International Contacts of the Portuguese Arabists (XVIIIth and XIXth centuries)," in Barbara Michalak-Pikulska and Andrzej Pikulski (eds.), *Authority, Privacy and Public Order in Islam: Proceedings of the 22nd Congress of L'Union Européenne des Arabisants et Islamisants* (Leuven and Paris and Dudley, 2006), pp. 369–386.

Kemnitz, Eva Maria von, "Muslims as Seen by the Portuguese Press 1974–1999," in Wasif Shadid and Pieter S. van Koningsveld (eds.), *Religious Freedom and the Neutrality of the State: The Position of Islam in the European Union* (Leuven, 2002), pp. 7–26.

Kemnitz, Eva Maria von, "O panorama das colecções museológicas islâmicas de Portugal," in Santiago Macias and Claúdio Torres (eds.), *Portugal Islâmico: Os Últimos Sinais do Mediterrâneo* (Lisbon, 1998), pp. 307–319.

Kemnitz, Eva Maria von, *Portugal e o Magrebe (séculos XVIII/XIX): Pragmatismo, inovação e conhecimento nas relações diplomáticas* (Lisbon, 2010).

Kolstø, Pål (ed.), *Myths and Boundaries in South-Eastern Europe* (London, 2005).

Koppelkamm, Stefan, *Der imaginäre Orient: Exotische Bauten des achtzehnten und neunzehnten Jahrhunderts in Europa* (Berlin, 1987).

Kottmann, Sina Lucia, "Mocking and Miming the 'Moor': Staging of the 'Self' and 'Other' on Spain's borders with Morocco," in *Journal of Mediterranean Studies* 20, no. 1 (2011), pp. 107–136.

Kottmann, Sina Lucia, "Moros en la Costa! – Mauren an christlichen Ufern: Abwehr und Inkorporation des Fremden im Süden Spaniens," in *Peripherie* 29, no. 114/15 (2009), pp. 282–303.

Kottmann, Sina Lucia, "Moros y Cristianos in Südspanien: Fiesta zwischen Spiel und Ernst," Master's thesis, Eberhard Karls Universität, Tübingen, 2004.

Krom, Maria J. C., "Festivals of Moors and Christians: Performance, Commodity and Identity in Folk Celebrations in Southern Spain," in *Journal of Mediterranean Studies* 18, no. 1 (2008), pp. 119–138.

Krumeich, Gerd, and Hartmut Lehmann (eds.), *"Gott mit uns": Nation, Religion und Gewalt im 19. und frühen 20. Jahrhundert* (Göttingen, 2000).

Krumeich, Gerd, and Susanne Brandt (eds.), *Schlachtenmythen: Ereignis – Erzählung – Erinnerung* (Cologne, 2003).

Kunz, Rudibert, and Rolf-Dieter Müller, *Giftgas gegen Abd el Krim: Deutschland, Spanien und der Gaskrieg in Spanisch-Marokko 1922–1927* (Freiburg im Breisgau, 1990).

Landwehr, Achim, "Diskurs und Diskursgeschichte: Version 1.0," in *Docupedia-Zeitgeschichte*, 11 Feb. 2010, http://docupedia.de/zg/ Diskurs_ und_Diskursgeschichte?oldid=75508 (accessed 17 Nov 2010).

Langewiesche, Dieter, "Die Idee Nation als Handlungsorientierung," in Lutz Raphael and Heinz-Elmar Tenorth (eds.), *Ideen als gesellschaftliche Gestaltungskraft im Europa der Neuzeit: Beiträge für eine erneuerte Geistesgeschichte* (Munich, 2006), pp. 359–368.

Langewiesche, Dieter, *Reich, Nation, Föderation: Deutschland und Europa* (Munich, 2008).

Lavajo, Joaquim Chorão, "Islão e christianismo, entre a tolerância e a guerra santa," in *História religiosa de Portugal*, vol. 1: *Formação e limites da cristandade* (Lisbon, 2000), pp. 127–133.

Leal, Ernesto Castro, "Nacionalismos portugueses: cultura e política no século XX," in *Revista da Faculdade de Letras de Lisboa* 26 (2002), pp. 29–39.

Leal, Ernesto Castro, "Poder, Memória e Glória," in *Revista Portuguesa de História* 36, no. 2 (2002–2003), pp. 313–334.

Leal, Ernesto Castro, *Nação e nacionalismos: A Cruzada Nacional D. Nuno Álvares Pereira e as origens do Estado Novo 1918–1938* (Lisbon, 1999).

Leal, João, *Etnografias Portuguesas (1870–1970): Cultura Popular e Identidade Nacional* (Lisbon, 2000).

Lécuyer, Marie Claude, and Carlos Serrano, *La Guerre d'Afrique et ses répercussions en Espagne 1859–1904* (Paris, 1976).

Lehmann, Hartmut (ed.), *Säkularisierung, Dechristianisierung, Rechristianisierung im neuzeitlichen Europa* (Göttingen, 1997).

Lepsius, M. Rainer, "The Nation and Nationalism in Germany," trans. by Jean A. Campbell, in *Social Research: An International Quarterly* 71, no. 3 (2004), pp. 481–500.

Liakova, Marina, "'Europa' und 'der Islam' als Mythen in den öffentlichen Diskursen in Bulgarien," in Heidi Hein-Kircher and Hans Henning Hahn (ed.), *Politische Mythen im 19. und 20. Jahrhundert in Mittel- und Osteuropa* (Marburg, 2006), pp. 225–242.

Livermore, Harold, "The 'Conquest of Lisbon' and its author," in *Portuguese Studies* 6 (1990), pp 1–16.

Llinares García, Mar, *Os mouros no imaxinario popular galego* (Santiago de Compostela, 1990).

Lopez Facal, Ramón, "La Historia enseñada en España," in Carlos Taibo (ed.), *Nacionalismo español: Esencias, memoria e instituciones* (Madrid, 2007), pp. 329–350.

López García, Bernabé, "Arabismo y Orientalismo en España: Radiografía y diagnóstico de un gremio escaso y apartadizo," in *Awraq*, supplement to vol. 11 (1990), pp. 35–69.

López García, Bernabé, "Origen, Gestión y Divulgación de la Historia de los Mozárabes de Francisco Javier Simonet (con una bibliografía del Simonet publicista)," in *Awraq* 22 (2001–2005), pp. 183–211.

López García, Bernabé, *Marruecos y España: Una historia contra toda lógica* (Seville, 2007).

López Sánchez, José María, "Im Dienste der Wissenschaft: Der Centro de estudios históricos und die Begründung eines liberalen Nationalbewußtseins in Spanien," in *Berichte zur Wissenschaftsgeschichte* 29, no. 2 (2006), pp. 121–136.

López-Baralt, Luce, *Islam in Spanish Literature: From the Middle Ages to the Present* (Leiden, 1992). First edition Madrid, 1985.

López-Cordón Cortezo, Maria Victoria, "La mentalidad conservadora durante la Restauración," in José Luis Garcia Delgado (ed.), *La España de la Restauración: Politica, Economia, Legislación y Cultura* (Madrid, 1985), pp. 71–109.

Lourenço, Eduardo, *Portugal como destino: Dramaturgia cultural portuguesa* (São Paulo, 1999).

Macagno, Lorenzo, *Outros Muçulmanos: Islão e narrativas coloniais* (Lisbon, 2006).

Machado, José Pedro, "Os estudos arábicos em Portugal," in ibid., *Ensaios arabico-portugueses* (Lisbon, 1997), pp. 109–144.

Machado, Paula Costa, and Hélder Ferreira: *Bugiada Valongo* (Valongo, 2002).

Machaqueiro, Mário Artur, "Estratégias, rivalidades e conflictos de poder identitário: Valy Mamede e a disputa pelo controlo das comunidades muçulmanas," http://run.unl.pt/bitstream/10362/2727/1/Valy%20Mamede%20e%20a%20disputa%20pelas%20comunidades%20isl%C3%A2micas.pdf (accessed 26 Jun. 2011).

Machaqueiro, Mário Artur, "Islão transnacional e os fantasmas do colonialismo português," in *Relações Internacionais: Revista do Instituto Portguês de Relações Internacionais da Universidad Nova de Lisboa*, June 2011, no. 30, pp. 71–82.

Machaqueiro, Mário Artur, "The Islamic Policy of Portuguese Colonial Mozambique, 1960–1973," in *The Historical Journal* 55, no. 4 (2012), pp. 1097–1116.

Macias, Santiago et al. (eds.), *Mesquita Igreja de Mértola* (Mértola, 2011).

Macias, Santiago, "Entrevista a António Borges Coelho," in ibid. (ed.), *Historiador em discurso directo: António Borges Coelho* (Mértola, 2003), pp. 15–42.

Macias, Santiago, and Cláudio Torres (eds.), *Portugal Islâmico: Os Últimos Sinais do Mediterrâneo* (Lisbon, 1998).

Madariaga, Maria Rosa de, "Imagen del moro en la memoria colectiva del pueblo español y retorno del moro en la Guerra Civil de 1936," in *Revista internacional de sociología* 46, no. 4 (1988), pp. 575–599.

Madariaga, Maria Rosa de, "Le nationalisme basque et le nationalisme catalan face au problème colonial au Maroc," in *Pluriel débat* 13 (1978), pp. 31–54.

Madariaga, Maria Rosa de, *Los moros que trajo Franco: La intervención de tropas coloniales en la Guerra Civil* (Barcelona, 2002).

Maestro González, Pilar, "La idea de España en la historiografía escolar del siglo XIX," in Antonio Morales Moya and Mariano Esteban de Vega (eds.), *¿Alma de España? Castilla en las interpretaciones del pasado español* (Madrid, 2005), pp. 141–194.

Maier, Charles S., "Hot Memory . . . Cold Memory: On the Political Half-Life of Fascist and Communist Memory," in *Transit: Tr@nsit online* 22 (2002), http://www.iwm.at/read-listen-watch/transit-online/hot-memory-cold-memory-on-the-political-half-life-of-fascist-and-communist-memory/ (accessed 28 Jan. 2015).

Majer, Hans Georg (ed.), *Die Staaten Südosteuropas und die Osmanen* (Munich, 1989).

Mansanet Ribes, José Luis, *La Fiesta de Moros y Cristianos de Alcoy y su Historia* (Alcoy, 1991).

Manzano Moreno, Eduardo "La creación de un esencialismo: la historia de al-Andalus en la visión del arabismo español," in Gonzalo Fernández Parilla and Manuel C. Feria García (eds.), *Orientalismo, exotismo y traducción* (Cuenca, 2000), pp. 23–37.

Manzano Moreno, Eduardo, "La construcción histórica del pasado nacional," in Juan Sisinio Pérez Garzón (ed.), *La gestión de la memória: la historia de España al servicio del poder* (Barcelona, 2000), pp. 33–62.

Marín, Manuela, "Arabistas en España: Un asunto de familia," in *Al-Qantara* 13, no. 2 (1992), pp. 379–393.

Marín, Manuela, "Orientalismo en España: Estudios árabes y acción colonial en Marruecos (1894–1943)," in *Hispania* 69, no. 231 (2009), pp. 117–146.

Mar-Molinero, Clare, and Angel Smith (eds.), *Nationalism and the Nation in the Iberian Peninsula: Competing and Conflicting Identities* (Oxford, 1996).

Marques, A. H. de Oliveira, *Geschichte Portugals und des portugiesischen Weltreichs* (Stuttgart, 2001).

Marques, João Lopes, "'Mouros forros' esquecidos," in *Público*, 10 Dec. 1996, p. 9.

Márquez Villanueva, Francisco, *Santiago: Trayectoria de un mito* (Barcelona, 2004). Averkorn, Raphaela, "Der Jakobus-Mythos: Die Entwicklung eines Mythos vom Mittelalter bis zur Gegenwart," in: Ulrich Müller and Werner Wunderlich (eds.), *Herrscher, Helden, Heilige*, 2nd ed. (St. Gallen, 2001), pp. 252–541.

Martín Corrales, Eloy (ed.), *Marruecos y el colonialismo español (1859–1912): De la Guerra de África a la penetración pacífica* (Barcelona, 2002).

Martín Corrales, Eloy, "El 'moro', decano de los enemigos exteriores de España:

Una larga enemistad (VIII–XXI)," in Xosé Manoel Núñez Seixas and Francisco Sevillano (eds.), *Los enemigos de España: Imagen del otro, conflictos bélicos y disputas nacionales, siglos XVI–XX* (Madrid, 2010), pp. 165–182.

Martín Corrales, Eloy, "El catalanismo y el andalucismo ante la aventura colonial en Marruecos," in *Actas del Tercer Congreso de Historia Catalano-Andaluza: Cataluña y Andalucía, 1898–1939* (Barcelona, 2003), pp. 155–191.

Martín Corrales, Eloy, "El cine en el protectorado español de Marruecos (1909–1939)," in *Cuadernos del Archivo Municipal de Ceuta* 10 (1996), pp. 227–240.

Martín Corrales, Eloy, "El nacionalismo catalán y la expansión colonial española en Marruecos: de la guerra de África a la entrada en vigor del Protectorado (1860–1912)," in ibid. (ed.), *Marruecos y el colonialismo español (1859–1912): De la Guerra de África a la penetración pacífica* (Barcelona, 2002), pp. 167–215.

Martín Corrales, Eloy, "Entre el 'moro' violador y el 'moro' seductor: la imagen de los marroquíes en la guerra civil según las fuerzas republicanas," in Ángeles Ramírez (ed.), *Antropología y antropólogos en Marruecos: Homenaje a David M. Hart* (Barcelona, 2002), pp. 221–236.

Martín Corrales, Eloy, *La imagen del magrebí en España: Una perspectiva histórica siglos XVI–XX* (Barcelona, 2002).

Martin-Márquez, Susan, *Disorientations: Spanish Colonialism in Africa and the Performance of Identity* (New Haven and London, 2008), pp. 220–299.

Marx, Christoph, "Grenzfälle: Zu Geschichte und Potential des Frontierbegriffs," in *Saeculum* 54, no. 1 (2003), pp. 123–143.

Mascarenhas, José Fernandes, *Elementos históricos sobre a freguesia de Santa Catarina da Fonte do Bispo e a batalha do "Desbarato" entre mouros e cristãos* (Tavira, 1972).

Mateo Dieste, Josep Lluís, *El "moro" entre los primitivos: El caso del Protectorado español en Marruecos* (Barcelona, 2003).

Matos, Sérgio Campos, "Conceitos de iberismo em Portugal," in *Revista de História das Ideias* 28 (2007), pp. 169–193.

Matos, Sérgio Campos, "Iberismo e identidade nacional (1851–1910)," in *Clio: Revista do Centro de História da Universidade de Lisboa* 14 (2006), pp. 349–400.

Matos, Sérgio Campos, "Was Iberism a Nationalism? Conceptions of Iberism in Portugal in the Nineteenth and Twentieth Centuries," in *Portuguese Studies* 25, no. 2 (2009), pp. 215–229.

Matos, Sérgio Campos, and David Mota Álvarez, "Portuguese and Spanish Historiography: Distance and Proximity," in Stefan Berger and Chris Lorenz (eds.), *The Contested Nation: Ethnicity, Class, Religion and Gender in National Histories* (London, 2008), pp. 339–365.

Matos, Sérgio Campos, *Consciência histórica e nacionalismo, Portugal, séc XIX e XX* (Lisbon, 2008).

Matos, Sérgio Campos, *História, mitologia, imaginário nacional: A História no Curso dos Liceus 1895–1939* (Lisbon, 1990).

Matos, Sérgio Campos, *Historiografia e Memória Nacional no Portugal do Séc. XIX 1846–1898* (Lisbon, 1998).

Mattoso, José, *A identidade nacional* (Lisbon, 1991).

Medina, João, *Historia Contemporanea de Portugal: Das invasões francesas aos nossos dias,* 7 vols. (n. p., 1990).

Medina, João, *Portuguesismo(s) acerca da identidade nacional* (Lisbon, 2006).

Meneses, Filipo Ribero de, *Salazar: A Political Biography* (New York, 2010).

Menny, Anna Lena, and Britta Voß (eds.), *Die Drei Kulturen und spanische Identitäten: Geschichts- und literaturwissenschaftliche Beiträge zu einem Paradigma der iberischen Moderne* (Gütersloh, 2011).

Menny, Anna Lena, *Spanien und Sepharad: Über den offiziellen Umgang mit dem Judentum im Franquismus und in der Demokratie* (Göttingen, 2013).

Metzger, Franziska, *Geschichtsschreibung und Geschichtsdenken im 19. und 20. Jahrhundert* (Bern, Stuttgart, and Vienna, 2011).

Millán, Jesús, "El País Valencià en l'inici de l'Estat centralista del vuit-cents: Una aproximació," in *L'Estat-nació i el conflicte regional: Joan Mañé i Flaquer, un cas paradigmàtic* (Barcelona, 2004), pp. 63–90.

Moliner, María (ed.), *Diccionario de uso del español*, 2nd ed. (Madrid, 1998).

Mónica, Maria Filomena, *Educação e sociedade no Portugal de Salazar* (Porto, 1978).

Monroe, James, *Islam and the Arabs in Spanish Scholarship: Sixteenth Century to the Present* (Leiden, 1970).

Monteiro, Fernando Amaro, "Moçambique 1964–1974: As comunidades islâmicas, o Poder e a Guerra," in *Africana* 5 (1989), pp. 81–124.

Monteiro, Fernando Amaro, "O Islão, o poder e a Guerra: Moçambique 1964–1974," Ph.D. thesis, Universidade Técnica de Lisboa, 1992.

Montoya Abat, Brauli, *Alacant: La llengua interrompuda* (Valencia, 1996).

Mora, Gloria, and Margarita Díaz-Andreu (eds.), *La cristalización del pasado: Génesis y desarrollo del marco institucional de la arqueología en España* (Málaga, 1997).

Morales Lezcano, Victor, "El norte de África, estrella del orientalismo español," in *Awraq*, supplement to vol. 11 (1990), pp. 17–34.

Morales Lezcano, Victor, "Orientalismo marroquista vs. Africanismo español (1859–1860 en adelante)," in José Antonio González Alcantud (ed.), *El orientalismo desde el Sur* (Barcelona, 2006), pp. 217–228.

Morant i Ariño, Toni, "'Der Caudillo wird nur durch seinen eigenen Willen begrenzt.' Der Franco-Mythos in Spanien, 1936–1945," in Benno Ennker and Heidi Hein-Kircher (eds.), *Der Führer im Europa des 20. Jahrhunderts* (Marburg, 2010), pp.–180.

Morawiec, Małgorzata, "Antemurale christianitatis: Polen als Vormauer des christlichen Europa," in *Jahrbuch für Europäische Geschichte* 2 (2001), pp. 249–260.

Moreno Luzón, Javier (ed.), *Construir España: Nacionalismo español y procesos de nacionalización* (Madrid, 2007).

Moreno Luzón, Javier and Xosé Manoel Núñez Seixas, *Ser españoles: Imaginarios nacionalistas en el siglo XX* (Barcelona, 2013).

Moser, Gerald M., "What Did the Old Man of the Restelo Mean?," in *Luso-Brazilian Studies* 17, no. 2 (1980), pp. 139–151.

Mosser, Alois (ed.), *"Gottes auserwählte Völker": Erwählungsvorstellungen und kollektive Selbstfindung in der Geschichte* (Frankfurt am Main, 2001).

Muñoz Cosme, Alfonso, *La conservación del patrimonio arquitectonico español* (Madrid, 1989).

Nascimento, Braulio do (ed.), *Euro-América: Uma realidade comum?* (Rio de Janeiro, 1996).

Nerín, Gustau, and Alfred Bosch, *El imperio que nunca existió: La aventura colonial discutida en Hendaya* (Barcelona, 2001).

Neto, Vítor, *O Estado, a Igreja e a sociedade em Portugal 1831–1911* (Lisbon, 1998).

Newitt, Malyn, *Portugal in Africa: The Last Hundred Years* (London, 1981).

Noltenius, Paul, "Die Nation und Schiller," in Helmut Scheuer (ed.), *Dichter und ihre Nation* (Frankfurt am Main, 1993), pp. 151–175.

Noltenius, Paul, *Dichterfeiern in Deutschland: Rezeptionsgeschichte als Sozialgeschichte am Beispiel der Schiller- und Freiligrath-Feiern* (Munich, 1984).

Nóvoa, António (ed.), *Dicionario de Educadores Portugueses* (Porto, 2003).

Nóvoa, António, *Le Temps des Professeurs: Analyse socio-historique de la profession enseignante au Portugal (XVIIIe–XXe siècle)*, 2 vols. (Lisbon, 1987).

Núñes Seixas, Xosé Manoel, *¡Fuera el Invasor! Nacionalismos y movilización bélica durante la Guerra Civil española* (Madrid, 2006).

Núñez Seixas, Xosé Manoel, "History of Civilization: Transnational or Post-Imperial? Some Iberian Perspectives (1870–1930)," in Stefan Berger and Chris Lorenz (eds.), *Nationalizing the Past: Historians as Nation-Builders* (Basingstoke, 2010), pp. 384–403.

Núñez Seixas, Xosé Manoel, "The Iberian Peninsula: Real and Imagined Overlaps," in Tibor Frank and Frank Hadler (eds.), *Disputed Territories and Shared Pasts: Overlapping National Histories in Modern Europe* (Basingstoke, 2010), pp. 329–348.

Núñez Seixas, Xosé Manoel, "The Region as Essence of the Fatherland: Regionalist Variants of Spanish Nationalism (1840–1936)," in *European History Quarterly* 31 (2001), pp. 483–518.

Núñez Seixas, Xosé Manoel, and António Costa Pinto, "Portugal and Spain," in Roger Eatwell (ed.), *European Political Cultures? Conflict or Convergence?* (London and New York, 1997), pp. 172–192.

Núñez Seixas, Xosé Manoel, *Patriotas y demócratas: El discurso nacionalista español después de Franco* (Madrid, 2010).

Ordieres Díez, Isabel, *Historia de la restauración monumental en España, 1835–1936* (Madrid, 1995).

Ordieres Díez, Isabel, *La formación de la conciencia patrimonial: Legislación e instituciones en la historia de la restauración arquitectónica en España* (Madrid, 1998).

Osterhammel, Jürgen, "Edward W. Said und die 'Orientalismus'-Debatte: Ein Rückblick," in *Asien Afrika Lateinamerika* 25 (1997), pp. 597–607.

Osterhammel, Jürgen, *Kolonialismus: Geschichte, Formen, Folgen*, 6th ed. (Munich, 2009).

Osterhammel, Jürgen, *The Transformation of the World: A Global History of the Nineteenth Century*, trans. by Patrick Camiller (Princeton, 2014).

Panadero Peropadre, Nieves, "Recuerdos de la Alhambra: Rafael Contreras y el Gabinete Árabe del Palacio Real de Aranjuez," in *Reales Sitios: Revista del Patrimonio Nacional* 31, no. 122 (1994), pp. 33–40.

Parafita, Alexandre, *A Mitologia dos Mouros: Lendas, mitos, serpentes, tesouros* (Canelas, 2006).

Parra Monserrat, David, "A Bridge between 'East' and 'West'? The View of the Muslim Past in 19th and 20th Century Spain," in Gabriele Haug-Moritz and Ludolf Pelizaeus (eds.), *Repräsentationen der islamischen Welt im Europa der Frühen Neuzeit,* (Münster, 2010), pp. 269–277.

Parra Monserrat, David, "Islam e identidad en la escuela franquista: Imágenes y tópicos a través de los manuales," in *Didáctica de las Ciencias Experimentales y Sociales* 21 (2007), pp. 15–32.

Parra Monserrat, David, "La Narrativa del Africanismo Franquista: Génesis y Prácticas Socio-Educativas," Ph.D. thesis, Universidad de Valencia, 2012.

Payne, Stanley G., *A History of Spain and Portugal,* 2 vols. (Madison, 1973).

Payne, Stanley G., *El catolicismo español* (Barcelona, 1984).

Peiro, Ignacio, "La difusión del libro de texto: autores y manuales de historia en los institutos del siglo XIX," in *Didáctica de las Ciencias Experimentales y Sociales* 7 (1993), pp. 39–57.

Peiro, Ignacio, and Gonzalo Pasamar Alzuria (eds.), *Dicionario Akal de historiadores espanoles* (Madrid, 2002).

Pelizaeus, Ludolf, "Die Konstruktion eines Islambildes in Spanien und Portugal als iberischer Integrationsfaktor," in Gabriele Haug-Moritz and Ludolf Pelizaeus (eds.), *Repräsentationen der islamischen Welt im Europa der Frühen Neuzeit* (Münster, 2010), pp. 177–205.

Pennell, C. Richard, *Morocco since 1830: A History* (London, 2001).

Perez, Rosa Maria (ed.), *Memórias Árabo-Islâmicas em Portugal* (Lisbon, 1998).

Pinto, António Costa, "Twentieth Century Portugal: An Introduction," in ibid. (ed.), *Contemporary Portugal: Politics, Society and Culture* (New York, 2003), pp. 1–46.

Pinto, Manuel, *A Bugiada: festa, luta e comunicação.* Paper presented at the 4th Encontro Lusófono de Ciências da Comunicação in São Vicente, Brasil, 19–22 Apr. 2000, http://www.bocc.ubi.pt/pag/_texto.php?html2=pinto-manuel-bugiada.html (accessed 20 Jan. 2008).

Pitarch, Vicent, "La llengua de l'administració eclesiàstica (País Valencià, segles XVII–XVIII)," in *L'espill* 6–7 (1980), pp. 41–76.

Poliakov, León, *Geschichte des Antisemitismus,* vol. IV: *Die Marranen im Schatten der Inquisition, mit einem Anhang: Die Morisken und ihre Vertreibung* (Worms, 1981).

Preston, Paul, *Franco: A Biography* (London, 1993).

Puccio-Den, Deborah, *Les Théâtres de "Maures et Chrétiens": Conflits politiques et dispositifs de reconciliation: Espagne, Sicile, XVIIe–XXIe siècles* (Turnhout, 2009).

Ramalhete, Ana Maria, "Ficcionalização de Contactos Culturais e Especifidade Nacional: Olhares Românicos sobre Modelos, Cristãos e Mouros," in Margarida L. Losa, Isménia de Sousa, and Gonçalo Vilas-Boas (eds.), *Literatura Comparada: Os Novos Paradigmas* (Porto, 1996), pp. 67–74.

Raphael, Lutz, "Ideen als gesellschaftliche Gestaltungskraft im Europa der Neuzeit," in ibid. and Heinz-Elmar Tenorth (eds.), *Ideen als gesellschaftliche Gestaltungskraft im Europa der Neuzeit: Beiträge für eine erneuerte Geistesgeschichte* (Munich, 2006), pp. 11–27.

Raposo, Paulo, "O Auto da Floripes: 'Cultura popular', etnógrafos, intelectuais e artistas, in *Etnografia* 2, no. 2 (1998), pp. 189–219.

Raquejo, Tonia, *El palacio encantado: La Alhambra en el arte británico* (Madrid, 1989).

Rauscher, Peter, "Die Erinnerung an den Erbfeind: Die 'Zweite Türkenbelagerung' Wiens 1683 im öffentlichen Bewusstsein Österreichs im 19. und 20. Jahrhundert," in Gabriele Haug-Moritz and Ludolf Pelizaeus (eds.), *Repräsentationen der islamischen Welt im Europa der Frühen Neuzeit* (Münster, 2010), pp. 278–305.

Rehrmann, Norbert, *Das schwierige Erbe von Sefarad: Juden und Mauren in der spanischen Literatur: Von der Romantik bis zur Mitte des 20. Jahrhunderts* (Frankfurt am Main, 2002).

Reinhard, Wolfgang, *Geschichte der europäischen Expansion*, vol. 4: *Dritte Welt Afrika* (Stuttgart, 1990).

Reis, António P. de M. dos, "Origem da 'Turquia' de Crasto," in *Almanaque de Ponte de Lima* (Ponte de Lima, 1980), pp. 143–148.

Reis, António, "Revolution und Demokratisierung," in Fernando Rosas (ed.), *Vom Ständestaat zur Demokratie: Portugal im 20. Jahrhundert* (Munich, 1997), pp. 89–106.

Renan, Ernest, "What is a Nation?," in Geoff Eley and Ronald Grigor Suny (eds.), *Becoming National: A Reader* (Oxford, 1996), pp. 42–55.

Rey Castelao, Ofelia, *Los mitos del apóstol Santiago* (Vigo, 2006).

Reyero, Carlos, *Imagen histórica de España, 1850–1900* (Madrid, 1987).

Ribas, Rogério de Oliveira, "Filhos de Mafoma: Mouriscos, cripto-islamismo e inquisição no Portugal quinhentista," 2 vols., Ph.D. thesis, Universidade de Lisboa, 2004.

Riedel, Sabine, "Die Politisierung islamischer Geschichte und Kultur am Beispiel Südosteuropas," in *Südost-Europa* 46, no. 1–2 (1997), pp. 539–561.

Ríos Saloma, Martin F., "De la Restauración a la Reconquista: la construcción de un mito nacional: Una revisión historiográfica: Siglos XVI–XIX," in *En la España Medieval* 28 (2005), pp. 379–414.

Ríos Saloma, Martin F., "La Reconquista: una invención historiográfica (siglos XVI–XIX)," in Daniel Baloup and Philippe Josserand (eds.), *Regards croisés sur la Guerre Sainte: Guerre, idéologie et religion dans l'espace méditerranéen latin (XIe–XIIIe siécle): Actes du Colloque international tenu à la Casa de Velázques (Madrid) du 11 au 13 avril 2005* (Toulouse, 2006), pp. 413–429.

Rivière Gómez, Aurora, "Arqueólogos y arqueología en el processo de construcción del Estado-nacional español (1834–1868)," in Gloria Mora and Margarita Díaz-Andreu (eds.), *La cristalización del pasado: Génesis y desarrollo del marco institucional de la arqueología en España* (Málaga, 1997), pp. 133–139.

Rivière Gómez, Aurora, *Orientalismo y nacionalismo español: Estudios árabes y hebreos en la universidad de Madrid 1843–1868* (Madrid, 2000).

Rocamora, José António, *El nacionalismo ibérico 1792–1936* (Valladolid, 1994).

Rodinson, Maxime, *Die Faszination des Islam* (Munich, 1985).

Rodríguez Campos, Xaquín "As festas patronais e a identidade en Galícia," in: *Galicia: Antropoloxía*, vol. 27: *Relixión. Crenzas. Festas* (A Coruña, 1997), pp. 354–375.

Rodríguez Domingo, José Manuel, "La Alhambra arqueológica (1847–1907):

Origen y evolución de un modelo anticuario," in Gloria Mora and Margarita Díaz-Andreu (eds.), *La cristalización del pasado: Génesis y desarrollo del marco institucional de la arqueología en España* (Málaga, 1997), pp. 341–350.

Rosado Llamas, María Dolores, and Manuel Gabriel López Payer, *La Batalla de Las Navas de Tolosa* (Madrid, 2002).

Rosas, Fernando, and José Maria Brandão Brito (eds.), *Dicionário da História do Estado Novo* (Lisbon, 1996).

Rotter, Ekkehart, *Abendland und Sarazenen: Das okzidentale Araberbild und seine Entstehung im Frühmittelalter* (Berlin and New York, 1986).

Rüegg, Walter (ed.), *Geschichte der Universität in Europa*, vol. 3: *Vom 19. Jahrhundert zum Zweiten Weltkrieg 1800–1945* (Munich, 2004).

Sáez-Arance, Antonio, "Constructing Iberia: National Traditions and the Problem(s) of a Peninsular History," in *European Review of History* 10, no. 2 (2003), pp. 189–202.

Said, Edward W., *Orientalism* (London, 1995). First edition 1978.

Salem, Abdelatif Ben, "La participación de los voluntarios árabes en las brigadas internacionales: Una memoria rescatada," in José Antonio González Alcantud (ed.), *Marroquíes en la Guerra Civil española: Campos equívocos* (Barcelona, 2003), pp. 111–129.

Sanchez Ruano, Francisco, *Islam y Guerra Civil española: moros con Franco y con la república* (Barcelona, 2004).

Santamarina Campos, Beatriz, "Moros y cristianos: De la batalla festiva a la discursiva," in *Gazeta de Antropologia* 24, no. 1 (2008), http://www.ugr.es/~pwlac/G24_16Beatriz_Santamarina_Campos.pdf (accessed 11 Feb. 2015).

Santos, Rui Afonso, "Comemorações/Festas oficiais," in Fernando Rosas and José Maria Brandão Brito (eds.), *Dicionário da História do Estado Novo* (Lisbon, 1996), pp. 162–167.

Santoveña Setién, Antonio, *Marcelino Menéndez Pelayo: revisión crítico-biográfica de un pensador católico* (Santander, 1994).

Schenk, Frithjof Benjamin, "Mental maps: Die Konstruktion von geographischen Räumen in Europa seit der Aufklärung," in *Geschichte und Gesellschaft* 28 (2002), pp. 493–514.

Schivelbusch, Wolfgang, *The Culture of Defeat: On National Trauma, Mourning, and Recovery* (London, 2004).

Schulze Wessel, Martin (ed.), *Nationalisierung der Religion und Sakralisierung der Nation im östlichen Europa* (Stuttgart, 2006).

Schulze, Reinhard, "Orientalism: Zum Diskurs zwischen Orient und Okzident," in Iman Attia (ed.), *Orient- und Islambilder: Interdisziplinäre Beiträge zu Orientalismus und antimuslimischem Rassismus* (Münster, 2007), pp. 45–68.

Schulze, Thies, *Dante Alighieri als nationales Symbol Italiens 1793–1915* (Tübingen, 2005).

Serrano, Carlos (ed.), *Nations en quête de passé: La péninsule ibérique XIXe–XXe siécles* (Paris, 2000).

Serrão, José, *Dicionário de História de Portugal* (Porto, 1984ff.).

Sevilla, Fabian, *Die "Drei Kulturen" und die spanische Identität: ein Konflikt bei Américo Castro und in der spanischsprachigen Narrativik der Moderne* (Tübingen, 2014).

Sewell, William H. Jr., *Work and Revolution in France: The Language of Labor from the Old Regime to 1848* (Cambridge, 1980).

Sidarus, Adel (ed.), *Islão e Arabismo na Península Ibérica: Actas do XI Congresso da Uniao Europeia de Arabistas e Islamólogos* (Évora, 1986).

Sidarus, Adel, "Os estudos árabes de Portugal (1772–1962)," in ibid. (ed.), *Islão e Arabismo na Península Ibérica: Actas do XI Congresso da Uniao Europeia de Arabistas e Islamólogos* (Évora, 1986), pp. 37–54.

Sievernich, Gereon, and Hendrik Budde (eds.), *Europa und der Orient 800–1900* (Gütersloh and Munich, 1989).

Silva, Antonio de Morais, *Novo Dicionário compacto da língua portuguesa*, 7th ed. (Lisbon, 1992).

Silva, Maria Cardeira da, "O sentido dos árabes no nosso sentido: Dos estudos sobre árabes e sobre muçulmanos em Portugal," in *Análise social* 39, no. 173 (2005), pp. 781–806.

Sobral, José Manuel, "A formação das nações e o nacionalismo: os paradigmas explicativos e o caso português," in *Análise social* 37 (2003), pp. 1093–1126.

Sobral, José Manuel, "O Norte, o Sul, a raça, a nação – representações da identidade nacional portuguesa (séculos XIX–XX)," in *Análise social* 39 (2004), pp. 255–284.

Stallaert, Christiane, *Etnogénesis y etnicidad: Una aproximación histórico-antropológica al casticismo* (Barcelona, 1998).

Stoll, André, "Woher kommt Dulcinea, und was schreibt Cide Hamete Benengeli? Cervantes' Erkundung der semitischen Zwischenwelten Kastiliens," in Christoph Strosetzki (ed.), *Miguel de Cervantes' Don Quijote: Explizite und implizite Diskurse im Don Quijote* (Berlin, 2005), pp. 99–135.

Storm, Eric, "El tercer centenario del Don Quijote en 1905 y el nacionalismo español," in *Hispania* 58, no. 199 (1998), pp. 625–654.

Storm, Eric, "Las conmemoraciones de héroes nacionales en la España de la Restauración: El centenario de El Greco de 1914," in *Historia y Política* 12 (2004), pp. 79–104.

Sundhaussen, Holm, "Kriegserinnerung als Gesamtkunstwerk und Tatmotiv: Sechshundertzehn Jahre Kosovo-Krieg (1389–1999)," in Dietrich Beyrau (ed.), *Der Krieg in religiösen und nationalen Deutungen der Neuzeit* (Tübingen, 2001), pp. 11–40.

Taboada Chivite, Xesus, "Moros y cristianos en tierras de Laza (Orense)," in ibid., *Ritos y creencias gallegas* (A Coruña, 1980), pp. 59–77. First published in *Revista de dialectología y tradiciones populares* 11, no. 3 (1955).

Taibo, Carlos (ed.), *Nacionalismo español: Esencias, memoria e instituciones* (Madrid, 2007).

Tercer Congreso Nacional de fiestas de moros y cristianos (Murcia, 2002).

Tiesler, Nina Clara, "Muçulmanos na margem: a nova presença islámica em Portugal," in *Sociologia: Problemas e práticas* 34 (2000), pp. 117–144.

Tiesler, Nina Clara, "Novidades no terreno: muçulmanos na Europa e o caso português," in *Análise social* 39, no. 173 (2005), pp. 827–849.

Tiesler, Nina Clara, "Portugal," in *Yearbook of Muslims in Europe* 2 (2010), pp. 413–423.

Tiesler, Nina Clara, and David Cairns, "Representing Islam and Lisbon Youth: Portuguese Muslims of Indian-Mozambican Origin," in *Lusotopie* 14, no. 1 (2007), pp. 223–238.

Todorova, Maria, "Die Osmanenzeit in der bulgarischen Geschichtsschreibung seit der Unabhängigkeit," in Hans Georg Majer (ed.), *Die Staaten Südosteuropas und die Osmanen* (Munich, 1989), pp. 127–161.

Todorova, Maria, "The Ottoman Legacy in the Balkans," in Leon Carl Brown (ed.), *Imperial Legacy: The Ottoman Imprint on the Balkans and the Middle East* (New York, 1996), pp. 45–77.

Todorova, Maria, *Imagining the Balkans* (New York and Oxford, 1997).

Torgal, Luís Reis, "A história em tempo de 'ditadura',"in Fernando Catroga, Luís Reis Torgal, and José Maria Amado Mendes, *História da História em Portugal séculos XIX–XX*, vol. 1, 2nd edition (n.p., 1998), pp. 272–310.

Torgal, Luís Reis, "Ensino da história," in Fernando Catroga, Luís Reis Torgal, and José Maria Amado Mendes, *História da História em Portugal séculos XIX–XX*, vol. 2, 2nd ed. (n.p. 1998), pp. 84–152.

Torre Gómez, Hipólito de la (ed.), *Portugal y España contemporáneos* (Madrid, 2000).

Torre Gómez, Hipólito de la, and António José Telo (eds.), *La mirada del otro: Percepctiones luso-españolas desde la historia* (Mérida, 2001).

Torre Gómez, Hipólito de la, and António José Telo, *Portugal e Espanha nos sistemas internacionais contemporâneos* (Lisbon, 2000).

Torres, Cláudio, "A arqueologia medieval e a historiografia portuguesa nos últimos anos," in *Actas do IV Congresso Internacional "A cerâmica medieval no mediterrâneo ocidental" organizado pelo Campo Arqueológico de Mértola, na Fundação Calouste Gulbenkian em Lisboa, 16–22 Novembro 1987* (Mértola, 1991), pp. 15–17.

Torres, Cláudio, "A arqueologia, o território e o desenvolvimento local," in *Efeitos sociais do património à escala local* (Mértola, 2001), pp. 21–26.

Torres, Cláudio, "Dignidad regional y desarollo," in *Jornadas andaluzas sobre: La función de la cultura en el desarollo local* (Córdoba, 1993), pp. 15–20.

Torres, Cláudio, "O Islão no ocidente ibérico," in Guilhermina Mota (ed.), *Minorias étnicas y religiosas em Portugal: História e actualidade: Actas do Curso de Inverno 2002* (Coimbra, 2003), pp. 91–100.

Torres, Cláudio, and Santiago Macias, *Museum von Mértola – islamische Kunst* (Mértola, 2003).

Torres, Cláudio, and Santiago Macias, *O legado islâmico em Portugal* (Lisbon, 1998).

Troebst, Stefan, "Introduction: What's in a Historical Region? A Teutonic Perspective," in *European Review of History* 10, no. 2 (2003), pp. 173–188.

Die Türken vor Wien. Europa und die Entscheidung an der Donau 1683, 2nd ed. (Vienna, 1983).

Vakil, AbdoolKarim, "Questões inacabadas: Colonialismo, Islão e Portugalidade," in Margarida Calafate Ribeiro and Ana Paula Ferreira (eds.), *Fantasmas e fantasias imperiais no imaginário português contemporâneo* (Porto, 2003), pp. 255–294.

Vakil, AbdoolKarim, "The Crusader Heritage: Portugal and Islam from Colonial to Postcolonial Identities," in Robert Shannan Peckham (ed.), *Rethinking Heritage: Cultures and Politics in Europe* (London, 2003), pp. 29–44.

Valente, Vasco Pulido, *Uma Educação Burguesa: Notas sobre a Ideologia do Ensino no Século XIX* (Lisbon, 1974).

Valls Montés, Rafael, "La imagen del islam en los actuales manuales escolares españoles de historia," in Luigi Cajani (ed.), *Conociendo al otro: El islam y*

Europa en sus manuales de historia (Madrid, 2008), pp. 73–122.

Valls Montés, Rafael, *Historiografía escolar española: Siglos XIX–XXI* (Madrid, 2007).

Varisco, Daniel Martin, *Reading Orientalism: Said and the Unsaid* (Seattle and London, 2007).

Vasconcelos, Damião Augusto de Brito, *Notícias Históricas de Tavira 1242–1840* (Tavira, 1999). First edition 1937.

Vasconcelos, José Leite de, *Etnografia Portuguesa* (Lisbon, 1997–2007). First edition 1933ff.

Vidal, César, *España frente al islam: de Mahoma a Ben Laden* (Madrid, 2004).

Vilanova Ribas, Mercedes, and Xavier Moreno Juliá, *Atlas de la evolución del analfabetismo en España de 1887 a 1981* (Madrid, 1992).

Viñes Millet, Cristina, *La Alhambra que fascinó a los románticos* (Granada, 2007).

Vocelka, Karl, "Die zweite Wiener Türkenbelagerung von 1683 und ihr Reflex in der Wissenschaft, den Schulbüchern und Jubiläumsveranstaltungen," in *Studia Austro-Polonica* 3 (1983), pp. 359–379.

Vones, Ludwig, *Geschichte der Iberischen Halbinsel im Mittelalter 711–1480* (Sigmaringen, 1993).

Weichlein, Siegfried, "Die Verlierer der Geschichte: Zu einem Theorem Carl Schmitts," in Christian Giordano, Jean-Luc Patry and François Rüegg (eds.), *Trugschlüsse und Umdeutungen: Multidisziplinäre Betrachtungen unbehaglicher Praktiken* (Berlin, 2009), pp. 147–165.

Weichlein, Siegfried, "Nationalismus und Nationalstaat in Deutschland und Europa: Ein Forschungsüberblick," in *Neue politische Literatur* 51, no. 2/3 (2006), pp. 265–351.

Weichlein, Siegfried, *Nationalbewegungen und Nationalismus in Europa* (Darmstadt, 2006).

Weller, Christoph, "Feindbilder – zwischen politischen Absichten und wissenschaftlichen Einsichten," in *Neue politische Literatur* 54, no. 1 (2009), pp. 87–103.

Werner, Michael, and Bénédicte Zimmermann, "Vergleich, Transfer, Verflechtung: Der Ansatz der Histoire croisée und die Herausforderung des Transnationalen," in *Geschichte und Gesellschaft* 28 (2002), pp. 607–637.

Winter, Ulrich (ed.), *Lugares de memoria de la guerra civil y del franquismo: representaciones literarias y visuales* (Madrid, 2006).

Wobring, Michael, "The Picturing of Islam in European History Textbooks (1970–2010)," in *Jahrbuch der Internationalen Gesellschaft für Geschichtsdidaktik/Yearbook of the International Society of History Didactics* 10 (2014), pp. 229–252.

Žanić, Ivo, "The Symbolic Identity of Croatia in the Triangle Crossroads-Bulkwark-Bridge," in Pål Kolstø (ed.), *Myths and Boundaries in South-Eastern Europe* (London, 2005), pp. 35–76.

Zimmer, Oliver, "Nation und Religion: Von der Imagination des Nationalen zur Verarbeitung von Nationalisierungsprozessen," in *Historische Zeitschrift* 283 (2006), pp. 617–656.

Index